DIGITAL IMAGE ENHANCEMENT AND RECONSTRUCTION

Hybrid Computational
Intelligence for Pattern Analysis
and Understanding Series

DIGITAL IMAGE
ENHANCEMENT
AND
RECONSTRUCTION

Series Editors

SIDDHARTHA BHATTACHARYYA

NILANJAN DEY

Edited by

SHYAM SINGH RAJPUT

NAFIS UDDIN KHAN

AMIT KUMAR SINGH

KARM VEER ARYA

ACADEMIC PRESS
An imprint of Elsevier

Notices

Knowledge and best practice in this field are constantly changing. As new research and experience
broaden our understanding, changes in research methods, professional practices, or medical
treatment may become necessary.

Practitioners and researchers must always rely on their own experience and knowledge in
evaluating and using any information, methods, compounds, or experiments described herein. In
using such information or methods they should be mindful of their own safety and the safety of
others, including parties for whom they have a professional responsibility.

To the fullest extent of the law, neither the Publisher nor the authors, contributors, or editors,
assume any liability for any injury and/or damage to persons or property as a matter of products
liability, negligence or otherwise, or from any use or operation of any methods, products,
instructions, or ideas contained in the material herein.

ISBN: 978-0-323-98370-9

For information on all Academic Press publications
visit our website at https://www.elsevier.com/books-and-journals

Publisher: Mara E. Conner
Editorial Project Manager: Ivy Dawn Torre
Production Project Manager: Sreejith Viswanathan
Cover Designer: Christian Bilbow

Typeset by VTeX

Working together
to grow libraries in
developing countries

www.elsevier.com • www.bookaid.org

Contents

List of contributors

Amrit Kumar Agrawal

Department of Computer Science & Engineering, Galgotias College of Engineering & Technology, Greater Noida, Uttar Pradesh, India

K.V. Arya

Multimedia and Information Security Research Group, ABV-Indian Institute of Information Technology and Management, Gwalior, India

Department of ICT, ABV-Indian Institute of Information Technology and Management, Gwalior, India

ABV-Indian Institute of Information Technology and Management, Gwalior, India

Vikas Baghel

Jaypee University of Information Technology, Solan, India

Abul Bashar

Prince Mohammad Bin Fahd University, Al Khobar, Saudi Arabia

Munish Bhardwaj

Jaypee University of Information Technology, Solan, India

Gaurav Bhatnagar

Department of Mathematics, IIT Jodhpur, Rajasthan, India

Cai Yee Chang

Department of Biomedical Engineering, Faculty of Engineering, Universiti Malaya, Kuala Lumpur, Malaysia

Shubhojeet Chatterjee

Maulana Azad National Institute of Technology, Bhopal, India

Antitza Dantcheva

Inria Sophia Antipolis, Biot, France

Manoj Diwakar

Department of CSE, Graphic Era Deemed to be University Dehradun, Uttarakhand, India

Srishty Dwivedi

Maulana Azad National Institute of Technology, Bhopal, India

Anna Jia Gander
Department of Applied IT, The University of Gothenburg, Gothenburg, Sweden

Manish Gaur
Department of Computer Science and Engineering, Institute of Engineering and Technology Lucknow, Dr. A.P.J. Abdul Kalam Technical University, Lucknow, India

Nidhi Goel
Department of ECE, IGDTUW, Delhi, India

Lalita Gupta
Maulana Azad National Institute of Technology, Bhopal, India

Feiran Huang
Jinan University, Guangzhou, China

Weichang Huang
Jinan University, Guangzhou, China

Ankush Jain
School of Computer Science Engineering & Technology (SCSET), Bennett University, Greater Noida, India

Indu Joshi
Inria Sophia Antipolis, Biot, France
Indian Institute of Technology Delhi, New Delhi, India

Prem Kumar Kalra
Indian Institute of Technology Delhi, New Delhi, India

Vineet Kansal
Department of Computer Science and Engineering, Institute of Engineering and Technology Lucknow, Dr. A.P.J. Abdul Kalam Technical University, Lucknow, India

Nafis Uddin Khan
Jaypee University of Information Technology, Solan, India

Riya Kothari
University of Southern California, Los Angeles, CA, United States

Pardeep Kumar
CSE and IT Jaypee University of Information Technology, Solan, India

Vinod K. Kurmi

KU Leuven, Leuven, Belgium

Khin Wee Lai

Department of Biomedical Engineering, Faculty of Engineering, Universiti Malaya, Kuala Lumpur, Malaysia

Zhiying Li

Jinan University, Guangzhou, China

Wenxiao Liu

Jinan University, Guangzhou, China

Wei Kit Loo

Department of Biomedical Engineering, Faculty of Engineering, Universiti Malaya, Kuala Lumpur, Malaysia

Zhihan Lv

College of Computer Science and Technology, Qingdao University, Qingdao, China

Monika Mathur

Department of ECE, IGDTUW, Delhi, India

P.V.S.S.R. Chandra Mouli

Department of Computer Science, Central University of Tamil Nadu, Thiruvarur, India

Surendra Nagar

CIDMR Laboratory, ABV-Indian Institute of Information Technology & Management, Gwalior, India

Department of Computer Science & Engineering, ASET, Amity University, Gwalior, India

Shyam Singh Rajput

Department of Computer Science and Engineering, National Institute of Technology Patna, Patna, India

Ciro R. Rodriguez

Dept of Software Engineering, Universidad National Mayor de San Marcos, UNMSM, Lima, Peru

Sumantra Dutta Roy

Indian Institute of Technology Delhi, New Delhi, India

Sima Sahu

Department of ECE, Malla Reddy Engineering College, Hyderabad, Telangana, India

Abhishek Singh

Department of Computer Science and Engineering, Institute of Engineering and Technology Lucknow, Dr. A.P.J. Abdul Kalam Technical University, Lucknow, India

Amit Kumar Singh

Department of Computer Science & Engineering, National Institute of Technology Patna, Patna, India

Prabhishek Singh

Amity School of Engineering and Technology, Amity University Uttar Pradesh, Noida, India

Pramod Kumar Singh

CIDMR Laboratory, ABV-Indian Institute of Information Technology & Management, Gwalior, India

Rini Smita Thakur

Maulana Azad National Institute of Technology, Bhopal, India

Anurag Singh Tomar

Multimedia and Information Security Research Group, ABV-Indian Institute of Information Technology and Management, Gwalior, India

Ayush Utkarsh

Independent Researcher, Ranchi, India

Santosh Kumar Vishwakarma

Manipal University, Jaipur, India

Haoxiang Wang

Cornell University, Ithaca, NY, United States

Jingyi Wu

College of Computer Science and Technology, Qingdao University, Qingdao, China

Shuxuan Xie

College of Computer Science and Technology, Qingdao University, Qingdao, China

Dilip Kumar Yadav

Department of Computer Science and Engineering, National Institute of Technology, Jamshedpur, India

Gaurav Yadav

Department of Computer Science and Engineering, National Institute of Technology, Jamshedpur, India

Ram Narayan Yadav

Maulana Azad National Institute of Technology, Bhopal, India

Preface

Digital Image Enhancement and Reconstruction as a subject nowadays is a constantly evolving and emerging area of image processing. The enhancement of different types of images along with the sufficient restoration of their important features have now become an interdisciplinary study and is one of the fastest-growing technologies around the world. In modern multimedia information systems, where a huge amount of images are utilized for image recognition and classification using Machine Learning and Deep Learning techniques, image enhancement and reconstruction are the primary steps of processing. The other major applications of image enhancement and reconstruction are agriculture and space sciences, medical imaging, image blockchain technology, watermarking, and steganography, etc. The performance of all these technologies is mostly affected by the natural aspects of the image, which are mainly diminished because of the defects or imperfections arising in the image during image sensing, digitization, and transmission processes. Therefore image enhancement and reconstruction are often considered as the first basic requirement in visual information processing and applications.

The main purpose of writing this book is to introduce recent advances, innovations, and research ideas in the area of Digital Image Enhancement and Reconstruction with their real-time applications. This book would surely help to promote the young researchers, academicians, and industry professionals to enhance their knowledge and to contribute significant research in this area.

Outline of the book and chapter synopsis

In view of the above, this book presents state-of-the-art intelligent approaches, design, and development of image enhancement and reconstruction techniques in the various demanding applications of multimedia systems; it consists of 15 chapters which are organized as follows:

Chapter 1 presents a novel image enhancement mechanism for low-resolution and low-quality video images. This method is based on a fusion of nonlocal features of the image, which proves to retain the low-frequency contents and deals with large motion blurs.

Chapter 2 provides the recent showcase investigations on the usefulness of uncertainty estimation to interpret fingerprint image preprocessing models.

The underwater image enhancement, which is one of the significant and prominent research problems in the emerging areas of image enhancement and reconstruction techniques, is the focus of Chapter 3. A review on a variety of ways to improve and restore underwater images that deal with common underwater issues, including extreme degradations and distortions, is discussed.

Chapter 4 presents an image denoising and enhancement algorithm for medical image modalities, such as ultrasound images, Magnetic Resonance images, and Computer Tomography images. The method uses the combination of a homomorphic filter and Haar wavelet decomposition to efficiently reduce the noise by recovering the essential features of the image.

Furthermore, the widespread use of Machine Learning-Based Convolutional Neural Networks in medical image enhancement and denoising has been explained in Chapter 5.

Chapter 6 mainly introduces the multimodal learning of social image representations. There is a large amount of social image data in social networks, and using the network information between images and multimodal content information is very useful for applications of social images.

Another comprehensive survey of conventional and Deep-Learning-Based models and different benchmark datasets and performance measures used for evaluating the underwater image enhancement techniques are discussed in Chapter 7.

Chapter 8 provides the comparative survey on workflow, methodologies, and performance analysis of image restoration techniques developed so far.

Chapter 9 presents a detailed comprehensive survey of learning-based face hallucination methods and a detailed description of Bayesian, Regularization, Subspace Learning, and Deep Learning methods with their issues and challenges are discussed.

Chapter 10 describes a fusion-based methodology for enhancement of region of interests of backlit images using Gradient Operator, Log Transformation, and Gamma Correction methods.

Chapter 11 focuses on recently used techniques for the enhancement of hyperspectral images with the help of image compression techniques, and also discusses the applications of the recently developed technique of hyperspectral imaging.

A thorough study on the classification of COVID-19 and non-COVID-19 Lung Computed Tomography images using different deep convolutional neural networks is presented in Chapter 12.

Chapter 13 provides a comprehensive survey on K-means clustering and fuzzy C-means clustering methods for detecting the location of brain tumors from MRI images. The survey depicts the effectivity of K-means clustering and fuzzy C-means clustering methods as robust unsupervised Machine Learning tools for brain tumor segmentation.

A novel multimodality medical image fusion technology based on shearlet transform is proposed in Chapter 14. The proposed technique decomposes input images using a nonsubsampled shearlet transform to extract low- and high-frequency components. Finally, the Indian face image dataset named IIITM Faces is presented in Chapter 15. This dataset can be used in numerous fields, such as image enhancement, image reconstruction, face recognition, face hallucination, object detection, biometrics, and surveillance to examine the performance of the developed models.

We especially thank the Hybrid Computational Intelligence for Pattern Analysis Series Editors, **Professor Siddhartha Bhattacharyya** and **Professor Nilanjan Dey** for their continuous support and valuable guidance.

We would also like to thank publishers and the editorial board at Elsevier, in particular *Mara Conner*, Publisher for Biomedical Engineering, Elsevier, and *Ivy Dawn C. Torre* Editorial Project Manager for their support and timely completion of the documentation and editing of this book.

We are sincerely thankful to all authors, editors, and publishers whose works have been cited directly and indirectly in this book.

Acknowledgments

The first and third authors gratefully acknowledge the authorities of the *National Institute of Technology Patna*, India, for their kind support to come up with this book.

The second author gratefully acknowledges the authorities of *Jaypee University of Information Technology*, Solan, India, for their kind support in connection to the composition of this book.

The fourth author gratefully acknowledges the authorities of *ABV-Indian Institute of Technology and Management Gwalior, India* for their kind support to the realization of this book.

Shyam Singh Rajput
Patna, India
Nafis Uddin Khan
Solan, India
Amit Kumar Singh
Patna, India
Karm Veer Arya
Gwalior, India

CHAPTER 1

Video enhancement and super-resolution

Zhihan Lv[a], Jingyi Wu[a], Shuxuan Xie[a], and Anna Jia Gander[b]
[a]College of Computer Science and Technology, Qingdao University, Qingdao, China
[b]Department of Applied IT, The University of Gothenburg, Gothenburg, Sweden

1.1 Introduction

Since the recent decades there have been increasing high-speed technological innovations, such as automatic industrial production, intelligent lifestyles, and digital information transmission and acquisition, with which original paper books and newspapers being gradually replaced by video images. For example, video images are widely used in a criminal inquiry, vehicle tracking, flow monitoring, and medical diagnosis. Under such conditions, the video image quality may directly determine relevant data and information acquisition effect, and, sometimes, low-quality images may cause property losses or threaten social and public security [1,2]. Therefore ever-more focus has been put on the low-quality video Image Enhancement (IE) through Artificial Intelligence (AI) algorithms.

By excavating useful information in video images, specific emergencies can be understood through the preset threshold parameters. In practical applications, due to environmental and equipment influences, the monitored video image quality is often too poor to be used for system automatic analysis. Therefore improving video quality has become the key to intellectualization [3]. For example, the application of a high-quality video monitoring system in a high-speed railway can help reduce costs, while improving efficiency to ensure the safe and stable operation of vehicles. In a criminal investigation, high-quality video surveillance can be used to pinpoint the suspect, thus greatly facilitating case detection speed [4,5].

Therefore video IE is essential to improve visual effects or visual features.

Deep Learning (DL) is one of the AI algorithms. The Convolutional Neural Network (CNN) has shown great potential in image recognition and has made many attempts in the field of IE of underlying vision. For example, the CNN can convert the IE problems into the regression from the degraded low-quality image to the original high-quality clear image,

Digital Image Enhancement and Reconstruction
https://doi.org/10.1016/B978-0-32-398370-9.00008-1

1

and the End-To-End (ETE) network training is realized through the sample pairs of low-quality image and high-quality image to learn and obtain this regression mapping [6]. However, there are two problems in the application of CNN to IE: firstly, CNN uses its powerful nonlinear representation ability to approximate clear images at the pixel level and does not learn the manifold distribution of the original high-quality clear images; secondly, most CNN learn more image features by designing deeper or wider networks to improve its representation ability, but they do not make full use of the inherent interdependence of feature channels. Generic Adversarial Networks (GAN) can force the distribution of the reconstructed image to approach the real image manifold distribution by adding additional adversarial networks, thus producing a reconstructed image with a better visual effect. The channel Attention Mechanism (AM) can give different weights to the feature channels so that the network can selectively emphasize the features conducive to IE and suppress the less useful features [7]. Finally, high-quality and clear real images, the same as the real image data, are generated, meeting the needs of data enhancement. Therefore using GAN to complete effective image data enhancement has important research significance.

In short, with the wider application of video images in all walks of life, it is of great practical significance to improve their quality. The innovation of this research is that given the shortcomings of traditional low illumination or low-resolution video IE algorithms and existing DL algorithms, the GAN in DL algorithm is introduced, and GAN is combined with AM. A video image super-resolution and deblurring model method based on high-order gated AM is constructed. The high-order gated AM is used to automatically learn different attention levels to realize the super-resolution and motion deblurring of the synthetic image. Finally, its performance is analyzed through comparative experiments, which provide an experimental reference for subsequent video image quality enhancement and application fields.

The contents of each section are as follows: Section 1.2, Recent Related Work, analyzes the current situation and trend of the application of video IE and machine vision in Image Processing (IP) and highlights the research methods by analyzing the research gaps; in Section 1.3, a low-quality video IE model based on DL algorithm is proposed, and its performance is evaluated by case analysis; Section 1.4, Results and Discussion, compares the proposed model algorithm with the other model algorithms in related fields and highlights the research results; Section 1.5, Conclusion, briefly expounds the research results, and analyzes the limitations and prospects.

1.2 Recent related work

1.2.1 Development status of video IE

Resolution-oriented IE is a heated topic in IP and has been widely studied and applied. Wang et al. (2017) proposed an Image Despeckling CNN (ID-CNN) for speckle contamination of Synthetic Aperture Radar (SAR) images to automatically remove speckle from input noisy images. Finally, synthetic and real SAR image experiments showed that the proposed method greatly outmatched the existing speckle suppression methods [8]. Yuan et al. (2018) nonlinearly mapped noisy Hyperspectral Image (HSI) to clean HSI combined with Spatial-Spectral Deep CNN (HSID-CNN) for hyperspectral image denoising. Simulation and actual data experiments proved that the proposed HSID-CNN was superior to many mainstream methods in quantitative evaluation index, visual effect, and HSI classification accuracy [9]. Jin et al. (2019) proposed a practical and accurate channel estimation framework based on the natural image of sparse millimeter-wave channel matrix and Fast and Flexible Denoising Convolutional Neural Network (FFDNET). The results indicated that FFDNET was suitable for a wide range of Signal-to-Noise Ratio (SNR) levels as the input of noise level mapping and could process natural images, such as buildings, efficiently [10]. To balance denoising performance and computing speed, Wang et al. (2020) selected a representative Multi-Wavelet CNN (MWCNN) as the backbone model to denoise the image. The results showed that the backbone model could extract more features from adjacent layers in a much shorter time and could well process seriously noisy images [11]. Panetta et al. (2021) proposed the first comprehensive underwater object tracking (UOT100) benchmark dataset to promote the development of tracking algorithms quite suitable for underwater environment. By testing the performance of 20 kinds of the most advanced target tracking algorithms, a cascade residual network model for underwater image enhancement is further introduced to improve the tracking accuracy and the success rate of the tracker. Finally, the experimental results prove the shortcomings of the existing underwater data tracking algorithms and how the GAN-based enhanced model can be used to improve the tracking performance. Meanwhile, compared with the existing GAN-based methods, the recognized quality index can evaluate the visual quality of the output of the constructed model and prove that it can produce better visual data [12]. Li et al. (2021) developed a CNN-based optical enhancement network. Firstly, a generation pipeline for converting daytime images into low light images is proposed and used to construct image pairs during model development. Then, they adopted the proposed light enhancement net (LE-net) for training and verified on the generated low light level image. Finally, they analyzed under various low light conditions to test the effectiveness of the proposed LE-net in real night conditions. The results indicated that the LE-net proposed is superior to the existing models qualitatively and quantitatively [13].

The relevant research and analysis on video IE suggest that most scholars only consider solving unbalanced data classification from a single dimension, rather than using rich and diverse data samples, but a single solution is not ideal. Meanwhile, in practical application, there is a need to consider the characteristics of dataset samples. Datasets have different characteristics, so the applicable data enhancement technologies are different. Then, the obtained data should conform to the distribution law of the original data, have low similarity with the original data, and can greatly improve the diversity of data samples, which is also the research direction of this study.

1.2.2 Application status and trend of Machine Vision (MV) in IP

IP methods are essential in the MV perception technology and have been studied extensively. Xin et al. (2018) added a parallel coil layer into an improved Deep CNN (DCNN) model to widen CNN. The improved DCNN could better extract image features with higher performance. The coiling layer preprocessed feature images through batch normalization, while network training was accelerated. The case analysis proved that the improved DCNN model could learn the image features faster for cervical cancer cells and minimize the classification error rate [14]; He et al. (2018) classified Hyperspectral Images (HSIS) through CNN and established a new hand-designed method to extract feature using Multiscale Covariance Maps (MCMs), finding that the proposed method had an explicit effect and could maximize the classification accuracy [15]. Jia et al. (2019) constructed a Multiverse Optimization (MVO) algorithm based on Lévy flight. Lévy flight was an effective strategy to diversify the population, minimize premature convergence, and avoid local optimization. Further simulation implied that the designed method was superior in image quality measurement, objective function, convergence performance, and robustness [16]. Kim et al. (2020) established a new ETE network for unsupervised image segmentation, which was composed of standardized and the differentiable clustering Argmax function. Then, a spatial continuity loss function was introduced, which alleviated the limitation of fixed-line segment boundary in previous work. Meanwhile, an extended segmentation method was put forward, which had better accuracy than the existing segmentation methods and could maintain efficiency. Finally, the proposed method was verified using multiple image segmentation benchmark datasets [17]. Yang et al. (2021) proposed a new face image coding framework, which used compression model and generation model to jointly support machine vision and human perception tasks. Firstly, they input an image into the system for feature analysis, and then reconstructed the image with compact structure and rich color features by using the generation model. The compact edge mapping was used as the basic layer of machine vision task, and the reference pixel was used as the enhancement layer to ensure the signal fidelity of human vision. Subsequently, they introduced an advanced generation model to train a decoding network to reconstruct the image from the compact structure and color representation, and control the output image effect between signal fidelity and visual realism. Finally, the experimental results and comprehensive performance analysis on face image datasets showed the superiority of the framework in human vision tasks and machine vision tasks, which provided useful evidence for the standardization of machine video coding [18]. Hu et al. (2021) analyzed the latest technologies and practices of various machine vision solutions under different operating conditions in a fine-grained quantitative manner. They also described the advantages and limitations of DL when applied to other algorithm models. In addition, through applicability evaluation, the role of DL in image classification, target detection, pixel segmentation, geometric scale quantization, and growth prediction was deployed and optimized. Finally, they summarized the current challenges and corresponding breakthrough directions to promote the further development of DL [19].

In summary, the analysis of the related works implies that the GAN model presents a considerable effect on natural images handling. Thus how to optimize the image generation effect of the GAN is worthy of in-depth research, and its application to the data enhancement field also has great research significance. To enhance low video image quality, this paper first introduces the GAN and AM, and then proposes an effective ETE DL network model, which has important practical research significance for the application of video images in various fields.

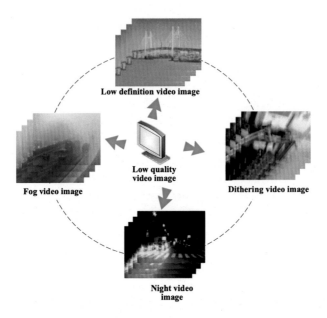

Figure 1.1 The mobile robot-mounted module diagram.

1.3 Analysis of low-quality video IE model based on DL algorithm

1.3.1 Demand Analysis (DA) of resolution-oriented video IE

With the in–depth application of AI algorithms in various fields, data amounts are surging over the Internet. Video images are an intuitive information expression, and information acquisition efficiency can be substantially boosted by improving image quality. For example, video images excavation technology can be employed to understand specific demands and predict event occurrence through the preset threshold parameters. In real scenarios, environmental and equipment factors often lead to poor quality video images, which can hardly be applicable in system automatic analysis [20,21]. Low–quality video is shown in Fig. 1.1.

Fig. 1.1 shows that the cause of low-quality video images is miscellaneous, such as poor weather conditions, for example, rain, snow, and fog, that might lead to reduced image contrast or blurriness in outdoor navigation, traffic monitoring, and target recognition. Hence low-quality video images have very limited applications in MV. Another resource of low-quality videos images is online applications because of frequent replication, transmission, and format conversion; additionally, the unstable equipment fixation also might result in video jitter and blurry images. Furthermore, illumination and equipment deficiencies in the dark environment might generate low contrasted, high noisy, and distorted images [22]. Therefore it is necessary to enhance the resolution of the low-quality video by restoring the image information and improving the detail and brightness of the image, which is also very important for subsequent video intelligence analysis.

At the same time, there are still the following problems in video IP: first, the generated image quality is poor, the detailed information is not obvious, and the resolution is not high. The early image generation technology Variable Autoencoder (VAE) mainly uses the approximation method, and its performance depends on the quality of the approximate distribution, which can easily lead to an unclear image. However, GAN contains two subnetworks, both of which are composed of Neural Networks (NN) and need to learn various data distribution. Besides, due to the small training sample size, the convolution layer of NN has less perception of image features and high randomness, which is easy to cause rasterization, poor image quality, unclear detail information, and low resolution. Therefore selecting the NN structure with better performance can better generate images with good quality and high resolution.

Second, the model is difficult to train, the parameters are large, and the model generalization ability is not enough. With the emergence of VGG-16 and RESNET, the number of NN layers increases to gain better image feature learning ability, with which, however, the parameters also increase, and the model is becoming harder to train. DNN is prone to gradient disappearance or gradient explosion. Additionally, when the dataset is too small, the NN may highly fit the distribution of training data. The accuracy of the test dataset is very low, and overfitting might occur, thereby reducing the network generalization ability.

Third, the processed image has few application scenarios and lacks practical value. At present, the resolution-oriented IE technology is still at the laboratory stage. Researchers mostly use the classic public dataset for parameter optimization and model adjustment and rarely analyze and process video images [23,24]. At present, resolution-oriented IE is only used in the field of image vision, such as image fine-grained emotion classification and target detection. In the future, it will be applied to the fields of text data, video data, and speech processing or recognition.

Given the above problems, such as low video image quality, difficult model training, and lack of practical value, this study introduces the GAN, improves it, creates relevant models to analyze the video image, and finally, uses the corresponding dataset to verify the effectiveness and feasibility of the proposed data enhancement method.

1.3.2 Analysis of the application of DL algorithm to video IP

As a simulation algorithm of neural connection structure of human brain, DL hierarchically describes the data features of image, sound, and text through multiple transformation stages. When the human visual system processes the image data, the processing order is edge detection → initial shape → forming a more complex visual shape. Similarly, DL integrates the low-level features, and then forms a higher-level abstract feature. Compared with shallow learning methods, such as support vector machine, DL actively learns hierarchical features through layer-by-layer feature transformation of original data samples, and produces more appropriate classification and visual features [25,26]. Since the DL is put forward, its application scope has expanded rapidly to speech recognition, autonomous driving (AD) systems, search technology, and Data Mining (DM). CNN and Deep Recurrent Neural Network (DRNN) are common in IP.

CNN includes a Convolution Layer (CL), pooling layer, and Fully Connected (FC) layer. Each pixel in the video image is scanned using the convolution kernel, and then the extracted eigenvalues are calculated by matrix multiplication [27]. The common feature extraction process of CNN for video images is shown in Fig. 1.2.

The parameters of the convolution layer are composed of some convolution kernels or convolution filters. A feature map will be generated in the convolution layer. It is often defined that the kth generated feature map is h^k, and the convolution kernel is composed of parameters W^k and b^k, respectively. Then

$$h_{ij}^k = f\left(\left(W^k * x\right)_{ij} + b^k\right). \tag{1.1}$$

In Eq. (1.1), $f(.)$ refers to an activation function, x represents an input feature graph, and the parameter W of the hidden layer can be expressed as a multidimensional vector.

The pooling layer exists in the continuous convolution layer. Its main function is to reduce the data dimension of the input architectural landscape image to reduce the size of the feature image and the parameters and calculation in the network, and finally, prevent overfitting. Assuming that the size of the input feature graph is V, the size of the filter is C, the step size is S, and the number of zero fills added to the boundary is P, then the

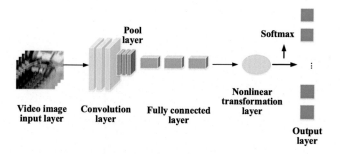

Figure 1.2 Flowchart of feature extraction of video image by CNN.

size of the output feature graph can be calculated as

$$(V - C + 2P)/S + 1. \tag{1.2}$$

The FC layer is the classifier of the whole CNN, which connects each point with all nodes of the previous layer and integrates all the features extracted in the earlier phase. The calculation of the FC layer reads as follows:

$$Fc_j = X_i W_j^T + b_j. \tag{1.3}$$

In Eq. (1.3), b represents the offset item.

In video IP, CNN is trained by minimizing the optimization target. The training does not stop until the network iteration reaches a threshold number or the optimization target converges. Assuming that the number of classification categories is c, the number of samples in the training set is c, the label corresponding to the nth sample is t^n, the actual output is y^n, and the Mean Square Error (MSE) is used as the loss function, then the total error loss is

$$E^N = \frac{1}{2} \sum_{n=1}^{c} \left\| t^n - y^n \right\|^2. \tag{1.4}$$

For simple description, only one sample is discussed here, and the error of the nth sample is expressed by Eq. (1.5):

$$E = \frac{1}{2} \left\| t^n - y^n \right\|^2. \tag{1.5}$$

According to the chain rule, it is necessary to calculate the partial derivative of the loss function E to each weight in the network, and l refers to the current layer of the network, then the output of the current layer is

$$x^l = \sigma\left(u^l\right) = \sigma\left(W^l x^{l-1} + b^l\right). \tag{1.6}$$

In Eq. (1.6), $\sigma()$ represents the excitation function. Generally, the Sigmoid or Rectified Linear Unit (ReLU) is used. The sensitivity of the basis of each neuron is defined as the error of Back Propagation (BP), as shown in Eq. (1.7):

$$\frac{\partial E}{\partial b} = \frac{\partial E}{\partial u}\frac{\partial u}{\partial b} = \delta. \tag{1.7}$$

The equation used for BP reads

$$\delta^l = \left(W^{l+1}\right)^T \delta^{l+1} * f'\left(u^l\right). \tag{1.8}$$

In Eq. (1.8), $*$ refers to convolution operation. The base sensitivity of the output layer is then calculated using Eq. (1.9):

$$\delta^L = f'\left(u^L\right) * \left(y^n - t^n\right). \tag{1.9}$$

Then, the chain rule is used to update the weight of the network. That is, for network layer l, the input of the current layer is multiplied by its sensitivity:

$$\frac{\partial E}{\partial W^l} = x^{l-1}\left(\delta^l\right)^T. \tag{1.10}$$

Finally, the weight update of the network layer l can be obtained by multiplying the partial derivative by a negative Learning Rate (LR), as shown in Eq. (1.11):

$$\Delta W^l = -\eta\frac{\partial E}{\partial W^l}. \tag{1.11}$$

η represents the LR.

However, with the continuous updating of CNN, the network layer of the improved CNN algorithms, such as VGG–16 and ResNet, increases, thereby showing better image feature learning ability; the parameters also increase, and the model training becomes more complex. The DNN is prone to gradient disappearance or gradient explosion.

GAN is an unsupervised DL structure, in which the training dataset does not necessarily obey a priori distribution. In GAN, the data dimension and generation complexity conform to a linear relation, and the calculation

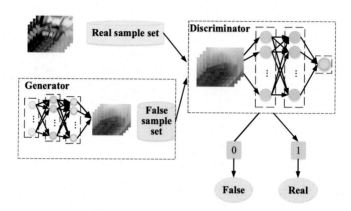

Figure 1.3 Flowchart of generating high-resolution video image by GAN.

will not be surge exponentially as the traditional model, because only the dimension of the Neural Network (NN) output is increased; besides, there is no explicit restriction on the distribution of data, to minimize the manual design of model distribution; furthermore, the data generated by GAN are clearer, which are the same as the connection mode of the Artificial Neural Network (ANN) [28,29]. GAN is composed of a pair of antagonistic DNN: Discriminator (D) and Generator (G). G strives to generate candidates verifiable by D as real samples, whereas the D endeavor to distinguish the generated candidates from real samples [30]. The objective function of the GAN model reads

$$\min_{G} \max_{D} E_{X \sim P_{data}(x)} \left[\ln D(x) \right] + E_{Z \sim P_z} \left[\ln \left(1 - D(x) \right) \right]. \tag{1.12}$$

In Eq. (1.12), x refers to the real picture, z represents the noise input to the G network, $G(z)$ denotes the picture generated by the network G, and $D(x)$ refers to the probability of the positive judgment by D network on the real image, in which $P_{data}(x)$ and P_z stand for the distribution of real data and synthetic data, respectively. In the generation of the high-quality video image, GAN aims is to generate a more realistic building pattern map as far as possible, so that the D can hardly discriminate the generated pattern map from real samples. The probability of the output result of the D is 0.5 for both true and false samples, thereby achieving a balanced ideal state as far as possible. The generation of high-resolution video images by the GAN is shown in Fig. 1.3.

The losses of G and D are shown in Eqs. (1.13) and (1.14), respectively:

$$L_d = -E_{X \sim P_{data}(x)} \left[\ln D(x) \right] - E_{Z \sim P_z} \left[\ln(1 - D(x)) \right], \qquad (1.13)$$

$$L_g = -E_{Z \sim P_z} \left[\ln(1 - D(x)) \right]. \qquad (1.14)$$

In Fig. 1.3, the D can learn the real sample set features of low-quality video images to distinguish the G samples from real samples using the DCNN structure, thus classifying the real video image data by 1 and classifying the generated high-quality video image data by 0. The G is designed to deceive the D as much as possible so that the D will be unable to identify the authenticity of generated realistic video image data. If the judgment of the D is close to 1, the video image of the G has the same main features as the real sample, and the G has successfully deceived the D.

When GAN is used for adversarial training, Image Discriminator (D) and Feature Discriminator (FD) are used respectively. Specifically, the D can distinguish the real image and the forged image by checking the pixel value, and the FD can distinguish them by checking the real image and the forged image, thus enabling the G to synthesize more meaningful high-frequency details [31,32]. To train the NN with the FD, the minimum loss function is defined as Eq. (1.15):

$$L_G = \alpha l_{enc} + \beta l_{perc} + \gamma l_{adv} + \lambda l_{feature_{adv}}. \qquad (1.15)$$

In Eq. (1.15), l_{perc} refers to the loss of perceptual similarity, which makes the forged image look similar to the real ground image in the training set; l_{adv} denotes the GAN loss of the image, in which the G synthesizes high-frequency details in the pixel domain; $l_{feature_{adv}}$ indicates the loss of feature GAN, in which the G synthesizes structural details in the feature domain; $\alpha, \beta, \gamma, \lambda$ means the weight of the corresponding item. Meanwhile, L_G has the additional function of GAN loss item $l_{feature_{adv}}$, which causes significant differences in perceived quality. To train the D and FD, the loss function l_{dis} and $l_{feature_{dis}}$ are minimized, and each of which corresponds to l_{adv} and $l_{feature_{adv}}$, respectively. The G, D, and FD are trained by alternatively minimizing $L_G, l_{dis}, l_{feature_{dis}}$. Furthermore, each loss item is described in more detail.

Clear details are obtained for super-resolution images through perceptual loss [33]. Unlike MSE loss, $G(I_{LR})$ and I_{HR} are first mapped to feature space using $\phi(\cdot)$, and then the distance between them is calculated. Therefore the loss function of perceptual loss is calculated by Eq. (1.16):

$$l_{perc} = E_{I_{LR} \sim P_L(l), I_{HR} \sim P_H(h)} \left\| \phi(G(I_{LR})) - \phi(I_{HR}) \right\|. \qquad (1.16)$$

In Eq. (1.16), $P_L(l)$ refers to the distribution of low–resolution images, $P_H(h)$ stands for the distribution of actual high-resolution images, and $G(I_{HR})$ means the forged images generated through the super-resolution network. For $\phi(\cdot)$, the first, second, and third convolution layers in the popular Visual Geometry Group-19 (VGG-19) network [34] are used in combination. Therefore both low–level and high–level features can be obtained simultaneously. The super-resolution network can be optimized by Eq. (1.17):

$$l_{adv} = -E_{I_{LR}\sim P_L(l), I_{HR}\sim P_H(h)} \left[\log \left(sigmoid \left(D \left(G(I_{LR}) \right) - D(I_{HR}) \right) \right) \right]. \quad (1.17)$$

Next, the D network is optimized by Eq. (1.18):

$$l_{dis} = -E_{I_{LR}\sim P_L(l), I_{HR}\sim P_H(h)} \left[\log \left(sigmoid \left(D(I_{HR}) - D \left(G(I_{LR}) \right) \right) \right) \right]. \quad (1.18)$$

Given a low-resolution image I_{LR} and its corresponding high-resolution image I_{HR}, MSE can be used to minimize the feature distance between the forged image and the high-resolution image, as calculated by Eq. (1.19):

$$l_{mse} = E_{I_{LR}\sim P_L(l), I_{HR}\sim P_H(h)} \| G(I_{LR}) - I_{HR} \|_F^2. \quad (1.19)$$

In Eq. (1.19), $\| \cdot \|_F$ refers to the Frobenius norm. The loss function of encoder loss is expressed as

$$l_{enc} = E_{I_{LR}\sim P_L(l), I_{HR}\sim P_H(h)} \| E \left(G(I_{LR}) \right) - E(I_{HR}) \|_{F'}^2. \quad (1.20)$$

In Eq. (1.20), $E(\cdot)$ refers to the coding network.

Since the features correspond to abstract image structures, the G can be encouraged to generate realistic high-frequency structures, rather than the illusion of noise. Both perceptual similarity loss and feature GAN loss are based on the feature map. However, in contrast to the loss of perceptual similarity that promotes perceptual consistency between $l_{feature_{adv}}$ and $l_{feature_{dis}}$, the loss of feature GAN makes it possible to synthesize perceptual effective image details.

Here, the video image is designed using the GAN, and the sample data generated by the G are sent to the D for judgment, the D will feedback an error gradient to the G, and the G will carry out further gradient descent training per these gradients to decrease the D deviation and generate high-quality video image.

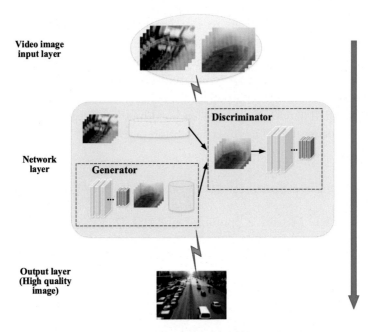

Figure 1.4 Flowchart of video image super-resolution and deblurring model based on high-order gated AM-optimized GAN.

1.3.3 Analysis of video image super-resolution and deblurring model based on high-order gated AM and improved GAN

Generally, low illumination or weak light will lead to dark or underexposure video images, with a low resolution of the object of interest and uneven illumination, which greatly hinders image classification and target tracking. This study aims at the shortcomings of traditional low illumination or low-resolution video IE algorithms and existing DL algorithms, and proposes a video image super-resolution and deblurring model method based on high-order gated AM. Firstly, an enhanced network structure is constructed using a multilayer residual module to improve the D network; then, the U–Net is used as the brightness attention module to predict the brightness distribution of the low illumination image, so that the network can pay more attention to the low illumination area of the image and avoid overexposure of the high brightness area. The flow of video image super-resolution and deblurring model based on high-order gated AM–optimized GAN is shown in Fig. 1.4.

In the proposed model, the first-order and second-order channel attention of deblurring and super-resolution feature extraction modules are calculated, respectively, and their combined third-order channel attention is calculated. The simple and direct combination of these high-order channels will lead to very complex attention and fitting phenomenon. Therefore the proposed network will randomly abandon some channel attention modules, making the network structure different in each training. This is similar to averaging many network structures, which greatly increases the robustness of the proposed network. Specifically, for the second-order channel attention module, the feature graph $F = [f_1, f_2, \cdots, f_C]$ with the size $H \times W \times C$ is changed into a feature matrix $[H \times W, C]$, and then the covariance matrix is calculated:

$$\Sigma = X \bar{I} X^T, \ \bar{I} = \frac{1}{s}\left(I - \frac{1}{s}\mathbb{1}\right). \tag{1.21}$$

In Eq. (1.21), I and $\mathbb{1}$ are unit matrix and unitary matrix, respectively, and the size is $s \times s$. Since covariance normalization plays an important role in more distinguishable signs, covariance normalization is performed on the obtained covariance matrix Σ, which is a symmetric and positive semidefinite matrix. Therefore singular value decomposition can be used:

$$\Sigma = U\Lambda U^T, \ \Lambda = diag\,(\lambda_1, \lambda_2, \ldots, \lambda_C). \tag{1.22}$$

U refers to the orthogonal matrix, Λ denotes diagonal matrix, and the eigenvalues are arranged in nonincreasing order and converted to the power of the eigenvalue:

$$\widehat{Y} = \Sigma^a = U\Lambda^a U^T, \ \Lambda^a = diag\left(\lambda_1^a, \lambda_2^a, \ldots, \lambda_C^a\right). \tag{1.23}$$

a refers to a positive real number. When $a = 1$, no normalization is performed. When $a < 1$, nonlinearly narrowing is performed on eigenvalues greater than 1, and eigenvalues less than 1 are pulled up. Normally, $a = 0.5$. Then, it is applied to the AM. If $\widehat{Y} = [y_1, y_2, \cdots, y_C]$, then the channel statistics can be obtained by narrowing $\widehat{Y}$. The calculation reads

$$z_c = GCP(y_C) = \frac{1}{c}\sum_{i=1}^{C} y_C(i). \tag{1.24}$$

$GCP()$ refers to global covariance pooling. In the gated AM, some attention modules are closed randomly with a probability of 0.5, and all these closed attention modules are set to 0.

$$r_i \sim Bernoulli(p), \tag{1.25}$$

$$\tilde{y} = concat(r * y). \tag{1.26}$$

Bernoulli( ) refers to a Bernoulli function, which aims to randomly generate tensors with probability p of all 0 or all 1, and *concat*( ) indicates the combination of these attention modules. Next, the modified feature is propagated forward, and then the loss is propagated back, whereas the parameters are updated according to the gradient descent algorithm on the unclosed attention module [35], as shown in Eq. (1.27):

$$z_i = \sigma \left(w_i \tilde{y} + b_i \right). \tag{1.27}$$

w_i refers to the weight parameter, b_i represents the offset, and $\sigma( )$ stands for the excitation function.

In the deblurring processing and high-resolution analysis on low-quality video images, there are samples x from real data. If the distribution function of real data is represented by $P(x)$, the pseudo-real data generation samples are random probability noise z under bell-shaped distribution, the probability distribution of the generation function is denoted by $P(z)$, the G network is $G(z)$, and the D network is $D(x)$, then, the GAN training process is an optimization task:

$$\min_{G} \max_{D} V(D, G), \tag{1.28}$$

$$V(D, G) = E_{x \sim pdata(x)} \left[\log D(x) \right] + E_{z \sim pz(z)} \left[\log(1 - D(G(z))) \right]. \tag{1.29}$$

In Eq. (1.29), the first item of $V(D, G)$ refers to the expectation that the real data is identified as true by D, and the second item indicates the expectation that the generated data does not deceive the D. Eq. (1.28) shows that the goal of GAN is to use the trained D to make the first item 1, that is, $D(x) = 1$, and the second item 0, that is, $D(G(z)) = 0$. In other words, the D determines the data from the real distribution as 1 and the data from the pseudo data distribution as 0. In a word, the goal of training is to maximize $V(D, G)$. By contrast, the training goal of the network for the G is to minimize $V(D, G)$ so that the D cannot distinguish the real data from the forged generated data. Therefore the optimization of GAN is to reach a balance between G and D, namely, Nash equilibrium, which, however, might not be reached, because D and G are trained separately. Furthermore, according to the analysis of Eq. (1.28), when the parameters of G are fixed, only the D is trained. When the input is true or pseudo-random sample x, the expression reads

$$P_r(x) \log D(x) + P_g(x) \log [1 - D(x)]. \tag{1.30}$$

The optimal-state D can be obtained through training. Thus after the extreme point of Eq. (1.30) is obtained, let the derivative of $D(x)$ be 0, and Eq. (1.31) can be obtained:

$$\frac{P_r(x)}{D(x)} - \frac{P_g(x)}{1 - D(x)} = 0. \tag{1.31}$$

According to Eq. (1.31), the optimal D is calculated by Eq. (1.32):

$$D^*(x) = \frac{P_r(x)}{P_r(x) + P_g(x)}. \tag{1.32}$$

When $D^*(x)$ in Eq. (1.32) is introduced into Eq. (1.28), Eq. (1.33) can be obtained:

$$V = E_{x \sim P_r} \log \frac{2P_r(x)}{P_r(x) + P_g(x)} + E_{x \sim P_g} \log \frac{2P_r(x)}{P_r(x) + P_g(x)} - 2 \log 2. \tag{1.33}$$

Eq. (1.33) suggests that when the D is trained well enough to always make correct decisions, $P_r(x) = 1$, $P_g(x) < 1$, $E_{x \sim pg} = 0$, the right side of Eq. (1.33) is 0, $V = \log 2 - \log 2 = 0$. That is, the G has not obtained an effective descent gradient and has not trained in the correct gradient direction, so the gradient disappears; similarly, the too-badly trained D will make wrong judgments on all data: $E_{x \sim pr} = 0$, $P_r(x) = 0$, the gradient obtained by the G is still 0, the training of the G has no directionality, and the gradient disappears.

Here, aiming at the gradient disappearance problem, the Least Squares GAN (LSGAN) is employed to improve the problems of unstable training and poor synthetic image effect in GAN, and the Least Square (LS) loss is used to replace the traditional Cross-Entropy (CE) loss [36]. The LS loss is shown in Eqs. (1.34) and (1.35):

$$\max_{D} L_{LSGAN}(D) = E_{X \sim P_{data}(x)} \left[(D(x) - b)^2 \right] + \frac{1}{2} E_{Z \sim P_z} \left[(D(G(z)) - a)^2 \right], \tag{1.34}$$

$$\min_{G} L_{LSGAN}(G) = \frac{1}{2}E_{Z \sim P_z}\left[(D(G(z)) - c)^2\right]. \qquad (1.35)$$

a and *b* refer to the encoding of the composite image and the target domain image; the purpose of the G is to map the image coding *a* to the image coding *c*, that is, the coding *c* represents the discrimination result of the D on the synthetic image against the optimal G; G(z) indicates the composite image of the G; D() stands for the judgment result of the D on the input image.

This research uses LS loss quantization G_1 and D to combat the loss. Since the input of the G replaces random noise with an image, the loss function changes accordingly, as shown in Eqs. (1.36) and (1.37):

$$\max_{D} L_{GAN_D}(D) = E_{X \sim P_{data}(Y)}\left[(D(x) - 1)^2\right] + \frac{1}{2}E_{x \sim G_1(x)}\left[(D(G_1(x)) - 1)^2\right], \qquad (1.36)$$

$$\min_{G_1} L_{GAN_{G_1}}(G_1) = E_{X \sim P_{data}(X)}\left[(D(G_1(x)) - 1)^2\right]. \qquad (1.37)$$

$X \sim P_{data}(X)$ means that the picture originates from the source domain X to be converted; $X \sim P_{date}(Y)$ represents the picture from the target domain Y; $D(G_1(x))$ stands for the judgment result of the D on the synthetic image of the G_1; $x \sim G_1(x)$ indicates that the image x is a forged result synthesized by the G_1. Here, $a = 0$, $b = c = 1$, that is, the encoding of the real image is set to 1, and the encoding of the generated image is set to 0.

After the training data are generated, high-quality image pairs are used to repeatedly train the network model. During D training, the generated samples are randomly mixed with real samples, and the mixed samples are input into the D again. To discriminate forged and real images, the D is trained, namely, the discrimination loss maximization. The algorithm flow of high-order gated AM-optimized GAN is shown in Fig. 1.5.

1.3.4 Experimental analysis

The performance of the proposed model is verified through a video image super-resolution and deblurring model system built according to the hardware (HW) and software (SW) design on the MATLAB® network simulation platform. The hyperparameters involved are: the iteration is 120 times. Flip and rotation are used to prevent overfitting for data enhancement. The batch size is set to 32, and the input image values are scaled to [0, 1]. The Adam optimizer is used for training, and the LR attenuation strategy is introduced. When the loss index stops improving, the LR

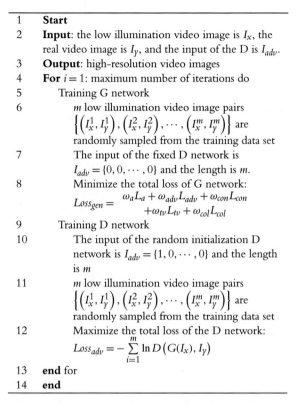

1	**Start**
2	**Input**: the low illumination video image is I_x, the real video image is I_y, and the input of the D is I_{adv}.
3	**Output**: high-resolution video images
4	**For** $i = 1$: maximum number of iterations do
5	Training G network
6	m low illumination video image pairs $\left\{ \left(I_x^1, I_y^1 \right), \left(I_x^2, I_y^2 \right), \cdots, \left(I_x^m, I_y^m \right) \right\}$ are randomly sampled from the training data set
7	The input of the fixed D network is $I_{adv} = \{0, 0, \cdots, 0\}$ and the length is m.
8	Minimize the total loss of G network: $Loss_{gen} = \begin{array}{c} \omega_a L_a + \omega_{adv} L_{adv} + \omega_{con} L_{con} \\ + \omega_{tv} L_{tv} + \omega_{col} L_{col} \end{array}$
9	Training D network
10	The input of the random initialization D network is $I_{adv} = \{1, 0, \cdots, 0\}$ and the length is m
11	m low illumination video image pairs $\left\{ \left(I_x^1, I_y^1 \right), \left(I_x^2, I_y^2 \right), \cdots, \left(I_x^m, I_y^m \right) \right\}$ are randomly sampled from the training data set
12	Maximize the total loss of the D network: $Loss_{adv} = - \sum\limits_{i=1}^{m} \ln D \left(G(I_x), I_y \right)$
13	**end** for
14	**end**

Figure 1.5 Algorithm flow chart of high-order gated AM combined with improved GAN.

is reduced by 50%. Spectral normalization and gradient penalty are used in D constraints. The HW and SW configuration is as follows: a computer with a CORE–i7-4720HQ-2.6GHZ CPU is chosen, the NN is built by using Google's open-source TensorFlow framework, which is a Machine Learning (ML) and DL programming framework based on vector flow graph, while the matrix operation is completed through an open-source matrix processing library, NumPy, and Pandas library that can facilitate data cleaning and data preprocessing.

The real dataset GoPro [37] and the synthetic dataset DIVerse 2K (div2k) [38] are selected as data sources to evaluate and analyze the performance of the proposed model.

The div2k dataset is a high-resolution and high-quality image dataset, including 800 images as the training set and 100 images as the test set. In this experiment, a training set with 21,995 images and a test set with 1123 images are made based on the dataset. The picture size is $100 * 1000$.

GoPro is a natural image sequence data set, in which there are 2023 images in the training set and 1019 images in the test set. The resolution of each image is $1280 * 720$. The blurred image uses bicubic interpolation to downsample the clear image to $320 * 180$. The motion blurred image of the GoPro dataset is generated by the proposed method.

Furthermore, the performance of the proposed video IE model is verified and compared with other related models in the latest literature, including GAN [39], Conditional GAN (CGAN) [40], Laplacian Pyramid of Adversarial Networks (LAPGAN) [41], Deep Convolutional GAN (DC-GAN) [42], and Self-Attention GAN (SA-GAN) [43] through quantitative analysis from Peak Signal-to-Noise Ratio (PSNR) and Structural Similarity (SSIM).

PSNR is a common index for evaluating images measured in dB, and PSNR calculation reads

$$PSNR = 10 \cdot \ln \frac{(2^n - 1)^2}{MSE}. \tag{1.38}$$

In Eq. (1.38), n represents the *byte* digits of each pixel value, *MSE* indicates the mean square error, and its calculation reads

$$MSE = \frac{1}{w \cdot h} \sum_{i=0}^{w-1} \sum_{j=0}^{h-1} \|X(i,j) - Y(i,j)\|^2. \tag{1.39}$$

In Eq. (1.39), the target image is represented by X, whereas Y indicates the source image, and w and h stand for the width and height of the image, respectively. The larger PSNR is, the less distortion is so that the restored target image has higher quality.

SSIM refers to an index that evaluates the structural similarity of two images by integrating image contrast, structural difference, and brightness. The mathematical expression reads

$$SSIM(X, Y) = l(X, Y)^\alpha gc(X, Y)^\beta gs(X, Y)^\gamma. \tag{1.40}$$

In Eq. (1.40), X and Y represent the source image and the target image, respectively, and $l(X, Y)$, $c(X, Y)$, and $s(X, Y)$ refer to the image brightness, contrast, and structure difference, respectively. Generally, the SSIM is usually set as $\alpha = \beta = \gamma = 1$. The larger the value is, the better the restored image effect is.

The recognition accuracy and data transmission performance are further compared and evaluated.

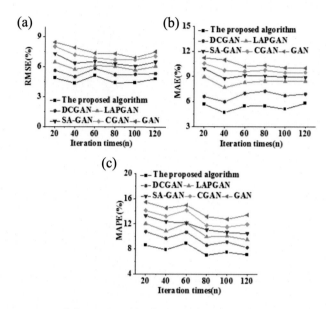

Figure 1.6 Histogram of the error (%) of different algorithms with the increase of the number of iterations under the synthetic data set div2k (a. RMSE; b. MAE; c. MAPE).

1.4 Results and discussion

1.4.1 Accuracy analysis of video image recognition based on different algorithms

The proposed video IE model is compared with GAN, CGAN, LAPGAN, DCGAN, and SA–GAN, and the video image recognition accuracy is analyzed from Root Mean Square Error (RMSE), MAE, and Mean Absolute Percentage Error (MAPE), as shown in Figs. 1.6 and 1.7.

Fig. 1.6 illustrates the changing results of RMSE, MAE, and MAPE of different algorithms with the rise of the iterations under the synthetic dataset div2k. Obviously, the average RMSE, MAE, and MAPE of the proposed video image super-resolution and deblurring model algorithm based on high-order gating AM combined with improved GAN are 4.78%, 5.79%, and 7.08% respectively; the proposed algorithm model outperforms largely other model algorithms in terms of recognition accuracy error.

Fig. 1.7 demonstrates the different algorithms changing results of RMSE, MAE, and MAPE with the increase of iteration times under the real dataset GoPro. Apparently, the average RMSE, MAE, and MAPE of the proposed video image super-resolution and deblurring model algo-

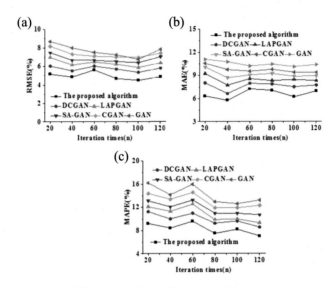

Figure 1.7 Histogram of different error (%) of different algorithms with the increase of iteration times under real dataset GoPro (a. RMSE; b. MAE; c. MAPE).

rithm based on high-order gating AM combined with improved GAN are 4.89%, 6.98%, and 7.08%, respectively; the recognition accuracy error of other model algorithms is significantly higher than that of the proposed algorithm model. Therefore the proposed model algorithm shows high video image recognition accuracy and better robustness under the synthetic dataset div2k and the real dataset GoPro.

1.4.2 Analysis of data transmission performance of different algorithms

Quantitative analysis is made for each algorithm from PSNR and SSIM under the synthetic dataset div2k and the real dataset GoPro, as shown in Figs. 1.8 and 1.9.

Fig. 1.8 reveals that the PSNR of each model algorithm shows an upward trend with the rise of iterations. Specifically, the PSNR of the proposed model algorithm obtains the best result. When the number of iterations is 120, the PSNR is 27.8 db, whereas the PSNR index of other model algorithms decreases slightly, indicating the effectiveness of the proposed method in reducing the number of model parameters. At the same time, there is no significant difference in PSNR between the synthetic dataset div2k and the real dataset GoPro, which shows that the PSNR of

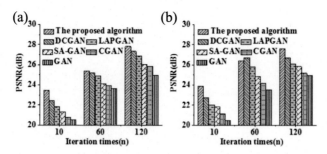

Figure 1.8 Influence curve of each algorithm on PSNR with the increase of iteration times under different datasets (a. synthetic data set div2k; b. real data set GoPro).

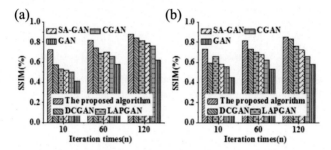

Figure 1.9 Influence curve of each algorithm on SSIM with the rise of iterations under different datasets (a. synthetic dataset div2k; b. real dataset GoPro).

the proposed model algorithm obtains the best results. Thus the proposed video image super-resolution and deblurring model algorithm based on high-order gated AM combined with improved GAN has less distortion and higher quality of the restored target image.

Fig. 1.9 illustrates that the SSIM of each model algorithm shows an upward trend with the increase of the number of iterations. Specifically, the SSIM of the proposed model algorithm obtains the best result when the number of iterations is 120, the SSIM of the proposed algorithm is 0.85, whereas the SSIM index of other model algorithms decreases slightly, which proves the effectiveness of this method in reducing the number of model parameters. At the same time, there is no significant difference in SSIM between the synthetic dataset div2k and the real dataset GoPro, which shows that the SSIM of the proposed model algorithm obtains the best results and has a stronger enhancement ability for low-resolution video images.

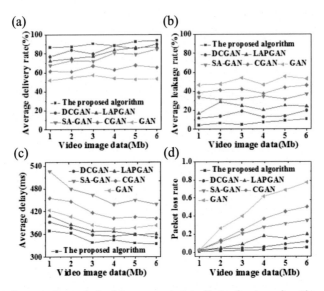

Figure 1.10 Comparative analysis of data transmission effects of various algorithms under different video image data volumes (a. average data delivery rate; b. average data leakage rate; c. average data delay; d. data Packet Loss Rate (PLR)).

1.4.3 Comparative analysis of acceleration efficiency of various NN algorithms

The performance of each algorithm model is analyzed from the data transmission of different model networks, as shown in Fig. 1.10.

The further analysis on transmission performance for video image data of each algorithm implies that with the increase of Energy Consumption (EC) data transmission, the Average Delivery Rate (ADR) of network data presents an upward trend, and the data delivery rate of the proposed algorithm is not less than 86.56% (Fig. 1.10a); the Average Leakage Rate (ALR) of video image data has no significant change, and the data message leakage rate of the proposed algorithm does not exceed 10.83% (Fig. 1.10b); in terms of average data delay, the average data delay decreases as the EC data transmission increases, and the average data delay of the proposed model algorithm finally stabilizes at about 336.85 ms (Fig. 1.10c). In terms of data PLR, CNN algorithm has a high PLR, which might be caused by hidden terminals. The PLR of the proposed algorithm is the lowest, no more than 5.23%, which may be caused by the equalization of the transmitted data (Fig. 1.10d). Therefore from the perspective of the transmission volume of different EC data, the proposed video image super-resolution and deblurring model based on the high-order gated AM-optimized GAN shows significantly higher ADR, the lowest ALR, and a low delay, so it has an excellent network secure transmission effect.

1.5 Conclusion

This research aims at the shortcomings of traditional low illumination or low-resolution video IE algorithms and existing DL algorithms and proposes a video image super-resolution and deblurring model based on high-order gated AM. Specifically, the high-order gated AM is used to automatically learn different attention levels to realize the super-resolution and motion deblurring of the synthetic image. Finally, experimental analysis finds that the proposed model algorithm has the best image recognition accuracy, with an error of about 5%, and the quantization result of the proposed image quality restoration method is PSNR = 27.8, SSIM = 0.85. Meanwhile, the advantages of the proposed algorithm are guaranteed in data transmission, which can provide a reference basis for the later video IE and resolution increase. However, this research also has some shortcomings. First, in reality, it is difficult to obtain paired low illumination or low-resolution video image datasets, and there are many lighting modes and styles. The synthetic lighting and noise are usually different from those in nature, resulting in the limited ability of these low illumination enhancement methods based on synthetic images to enhance low illumination images from the real world. Unsupervised learning, such as CycleGAN, can be used to convert low illumination images to real images. Moreover, low illumination or low-resolution video images have a large loss of content information due to uneven illumination distribution and various noises. How to model multi-scale to extract weak light image information and reduce the feature loss caused by the deepening of the network is also a research direction in the future. Additionally, the experiment only focuses on the research of video image data enhancement and uses the classic image dataset. However, to apply the data enhancement technology to such actual scenes as the industrial or the medical field, it needs to collect images exclusively, with an extremely huge workload and a longer time cost. Hence there is a need to design targeted models for different datasets and adjust and set appropriate parameters, which is surely feasible, given the development of big data and hardware equipment. Lastly, expanding data enhancement technology to text data enhancement, voice enhancement, and video data enhancement is also a future research direction.

Acknowledgment

This research is financially supported by the Ministry of Science and Technology, Taiwan, ROC under the project number 108-2410-H-019-012-SSS and MOST: 106-2410-H-019-020.

References

[1] Q. Ding, L. Shen, L. Yu, H. Yang, M. Xu, Patch-wise spatial-temporal quality enhancement for HEVC compressed video, IEEE Transactions on Image Processing 30 (2021) 6459–6472.
[2] M. Stein, H. Janetzko, A. Lamprecht, T. Breitkreutz, P. Zimmermann, B. Goldlücke, T. Schreck, G. Andrienko, M. Grossniklaus, D.A. Keim, Bring it to the pitch: Combining video and movement data to enhance team sport analysis, IEEE Transactions on Visualization and Computer Graphics 24 (1) (2017) 13–22.
[3] K. Bairagi, S. Mitra, U. Bhattacharya, Coverage aware scheduling strategies for 3D wireless video sensor nodes to enhance network lifetime, IEEE Access 9 (2021) 124176–124199.
[4] S. Ma, X. Zhang, C. Jia, Z. Zhao, S. Wang, S. Wang, Image and video compression with neural networks: A review, IEEE Transactions on Circuits and Systems for Video Technology 30 (6) (2019) 1683–1698.
[5] Z. Guan, Q. Xing, M. Xu, R. Yang, T. Liu, Z. Wang, MFQE 2.0: A new approach for multi-frame quality enhancement on compressed video, IEEE Transactions on Pattern Analysis and Machine Intelligence 43 (3) (2019) 949–963.
[6] Y. Zhou, L. Tian, C. Zhu, X. Jin, Y. Sun, Video coding optimization for virtual reality 360-degree source, IEEE Journal of Selected Topics in Signal Processing 14 (1) (2019) 118–129.
[7] H. Wang, D. Su, C. Liu, L. Jin, X. Sun, X. Peng, Deformable non-local network for video super-resolution, IEEE Access 7 (2019) 177734–177744.
[8] P. Wang, H. Zhang, V.M. Patel, SAR image despeckling using a convolutional neural network, IEEE Signal Processing Letters 24 (12) (2017) 1763–1767.
[9] Q. Yuan, Q. Zhang, J. Li, H. Shen, L. Zhang, Hyperspectral image denoising employing a spatial-spectral deep residual convolutional neural network, IEEE Transactions on Geoscience and Remote Sensing 57 (2) (2018) 1205–1218.
[10] Y. Jin, J. Zhang, S. Jin, B. Ai, Channel estimation for cell-free mmWave massive MIMO through deep learning, IEEE Transactions on Vehicular Technology 68 (10) (2019) 10325–10329.
[11] S.F. Wang, W.K. Yu, Y.X. Li, Multi-wavelet residual dense convolutional neural network for image denoising, IEEE Access 8 (2020) 214413–214424.
[12] K. Panetta, L. Kezebou, V. Oludare, S. Agaian, Comprehensive underwater object tracking benchmark dataset and underwater image enhancement with GAN, IEEE Journal of Oceanic Engineering (2021) 1–17.
[13] G. Li, Y. Yang, X. Qu, D. Cao, K. Li, A deep learning based image enhancement approach for autonomous driving at night, Knowledge-Based Systems 213 (2021) 106617.
[14] X.I.E. Xin, X.I.A. Zhelei, Image recognition of cervical cancer cells based on deep convolution neural networks, Journal of China University of Metrology 2 (2018) 14.
[15] N. He, M.E. Paoletti, J.M. Haut, L. Fang, S. Li, A. Plaza, J. Plaza, Feature extraction with multiscale covariance maps for hyperspectral image classification, IEEE Transactions on Geoscience and Remote Sensing 57 (2) (2018) 755–769.
[16] H. Jia, X. Peng, W. Song, C. Lang, Z. Xing, K. Sun, Multiverse optimization algorithm based on Lévy flight improvement for multi-threshold color image segmentation, IEEE Access 7 (2019) 32805–32844.

[17] W. Kim, A. Kanezaki, M. Tanaka, Unsupervised learning of image segmentation based on differentiable feature clustering, IEEE Transactions on Image Processing 29 (2020) 8055–8068.

[18] S. Yang, Y. Hu, W. Yang, L.Y. Duan, J. Liu, Towards coding for human and machine vision: Scalable face image coding, IEEE Transactions on Multimedia 23 (2021) 2957–2971.

[19] W. Hu, W. Wang, C. Ai, J. Wang, W. Wang, X. Meng, J. Liu, H. Tao, S. Qiu, Machine vision-based surface crack analysis for transportation infrastructure, Automation in Construction 132 (2021) 103973.

[20] K. Jiang, Z. Wang, P. Yi, G. Wang, T. Lu, J. Jiang, Edge-enhanced GAN for remote sensing image superresolution, IEEE Transactions on Geoscience and Remote Sensing 57 (8) (2019) 5799–5812.

[21] D. Liu, B. Cheng, Z. Wang, H. Zhang, T.S. Huang, Enhance visual recognition under adverse conditions via deep networks, IEEE Transactions on Image Processing 28 (9) (2019) 4401–4412.

[22] C.O. Ancuti, C. Ancuti, C. De Vleeschouwer, P. Bekaert, Color balance and fusion for underwater image enhancement, IEEE Transactions on Image Processing 27 (1) (2017) 379–393.

[23] C. Dai, X. Liu, J. Lai, P. Li, H.C. Chao, Human behavior deep recognition architecture for smart city applications in the 5G environment, IEEE Network 33 (5) (2019) 206–211.

[24] M. Han, Z. Lyu, T. Qiu, M. Xu, A review on intelligence dehazing and color restoration for underwater images, IEEE Transactions on Systems, Man, and Cybernetics: Systems 50 (5) (2018) 1820–1832.

[25] V. Monga, Y. Li, Y.C. Eldar, Algorithm unrolling: Interpretable, efficient deep learning for signal and image processing, IEEE Signal Processing Magazine 38 (2) (2021) 18–44.

[26] L. Jiao, J. Zhao, A survey on the new generation of deep learning in image processing, IEEE Access 7 (2019) 172231–172263.

[27] P. Yi, Z. Wang, K. Jiang, J. Jiang, T. Lu, J. Ma, A progressive fusion generative adversarial network for realistic and consistent video super-resolution, IEEE Transactions on Pattern Analysis and Machine Intelligence 44 (5) (2020) 2264–2280.

[28] F. Wu, X.Y. Jing, Z. Wu, Y. Ji, X. Dong, X. Luo, Q. Huang, R. Wang, Modality-specific and shared generative adversarial network for cross-modal retrieval, Pattern Recognition 104 (2020) 107335.

[29] A. Lucas, S. Lopez-Tapia, R. Molina, A.K. Katsaggelos, Generative adversarial networks and perceptual losses for video super-resolution, IEEE Transactions on Image Processing 28 (7) (2019) 3312–3327.

[30] L. Zhu, S. Kwong, Y. Zhang, S. Wang, X. Wang, Generative adversarial network-based intra prediction for video coding, IEEE Transactions on Multimedia 22 (1) (2019) 45–58.

[31] T.A. Song, S.R. Chowdhury, F. Yang, J. Dutta, PET image super-resolution using generative adversarial networks, Neural Networks 125 (2020) 83–91.

[32] L.H. Chen, C.G. Bampis, Z. Li, A.C. Bovik, Learning to distort images using generative adversarial networks, IEEE Signal Processing Letters 27 (2020) 2144–2148.

[33] J. Yang, Z. Zhao, H. Zhang, Y. Shi, Data augmentation for X-ray prohibited item images using generative adversarial networks, IEEE Access 7 (2019) 28894–28902.

[34] L.E. Falqueto, J.A. Sá, R.L. Paes, A. Passaro, Oil rig recognition using convolutional neural network on Sentinel-1 SAR images, IEEE Geoscience and Remote Sensing Letters 16 (8) (2019) 1329–1333.

[35] C. Jia, X. Zhang, S. Wang, S. Wang, S. Ma, Light field image compression using generative adversarial network-based view synthesis, IEEE Journal on Emerging and Selected Topics in Circuits and Systems 9 (1) (2018) 177–189.

[36] M. Yang, K. Hu, Y. Du, Z. Wei, Z. Sheng, J. Hu, Underwater image enhancement based on conditional generative adversarial network, Signal Processing: Image Communication 81 (2020) 115723.

[37] K. Zhang, W. Luo, Y. Zhong, L. Ma, W. Liu, H. Li, Adversarial spatio-temporal learning for video deblurring, IEEE Transactions on Image Processing 28 (1) (2018) 291–301.

[38] Q. Li, X. Wang, X. Wang, B. Ma, C. Wang, Y. Xian, Y. Shi, A novel grayscale image steganography scheme based on chaos encryption and generative adversarial networks, IEEE Access 8 (2020) 168166–168176.

[39] P. Xiang, L. Wang, F. Wu, J. Cheng, M. Zhou, Single-image de-raining with the feature-supervised generative adversarial network, IEEE Signal Processing Letters 26 (5) (2019) 650–654.

[40] F. Dong, Y. Zhang, X. Nie, Dual discriminator generative adversarial network for video anomaly detection, IEEE Access 8 (2020) 88170–88176.

[41] Y. Fan, G. Wen, F. Xiao, S. Qiu, D. Li, Detecting anomalies in videos using perception generative adversarial networks, Circuits, Systems, and Signal Processing (2021) 1–25.

[42] J.U. Yun, B. Jo, I.K. Park, Joint face super-resolution and deblurring using the generative adversarial network, IEEE Access 8 (2020) 159661–159671.

[43] Y. Pang, J. Xie, X. Li, Visual haze removal by a unified generative adversarial network, IEEE Transactions on Circuits and Systems for Video Technology 29 (11) (2018) 3211–3221.

CHAPTER 2

On estimating uncertainty of fingerprint enhancement models

Indu Joshi[a,e], Ayush Utkarsh[b], Riya Kothari[c], Vinod K. Kurmi[d], Antitza Dantcheva[a], Sumantra Dutta Roy[e], and Prem Kumar Kalra[e]

[a]Inria Sophia Antipolis, Biot, France
[b]Independent Researcher, Ranchi, India
[c]University of Southern California, Los Angeles, CA, United States
[d]KU Leuven, Leuven, Belgium
[e]Indian Institute of Technology Delhi, New Delhi, India

2.1 Introduction

The ubiquitous nature of fingerprints and the robust performance of automated fingerprint recognition systems (AFRS) promotes its application in forensics, law enforcement, access control, and a wide range of other applications. An AFRS typically constitutes of five modules: acquisition, region of interest (ROI) segmentation, enhancement, feature extraction, and matching. The performance of an AFRS majorly depends on feature extraction and matching modules. ROI segmentation and enhancement modules are typically designed to improve the performance of the fingerprint extraction module. While acquiring a fingerprint image, the quality of obtained fingerprint image depends on various factors, such as fingerprint sensing technology used, the physical condition of the fingertip (fingertip skin quality, aging, scars, cuts, wrinkles, dry or wet skin), and physical contact between fingertip and sensor, i.e., exertion of excessive or too low pressure. Poor skin conditions lead to spurious minutiae or fading away of genuine minutiae. Dry fingertips are difficult to image and result in blurred ridges. Wet fingertips often lead to thickened ridges, unclear valleys and sometimes may lead to false minutiae due to false joining of ridges. Similarly, inappropriate contact with fingerprint sensors leads to fingerprint images with poor contrast. Various studies report the correlation between fingerprint image quality and performance of AFRS and the challenges of state-of-the-art AFRS on poor quality fingerprints. Fig. 2.1 presents sample poor quality fingerprints used for the experiments and analysis presented in this chapter. To alleviate the limitation of AFRS on poor quality fingerprint images, the fingerprint *enhancement* module plays a key role.

Digital Image Enhancement and Reconstruction
https://doi.org/10.1016/B978-0-32-398370-9.00009-3
29

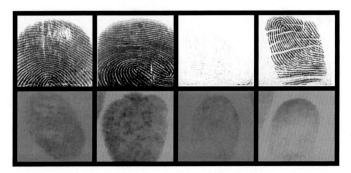

Figure 2.1 *Sample poor quality fingerprints used for the experiments and analysis presented in this chapter.* Rural Indian fingerprint database [46] comprises of distorted fingerprints with unclear ridges due to warts, scars, and creases along with dry and wet fingerprint images (see the first row). IIITD-MOLF database [55] comprises of samples with unclear ridge details, background noise, and overlapping fingerprints in the background (see the second row).

A fingerprint enhancement module improves the contrast of a fingerprint image, removes background noise, improves ridge–valley clarity, and predicts the missing ridge information due to poor skin condition, overlapping text, or overlapping fingerprints in the background (usually found in case of latent fingerprints). As a result, the quality of a fingerprint image is generally improved after fingerprint enhancement. The improved quality of the fingerprint image improves its suitability for authentication by promoting accurate minutiae extraction. Accurate minutiae extraction, by consequence, improves the authentication performance of AFRS. Although fingerprint enhancement module is an essential part of an AFRS, enhancement is especially critical for nonideal fingerprints (such as fingerprints of aging and elderly population), people involved in excessive manual work (such as the rural population of undeveloped or developing nations), fingerprints with cosmetics (such as henna and fingerprints found at crime scenes; latent fingerprints). State-of-the-art fingerprint enhancement models are mostly based on deep neural networks that often perform enhancement like a black box and do not specify cases for which the model is expected to fail. Failure of fingerprint enhancement models and subsequently of AFRS on genuine samples often leads to undue inconvenience to genuine users. Estimating *uncertainty* of a predictive model allows interpreting the confidence of a model in its prediction. A reliable measure of uncertainty of a fingerprint enhancement model can be especially useful to identify the samples for which model is highly likely to generate an erroneous enhanced image. Such cases can be segregated for manual evaluation.

Uncertainty can also be useful for a human operator to understand what is causing the model to fail. Thus to interpret the otherwise black–box behavior of standard fingerprint enhancement models, the notion of uncertainty is introduced in fingerprint enhancement models.

Uncertainty originating in a fingerprint enhancement model can be broadly categorized as either *model uncertainty* or *data uncertainty*. Model uncertainty signifies the uncertainty in model parameters due to the limited availability of training data. Model uncertainty can asymptotically vanish in the limit of infinite training data. Model uncertainty is usually higher for out-of-distribution samples, i.e., fingerprints with noise patterns that are not seen during training. As a result, the fingerprint samples with noise patterns unseen during training, and for which the fingerprint enhancement generates an erroneous enhanced image, the predicted model uncertainty is usually high, whereas data uncertainty is the uncertainty originating due to noise present in a given fingerprint sample. Occlusion due to text or overlapping fingerprints in the background, sensor noise, unclear ridge information due to injuries, aging, or creases results in high data uncertainty. Data uncertainty cannot be explained away even in the limit of infinite training data as it captures the inherent noise in a fingerprint sample. As a result, both these uncertainties extract different but complementary information that imparts interpretability to fingerprint enhancement models. Fig. 2.2 illustrates both model uncertainty and data uncertainty observed during fingerprint enhancement by a state-of-the-art fingerprint enhancement model FP-E-GAN. We observe that introducing either type of uncertainty improves the performance of the baseline fingerprint enhancement model. Additionally, the predicted spatial uncertainty maps impart interpretability to the fingerprint enhancement model.

Research contributions

The research contributions in this chapter are as follows:

- This chapter is based on recent researches in the fingerprints domain [26], [28], and [29], and discusses in detail how to interpret model and data uncertainty from deep learning-based fingerprint enhancement models.
- A rigorous analysis of model parameters, computation time, and model performance is presented to understand the effect of both the kind of uncertainties.
- A detailed analysis of predicted uncertainties is provided to share insights on model and data uncertainty.

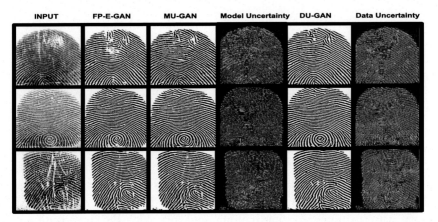

| INPUT | FP-E-GAN | MU-GAN | Model Uncertainty | DU-GAN | Data Uncertainty |

Figure 2.2 *Visualization of uncertainty estimated for a fingerprint enhancement model.* MU-GAN and DU-GAN represent the fingerprint enhancement model obtained by introducing model uncertainty and data uncertainty respectively into the baseline fingerprint enhancement model FP-E-GAN. The visualization of both the uncertainties illustrates that higher model uncertainty is predicted for the pixels where the enhancement model generates spurious patterns (first row) or erroneously enhances background noise (last row). The fingerprint enhancement model predicts higher data uncertainty for noisy and background pixels, which in turn, helps the model to minimize erroneous predictions on noisy pixels.

- For analyzing the effect of uncertainty on fingerprint enhancement, both data uncertainty and model uncertainty are introduced into two different state-of-the-art fingerprint enhancement models.
- Three challenging databases corresponding to the fingerprints acquired from the rural Indian population and latent fingerprints are used to evaluate the effectiveness of modeling model and data uncertainties.
- To evaluate the generalization ability of modeling data and model uncertainties on fingerprint preprocessing models, their effect on fingerprint segmentation is analyzed. Experiments on fingerprint ROI segmentation are conducted on twelve challenging publicly available fingerprints databases.

2.2 Related work

2.2.1 Fingerprint enhancement

2.2.1.1 Classical image processing techniques for enhancement

Traditional approaches for fingerprint enhancement perform *filtering* either in spatial or frequency domain to exploit cues such as ridge orientation or ridge continuity to recover the corrupted or unclear regions of a fingerprint image [9,19–21,23,52,63,67]. Hong et al. [23] work on a normalized fingerprint image to compute ridge orientation through gradients and ridge frequency by modeling a sinusoid wave along a direction normal to the ridge orientation. The enhanced image is obtained by applying Gabor filters tuned to the computed orientation and frequency. Gottschlich and Schönlieb [21] perform locally adaptive fingerprint enhancement through anisotropic filtering along the direction of local ridge orientations. Turroni et al. [63] exploit context defined by local orientation, frequency, and quality to adapt the filter characteristics for a specific fingerprint region. The authors propose to iteratively apply contextual filtering, starting from high-quality regions to low-quality regions so that the contextual information from low-quality regions can be reliably predicted. Ramos et al. [52] apply adaptive Gabor filtering such that the standard deviation of Gaussian function in the Gabor filter is adapted based on the signal frequency. Wang et al. [67] argue that Gabor filters have limited bandwidth, whereas the log-Gabor filters can be designed with any arbitrary bandwidth. Consequently, log-Gabor filters are better suited for oriented-textured patterns, such as fingerprints. The authors calculate the orientation and ridge frequency as defined in [23], whereas the curvature information is used to find the angular bandwidth for filtering with log-Gabor filter. Gottschlich [20] argues that the curved Gabor filter is highly suited for fingerprints due to their inherent curvature and uses it for filtering fingerprint ridges. Chikkerur et al. [9] exploit short-time Fourier transform (STFT) to estimate ridge orientation and ridge frequency. Context filtering using the estimated filters is used to obtain the enhanced image. Ghafoor et al. [19] propose a method that offers the advantages of filtering in both frequency and spatial domain. The authors propose band-pass filtering in the frequency domain so that only ridge patterns are filtered. Furthermore, directional filtering is applied in the spatial domain to smooth ridges along the ridge directions.

Hsieh et al. [24] observe that the approaches presented above focus only on local information, such as ridge orientation and ignore global information. The authors propose to perform wavelet decomposition to obtain different spatial or frequency subimages. These subimages are converted into texture spectrum domain and use global information to improve under- or overinked regions. Directional filtering followed by wavelet reconstruction is used to obtain the enhanced fingerprint image. Jirachaweng and Areekul [25] argue that the Gabor filters result in ridge discontinuity and blocking artifacts around regions with high curvatures. Furthermore, the computational complexity of enhancement algorithms due to the computation of fast Fourier transform (FFT) is very high. To address these limitations, the authors propose to apply filtering on the discrete cosine transform (DCT) domain. Yoon et al. [71] estimate fingerprint rotation and skin distortion model to estimate orientation field. Furthermore, they also estimate orientations from singular points using the zero–pole method. Both the manual marked region of interest and singular points information are exploited to obtain the orientation field for a given input fingerprint. The orientation field is then used to tune the Gabor filter and obtain an enhanced fingerprint image.

A general shortcoming of classical image processing-based fingerprint enhancement methods is that their performance is heavily dependent upon the quality of contextual information, i.e., ridge orientation and ridge frequency. Quite often, the contextual information extracted by these methods around fingerprint regions with high distortions is not reliable. Consequently, these methods generally obtain poor performance on highly distorted fingerprint regions. To address the abovementioned limitation, learning-based fingerprint enhancement methods are proposed.

2.2.1.2 Learning-based enhancement models

Many algorithms use *dictionary based approach* for approximating orientation field [7,8,12,36,70]. Feng et al. [12] argue that the orientation estimation is analogous to spelling correction in a sentence. They propose to create a dictionary of orientation patches and claim that it helps to eliminate nonwords errors, i.e., prediction of such orientations that cannot exist in real life. To begin with, the authors compute an initial estimate of the orientation field using STFT and compare the initial estimate with each dictionary element to identify potential candidates. Furthermore, they use compatibility between the neighboring patches to find the optimal candidate. Orientation information of all orientation patches is then summarized to obtain the final orientation field. Yang et al. [70] utilize spatial locality information to improve orientation estimation. The authors claim that only specific orientations occur at a given location. To exploit this information, they introduce localized dictionaries, i.e., create a dictionary for every location in a fingerprint. Due to this, each dictionary contains only a limited number of orientations leading to faster dictionary look-ups and fewer nonword errors. Chen et al. [8] observe that the average size of noise varies depending upon the quality of fingerprints. For a poor quality image, one can obtain better results by using a dictionary with bigger patch size and vice-versa. Motivated by this observation, the authors create multiscale dictionaries, i.e., dictionaries of different patch sizes, and use compatibility between neighbors across different scales to find the optimal orientation patch for a given estimate. Liu et al. [36] propose sparse coding for denoising of orientation patches. Authors create multiscale dictionaries from good quality fingerprints. After computing the initial estimate, they then reconstruct the orientation using the dictionary of the smallest size with sparse coding. The quality of an orientation patch is then estimated based on compatibility with the neighbors. If the quality is below a certain threshold, then the orientation patch is reconstructed using a dictionary of bigger patches. This process is continued until the quality of the reconstructed orientation patch is satisfactory. Chaidee et al. [7] propose sparse-coded dictionary learning in the frequency domain, which fuses responses from Gabor and curved filters. The dictionary is constructed from the frequency response. During testing, spectral response is computed and encoded by the spectral encoder. The sparse representation of the spectral code is computed and decoded by the spectral decoder to reconstruct the Fourier spectrum. A weighted sum of the reconstructed image is obtained from both the filters is computed to obtain the final enhanced image.

A common shortcoming of dictionary-based orientation estimation approaches is that the dictionary is constructed from good quality fingerprint patches, due to which the orientation is not reliably predicted for noisy fingerprint regions. To address this limitation, *orientation prediction networks* are proposed [3,48]. Cao and Jain [3] pose orientation field estimation as a classification problem and exploit a CNN-based classification model. K-means clustering is performed on orientation patches of good quality images to select 128 representative orientation patch classes. The authors extract 1000 orientation patches for each orientation class and train the network with the corresponding simulated poor quality fingerprint. During testing, for each patch in the input fingerprint, an orientation class is predicted by the model. Qu et al. [48] propose a deep regression neural network to predict orientation angle values. The input fingerprint image is first preprocessed using total variation decomposition and Log-Gabor filtering. The preprocessed image is presented as input to the network and orientation is estimated. Boosting is performed to further improve the prediction accuracy. Later, researchers make a paradigm shift in fingerprint enhancement by working towards *directly constructing the enhanced image* [35,47,50,54,56,60,69], rather than predicting the orientation field and filtering through the Gabor filter tuned at the predicted orientation.

Sahasrabudhe and Namboodiri [54] propose a deep belief network for the enhancement of fingerprints. The network is trained using a greedy strategy such that the first layer learns oriented ridges, while the second layer learns higher-level features. Hierarchical probabilistic inference from the second layer is used for reconstructing enhanced fingerprints. Schuch et al. [56] propose a deconvolutional autoencoder (DeConvNet) for enhancement of fingerprint images. Svoboda et al. [60] propose an autoencoder network that is trained to minimize gradient and orientation between the output and target enhanced image. Qian et al. [47] exploit DenseUNet to enhance poor quality fingerprint patches. Wong and Lai [69] propose a multi-task learning model that is trained to generate not only an enhanced image but also perform orientation correction. Li et al. [35] propose a multitask learning-based enhancement algorithm that accepts texture component of fingerprint image (preprocessed using total variation decomposition) as an input for the proposed model. The proposed solution is based on encoder-decoder architecture trained with a multi-task learning loss. One branch enhances the fingerprint, and the other branch predicts orientation. Schuch et al. [57] present rigorous comparisons between several relevant fingerprint enhancement methods.

To summarize, most of the learning-based fingerprint enhancement methods utilize autoencoder architectures at their core and improve their representations either through predicting related information or using an adversarial discriminator. We also observe that all the models proposed so far are black-box models and do not provide any information on the model's confidence in the prediction. All these observations motivate the discussions in this chapter.

2.2.2 Uncertainty estimation

Uncertainty estimation techniques can be broadly categorized into four different categories: *single network deterministic techniques, ensemble techniques, test-time augmentation techniques,* and *Bayesian techniques.* Single network deterministic techniques for uncertainty estimation are the methods in which only a single forward pass is required to make a prediction. The uncertainty is either directly predicted by the model or an external network is exploited to predict it. Ensemble techniques combine the predictions of several deterministic models and estimate the predictive uncertainty. Test-time augmentation techniques also exploit a single deterministic model to make a prediction. However, during testing, these techniques augment the test input to obtain various predictions and later exploit these predictions to estimate predictive uncertainty. Bayesian techniques are the methods that exploit stochastic deep models to make a prediction. Because of the stochastic nature of the model, different predictions are obtained for the same input during different inferences. These different predictions are then used to estimate the predictive uncertainty.

2.2.2.1 Uncertainty estimation through single network deterministic techniques

A deterministic model is characterized by fixed model weights. Subsequently, in a deterministic network, the prediction is always the same after forwarding the same input. The uncertainty for a deterministic model is either obtained by using an external network [49,51] or directly predicted by the network itself [38,40,58]. Prior networks and Gradient penalty-based methods are among the most widely used methods in this category. In the Prior networks [39], the Dirichlet distribution is modeled for a network's output to obtain the distribution of uncertainty. To train the model, Kullback–Leibler divergence (KLD) is minimized between the predictions of in-distribution data with a sharp Dirichlet distribution. For the out-of-distribution data, the prediction is KLD is minimized between a flat Dirichlet distribution and the predictions. On the other hand, the gradient penalty-based method [65] enforces the detectability of changes to obtain the out-of-distribution (OOD) data. Similarly, methods proposed in [34,44] use the gradient metric, such as norms, to define the uncertainty of the prediction. A major limitation of this category of techniques is high sensitivity to initial model weights [18].

2.2.2.2 Uncertainty estimation through ensemble techniques

An ensemble model combines the prediction from different models. Ensemble techniques for uncertainty estimation model network parameters as random variables of some prior distribution. For each forward pass, the model parameters are sampled from this distribution. As a result, stochastic model outputs are obtained and uncertainty of these predictions is quantified. An ensemble model can be obtained in different ways, such as data shuffle [33], random initialization, bagging, boosting [1], and employing different architectures. Other ensemble-based approaches for uncertainty estimation include subsample [64] and batch samples [68]. These methods aim towards lowering the memory and computational requirements through sharing of parts among the single members. Deep ensemble [14] is one of the most frequently used ensemble-based techniques to obtain the uncertainty in deep learning models. Gustafsson et al. [22] show comparisons between ensemble and Monte Carlo dropout sampling based uncertainty. Ovadia et al. [45] evaluate different uncertainty methods for a task in which the test set has a distributional shift. Vyas et al. [66] show that the OOD detection is improved in case of ensemble models. High memory requirements for training and testing is a key limitation of this category of approaches for uncertainty estimation [18].

2.2.2.3 Uncertainty estimation through test-time augmentation techniques

It is an easy to implement category of uncertainty estimation techniques. The basic working principle behind these techniques is to exploit different views from a given test data by augmenting it. All the augmented samples are used to obtain the final prediction and the associated uncertainty. The techniques in this category are especially useful for applications with very limited data, such as medical image processing. Shanmugam et al. [59] argue that several factors, such as size of the training set, nature of problem, network architecture and kind of augmentation, must be taken into consideration while choosing a test-time augmentation strategy. In particular, the authors propose an aggregation function to aggregate the predictions obtained for the various augmented inputs. Kim et al. [32] propose to learn a loss predictor such that the test-time augmentation with the minimum loss for an input sample is selected. Lyzhov et al. [37] propose greedy policy search to design a test-time augmentation policy that selects augmentations to be performed. High inference time is a major limitation of this class of uncertainty estimation techniques [18].

2.2.2.4 Uncertainty estimation through Bayesian techniques

Bayesian techniques for uncertainty estimation model a deterministic deep model into a Bayesian neural network (BNN). These methods estimate posterior distribution over model parameters (conditioned on the training data) is obtained using a prior distribution. The BNN posterior can capture the uncertainty in model parameters, which can obtain the uncertainty in the predictions. This uncertainty occurs due to uncertainty in model parameters and called model uncertainty. There are many works proposed to estimate and model the uncertainty in the deep learning models. In the classification problem, Szegedy et al. [61] propose to treat softmax output as one source of uncertainty. However, imperceptible perturbations to a real image can change a deep network's softmax output to arbitrary values due to which softmax output is not a good estimate of the uncertainty. Another way is to obtain uncertainty through OOD. Some of the works proposed methods for OOD are likelihood test ratio [53], density estimation, and bias detection. Gal [15] model two types of uncertainties in deep learning models, namely epistemic and aleatoric uncertainty. Traditionally, BNNs have been computationally complex and far more complicated than non-Bayesian NNs. Monte Carlo dropout is a practical way to approximate BNNs [16]. Concrete dropout [17] explores the dropout probabilities to obtain the variation inference using dropout. A major advantage of these approximation-based methods is that these only require ensemble of prediction at test time, which makes these methods widely applied in many downstream tasks [31,41]. Malinin [38] propose data uncertainty using the entropy measurement. Low memory requirements and low sensitivity to choice of initial model weights [18] encourage the use of Bayesian techniques for estimating uncertainty of fingerprint enhancement models.

2.3 Model uncertainty estimation

Uncertainty in a fingerprint enhancement can originate either because of uncertainty in model parameters termed as model uncertainty or uncertainty as a result of noise in the input fingerprint image. State-of-the-art deep learning-based fingerprint enhancement models are deterministic models that output point estimates of prediction. To exploit Bayesian techniques for approximating uncertainty from a deterministic model, it is converted into a probabilistic model so that the statistical analysis of model's prediction can be conducted. Estimating model uncertainty in a fingerprint enhancement model aims at understanding what the fingerprint enhancement model does not know. State-of-the-art deep models for fingerprint enhancement do not output model uncertainty. Studies indicate that the predictive probabilities output by deep models cannot correctly indicate the model's confidence in the prediction. Gal and Ghahramani [16] demonstrate that an uncertain deep model may also output a high predictive probability through the output of softmax. Therefore a high predictive probability cannot be regarded as a reliable measure to infer the model's confidence. Bayesian deep learning offers a practical mechanism to infer uncertainty from deep learning-based fingerprint enhancement models. Estimating model uncertainty allows to know the confidence with which output of the fingerprint enhancement can be trusted. To formalize, model uncertainty is modeled as placing a prior distribution over the weights of a model, and then estimating how much these weights vary given the training data. Monte Carlo dropout is a computationally efficient mechanism to estimate model uncertainty from a deep fingerprint enhancement model. The spatial uncertainty maps output during inference indicate the fingerprint enhancement model's per-pixel confidence. We now share details on Monte Carlo dropout-based model uncertainty estimation.

2.3.1 Bayesian neural networks

Assuming that the training set of input fingerprint images is denoted by $X = \{x_1, x_2...x_M\}$, the set of corresponding enhanced images is denoted as $Y = \{y_1, y_2...y_M\}$, and the baseline fingerprint enhancement model is represented as $y = f^\theta(x)$. A Bayesian neural network (BNN) aims to infer the distribution over model weights θ that are likely to have generated the set of enhanced images; Y for a given training set of input fingerprint images X and baseline fingerprint enhancement model. The probability distribution of an enhanced image, given an input fingerprint, is denoted as $p(y|x, \theta)$. Training of a BNN implies learning the posterior distribution $p(\theta|X, Y)$ and finding the most probable model weights, given the set of input fingerprints and corresponding enhanced fingerprints images. For a given test input fingerprint image x_{test}, the output probability is defined as

$$p(y_{test}|x_{test}, X, Y) = \int p(y_{test}|x_{test}, \theta) p(\theta|X, Y) \, d\theta,$$

$$p(\theta|X, Y) = \frac{p(X, Y|\theta) p(\theta)}{\int p(X, Y|\theta) p(\theta) \, d\theta}.$$

Obtaining the posterior probability distribution, however, requires marginalizing the product of the likelihood ($p(X, Y|\theta)$) and the prior ($p(\theta)$) over all the possible combinations of model weights. Deep models have an extremely high number of model weights, due to which marginalizing is impractical. As a result, posterior probability distribution $p(\theta|X, Y)$ of a deep model is intractable. However, to conduct from inference a BNN, the posterior probability is required. To overcome this limitation of BNNs, the variational inference is a widely used technique to approximate the posterior of model weights. It requires defining an approximating variational distribution $q_w(\theta)$ such that $q_w(\theta)$ is close to the true posterior of model weights. Here w denotes the variational parameters of the approximated distribution:

$$p(y_{test}|x_{test}, X, Y) \approx \int p(y_{test}|x_{test}, \theta) q_w(\theta) \, d\theta.$$

2.3.2 Approximating inference via Monte Carlo dropout

For a given neural network of any arbitrary depth and non–linearities, Gal and Ghahramani [16] in their seminal work show that by introducing a Bernoulli distribution over approximating variational distribution placed over every layer of model weights, the model effectively minimizes the KLD between the posterior and the approximate distribution. This enables approximation of variational inference from a deterministic deep neural network by reparameterizing the variational distribution as a Bernoulli distribution. Dropout allows sampling of a binary variable for each input fingerprint image and every output unit in each layer of the model. Assume y_k represents the output of layer k. After the introduction of dropout, the output is modified as

$$y_k = p_k * y_k,$$
$$y_k = Bernoulli(p_k)\, y_k.$$

This result signifies that the introduction of dropout is essentially placing a Bernoulli variational distribution over model weights. Therefore for any deterministic deep model, approximation of Bayesian inference can be obtained by applying dropout before every layer of model weights. Monte Carlo integration is a practical approximation mechanism for evaluating the integral for variational inference. Here, the Monte Carlo integration of the model outputs after introducing dropout is carried out, due to which the method is termed as *Monte Carlo dropout*.

$$p(y_{test}|x_{test}, X, Y) \approx \int p(y_{test}|x_{test}, \theta)\, q_w(\theta)\, d\theta$$
$$= \frac{1}{S} \sum_{s=1}^{S} p(y_{test}|x_{test}, \tilde{\theta}_s),$$

where $\tilde{\theta}_s \sim q_w(\theta)$ and $q_w(\theta)$ is the dropout distribution. The above result implies that the output of the model is approximated by averaging the output of S stochastic outputs (a stochastic output is the model output obtained after forward pass over the model with dropout).

2.3.3 Estimating model uncertainty

Model uncertainty is quantified as the variance of the model predictions. Model uncertainty through Monte Carlo dropout-based deep Bayesian

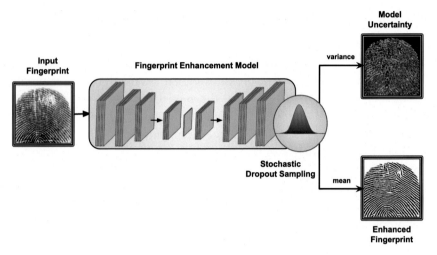

Figure 2.3 *Model uncertainty estimation in a fingerprint enhancement model.* At test time, dropout is introduced into the baseline fingerprint enhancement model. The average of stochastic outputs obtained for the Monte Carlo samples serves as the enhanced fingerprint. Variance of these Monte Carlo samples is the estimated model uncertainty of the fingerprint enhancement model.

model can be computed as

$$var(y_{test}) = \frac{1}{S} \sum_{s=1}^{S} (p(y_{test}|x_{test}, \tilde{\theta}_s))^T p(y_{test}|x_{test}, \tilde{\theta}_s) - E(y_{test}^T) E(y_{test}),$$

where

$$E(y_{test}) = \frac{1}{S} \sum_{s=1}^{S} (p(y_{test}|x_{test}, \tilde{\theta}_s)).$$

To estimate Bayesian inference from the baseline fingerprint enhancement model, dropout is introduced before each layer of the model. Consequently, as a result of introducing dropout, the output of a model may change for each iteration. Due to this, the model output is now referred to be a *stochastic output*. For a test input fingerprint image x_{test}, the model output ($E(y_{test})$) is approximated as the mean of S stochastic samples. Model uncertainty is the variance of S stochastic outputs ($var(y_{test})$) (see Fig. 2.3).

2.4 Data uncertainty estimation

Noise in a fingerprint image can arise due to various reasons, such as sensor noise, dust or grease on the fingerprint sensing device, unclear or blurred boundaries (due to wet or dry fingertips), or false traces from previously acquired fingerprints. Data uncertainty of a fingerprint enhancement model accounts for uncertainty due to noise in a fingerprint image. As a result, data uncertainty, unlike model uncertainty, cannot be reduced even if an infinitely large training database is available to train the fingerprint enhancement model. Separately quantifying model and data uncertainties is a good idea as it helps to understand which uncertainties can be reduced, and which are unlikely to be reduced. Data uncertainty can be approximated as either *homoscedastic* or *heteroscedastic* uncertainty. Homoscedastic uncertainty assumes that the noise observed by the model is uniformly distributed across the input fingerprint image. In other words, homoscedastic uncertainty implies that the data uncertainty is invariant to the choice of input to the model. However, the assumption of a uniform noise model may not always be satisfied. To address the limitation of homoscedastic uncertainty estimation, heteroscedastic uncertainty estimation assumes that the noise is a random variable, whose mean and variance need to be estimated. To put it simply, heteroscedastic uncertainty means that the data uncertainty or the noise in the input is dependent on the input to the model. Various regions in a fingerprint image observe the different levels of noise. For instance, background regions are expected to be noisier than the foreground fingerprint region. Therefore data uncertainty is modeled as heteroscedastic uncertainty for fingerprint enhancement models. Bayesian deep learning can be successfully utilized to estimate data uncertainty in fingerprint enhancement models.

To formalize, data uncertainty is modeled by placing a distribution over the model of the output. We assume that the output of the fingerprint enhancement model is corrupted by zero-mean Gaussian noise. Data uncertainty estimation, in this case, aims at approximating the variance of the noise. As data uncertainty is modeled as heteroscedastic, the noise variance is learnt as a function of the input fingerprints, rather than a constant value for all fingerprint images. Furthermore, the uncertainty is learned as spatial maps with pixel level correspondence to the input fingerprint image. To estimate heteroscedastic data uncertainty originating in fingerprint enhancement, network architecture of the baseline fingerprint enhancement model is modified. In the modified architecture, not only enhanced fingerprint but also the data uncertainty is learnt as a function of the input

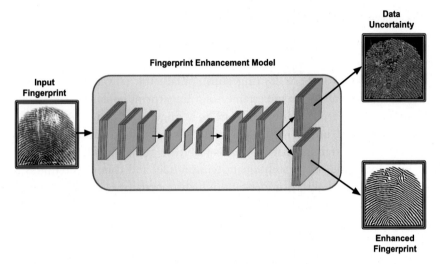

Figure 2.4 *Data uncertainty estimation in a fingerprint enhancement model.* An additional branch is introduced into the final layer of the baseline fingerprint enhancement model. One branch of the final layer predicts the enhanced fingerprint. The newly introduced branch is dedicated to learn data uncertainty prediction.

fingerprint image [15]. To achieve this, both the functions are tied together by splitting the last layer into two branches. Both the branches are trained in a multitask manner. The first task is to predict the enhanced fingerprint image, whereas the other task is to predict the data uncertainty (see Fig. 2.4). The branch predicting the enhanced fingerprint image is trained in a fully supervised manner, using noisy synthetic fingerprints and the corresponding good quality binarized fingerprint images. The data uncertainty branch, on the other hand, is trained in an unsupervised manner. A prior over the weights of noise variance (data uncertainty) is placed. To ensure training of the resulting architecture, the loss function is also modified, depending upon the functional form of the loss function. The loss function of a fingerprint enhancement model can be either regression-based or cross-entropy-based. In case of a regression-based loss function, change in the model output can be directly computed, whereas for cross-entropy loss-based fingerprint enhancement models, change in the logits is computed instead of change in output of softmax (output probabilities). In the following subsections, we describe how the loss function of fingerprint enhancement models should be adapted to also estimate data uncertainty in addition to predicting enhanced fingerprint image.

2.4.1 Estimating data uncertainty for regression loss-based fingerprint enhancement models

Assuming loss function of a fingerprint enhancement model is originally defined to be $\frac{1}{P}\sum_{k=1}^{P}\|y_k - f_e(x_k)\|^2$, where P represents the total number of training pixels, and x_k signifies pixel k in the input fingerprint image x. y_k and $f_e(x_k)$ denote the ground annotation and output of fingerprint enhancement model for pixel k. We assume that $f_e(x_k)$ is adulterated with a zero mean Gaussian noise, whose variance is $\sigma(x_k)$. Estimating data uncertainty aims at learning the noise variance $\sigma(x_k)$. To learn $\sigma(x_k)$ as a function of input fingerprints, the loss function is adapted as

$$\frac{1}{P}\sum_{i=1}^{P}\frac{1}{2\sigma(x_k)^2}\|y_k - f_e(x_k)\|^2 + \frac{1}{2}\log\sigma(x_k)^2.$$

Intuitively, adapting the loss function as above allows the fingerprint enhancement model to alleviate the residual error term by a factor of $\sigma(x_k)$. As $\sigma(x_k)$ is a function of input fingerprint, the adaptation of loss function enables the fingerprint enhancement model to attenuate the residual error obtained on noisy pixels. To achieve this, the fingerprint enhancement model outputs high data uncertainty ($\sigma(x_k)$) on noisy pixels. This, in effect, makes the fingerprint enhancement model achieve *noise-aware* enhancement and predict high uncertainty on noisy pixels to promote a lower effect on the overall loss. However, to ensure that predicted uncertainty is indeed dependent on the input fingerprint, the fingerprint enhancement model is discouraged from predicting high uncertainty on all input pixels. This is achieved by introducing $\log\sigma(x_k)^2$ term in the new loss function. High predicted uncertainty leads to higher contribution from the $\log\sigma(x_k)^2$ term in the loss function, whereas lower predicted uncertainty leads to high loss due to $\sigma(x_k)^2\|y_k - f_e(x_k)\|^2$. As a result, the fingerprint enhancement model learns to predict higher uncertainty on noisy and erroneous pixels, whereas lower uncertainty on the rest of the pixels in the input fingerprint image.

2.4.2 Estimating data uncertainty for cross-entropy loss-based fingerprint enhancement models

As explained above, predicting heteroscedastic uncertainty in regression loss–based fingerprint enhancement models enables them to attenuate loss function on noisy pixels. It is a desirable characteristic for cross–entropy loss–based fingerprint enhancement models as well. However, directly quantifying change in model output for cross–entropy loss-based finger-print enhancement models is not possible. Therefore the idea of predicting heteroscedastic uncertainty in cross–entropy loss-based fingerprint enhancement models is extended in the *logit space*. To implement this idea, heteroscedastic regression uncertainty is placed over the logit space and marginalized. We now provide details about this method. Let $f_e(x_k)$ denote the vector of binary variable (logit) for a pixel i of the input fingerprint image (x). This vector is adulterated with a random zero–mean Gaussian noise. The adulterated logit is denoted by $\hat{x}_k$. The corrupted logit is then converted to a probability score p_k by the softmax function:

$$\hat{x}_k \sim \mathcal{N}(f_e(x_k), \sigma(x_k)^2),$$

$$\hat{p}_k = \text{Softmax}(\hat{x}_k).$$

To learn $\sigma(x_k)^2$ and the parameter of feature extractor (f_e) of the fingerprint enhancement model, Monte Carlo integration of softmax probabilities of sampled logits is carried out. To achieve this, the loss function is adapted to be

$$\hat{x}_{k,s} = f_e(x_k) + \sigma(x_k)\,\alpha_s, \quad \alpha_s \sim \mathcal{N}(0, I),$$

$$\frac{1}{P}\sum_{k=1}^{P}\log\frac{1}{S}\sum_{s=1}^{S}\exp(\hat{x}_{k,s,\hat{l}} - \log\sum_{\hat{l}}\exp(\hat{x}_{i,s,\hat{l}})).$$

$\hat{x}_{k,s}$ represents corrupted logit obtained for input x_k and stochastic sample s. $\hat{x}_{k,s,\hat{l}}$ represents the $\hat{l}$ element in the logit vector $\hat{x}_{k,s}$. $\hat{l}$, S, and P represent the total number of class labels, the number of Monte Carlo samples, and the total number of pixels in training images, respectively. Similar to the adapted loss function for regression, the abovementioned modified cross-entropy loss, this loss function can also be interpreted as learning an attenuation of loss.

2.5 Experimental evaluation

2.5.1 Databases

Poor quality fingerprint images generally result either due to poor skin conditions or structured noise in the background. To study the effect of uncertainty estimation on fingerprint enhancement models, we evaluate the performance of the resulting models on three challenging fingerprint databases. Two rural Indian fingerprint databases are analyzed to examine the effect on poor quality fingerprints. On the other hand, performance on latent fingerprints is investigated to evaluate the performance on noisy backgrounds. Please note that the training of the all the fingerprint enhancement models studied in this chapter is executed on the same training database as performed in [26]. Details about the testing datasets are presented next.

1. *Rural Indian fingerprint database*: This is a publicly available fingerprint database that has fingerprint samples acquired from the rural Indian population. The volunteers constitute farmers, carpenters, and housewives who are rigorously involved in manual work. This database has total of 1631 fingerprint samples.

2. A private rural Indian fingerprint database that has challenging samples of elderly population and poor quality fingertips. This database has 1000 fingerprint images.

3. *IIITD-MOLF*: This is the largest latent fingerprint database available in the public domain. This database has 4400 latent fingerprints and corresponding fingerprints obtained from optical sensors.

In Section 2.6.3, we analyze the generalization ability of the Bayesian deep learning for uncertainty estimation of fingerprint ROI segmentation methods. The experiments on fingerprint ROI segmentation are conducted on fingerprint verification competition (FVC) databases: FVC 2000, FVC 2002, and FVC 2004. Each of these databases constitutes of four subdatabases, out of which fingerprints in three databases (DB1–DB3) are collected from fingerprint sensors with varying sensing technologies. DB4 for each of these databases contains synthetic fingerprints obtained from Anguli [2], an open-source implementation of SFinGe [6]. Each subdatabase is divided into two parts: set A and set B. Set B is used for training the ROI segmentation model, whereas set A is used to evaluate the ROI segmentation performance. In total, 960 images are used for training, whereas 9600 images are used for testing. The ground truth constituting of manually marked segmentation masks of ROI is taken from [62].

2.5.2 Evaluation metrics

We now present the evaluation metrics used to assess the effectiveness of fingerprint enhancement models after adapting them to also estimate model and data uncertainty.

1. *Ridge structure preservation ability*: Biometric identity of a person lies in the ridge details of his/her fingerprints. Therefore it is critical that a fingerprint enhancement model must be able to preserve the finest ridge details, while enhancing the fingerprint. To evaluate the ridge preservation ability of fingerprint enhancement models, we generate some noisy synthetic fingerprints and calculate the peak signal-to-noise-ratio (PSNR) [42] between enhanced fingerprint and ground truth binarized image. Synthetic (noisy) test samples are generated by introducing varying backgrounds and noise into good quality synthetic fingerprints. The ground truth binarized fingerprints images are obtained using NBIS.

2. *Fingerprint quality assessment*: The goal of a fingerprint enhancement model is to improve the quality of an input fingerprint. The quality of a fingerprint image is characterized by various factors, such as uniform contrast, clarity of ridges and valleys, the flow of ridge orientations, number and quality of minutiae, etc. We adopt the NFIQ module of NBIS (NIST biometric image software) [43] to evaluate the quality of enhanced fingerprints. NFIQ outputs a score for each input fingerprint image. The score value is within the range of one to five. One represents the best quality, whereas five signifies the worst quality. Ideally, fingerprint quality score should improve (value should reduce in this case) after enhancement.

3. *Fingerprint matching performance*: An enhanced fingerprint image is expected to obtain a higher match score and an accurate fingerprint matching performance. To assess fingerprint matching performance obtained on enhanced fingerprints, the fingerprint matching performance is evaluated under both verification and identification setting. Under verification mode, a fingerprint matching system is required to output whether the input fingerprint matches with any fingerprint in the gallery or not. Whereas, during the identification mode of operation, a fingerprint matching system is required to identify a list of potential matches from the gallery. The rural Indian fingerprint databases are evaluated under verification mode. For each of these databases, the average equal error rate (EER) is computed, and the detection error tradeoff (DET) curve is plotted. On the other hand, performance on latent fingerprints is evaluated for the identification mode. Rank-50 accuracy and cumulative matching characteristics (CMC) curve is computed. Please note that Bozorth [43] and MCC [5], [4], and [13] are used for conducting fingerprint matching.

2.5.3 Effect of estimating model uncertainty

To analyze the effect of estimating model uncertainty of a fingerprint enhancement model, we introduce Monte Carlo dropout into the following fingerprint enhancement models: DeConvNet [56] and FP-E-GAN [27]. The resulting architectures are termed as *MU-DeConvNet* and *MU-GAN*, respectively. The modified architectures are expected to achieve better performance as compared to the baseline due to the *model averaging* effect introduced by Monte Carlo dropout.

2.6 Results and analysis

During visual inspection of enhanced samples (see Fig. 2.5), we find that the ridge-valley clarity and smoothness of ridges are improved after introducing Monte Carlo dropout. Furthermore, the ridge prediction ability has also improved. To quantify these observations, we quantitatively analyze the enhancement performance of both these architectures. Firstly, we evaluate the effect on the ridge preservation ability of the fingerprint enhancement model after introducing Monte Carlo dropout. Sample synthetic test cases and the obtained enhanced images generated by MU-GAN are compared

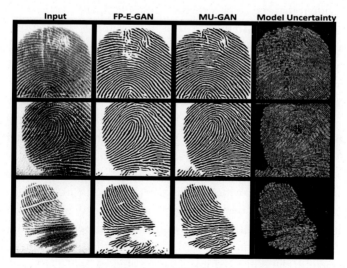

Figure 2.5 Sample cases demonstrating the enhanced fingerprints generated by MU-GAN and the corresponding predicted model uncertainties. Results indicate that high model uncertainty is predicted at the enhanced fingerprint regions with spurious ridge structure, whereas low uncertainty is predicted on enhanced regions with smooth and clear ridge details.

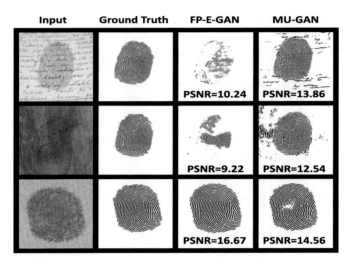

Figure 2.6 Test examples quantifying the progression in the ridge preservation proficiency after introducing Monte Carlo dropout. Higher PSNR scores between the enhanced fingerprints and the ground truth binarized fingerprints are obtained for MU-GAN as compared to the baseline FP-E-GAN. The improvement by MU-GAN is attributed to the model averaging effect introduced by the Monte Carlo dropout.

with the baseline FP-E-GAN and the ground truth in Fig. 2.6. It is even visually evident that the ridge structure ability of MU-GAN is far better in contrast to FP-E-GAN. To quantify this improvement, we calculate PSNR between the ground truth and the enhanced images. Higher PSNR is attained by the model with Monte Carlo dropout, which illustrates that the improved ridge preservation ability.

Next, we evaluate the fingerprint quality of the enhanced images output by both these models. We find that the average NFIQ fingerprint quality score has improved (or at least competitive with the baseline) after introducing Monte Carlo dropout (see Table 2.1, Table 2.3, and Table 2.5). For better understanding of distribution of obtained NFIQ quality scores, the histogram of scores is provided in Fig. 2.7(a), Fig. 2.8(a), and Fig. 2.9(a). All these results indicate that the fingerprint quality of enhanced images is indeed improved after introducing Monte Carlo dropout as a model uncertainty estimation technique. Lastly, we assess the fingerprint matching performance on the enhanced images generated by MU-DeConvNet and MU-GAN. For both the rural Indian fingerprint databases, we compute the average EER and find that the average EER on the enhanced images has reduced significantly (see Table 2.2 and Table 2.4). The corresponding

Table 2.1 Average fingerprint quality scores attained on the rural Indian fingerprint database. Competitive fingerprint quality of enhanced images is obtained after incorporating model uncertainty estimation.

Enhancement Model	Avg. NFIQ Score ($\downarrow$)
Raw Image	2.94
DeConvNet [56]	1.95
MU-DeConvNet	*1.68*
MU-GAN	1.33
FP-E-GAN [27]	**1.31**

Table 2.2 Verification performance obtained on the rural Indian fingerprint database. Reduced average EER indicates improved matching performance on enhanced images generated after incorporating model uncertainty estimation.

Enhancement Model	Matching Algorithm	Avg. EER ($\downarrow$)
Raw Image	Bozorth	16.36
DeConvNet [56]	Bozorth	10.93
MU-DeConvNet	Bozorth	*8.48*
FP-E-GAN [27]	Bozorth	**7.30**
MU-GAN	Bozorth	7.46
Raw Image	MCC	13.23
DeConvNet [56]	MCC	10.86
MU-DeConvNet	MCC	*7.56*
FP-E-GAN [27]	MCC	5.96
MU-GAN	MCC	**5.06**

Table 2.3 Average fingerprint quality scores attained on the private fingerprint database. Fingerprint quality of enhanced images has improved significantly after incorporating model uncertainty estimation.

Enhancement Model	Avg. NFIQ Score ($\downarrow$)
DeConvNet [56]	4.12
FP-E-GAN [27]	2.28
MU-GAN	**1.92**

DET curves are presented in Fig. 2.7(b)–(c) and Fig. 2.8(b)–(c), respectively. These results illustrate the fact that for the rural Indian fingerprint

Table 2.4 Verification performance obtained on the private Indian fingerprint database. Reduced average EER indicates improved matching performance on enhanced images generated after incorporating model uncertainty estimation.

Enhancement Model	Matching Algorithm	Avg. EER ($\downarrow$)
DeConvNet [56]	Bozorth	28.75
FP-E-GAN [27]	Bozorth	17.06
MU-GAN	Bozorth	**12.75**
DeConvNet [56]	MCC	26.80
FP-E-GAN [27]	MCC	15.85
MU-GAN	MCC	**11.55**

Table 2.5 Comparison of average quality scores obtained using NFIQ on IIITD-MOLF database.

Enhancement Model	Avg. NFIQ Score ($\downarrow$)
Raw Image	4.96
DeConvNet [56]	4.09
FP-E-GAN [27]	1.91
MU-GAN	**1.48**

databases, incorporating Monte Carlo dropout results in a significant increase in the matching performance obtained for the enhanced images. For evaluating the matching performance obtained on the enhanced images generated for latent fingerprints from IIITD-MOLF database, we calculate Rank-50 accuracy. Different from the rural Indian fingerprint databases, we find that instead of improvement, rather the fingerprint matching performance decreases on enhanced fingerprints obtained after introducing model uncertainty. Table 2.6 reports the obtained Rank-50 accuracies. The corresponding CMC curves are presented in Fig. 2.9(b)–(c). The obtained results indicate that the performance in enhancement performance does not generalize on latent fingerprints. We understand that generalization on latent fingerprints with varying complex background noise poses a significant challenge on fingerprint enhancement models. These challenges are increased more after introducing model uncertainty as the model is trained on synthetic training examples and able to perform well on similar noise patterns but not the ones as seen in real latent fingerprints.

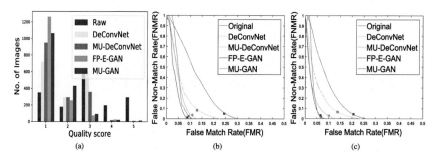

Figure 2.7 Enhancement performance on the rural Indian fingerprint database after introducing model uncertainty estimation: (a) histogram of NFIQ scores; DET curves obtained using (b) Bozorth and (c) MCC.

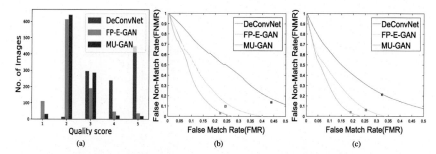

Figure 2.8 Enhancement performance on the private fingerprint database after introducing model uncertainty estimation: (a) histogram of NFIQ scores; DET curves obtained using (b) Bozorth and (c) MCC.

Table 2.6 Comparison of identification performance obtained on IIITD-MOLF database when matched across Lumidigm gallery.

Enhancement Model	Bozorth (↑)	MCC (↑)
Raw Image	5.45	6.06
DeConvNet [56]	14.02	14.27
Svoboda et al. [60]	N.A.	22.36
FP-E-GAN [27]	**28.52**	**34.43**
MU-GAN	25.09	28.61

2.6.1 Effect of estimating data uncertainty

Having analyzed the effect of estimating model uncertainty, we now shift attention towards analyzing the effect of data uncertainty estimation on fingerprint enhancement models. To achieve this, we modify the architecture of DeConvNet [56] and FP-E-GAN [27] (as suggested in Section 2.4). The modified fingerprint enhancement models are termed as

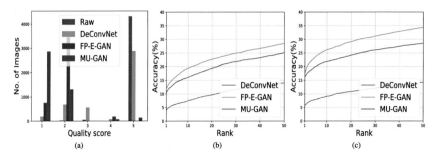

Figure 2.9 Comparison of results on IIITD-MOLF database by DeConvNet [56], FP-E-GAN, and MU-GAN: (a) histogram of NFIQ scores; CMC curve comparing the identification performance obtained using (b) Bozorth and (c) MCC.

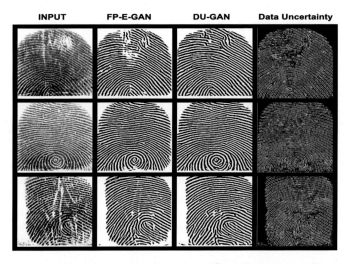

Figure 2.10 Sample cases demonstrating the enhanced fingerprints generated by DU-GAN and the corresponding predicted data uncertainties. Results indicate that high data uncertainty is predicted at the poor quality and noisy fingerprint regions in the input fingerprint image, whereas low uncertainty is predicted on good quality fingerprint regions with ridge-valley clarity.

DU-DeConvNet and *DU-GAN*, respectively. Modifying a fingerprint enhancement model to estimate data uncertainty enables it to attenuate the loss function such that noise–aware enhancement can be conducted. As a result, DU–DeConvNet and DU–GAN are expected to attain superior enhancement performance than the baselines DeConvNet and FP–E-GAN, respectively. Fig. 2.10 presents sample enhanced fingerprints generated by DU–GAN. DU–GAN outperforms the baseline in predicting the missing

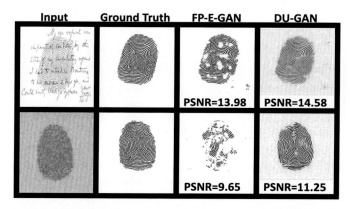

Figure 2.11 Test examples quantifying the progression in the ridge preservation proficiency after introducing data uncertainty estimation. Higher PSNR scores between the enhanced fingerprints and the ground truth binarized fingerprints are obtained for DU-GAN as compared to the baseline FP-E-GAN. The improvement by DU-GAN is attributed to the noise adaptive enhancement achieved as a result of learning of loss attenuation.

ridge details. Furthermore, the enhanced fingerprints generated by DU-GAN have smoother ridges and higher ridge-valley clarity. Additionally, we also observe that DU-GAN predicts higher data uncertainty on noisy pixels. These results help to qualitatively evaluate the enhancement performance of DU-GAN.

To quantitatively evaluate the fingerprint enhancement performance obtained using DU-GAN, we first assess the ridge preservation ability of DU-GAN. Fig. 2.11 illustrates the enhanced fingerprints obtained for synthetic test cases. The sample cases present in the figure demonstrate that DU-GAN enhances unclear ridge details, while preserving them. These results qualitatively signify that DU-GAN has better ridge preservation ability than baseline FP-E-GAN. We also calculate the PSNR value between ground truth binarized image and the enhanced fingerprint to quantitatively assess the ridge preservation ability. High PSNR values are obtained for DU-GAN as compared to FP-E-GAN, which indicates that ridge preservation ability is improved after incorporating data uncertainty estimation into fingerprint enhancement models. Next, we assess the fingerprint quality of enhanced fingerprints generated after introducing data uncertainty estimation into baseline fingerprint enhancement models. Table 2.7 and Table 2.9 demonstrate that for the rural Indian fingerprints, we observe that the fingerprint quality improves after enhancement. The corresponding histograms of NFIQ values are plotted in Fig. 2.12(a) and Fig. 2.13(a).

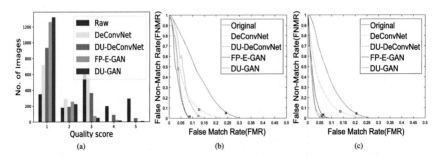

Figure 2.12 Enhancement performance on the rural Indian fingerprint database after introducing data uncertainty estimation: (a) histogram of NFIQ scores; DET curves obtained using (b) Bozorth and (c) MCC.

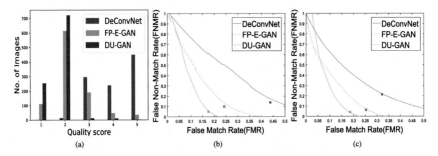

Figure 2.13 Enhancement performance on the private fingerprint database after introducing data uncertainty estimation: (a) histogram of NFIQ scores; DET curves obtained using (b) Bozorth and (c) MCC.

However, for latent fingerprints, the fingerprint quality rather degrades after enhancement, as reported in Table 2.11. Fig. 2.14 presents the corresponding histogram of NFIQ scores.

Lastly, we evaluate the fingerprint matching performance obtained on enhanced fingerprints generated after incorporating data uncertainty estimation in fingerprint enhancement models. For both the rural Indian fingerprint databases, we compute the average EER and find that the average EER on the enhanced images has reduced significantly (see Table 2.8 and Table 2.10). The corresponding DET curves are presented in Fig. 2.12(b)–(c) and Fig. 2.13(b)–(c), respectively. These results illustrate the fact that for the rural Indian fingerprint databases, the matching performance on the enhanced images has increased significantly after introducing data uncertainty. For latent fingerprints from IIITD-MOLF database, we find that the fingerprint matching performance decreases on enhanced fingerprints obtained after introducing data uncertainty. Table 2.12 re-

Table 2.7 Comparison of average quality scores attained using NFIQ on the rural Indian fingerprint database. Fingerprint quality of enhanced images improves after incorporating data uncertainty estimation.

Enhancement Model	Avg. NFIQ Score ($\downarrow$)
Raw Image	2.94
DeConvNet [56]	1.95
DU-DeConvNet	*1.84*
FP-E-GAN [27]	1.31
DU-GAN	**1.26**

Table 2.8 Verification performance obtained on the rural Indian fingerprint database. Reduced average EER indicates improved matching performance on enhanced images generated after incorporating data uncertainty estimation.

Enhancement Model	Matching Algorithm	Avg. EER ($\downarrow$)
Raw Image	Bozorth	16.36
DeConvNet [56]	Bozorth	10.93
DU-DeConvNet	Bozorth	*8.71*
FP-E-GAN [27]	Bozorth	7.30
DU-GAN	Bozorth	**7.13**
Raw Image	MCC	13.23
DeConvNet [56]	MCC	10.86
FP-E-GAN [27]	MCC	5.96
DU-DeConvNet	MCC	*5.36*
DU-GAN	MCC	**5.13**

ports the obtained Rank-50 accuracies. The corresponding CMC curves are presented in Fig. 2.14(b)–(c). The obtained results indicate that the performance in enhancement performance does not generalize on latent fingerprints. We understand that generalization on latent fingerprints with varying complex background noise poses a significant challenge on fingerprint enhancement models. The fingerprint enhancement model is trained on synthetic training examples and able to perform well on similar noise patterns, but not the ones as seen in real latent fingerprints. These challenges are increased more after introducing data uncertainty. As a result, matching performance degrades for latent fingerprints.

Table 2.9 Average fingerprint quality scores attained on the private fingerprint database. Fingerprint quality of enhanced images has improved significantly after incorporating data uncertainty estimation.

Enhancement Algorithm	Avg. NFIQ Score ($\downarrow$)
DeConvNet [56]	4.12
FP-E-GAN [27]	2.28
DU-GAN	**1.79**

Table 2.10 Verification performance obtained on the private Indian fingerprint database. Reduced average EER indicates improved matching performance on enhanced images generated after incorporating model uncertainty estimation.

Enhancement Algorithm	Matching Algorithm	Avg. EER ($\downarrow$)
DeConvNet [56]	Bozorth	28.75
FP-E-GAN [27]	Bozorth	17.06
DU-GAN	Bozorth	**11.24**
DeConvNet [56]	MCC	26.80
FP-E-GAN [27]	MCC	15.85
DU-GAN	MCC	**11.50**

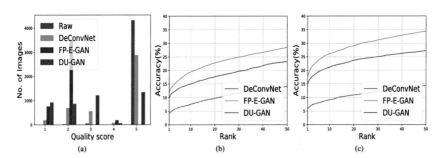

Figure 2.14 Comparison of results on IIITD-MOLF database by DeConvNet [56], FP-E-GAN, and DU-GAN: (a) histogram of NFIQ scores; CMC curve comparing the identification performance obtained using (b) Bozorth and (c) MCC.

2.6.2 Comparison of model and data uncertainty

This section provides a detailed comparison between model and data uncertainty estimation in fingerprint enhancement models. We compare the model complexity and computational cost to estimate model and data un-

Table 2.11 Comparison of average quality scores obtained using NFIQ on IIITD-MOLF database.

Enhancement Algorithm	Avg. NFIQ Score ($\downarrow$)
Raw Image	4.96
DeConvNet [56]	4.09
FP-E-GAN [27]	**1.91**
DU-GAN	3.01

Table 2.12 Comparison of identification performance obtained on IIITD-MOLF database when matched across Lumidigm gallery.

Enhancement Algorithm	Bozorth ($\uparrow$)	MCC ($\uparrow$)
Raw Image	5.45	6.06
DeConvNet [56]	14.02	14.27
Svoboda et al. [60]	N.A.	22.36
FP-E-GAN [27]	**28.52**	**34.43**
DU-GAN	23.16	27.21

certainty. The comparisons are provided in terms of model parameters and inference time. All the relevant discussions are presented next.

2.6.2.1 Comparison of model complexity

To give insights on the computational complexity introduced by model and data uncertainty estimation, we demonstrate whether any additional model complexity is introduced by uncertainty estimation. In this research, uncertainty estimation is introduced in the generator subnetwork of the baseline fingerprint enhancement model FP-E-GAN. Therefore, in Table 2.13, we compare the model parameters in the generator subnetwork of the FP-E-GAN, MU-GAN, and DU-GAN. As expected, the model parameters of FP-E-GAN and MU-GAN are the same, because the architecture of MU-GAN is similar to FP-E-GAN, just with an additional introduction of dropout. As a result, the model parameters are exactly the same as the baseline. In contrast, data uncertainty is learnt as a function of the input and requires the introduction of an additional branch in the model architecture. Therefore few additional parameters are introduced without significantly increasing the model complexity. Subsequently, DU-GAN has more parameters than the baseline FP-E-GAN. These results help us to conclude that model uncertainty estimation does not increase the model complexity,

Table 2.13 Comparison of model parameters introduced by model and data uncertainty estimation. The reported parameters are the total number of model parameters in the generator sub-network of the model. Model uncertainty estimation using Monte Carlo dropout does not introduce any additional model parameters, whereas data uncertainty estimation introduces only a few additional parameters. These results indicate that uncertainty estimation does not significantly affect the model complexity.

Enhancement Model	Parameters
FP–E–GAN [27]	11376129
MU–GAN	11376129
DU–GAN	11386178

Table 2.14 Comparison of inference time for estimating model and data uncertainty. Data uncertainty estimation requires the introduction of one more branch in the final layer of the baseline network. Therefore inference time is not significantly increased. However, model uncertainty estimation using Monte Carlo dropout requires averaging of stochastic output obtained for each Monte Carlo sample. In this study, ten Monte Carlo are used. As a result, inference time of MU-GAN is about tenfold in contrast to FP-E-GAN.

Enhancement Model	Time (ms)
FP–E–GAN [27]	5.13
DU–GAN	5.87
MU–GAN	49.32

whereas data uncertainty estimation increases it, but the increase is insignificant as compared to the baseline.

2.6.2.2 Comparison of inference time

Next, we compare the inference time for model and data uncertainty estimation. For this, we compute the inference time of baseline FP-E-GAN, MU-GAN, and DU-GAN on a Tesla T4 GPU. The inference time is reported in Table 2.14. We find that the inference time after introducing data uncertainty is comparable to the baseline model. In contrast, the inference time is significantly increased after incorporating Monte Carlo dropout-based model uncertainty. As the model uncertainty estimation requires averaging the stochastic outputs, thus the inference time is directly dependent on the number of samples used on which Monte Carlo integration is performed. For MU-GAN, we have used ten Monte Carlo samples.

Subsequently, the inference time of MU–GAN is about ten folds in contrast to that of the baseline FP-E-GAN. On the other hand, inference time of DU–GAN is competitive to that of FP-E-GAN. These results indicate that the high computational time is required to estimate model uncertainty while data uncertainty can be estimated without significant increase in inference time.

2.6.3 Generalization on fingerprint ROI segmentation

This section investigates whether the usefulness of estimating model and data uncertainty generalizes to fingerprint preprocessing. In this direction, we study the effect of estimating model and data uncertainty in a fingerprint ROI segmentation model. As motivated in [30], we work with Recurrent Unet (RUnet) as the baseline fingerprint ROI segmentation model. We introduce Monte Carlo dropout and data uncertainty estimation into RUnet, and the resulting fingerprint ROI segmentation models are termed as *MU-RUnet* and *DU-RUnet*, respectively. We analyze both predicted uncertainty values and segmentation performance after introducing model and data uncertainty. The detailed analysis is presented next.

2.6.3.1 Predicted uncertainty

Theoretically, model uncertainty should be high on pixels, where a fingerprint ROI segmentation model is probable to predict an incorrect output. In contrast, data uncertainty, is expected to be high on noisy pixels. To analyze the uncertainty predicted on these pixels, we calculate the average uncertainty predicted for foreground as opposed to background pixels. We also compare the average uncertainty predicted for correctly as opposed to incorrectly classified pixels. The annotation of foreground and background is the same as provided in the ground truth annotations. Similarly, a pixel is regarded correctly or incorrectly classified based on manual annotations. Please note that a similar analysis of predicted uncertainty values is not conducted for fingerprint enhancement models due to the unavailability of ground truth annotations. Fig. 2.15(a) compares predicted model uncertainty for foreground and background pixels. In general, background pixels are far more challenging for segmentation as compared to the foreground. Therefore, as expected, predicted model uncertainty is higher for background pixels in contrast to foreground pixels. Likewise, by definition, model uncertainty should be high for pixels that are likely to be incorrectly classified. As presented in Fig. 2.15(b), the predicted model uncertainty is significantly higher for incorrectly classified pixels in contrast to

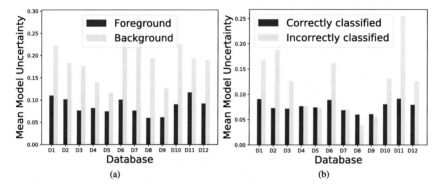

Figure 2.15 Analysis of the efficacy of the predicted model uncertainty. Model uncertainties are predicted for all the FVC databases, from FVC 2000 DB1 (represented as D1) to FVC 2004 DB4 (represented as D12). A comparison of mean model uncertainties is provided for (a) foreground versus background pixels, (b) correctly versus incorrectly classified pixels. Lower model uncertainty values are estimated for foreground and correctly classified pixels as compared to background and incorrectly classified pixels, respectively. These results indicate the usefulness and efficacy of predicted model uncertainty.

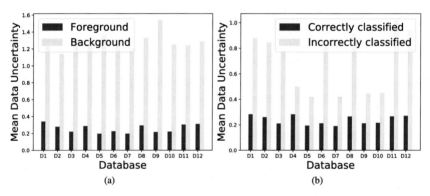

Figure 2.16 Analysis of the efficacy of the predicted data uncertainty. Data uncertainties are predicted for all the FVC databases, from FVC 2000 DB1 (represented as D1) to FVC 2004 DB4 (represented as D12). A comparison of mean data uncertainties is provided for (a) foreground versus background pixels, (b) correctly versus incorrectly classified pixels. Lower data uncertainty values are estimated for foreground and correctly classified pixels as compared to background and incorrectly classified pixels respectively. These results indicate the usefulness and efficacy of predicted data uncertainty.

the correctly classified pixels. The obtained results demonstrate the efficacy of predicted model uncertainty.

Next, we analyze the predicted data uncertainty. Fig. 2.16(a) compares the predicted data uncertainty for foreground and background pixels. By

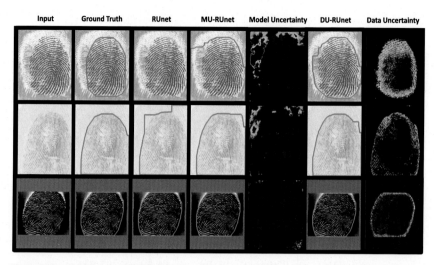

| Input | Ground Truth | RUnet | MU-RUnet | Model Uncertainty | DU-RUnet | Data Uncertainty |

Figure 2.17 Sample cases illustrating the estimated model and data uncertainty. Results show that estimating both the kind of uncertainties promotes improved segmentation efficacy in contrast to baseline RUnet. Both these uncertainties provide different but complementary information. Model and data uncertainties capture similar information for a segmentation model, as observed for an enhancement model. Here also model uncertainty signifies the confidence of the model in its output. As a result, lower uncertainty is attained on correctly segmented pixels as compared to incorrectly segmented pixels. Likewise, data uncertainty signifies noise in the input fingerprints. Therefore lower uncertainty values are predicted for foreground pixels as compared to pixels in the boundaries and background.

definition, data uncertainty should be high for noisy pixels. Generally, background pixels in a fingerprint image are noisier than the foreground. Therefore, as expected, we observe that significantly lower data uncertainty is predicted for foreground pixels in contrast to the background pixels. Likewise, a fingerprint ROI segmentation model is more likely to be incorrectly classifying noisy pixels. In Fig. 2.16(b), we compare the predicted data uncertainty values for correctly classified and incorrectly classified pixels. We find that much lower data uncertainty values are output by the model for correctly classified pixels in contrast to incorrectly classified pixels, which confirm the efficacy of predicted data uncertainty. Lastly, in Fig. 2.17, we illustrate the sample cases demonstrating the segmentation obtained after introducing uncertainty estimation and predicted uncertainties. We find that segmentation performance improves after introducing either kind of uncertainty. These results also show that predicted model uncertainty is higher for pixels that are incorrectly segmented and low for correctly segmented pixels. Furthermore, higher data uncertainty is predicted for noisy back-

Table 2.15 Quantification of improved segmentation performance obtained after incorporating Monte Carlo dropout. MU-RUnet attains higher Jaccard similarity and Dice scores in contrast to RUnet, which highlight the improvement after estimating model uncertainty.

Database	Jaccard Similarity (↑)		Dice Score (↑)	
	RUnet	MU-RUnet	RUnet	MU-RUnet
2000DB1	**88.15**	87.97	**93.34**	93.14
2000DB2	86.40	**88.43**	92.39	**93.58**
2000DB3	93.74	**95.39**	96.50	**97.57**
2000DB4	94.28	**94.89**	97.04	**97.36**
2002DB1	**96.95**	96.83	**98.44**	98.38
2002DB2	94.88	**95.13**	97.28	**97.40**
2002DB3	91.83	**93.87**	95.53	**96.73**
2002DB4	91.17	**91.53**	95.32	**95.54**
2004DB1	98.78	**98.98**	99.38	**99.49**
2004DB2	93.94	**95.98**	96.69	**97.93**
2004DB3	94.62	**95.29**	97.17	**97.55**
2004DB4	94.73	**96.18**	97.21	**98.03**

ground pixels as compared to the foreground. These results demonstrate that model and data uncertainties represent different and useful information for improving the performance of the fingerprint ROI segmentation model.

2.6.3.2 Segmentation performance

We also assess the fingerprint ROI segmentation performance obtained after introducing the model and data uncertainty into the baseline fingerprint ROI segmentation model. To quantify the segmentation ability, we compute standard segmentation metrics: Jaccard similarity [10] and Dice score [11]. Table 2.15 compares the segmentation ability of MU-RUnet as opposed to RUnet. We find that both Dice score and Jaccard similarity values have significantly improved after introducing model uncertainty. Fig. 2.18 presents the sample cases illustrating the improved efficacy of segmentation attained by MU-RUnet in contrast to RUnet. The improved efficacy of segmentation attained by MU-RUnet is attributed to the model averaging effect introduced by Monte Carlo dropout. This averaging effect reduces model over-fitting for MU-RUnet. This justifies the improvement in segmentation efficacy.

At last, we evaluate the segmentation performance obtained after introducing data uncertainty. Table 2.16 compares the Jaccard similarity and

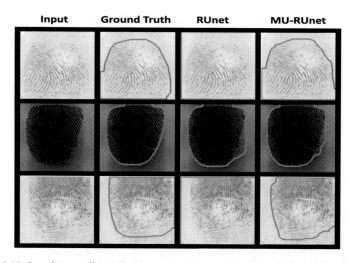

Figure 2.18 Sample cases illustrating the improvement in the segmentation performance after introduction of Monte Carlo dropout uncertainty into the baseline RUnet architecture.

Dice scores attained by DU-RUnet in contrast to RUnet. Higher values for both the evaluation metrics are attained by DU-RUnet as opposed to RUnet. Fig. 2.19 presents sample cases that highlight that improved segmentation performance is obtained after the introduction of data uncertainty into the baseline fingerprint ROI segmentation model. The improved performance obtained after introducing data uncertainty is attributed to the fact that data uncertainty estimation enables DU-RUnet to identify noisy pixels. As a result, it makes better predictions on noisy pixels, which results in overall improved segmentation performance.

2.7 Conclusion

In this chapter, we share details on uncertainty estimation for fingerprint enhancement models. We discuss estimating both model and data uncertainty for a fingerprint enhancement model. Through extensive experimentation, we find that modeling both kinds of uncertainties is useful. Both these uncertainties capture different but complementary information, which helps to improve the enhancement performance. We also demonstrate that the proposed uncertainty estimation techniques generalize on fingerprint ROI segmentation. Analysis of predicted uncertainty is performed, which indicates the efficacy and usefulness of predicted uncertainty values. The model complexity is analyzed, and we find that model uncer-

Table 2.16 Quantification of improved segmentation performance obtained after estimating data uncertainty. Higher Jaccard similarity and Dice scores are attained by DU-RUnet in contrast to RUnet, which highlight the improvement after estimating data uncertainty.

Database	Jaccard Similarity (↑)		Dice Score (↑)	
	RUnet	DU-RUnet	RUnet	DU-RUnet
2000DB1	88.15	**88.52**	93.34	**93.62**
2000DB2	86.40	**88.07**	92.39	**93.42**
2000DB3	93.74	**95.36**	96.50	**97.55**
2000DB4	94.28	**94.97**	97.04	**97.40**
2002DB1	96.95	**97.07**	98.44	**98.50**
2002DB2	94.88	**95.43**	97.28	**97.60**
2002DB3	91.83	**93.06**	95.53	**96.25**
2002DB4	91.17	**91.89**	95.32	**95.74**
2004DB1	98.78	**99.00**	99.38	**99.50**
2004DB2	93.94	**96.37**	96.69	**98.14**
2004DB3	94.62	**95.47**	97.17	**97.65**
2004DB4	94.73	**95.61**	97.21	**97.70**

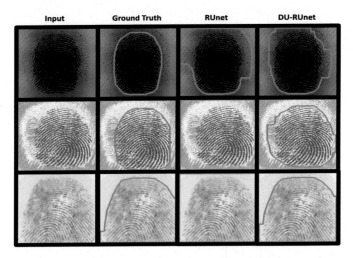

Figure 2.19 Sample cases illustrating the improvement in the segmentation performance after introduction of data uncertainty estimation into the baseline RUnet architecture.

tainty estimation does not increase the model complexity at all, whereas data uncertainty estimation adds only a few parameters, which are insignificant compared to the model complexity of the baseline fingerprint enhancement model. We also compare the inference time for model and data uncertainty and observe that model uncertainty estimation significantly increases the inference time by a factor of the number of Monte Carlo samples. In contrast, the inference time for data uncertainty estimation is comparable to that of the baseline fingerprint enhancement model. The discussions presented in this chapter show the efficacy and usefulness of uncertainty estimation as an interpretability mechanism for a fingerprint enhancement model. We understand that model interpretability is a desired characteristic for all the components of an automated fingerprint recognition system. In the future, the techniques presented in this chapter can be extended to other modules of a fingerprint matching system as well.

References

[1] O. Achrack, R. Kellerman, O. Barzilay, Multi-loss sub-ensembles for accurate classification with uncertainty estimation, arXiv preprint, arXiv:2010.01917, 2020.

[2] A.H. Ansari, Generation and Storage of Large Synthetic Fingerprint Database, Technical Report, Indian Institute of Science Bangalore, 2011.

[3] K. Cao, A.K. Jain, Latent orientation field estimation via convolutional neural network, in: Proc. International Conference on Biometrics (ICB), 2015, pp. 349–356.

[4] R. Cappelli, M. Ferrara, D. Maltoni, Fingerprint indexing based on minutia cylinder-code, IEEE Transactions on Pattern Analysis and Machine Intelligence 33 (2010) 1051–1057.

[5] R. Cappelli, M. Ferrara, D. Maltoni, Minutia cylinder-code: A new representation and matching technique for fingerprint recognition, IEEE Transactions on Pattern Analysis and Machine Intelligence 32 (2010) 2128–2141.

[6] R. Cappelli, D. Maio, D. Maltoni, SFinGe: An approach to synthetic fingerprint generation, in: Proc. International Workshop on Biometric Technologies, 2004, pp. 147–154.

[7] W. Chaidee, K. Horapong, V. Areekul, Filter design based on spectral dictionary for latent fingerprint pre-enhancement, in: Proc. International Conference on Biometrics (ICB), 2018, pp. 23–30.

[8] C. Chen, J. Feng, J. Zhou, Multi-scale dictionaries based fingerprint orientation field estimation, in: Proc. International Conference on Biometrics (ICB), 2016, pp. 1–8.

[9] S. Chikkerur, A.N. Cartwright, V. Govindaraju, Fingerprint enhancement using STFT analysis, Pattern Recognition 40 (2007) 198–211.

[10] S.S. Choi, S.H. Cha, C.C. Tappert, A survey of binary similarity and distance measures, Journal of Systemics, Cybernetics and Informatics 8 (2010) 43–48.

[11] L.R. Dice, Measures of the amount of ecologic association between species, Ecology 26 (1945) 297–302.

[12] J. Feng, J. Zhou, A.K. Jain, Orientation field estimation for latent fingerprint enhancement, IEEE Transactions on Pattern Analysis and Machine Intelligence 35 (2013) 925–940.

[13] M. Ferrara, D. Maltoni, R. Cappelli, Noninvertible Minutia Cylinder-Code representation, IEEE Transactions on Information Forensics and Security 7 (2012) 1727–1737.

[14] S. Fort, H. Hu, B. Lakshminarayanan, Deep ensembles: A loss landscape perspective, arXiv preprint, arXiv:1912.02757, 2019.

[15] Y. Gal, Uncertainty in Deep Learning, Ph.D. thesis, University of Cambridge, 2016.

[16] Y. Gal, Z. Ghahramani, Dropout as a Bayesian approximation: Representing model uncertainty in deep learning, in: Proc. International Conference on Machine Learning (ICML), 2016, pp. 1050–1059.

[17] Y. Gal, J. Hron, A. Kendall, Concrete dropout, arXiv preprint, arXiv:1705.07832, 2017.

[18] J. Gawlikowski, C.R.N. Tassi, M. Ali, J. Lee, M. Humt, J. Feng, A. Kruspe, R. Triebel, P. Jung, R. Roscher, et al., A survey of uncertainty in deep neural networks, arXiv preprint, arXiv:2107.03342, 2021.

[19] M. Ghafoor, I.A. Taj, W. Ahmad, N.M. Jafri, Efficient 2-fold contextual filtering approach for fingerprint enhancement, IET Image Processing 8 (2014) 417–425.

[20] C. Gottschlich, Curved-region-based ridge frequency estimation and curved Gabor filters for fingerprint image enhancement, IEEE Transactions on Image Processing 21 (2011) 2220–2227.

[21] C. Gottschlich, C.B. Schönlieb, Oriented diffusion filtering for enhancing low-quality fingerprint images, IET Biometrics 1 (2012) 105–113.

[22] F.K. Gustafsson, M. Danelljan, T.B. Schon, Evaluating scalable Bayesian deep learning methods for robust computer vision, in: Proc. IEEE International Conference on Computer Vision and Pattern Recognition Workshops (CVPRW), 2020, pp. 318–319.

[23] L. Hong, Y. Wan, A. Jain, Fingerprint image enhancement: Algorithm and performance evaluation, IEEE Transactions on Pattern Analysis and Machine Intelligence 20 (1998) 777–789.

[24] C.T. Hsieh, E. Lai, Y.C. Wang, An effective algorithm for fingerprint image enhancement based on wavelet transform, Pattern Recognition 36 (2003) 303–312.

[25] S. Jirachaweng, V. Areekul, Fingerprint enhancement based on discrete cosine transform, in: Proc. International Conference on Biometrics (ICB), 2007, pp. 96–105.

[26] I. Joshi, A. Anand, S. Dutta Roy, P.K. Kalra, On training generative adversarial network for enhancement of latent fingerprints, in: AI and Deep Learning in Biometric Security, 2021, pp. 51–79.

[27] I. Joshi, A. Anand, M. Vatsa, R. Singh, S. Dutta Roy, P. Kalra, Latent fingerprint enhancement using generative adversarial networks, in: IEEE Winter Conference on Applications of Computer Vision (WACV), 2019, pp. 895–903.

[28] I. Joshi, R. Kothari, A. Utkarsh, V.K. Kurmi, A. Dantcheva, S. Dutta Roy, P.K. Kalra, Explainable fingerprint ROI segmentation using Monte Carlo dropout, in: IEEE Winter Conference on Applications of Computer Vision Workshops (WACVW), 2021, pp. 60–69.

[29] I. Joshi, A. Utkarsh, R. Kothari, V.K. Kurmi, A. Dantcheva, S. Dutta Roy, P.K. Kalra, Data uncertainty guided noise-aware preprocessing of fingerprints, in: International Joint Conference on Neural Networks (IJCNN), 2021, pp. 1–8.

[30] I. Joshi, A. Utkarsh, R. Kothari, V.K. Kurmi, A. Dantcheva, S. Dutta Roy, P.K. Kalra, Sensor-invariant fingerprint ROI segmentation using recurrent adversarial learning, in: International Joint Conference on Neural Networks (IJCNN), 2021, pp. 1–8.

[31] A. Kendall, Y. Gal, What uncertainties do we need in Bayesian deep learning for computer vision?, in: Proc. Advances in Neural Information Processing Systems (NIPS), 2017, pp. 5574–5584.

[32] I. Kim, Y. Kim, S. Kim, Learning loss for test-time augmentation, arXiv preprint, arXiv:2010.11422, 2020.

[33] B. Lakshminarayanan, A. Pritzel, C. Blundell, Simple and scalable predictive uncertainty estimation using deep ensembles, arXiv preprint, arXiv:1612.01474, 2016.

[34] J. Lee, G. AlRegib, Gradients as a measure of uncertainty in neural networks, in: Proc. IEEE International Conference on Image Processing (ICIP), 2020, pp. 2416–2420.

[35] J. Li, J. Feng, C.C.J. Kuo, Deep convolutional neural network for latent fingerprint enhancement, Signal Processing: Image Communication 60 (2018) 52–63.

[36] S. Liu, M. Liu, Z. Yang, Sparse coding based orientation estimation for latent finger-prints, Pattern Recognition 67 (2017) 164–176.

[37] A. Lyzhov, Y. Molchanova, A. Ashukha, D. Molchanov, D. Vetrov, Greedy policy search: A simple baseline for learnable test-time augmentation, in: Proc. Conference on Uncertainty in Artificial Intelligence (UAI), 2020, pp. 1308–1317.

[38] A. Malinin, Uncertainty Estimation in Deep Learning with Application to Spoken Language Assessment, Ph.D. thesis, University of Cambridge, 2019.

[39] A. Malinin, M. Gales, Predictive uncertainty estimation via prior networks, in: Proc. Advances in Neural Information Processing Systems (NIPS), 2018, pp. 7047–7058.

[40] M. Możejko, M. Susik, R. Karczewski, Inhibited softmax for uncertainty estimation in neural networks, arXiv preprint, arXiv:1810.01861, 2018.

[41] J. Mukhoti, Y. Gal, Evaluating Bayesian deep learning methods for semantic segmen-tation, arXiv preprint, arXiv:1811.12709, 2018.

[42] P. Ndajah, H. Kikuchi, M. Yukawa, H. Watanabe, S. Muramatsu, An investigation on the quality of denoised images, International Journal of Circuit, Systems, and Signal Processing 5 (2011) 423–434.

[43] NIST, NBIS- NIST biometric image software, http://biometrics.idealtest.org/.

[44] P. Oberdiek, M. Rottmann, H. Gottschalk, Classification uncertainty of deep neu-ral networks based on gradient information, in: Proc. IAPR Workshop on Artificial Neural Networks in Pattern Recognition, 2018, pp. 113–125.

[45] Y. Ovadia, E. Fertig, J. Ren, Z. Nado, D. Sculley, S. Nowozin, J. Dillon, B. Laksh-minarayanan, J. Snoek, Can you trust your model's uncertainty? Evaluating predictive uncertainty under dataset shift, in: Proc. Advances in Neural Information Processing Systems (NIPS), 2019, pp. 13991–14002.

[46] C. Puri, K. Narang, A. Tiwari, M. Vatsa, R. Singh, On analysis of rural and urban Indian fingerprint images, in: Proc. International Conference on Ethics and Policy of Biometrics, 2010, pp. 55–61.

[47] P. Qian, A. Li, M. Liu, Latent fingerprint enhancement based on DenseUNet, in: Proc. International Conference on Biometrics (ICB), 2019, pp. 1–6.

[48] Z. Qu, J. Liu, Y. Liu, Q. Guan, C. Yang, Y. Zhang, OrieNet: A regression system for latent fingerprint orientation field extraction, in: Proc. International Conference on Artificial Neural Networks, 2018, pp. 436–446.

[49] M. Raghu, K. Blumer, R. Sayres, Z. Obermeyer, B. Kleinberg, S. Mullainathan, J. Kleinberg, Direct uncertainty prediction for medical second opinions, in: Proc. Inter-national Conference on Machine Learning (ICML), 2019, pp. 5281–5290.

[50] R.K. Rama, A.M. Namboodiri, Fingerprint enhancement using hierarchical Markov random fields, in: Proc. IEEE International Joint Conference on Biometrics (IJCB), 2011, pp. 1–8.

[51] T. Ramalho, M. Miranda, Density estimation in representation space to predict model uncertainty, in: Proc. International Workshop on Engineering Dependable and Secure Machine Learning Systems, 2020, pp. 84–96.

[52] R.C. Ramos, E.V.C. de Lima Borges, I.L.P. Andrezza, J.J.B. Primo, L.V. Batista, H.M. Gomes, Analysis and improvements of fingerprint enhancement from Gabor itera-tive filtering, in: SIBGRAPI Conference on Graphics, Patterns and Images, 2018, pp. 266–273.

[53] J. Ren, P.J. Liu, E. Fertig, J. Snoek, R. Poplin, M.A. DePristo, J.V. Dillon, B. Lak-shminarayanan, Likelihood ratios for out-of-distribution detection, arXiv preprint, arXiv:1906.02845, 2019.

[54] M. Sahasrabudhe, A.M. Namboodiri, Fingerprint enhancement using unsupervised hierarchical feature learning, in: Proc. IAPR- and ACM-sponsored Indian Conference on Computer Vision, Graphics and Image Processing (ICVGIP), 2014, pp. 1–8.

[55] A. Sankaran, M. Vatsa, R. Singh, Multisensor optical and latent fingerprint database, IEEE Access 3 (2015) 653–665.

[56] P. Schuch, S. Schulz, C. Busch, De-convolutional auto-encoder for enhancement of fingerprint samples, in: Proc. International Conference on Image Processing Theory, Tools and Applications (IPTA), 2016, pp. 1–7.

[57] P. Schuch, S. Schulz, C. Busch, Survey on the impact of fingerprint image enhancement, IET Biometrics (2017) 102–115.

[58] M. Sensoy, L. Kaplan, M. Kandemir, Evidential deep learning to quantify classification uncertainty, arXiv preprint, arXiv:1806.01768, 2018.

[59] D. Shanmugam, D. Blalock, G. Balakrishnan, J. Guttag, When and why test-time augmentation works, arXiv preprint, arXiv:2011.11156, 2020.

[60] J. Svoboda, F. Monti, M.M. Bronstein, Generative convolutional networks for latent fingerprint reconstruction, in: Proc. IEEE International Joint Conference on Biometrics (IJCB), 2017, pp. 429–436.

[61] C. Szegedy, W. Zaremba, I. Sutskever, J. Bruna, D. Erhan, I. Goodfellow, R. Fergus, Intriguing properties of neural networks, arXiv preprint, arXiv:1312.6199, 2013.

[62] D.H. Thai, C. Gottschlich, Global variational method for fingerprint segmentation by three-part decomposition, IET Biometrics 5 (2016) 120–130.

[63] F. Turroni, R. Cappelli, D. Maltoni, Fingerprint enhancement using contextual iterative filtering, in: Proc. International Conference on Biometrics (ICB), 2012, pp. 152–157.

[64] M. Valdenegro-Toro, Deep sub-ensembles for fast uncertainty estimation in image classification, arXiv preprint, arXiv:1910.08168, 2019.

[65] J. Van Amersfoort, L. Smith, Y.W. Teh, Y. Gal, Uncertainty estimation using a single deep deterministic neural network, in: Proc. International Conference on Machine Learning (ICML), 2020, pp. 9690–9700.

[66] A. Vyas, N. Jammalamadaka, X. Zhu, D. Das, B. Kaul, T.L. Willke, Out-of-distribution detection using an ensemble of self supervised leave-out classifiers, in: Proc. European Conference on Computer Vision (ECCV), 2018, pp. 550–564.

[67] W. Wang, J. Li, F. Huang, H. Feng, Design and implementation of log-Gabor filter in fingerprint image enhancement, Pattern Recognition Letters 29 (2008) 301–308.

[68] Y. Wen, D. Tran, J. Ba, BatchEnsemble: An alternative approach to efficient ensemble and lifelong learning, arXiv preprint, arXiv:2002.06715, 2020.

[69] W.J. Wong, S.H. Lai, Multi-task CNN for restoring corrupted fingerprint images, Pattern Recognition 101 (2020) 107203–107213.

[70] X. Yang, J. Feng, J. Zhou, Localized dictionaries based orientation field estimation for latent fingerprints, IEEE Transactions on Pattern Analysis and Machine Intelligence 36 (2014) 955–969.

[71] S. Yoon, J. Feng, A.K. Jain, On latent fingerprint enhancement, in: Biometric Technology for Human Identification VII, 2010, pp. 766707–766716.

CHAPTER 3

Hardware and software based methods for underwater image enhancement and restoration

Monika Mathur[a], Nidhi Goel[a], and Gaurav Bhatnagar[b]
[a]Department of ECE, IGDTUW, Delhi, India
[b]Department of Mathematics, IIT Jodhpur, Rajasthan, India

3.1 Introduction

Much of our planet is covered by oceans, and the life of our planet is controlled by these water resources. Therefore it is important to examine and study the hidden features of these widespread bodies of water. Underwater photos and videos play an important role in exploring and protecting the underwater world. The underwater environment is home to a variety of attractions, such as marine animals, plants, amazing sea creatures, and mysterious shipwrecks. Underwater images thus attract marine scientists and researchers to study this untested vast underwater world.

In today's world, the use of visual aids is inevitable. This has led many researchers to work in the field of prescreening their images and applications [1], [2], [3], [4]. One such field is underwater image restoration and enhancement. Due to vast diversity of aquatic organisms and fish species, the widespread use of robotic optical, and marine engineering, the underwater world is now earning a lot of interest.

Underwater photography is an important tool used to record and recreate areas of biological or historical interest that are inaccessible to many social and scientific communities. In underwater photography, many scientific and specialized equipments are used, including optical camera, sonar, laser, and infrared. In current underwater photography, high-quality optical cameras are often selected for the scene collection. However, underwater photography production and the assurance of the dynamic nature of imagery have faced a number of important challenges.

The development of underwater photography is one of the latest research areas under investigation. Details of underwater mines, telecommunications, coral reefs, shipwrecks, pipelines, and the underwater environ-

Digital Image Enhancement and Reconstruction
https://doi.org/10.1016/B978-0-32-398370-9.00010-X

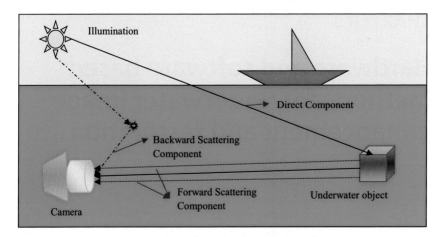

Figure 3.1 Forward scattering, backward scattering, and direct components of light in seawater [5].

ment are taken from private underwater vehicles and long-distance vehicles. Blurred vision, low contrast, contrast light, brightness, sound, and other distortions are the main features of underwater images. The clear reduction of light in the water makes the underwater images less clear and slightly different. Underwater visibility is reduced by about 20 feet [7 m] compared with freshwater. In turbulent waters, the range drops to 15 feet [5 m] or less. Underwater images are affected by the absorption and distribution of light in water.

Fig. 3.1 shows the propagation model of light in the ocean representing direct component, backward scattering component, and forward scattering component. Direct component is the component of light, which is directly coming from the object to the camera without any deviation and represented by a solid line in the Fig. 3.1. Forward scattering component is the component of light that is deviated on its way from the object to the camera due to marine snow and dust particles present in the water and leads to the blurriness of underwater images. Dotted lines in Fig. 3.1 represents these forward scattering components of light. Backward scattering component is the fraction of light that reaches the camera before actually reaching to the object present in water. Backward scattering component represented by dotted and hashed lines in Fig. 3.1 leads to the reduced contrast and haziness in underwater images. Underwater images are combination of these three components mentioned above.

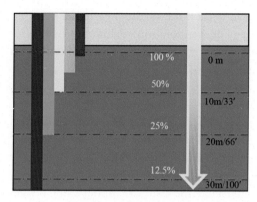

Figure 3.2 Absorption of red, orange, yellow, green, and blue wavelengths in ocean with depth [6].

Fig. 3.2 shows absorption pattern of different colors in the sea water. Red color is absorbed first due to longest wavelength, whereas blue is the last to get absorbed due to shortest wavelength. Orange color vanishes at the depth of 5–7 meters, whereas yellow color is absorbed completely at depth of 10 meters under the surface of water. Green color travels up to the distance of 20 meters below the surface of ocean. This absorption of light depends on the wavelength of the particular color and produces dullness in underwater images.

The distribution of light is caused not only by water, but also by the diversity of living things and dust particles present in the oceans. The artificial light incident on the scene increases the visibility range, but there is a problem of producing a bright light in the middle of the image and the negative lighting areas surrounding the scene. Therefore artificial light in the underwater environment decreases the problem of inconsistent light. As the depth increases, the amount of light decreases and colors start fading due to the decrease in the wavelength.

Underwater photography is not only influenced by absorption and scattering, but also by optical noise, wave disturbance, light stability, bright balance, temperature variations, and other environmental variables, making underwater measurement one of the most difficult tasks. Image processing techniques can help researchers provide a solution to these underwater photography problems. Therefore various methods are designed to enhance and restore underwater images with different lighting conditions.

This chapter focuses on reviewing the various enhancement and restoration techniques used to overcome the issues of underwater images. To date, various studies have been done in the area underwater image processing. These enhancement and restoration techniques have also been reviewed from time to time and all these review works are only based on the different software algorithms used by these techniques.

But the present chapter focuses on the review of both hardware- and software-based methods used in literature for enhancement and restoration of underwater images. The chapter reviews and summarizes the techniques used for enhancement and restoration by the hardware equipments and laboratory setups and the software algorithms. The chapter further prepares a platform for the beginners and researchers in the area of underwater images to better understand the issues of underwater image processing and formulate their research problems.

The rest of the chapter is organized as follows: Section 3.2 presents detailed survey of the software- and hardware-based methods for underwater images, Section 3.3 highlights the research gaps in the literature and Section 3.4 concludes the chapter with future scope of this area.

3.2 Literature survey

Enhancement strategies are frequently used for improving color, assessment, and element in underwater images. This has attracted lot of attention during the last decade, however it's a very undeveloped area compared to nature images. This section looks at few methods to enhance underwater images proposed during the last decade. These strategies can be categorized as hardware and software program techniques. Hardware used in enhancement includes lasers and aqua tripods. They are frequently used in hardware-supported systems to enhance underwater pictures. On the other hand, software program-based techniques create an operating environment using specific software to enhance underwater pictures. Some of the commonly used hardware- and software-based method are shown in Fig. 3.3.

3.2.1 Hardware-based methods

Hardware techniques used for image restoration and enhancement often require devoted hardware for enhancing underwater images. This study emphasizes gating imaging models and polarizers, as they are widely used for enhancement purpose. The size, separation, and length of the wavelength are important elements of light. Natural light is flawless, but the camera light sensor that reaches the light has a partial separation problem. Some studies confirm that simple separation can reduce the back scattering

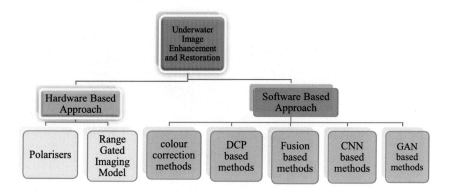

Figure 3.3 Classification of hardware- and software-based methods.

from underwater images [7]. A rotating filter-based hardware approach is proposed by Laschi et al. [8] to restore the images of underwater scenes. The rotating cooling filter model is analyzed for different images with angles ranging between 0 to 180 degrees in a different light conditions.

Three-dimensional (3D) range-gated imaging suppresses backscatter and finds application in underwater navigation, target detection, and marine research. Turbid water leads to apparent back-scatter and further reduces accuracy for 3D reconstruction of images. To overcome this issue, Wang et al. [9] uses propagation property of light in water and proposed a 3D range-gated-intensity correlation imaging method. This method calculates the depth–noise maps (DNM) of target gate images by using the reference image and water attenuation coefficient. New denoised gate images are obtained by subtracting the DNMs from target gate images. Finally, the denoised gate images are used for reconstruction of 3D images with high accuracy and range resolution. The experimental setup for 3D range-gated imaging model is also shown below in Fig. 3.4.

Similarly, the polarization imaging model is proposed by Liu et al. [10] by considering effects of diffusion in water. In addition to these effects, the polarization details are also emphasized, which means that the target light is completely separate and the back-scattered light is slightly separated in the enhancement process. This model also estimates that light absorption causes color loss due to which it receives accurate target light.

Li et al. [11] has developed an enhancement approach based on polarimetric underwater images. This algorithm shows orthogonal separation by an extended histogram. Results analysis shows that the images show improvement in their quality even in turbid waters. An extended dark channel

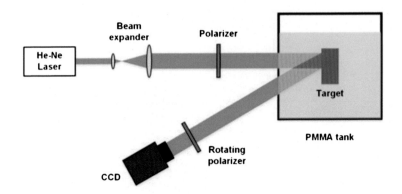

Figure 3.4 Experimental setup for 3D range gated imaging model. Image source [9].

prior (DCP) approach was also proposed by Hajjami et al. [12] to reduce the impact of underwater exposure by installing a polarimetric imaging system.

The polarization imaging model proposed by Linghao et al. [13] combines two joint regularization schemes for underwater image enhancement. It offers transmission map with depth-chromaticity regularization and image enhancement with chromaticity-depth compensation regularization. The irradiance image and transmission map promotes each other. The effectiveness of the algorithm lies in the fact that it enhances the visibility of underwater images without amplifying the noise.

Results of the polarization imaging model are also shown below in Fig. 3.5. Comparisons with various state-of-the art methods, such as CLAHE (Contrast limited adaptive histogram equalization), GC (Generalized unsharp masking), HE (Histogram equalization), ICM (Integrated color model), RD (Rayleigh distribution), RGHS (Relative global histogram stretching), and UCM (Unsupervised color model) are highlighted in Fig. 3.3. Result analysis proves that polarization imaging model outperforms all the abovementioned methods in terms of both contrast and colors. Huang et al. [14] also proposed an enhancement method of underwater images by calculating the polarized-difference image of the target signal.

The measurement hardware proposed by Sun et al. [15] is based on analysis of frequency and computational estimates to put off the unfold of underwater pictures. This hardware is effective in doing away with backscatter noise and improving underwater images. In addition Mariani et al. [16] has proposed a high-resolution camera with integrated gates

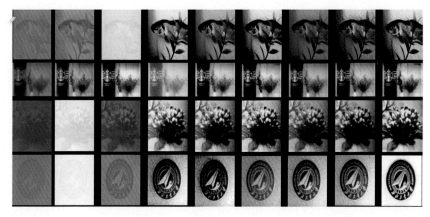

Figure 3.5 Results for polarization imaging model and various state-of-the-art techniques for different underwater scenes (a) Original, (b) CLAHE, (c) GC, (d) HE, (e) ICM, (f) RD, (g) RGHS, (h) UCM, (i) Polarization imaging model. Image source [13].

by combining "time of flight" (tof) sensors with laser light from incident source. The version also complements photographs through putting off background coverage and providing a range of every illuminated object. This model works well for prolonged intensity range. Treibitz et al. [17] proposes the fluorescence imaging gadget (fluoris) to enhance chlorophyll sensitivity.

Zeng et al. [18] propelled the development process by combining thinking technology separated from tail cutting technology. The addition of a polarizer to the light source and a polarization analyzer to the light collection unit leads to an improved version of the comprehensive recording system. Further testing in a water tank with magnesium hydroxide as dispersed particles were made for comparison. The Job transfer exchange is used as a test parameter for image correction. The results of combining polarization technology with gating improve the imaging solution in stagnant water.

The light field camera thinking system is proposed by Yu et al. [19] to enhance underwater images. This method also creates a three-dimensional image from various underwater locations. Some experiments were performed with 2-D imaging and 3-D reconstruction using a bright field camera list. 3-D measurements of underwater scenes are obtained by analyzing and refocusing the light of the target scenes in turbulent waters. Various tests confirm the reliability of the field camera light system by comparing the structural similarity index measure (SSIM) system in hot water with the single SSIM camera assumption, which ensures that the forward water distribution does not affect the lighting field system.

To overcome the challenges of underwater scenario, high-definition sonars are used now-a-days, which provide high frame rates for acoustic imagery. But there are difficulties in image registration of sonar data, which is prior for motion estimation and mosaicing applications. Hurtos et al. [20] proposed a Fourier-based image registration technique for sonar images, as it can overcome the issues of noise, low resolution, and artifacts. This technique outperforms the various state-of-the-art techniques in the terms of the higher robustness in featureless environment and alignment of both consecutive and nonconsecutive views. For high resolution and better details of images, pose constrains between sonar frames are computed and integrated in an aligned framework.

Photometric stereo is widely used for scattering media, such as water, fog, and biological tissue, because of forward scattered light from both the source and object, also light scattered back from the medium (backscatter). To alleviate the need to handle light source, Murez et al. [21] proposed a method in which a single-scattered light from a source is approximated by a point light source with a single direction. Next, a deconvolution method is used to model the blur due to scattering of light from the object. Finally to increase the signal-to-noise ratio, imaging fluorescence emission eliminates the back-scatter component and enhances the underwater images.

Hardware-based techniques are not widely used, as they emphasize the choice of unique hardware or laboratory gadget, and furthermore those techniques are high-priced and time-consuming. To overcome this short-coming, many researchers are attracted by software programs to improve underwater images, as they are simpler and fast compared to hardware methods.

3.2.2 Software-based methods

Software methods help to enhance underwater images using practical techniques. These software methods can be categorized as image restoration methods, color correction methods, DCP methods, integration-based methods, methods based on convolutional neural networks (CNNs) and generative adversarial networks (GAN) based methods.

3.2.2.1 Image restoration methods

Image restoration techniques generally require a degradation model and image formation model to restore the images. These techniques generally require various parameters, such as attenuation coefficient, diffusion coefficient and depth of the scene from surface of water. Based on the above restoration model, Wang et al. [22] restored underwater images using an in-depth approach based on Poisson's equation. This approach also works well on removing the interference in the green underwater images. The novel underwater image enhancement method proposed by Chen et al. [23] depends on debugging process. Mapping depth is calculated using a method to eliminate the power of the separation between the back and front area inside the water. The size of the front and back light are the same and their differences are used to determine the presence of an artificial light source. Thereafter the depth of the water is measured by calculating remaining residual energy of the different colors present in the background light.

Chang et al. [24] proposed a new restoration model for single underwater images by considering a simplified image formation model. The restoration model developed two distinct transmission coefficient estimation approaches. The first approach relies on the optical characteristics, whereas the second coefficient depends on the knowledge of underwater image processing. Furthermore, these two transmission maps with their respective saliency maps are fused to obtain the resultant image. The restoration model is tested on various underwater images with different scenes, and result analysis demonstrates the superiority of the proposed algorithm.

Underwater image restoration method proposed by Zhou [25] is based on secondary guided transmission map for better restoration of visibility, colors, and overall appearance of underwater image. The transmission map has been refined by the aid of guided filter. Guided filter decomposed the rough transmission map into the basic and the detailed image. Finally, the images are processed, respectively, to construct the refined transmission map. Furthermore, contrast of restored image is improved by auto-level processing. Comparison of experimental results with state-of-the-art methods shows the improvement in visibility, color, and contrast of restored images.

3.2.2.2 Color correction methods

Colors in underwater images get absorbed as light travels deep in the ocean. Therefore color correction in underwater images is very important task to restore perceptual visibility and good colors. Daway et al. [26] suggested an approach that uses the RGB model to restore colors and YCbCr space for color conversion. Comparison of state-of-the-art methods with Rayleigh integrated color model, in terms of qualitative and quantitative results, shows the effectiveness of this model. Pan et al. [27] proposed a technique based on compensation for low color channels in dedicated fractions. This method calculates the rate of variation between the upper and lower color channels to the lower color channels. In addition, each color channel is used with an algorithm to enhance the dynamic brightness to extract the front and back extended images. These front and back extensions include enhancing the overall brightness of the resulting image. The resulting image is processed through a subtle encryption process to sharpen the entire image. Measurement and quality results continue to prove the efficacy of the proposed algorithms.

To improve the quality of underwater images, Dong et al. [28] proposed an approach based on bi-interval contrast enhancement and color correction. Subinterval linear transformation based color correction method is employed to address color distortion. To decompose the underwater image into low- and high-frequency component, L channel of image is treated with Gaussian low-pass filter. Bi-interval histograms are used to enhance the low- and high-frequency components of decomposed image. Finally, S-shaped function is used to highlight image details and enhance image contrast. Enhanced high- and low-frequency components are integrated by the multiscale fusion.

3.2.2.3 DCP-based methods

The DCP-based method utilizes the dark channel of underwater images and depth map for improving the visual quality. Yang et al. [29] has proposed a background light measurement system capable of enhancing underwater images within a depth of 30–60 meters utilizing an artificial illumination source. This system combines deep learning with DCP to extract the red channel details and to enhance the color variations in the image. Cosman et al. [30] proposed DCP-based approach for image enhancement in moderate light conditions. Pardo et al. [31] anticipated red channel-based method to enhance the contrast of underwater images by variations in DCP approach. It enhances the images of underwater scenes by the aid of red channel, which has the shortest wavelength.

To enhance the quality of underwater images Yu et al. [32] proposed a dehazing algorithm, which comprises of homomorphic filtering, followed by double transmission map and wavelet fusion. Homomorphic filtering is used to remove the color deviation from the underwater images. The difference between the dark and light channels is used to obtain the transmission map of enhanced image. The depth map from DCP is also used to obtain the enhanced version of the image. Finally, both the enhanced images are combined together by dual-image wavelet fusion technique. The fused image is further contrast enhanced by the CLAHE method. Result analysis proves that the enhanced images from proposed method have high contrast and better effect on average gradient and entropy. Underwater color image quality evaluation (UCIQE) is also better in case of proposed double transmission map method when compared with state-of-the-art methods.

Since traditional DCP has certain limitations and tends to show unsatisfactory results for underwater image restoration, to overcome this issue Wu et al. [33] proposed an optimized red dark channel prior (ORDCP) method by considering the differences between light attenuation in water and atmosphere. Furthermore, a double threshold method is used to determine the red channel transmission map and main color tone of underwater images. After obtaining the transmission maps and background light, restoration can be done using conventional DCP. The qualitative analysis depicts the better performance of ORDCP in terms of images edge detail, contrast, and saturation. In addition, quantitative analysis shows that the performance of ORDCP increases by 32.32%. ORDCP method is also capable of removing the blurriness and noise in underwater images and outperforms various state-of-the-art techniques.

3.2.2.4 Fusion-based methods

Fusion-based methods generally fuse two or more results from different algorithms, depending on the assigned weighted maps for each algorithm. Based on the same principle, Ancuti et al. [34] suggested a fusion process for underwater image enhancement. This technique enhances the images by combining real-time image versions with white and color balance versions, as shown in Fig. 3.6. This fusion method relies on two types of real image with related weight maps to enhance the color brightness and edges of the enhanced output. The resultant images from the abovementioned fusion process are shown in Fig. 3.7 and Ghani et al. [35] also proposed a double-image wavelength integration method that includes standard histogram specification (CLAHS) and homomorphic filters to enlarge underwater images. Qu et al. [36] has proposed an optical property-based approach by incorporating its underwater model design. The results show good performance and functional balance of optical properties.

Simple fusion network (LAFFNet) is proposed by Yang et al. [37] overcoming the cost issues of the model parameter and the fusion network memory. LAFFNet has many flexibility feature modules. Multifeature maps

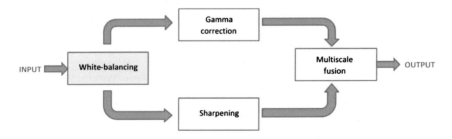

Figure 3.6 Fusion algorithm proposed by Ancuti et al. Image source [34].

Figure 3.7 Results of fusion algorithm proposed by Ancuti et al. Image source [34].

are generated in different kernel sizes to include multiple branches in fusion feature modules. LAFFNet reduces the number of parameters by 94% (e.g. from 2.5M to 0.15M) and exceeds high-level techniques by improving high-quality viewing functions, such as single-image depth measurement and salience object detection.

3.2.2.5 Integrated methods

Integrated methods are the methods where two or more algorithms are integrated together by providing output of one technique as input to the next one. Based on the color line elements, Wu et al. [38] has suggested an algorithm to reduce the scattering of input light. The color line model also recovers the dot color line of the image by refining the pre-colored markers. This model also measures the local distribution and restores the contrast and color of the underwater images. Lu et al. [39] suggested a process to improve underwater images by combining the spectral properties of the camera in muddy water with a trigonometric filter. This approach compensates for the inconsistencies in the reduction of the distribution method. Hou et al. [40] introduces an underwater image enhancement method using Hue-

| | Ancuti1 | Ancuti3 | Reef3 | Dark1 | Dark2 |

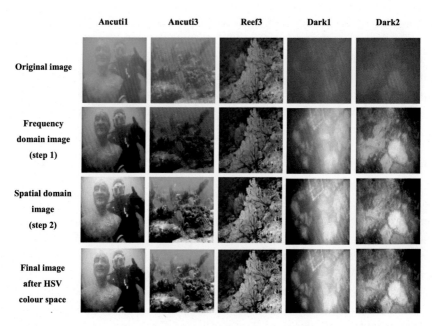

Figure 3.8 Stepwise results of integrated algorithm proposed by Mathur et al. Image source [42].

Saturation-Intensity (HSI) and Hue–Saturation–Value (HSV) color models by keeping the Hue (H) component stable in both conditions.

Li et al. [41] has suggested a development approach based on the Bayesian retinex algorithm. A color correction algorithm is used to address color distribution and multiorder gradient calculations in appearance and brightness. The Bayesian retinex algorithm easily overcomes a variety of challenging applications. Furthermore, Mathur et al. [42] proposed a novel method based on Rayleigh stretching of different bands of RGB image to enhance the colors and contrast of underwater images. It works well for all types of nonuniformly illuminated underwater images. Stepwise results for the same are also shown in Fig. 3.8. Comparison of Rayleigh-based method with state-of-the-art method is also shown in Fig. 3.9. A color and contrast enhancement method proposed by Mathur et al. [43] is based on histogram stretching and white balancing. It improves the visibility of images in all types of underwater environment, ranging from clear to turbid waters.

Taguchi et al. [44] proposed a solution to enhance the contrast and remove the color cast from underwater images. Gray World (GW) method is used to improve the color cast, but still the resultant image is not visually good. Therefore an integrated approach is proposed by using differential histogram equalization (DHE) and adaptive GW (AGW). DHE enhances the contrast of underwater images, whereas AGW improves the color cast. Finally, enhanced image is formed by combining the intensity components of DHE and chromaticity components of AGW algorithm. Qualitative and quantitative measures are used for result evaluation. The integrated method is compared with three state-of-the-art methods and shows better visibility of underwater images.

3.2.2.6 CNN-based methods

The use of neural underwater image enhancement (UIE) networks is becoming increasingly important in this current situation. Based on this, Hu et al. [45] proposes a two-component novel CNN, which separates enhanced image brightness and colorization using HSV color space material to differentiate firmness and chrominance. The RGB input image is converted to HSV image and is divided into HS and V channels to function as input to both branches, respectively. Subsequently, the construction of a productive resistance network acts as a branch of color removal to improve the H and S channels. The traditional CNN acts as a comparison branch that improves the V–channel. The final enhanced image is obtained by merging the effects from two branches and converting them back to an RGB image. The above approach exceeds the various modes for improving the quality of underwater images.

A CNN-based network, called UIE–Net, is proposed by Wang et al. [46]. UIE–Net is the final framework that trains a network in 200,000 images of haze removal and color correction. The pixel interference process is used to remove natural features from local dots to improve the accuracy and speed of conversion. Li et al. [47] has proposed an image enhancement model called Underwater-CNN (UWCNN) based on the automated training model. The details of the underwater images are widely used in this data-driven model. Lu et al. [48] also suggested a similar model based on CNN, which enhances images with integrated retrieval filters and a variation of the DCP method.

Porikli et al. [49] proposed an underwater convolutional neural network, also referred to as UWCNN, which is based on CNN's lightweight model. It reconstructs underwater images from the underwater scenes and doesn't utilize image parameters from the image model. Underwater convolutional neural network shows excellent results on various types of images, ranging between clear and turbid water. A two-phase dust removal method for turbid scene images has been suggested by Xu et al. [50]. Scattering due to fine dust has been removed by a reddish–green water channel and, furthermore, a deep CNN has been utilized for elimination of hazy appearance from turbid underwater images.

In addition, Hu et al. [51] has proposed an efficient and automated process that uses neural networks, including A-network and transmission network (T-network). The T-network relies on multi-level measurements and layer connections to maintain edges and avoid halo art objects. Hu et al. [51] has developed a novel training method for imitating images taken in various waters. Shin et al. [52] reveals a process that uses the CNN architecture to transmit and measure optical light. Available transmission map and lighting enhance the quality of underwater images by burning them with fire.

Kwong et al. [53] has raised an underwater photo booth containing 950 underwater images. 890 of the 950 images with corresponding references and the remaining 60 images without reference images are considered challenging data. In addition, a water-based image enhancement project was proposed and trained. Moghimi et al. [54] has come up with two powerful steps to improve the underwater photography algorithm. The first step is to adjust the color of the underwater images and improve the image quality by minimizing harmful and dark objects. The second step enhances image processing using Convolutional neural network (CNN) for images with high-precision underwater under different artistic conditions and at different depths.

3.2.2.7 GAN-based methods

These days, the GAN has also been broadly used for underwater image enhancement. Takahashi et al. [55] proposed one such GAN for contrast enhancement of underwater images. The underwater images are enhanced by training the loss feature of network. Unique multiscale dense GAN has also been proposed by Guo et al. [56] for enhancing images of underwater scenes. This generator utilizes the multiscale dense block for residual features, and hence improves the detailing of the images.

Hong et al. [57] suggested a GAN-based design to enhance underwater images with nonresponsive image conversion, i.e., from underwater photography (area X) to high-resolution images (background Y), reducing the need for aligned image pairing. The depth of the internal depth of the underwater images is explored to create a new purposeful work, which increases the sensitivity of the depth. An additional model is trained based on an unequal image balance database, called Unaligned underwater image enhancement (UUIE) dataset. The analysis of the results and the magnitude of the results show that this method improves the visual quality of underwater images.

Dhall et al. [58] proposed an underwater generative adversarial network (UW-GAN) for depth estimation from single underwater image. UW-GAN consists of underwater coarse-level generative network (UWC-Net) and underwater fine-level network (UWF-Net) for estimation of coarse-level depth map and fine-level depth map, respectively. Estimated coarse-level depth map and the input image are together fed as input to the UWF-Net. For fine-level depth estimation, spatial and channel-wise squeeze and excitation block are used. UW-GAN is evaluated on underwater images having different lighting conditions, contrast, and color casts. Result analysis proves that UW-GAN outperforms the state-of-the-art enhancement techniques.

To address the limitation of scattering and absorption of light in underwater images, Han et al. [59] proposed a novel spiral-GAN framework, which can effectively enhance the underwater images with better contrast, bright colors and significant details. Pixel-wise losses are used for color correction and training of the framework. Objective function of the framework consists of angle error and mean squared error. Furthermore, a generator is designed with deconv-conv blocks to preserve the details from the original distorted images. Finally, a spiral learning strategy is modeled to effectively recover the real-world underwater images. Qualitative and quantitative evaluations suggest that spiral-GAN framework can efficiently enhance the quality of underwater images and can be further used for underwater object detection. Most of the abovementioned software methods generally relies on F4K datasets for evaluation of their algorithms. Some standard test images used for testing and result analysis from this dataset are as shown in Fig. 3.9.

The study describes methods based on the development and restoration of underwater images. The above discussion shows that software-based methods are better compared to hardware-based methods due to less computation time, easier design, easy flexibility, and no complex hardware. The following section describes some of the research gaps available for the development of underwater images. Furthermore, Table 3.1 and Table 3.2 highlight the major advantages and disadvantages of both the hardware- and software-based methods.

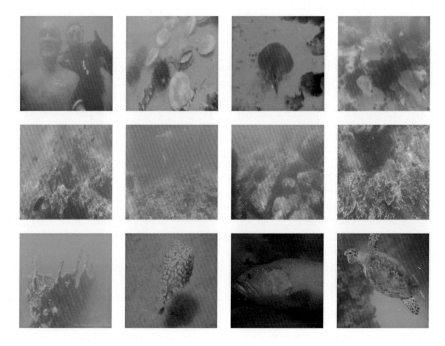

Figure 3.9 Some standard test images from F4K dataset used by software-based methods [60].

3.3 Research gaps

As mentioned in the above section, various methods of improvement and restoration have been used in the literature to improve the visibility of underwater images. Such methods have a variety of disadvantages of blurred appearance, low contrast, and distorted colors, which impair their performance by undermining their significant achievements. Apart from a lot of research, there are still various research gaps in this underwater image development area. Some of which include the following:

1. Noises present in underwater images are the main source of degradation for these images. These noises occur during acquisition and transmission processes of underwater images. Various noises present in underwater images include Gaussian noise, salt and pepper noise, speckle noise, fixed mode device, correlated noise, and signal-related noise. But many current methods of enhancement and restoration ignore the problem of noises present in underwater images. Underwater noise removal should be considered as a preprocessing step along with

Table 3.1 Advantages and disadvantages of hardware-based methods.

Hardware-Based Methods

Advantages

1. Results are better from hardware methods, as hardware equipment works in real environment with all the parameters properly balanced.
2. Hardware methods are more reliable for real-time problems.
3. The hardware approach mitigates the problems induced by water in the captured underwater images.

Disadvantages

1. Unique hardware and laboratory setups are required for restoration and enhancement purpose.
2. Hardware methods are very expensive, as large funding is required for lab setups and equipments.
3. Hardware methods are time-consuming; they can take several months for proper setup and experimentation.
4. One cannot handle these methods individually; a team work is required for proper execution.
5. Skilled manpower is one more problem in hardware-based methods for proper handling of instruments.

the main enhancement algorithm to facilitate obtaining better improvement results.

2. Most of the enhancement methods focus on the enhancement and clearing the foreground, but the background is left unattended. Sometimes background also covers some important information along with foreground. Background can help to identify the particular location for a specific species of sea plants and animals. Skipping background information results in the loss of partial information. Therefore background should also be worked properly to get full details of the underwater scene. Algorithm that can enhance both background and foreground details should be developed.

3. Underwater images always have issues regarding the lighting conditions. The intensity of light decreases as we go deep in the water along with fading of colors. There are different lighting conditions for different depths. So, underwater scenes are generally captured by the aid of artificial lighting, but images captured with these lighting sources give unnatural and degraded scenes with nonuniform brightness. The images have bright spot at the center, followed by the dark or less illuminated area around it. Most algorithms focus either on the en-

Table 3.2 Advantages and disadvantages of software-based methods.

Software-Based Methods

Advantages

1. Software-based methods are less complex as they don't require complex hardware.
2. These methods are fast as computational complexity is low.
3. Software-based methods are cheaper as compared to hardware-based approaches.
4. Software-based methods are more flexible as compared to hardware-based approaches, as change in single line of code can change the whole result.
5. There is no need of professionals for software-based methods, which is required in hardware-based methods.
6. Reduction in manpower, as software can handle lots of things.

Disadvantages

1. Comparative results are less accurate as compared to hardware-based methods.
2. Underwater images used in software-based methods suffer from various water effects, which can mar the results.
3. Software-based methods are less effective in real-time environment.

---

hancement of objects present in the scenes or the overall enhancement of the image, neglecting the issue of lighting in the scene. This issue of nonuniform lighting in the underwater images is ignored by most of the enhancement algorithm. Nonuniform lighting should be taken into consideration for further advancement in the restoration and enhancement algorithms.

4. Most of the underwater image development strategies work with the RGB (red, green, and blue) color space. Comparison of RGB with other color spaces, such as HSV (hue saturation value), CIELAB, CMY (cyan, magenta, yellow), CMYK (cyan, magenta, yellow, black), HSI (hue saturation intensity), etc., should also be done for the restoration and enhancement of the underwater images. There is a gap in literature that all algorithms focus on RGB images leaving other color spaces unexplored for underwater images.

5. Once underwater images are enhanced, some image quality measures are required for measuring the output results of the algorithm. But as we survey the literature, there are no such image quality measures that are suitably meant for underwater images. Most of the researchers rely on the measures meant for aerial images. These measures require orig-

inal image for comparison of input and output results, but the absence of original images in case of underwater images makes these measures unreliable for underwater scenario. So, there is requirement of the blind image quality metrics suitable for retrieval analysis and optimization algorithms meant for underwater images.

The next section concludes the chapter. Recommendations and suggestions for future work are also highlighted in this section.

3.4 Conclusion and future scope

Underwater images are becoming more and more important for research purposes over the past decade. Various strategies for improvement and restoration have been proposed as outlined in the literature review. The current chapter reviews various ways to improve the underwater images. It summarizes the findings, conclusions, and research gaps taken from various research papers in underwater image enhancement. The chapter also helps marine researchers and scientists to understand the background and challenges of underwater photography. Hardware- and software-based approaches provide in-depth knowledge of underwater image enhancement techniques to better assess the value and application of an underwater environment.

Although the methods of enhancing and restoring images under water have made great strides, measuring the quality of these images after enhancement is a difficult task, as the original images for underwater scenes are not available. Therefore the reference quality metrics available for aerial photographs do not apply to underwater images. There are only few blind measures available for underwater images and those too have some limitations. Future research will be on the index to raise the blind metrics for measuring the performance of improved underwater images. Photographs taken in the deep sea are usually very dark, as there is no light, and it is very difficult to enhance such images. The use of artificial lights spread nonuniform lighting on the scene, which further undermines the quality of underwater images. So, future work would also focus on the enhancement of these dark underwater images.

References

[1] A.K. Bhunia, G. Kumar, P.P. Roy, R. Balasubramanian, U. Pal, Text recognition in scene image and video frame using color channel selection, Multimedia Tools and Applications 77 (7) (2017) 8551–8578.

[2] R. Sethi, S. Indu, Fusion of underwater image enhancement and restoration, International Journal of Pattern Recognition and Artificial Intelligence 34 (03) (2020) 1–23.

[3] G. Bhatnagar, Q.M.J. Wu, A fractal dimension based framework for night vision fusion, IEEE/CAA Journal of Automatica Sinica 6 (1) (2019) 220–227.

[4] P. Pandey, R. Gupta, N. Goel, A fast and effective vision enhancement method for single foggy image, Engineering Science and Technology, an International Journal 24 (2021) 1478–1489.

[5] R. Schettini, S. Corchs, Underwater image processing: State of the art of restoration and image enhancement methods, EURASIP Journal on Advances in Signal Processing 2010 (1) (2010) 1–14.

[6] L. Chao, M. Wang, Removal of water scattering, in: 2nd International Conference on Computer Engineering and Technology, vol. 2, 2010, pp. 35–39.

[7] J.S. Tyo, M.P. Rowe, E.N. Pugh, N. Engheta, Target detection in optically scattering media by polarization-difference imaging, Applied Optics 35 (11) (1996) 1855–1870.

[8] M. Calisti, G. Carbonara, C. Laschi, A rotating polarizing filter approach for image enhancement, in: OCEANS, 2017, pp. 1–4.

[9] M. Wang, X. Wang, L. Sun, Y. Yang, Y. Zhou, Underwater 3D deblurring-gated range-intensity correlation imaging, Optical Letter 45 (6) (2020) 1455–1458.

[10] F. Liu, Y. Wei, P. Han, K. Yang, L. Bai, X. Shao, Polarization-based exploration for clear underwater vision in natural illumination, Optics Express 27 (3) (2019) 3629–3641.

[11] X. Li, H. Hu, L. Zhao, Polarimetric image recovery method combining histogram stretching for underwater imaging, Scientific Reports 8 (1) (2018) 1–10.

[12] K.O. Amer, M. Elbouz, A. Alfalou, C. Brosseau, J. Hajjami, Enhancing underwater optical imaging by using a low-pass polarization filter, Optical Express 27 (2) (2019) 621–643.

[13] L. Shen, Y. Zhao, Underwater image enhancement based on polarization imaging, in: ISPRS - International Archives of the Photogrammetry, Remote Sensing and Spatial Information Sciences, XLIII-B1-2020, 2020, pp. 579–585.

[14] B. Huang, T. Liu, H. Hu, J. Han, M. Yu, Underwater image recovery considering polarization effects of objects, Optical Express 24 (9) (May 2016) 9826–9838.

[15] X. Wang, M. Wang, Y. Yang, L. Sun, Y. Zhou, Underwater de-scattering range-gated imaging based on numerical fitting and frequency domain filtering, Intelligent Robotics and Applications 11741 (2019) 195–204.

[16] P. Mariani, I. Quincoces, K.H. Haugholt, Y. Chardard, A.W. Visser, C. Yates, G. Piccinno, G. Reali, P. Risholm, J.T. Thielemann, Range-gated imaging system for underwater monitoring in ocean environment, Sustainability 162 (11) (2019) 1–14.

[17] T. Reibitz, B. Neal, D. Kline, Wide field-of-view fluorescence imaging of coral reefs, Scientific Reports 5 (1) (2015) 7694, pp. 1–9.

[18] X. Zeng, Z. Li, H. Yu, W. Du, J. Han, Underwater image enhancement by method combined the tail-gating and active polarization imaging technology, in: Seventh Symposium on Novel Photoelectronic Detection Technology and Applications, vol. 11763, 2021, pp. 1829–1835.

[19] F. Ouyang, J. Yu, H. Liu, Z. Ma, X. Yu, Underwater imaging system based on light field technology, IEEE Sensors Journal 21 (12) (2021) 13753–13760.

[20] N. Hurtós, D. Ribas, X. Cufí, Y. Petillot, J. Salvi, Fourier-based registration for robust forward-looking sonar mosaicing in low-visibility underwater environments, Journal of Field Robotics 32 (1) (2015) 123–151.

[21] Z. Murez, T. Treibitz, R. Ramamoorthi, D.J. Kriegman, Photometric stereo in a scattering medium, IEEE Transactions on Pattern Analysis and Machine Intelligence 39 (9) (2017) 1880–1891.

[22] W. Yongxin, M. Diao, A novel underwater image restoration algorithm, International Journal of Performability Engineering 14 (2018) 1513–1520.

[23] J.Y. Chiang, Y. Chen, Underwater image enhancement by wavelength compensation and dehazing, IEEE Transactions on Image Processing 21 (4) (2012) 1756–1769.

[24] H.H. Chang, Single underwater image restoration based on adaptive transmission fusion, IEEE Access 8 (2020) 38650–38662.

[25] J. Zhou, Z. Liu, W. Zhang, Underwater image restoration based on secondary guided transmission map, Multimedia Tools and Applications 80 (2021) 7771–7788.

[26] H.H. Kareem, H.G. Daway, E.G. Daway, Underwater image enhancement using colour restoration based on YCbCr colour model, IOP Conference Series: Materials Science and Engineering 571 (2019) 1–7.

[27] W. Zhang, X. Pan, X. Xie, L. Li, Z. Wang, C. Han, Color correction and adaptive contrast enhancement for underwater image enhancement, Computers and Electrical Engineering 91 (2021) 106981.

[28] W. Zhang, L. Dong, T. Zhang, W. Xu, Enhancing underwater image via color correction and bi-interval contrast enhancement, Signal Processing: Image Communication 90 (2021) 116030.

[29] S. Yang, Z. Chen, Z. Feng, X. Ma, Underwater image enhancement using scene depth-based adaptive background light estimation and dark channel prior algorithms, IEEE Access 7 (2019) 165318–165327.

[30] Y. Peng, K. Cao, P.C. Cosman, Generalization of the dark channel prior for single image restoration, IEEE Transactions on Image Processing 27 (6) (2018) 2856–2868.

[31] A. Galdran, D. Pardo, A. Picón, A. Alvarez-Gila, Automatic red-channel underwater image restoration, Journal of Visual Communication and Image Representation 26 (C) (2015) 132–145.

[32] H. Yu, X. Li, Q. Lou, Underwater image enhancement based on DCP and depth transmission map, Multimedia Tools and Applications 79 (2020) 20373–20390.

[33] Q. Wu, Y. Guo, J. Hou, Underwater optical image processing based on double threshold judgements and optimized red dark channel prior method, Multimedia Tools and Applications 80 (2021) 29985–30002.

[34] C.O. Ancuti, C. Ancuti, C. De Vleeschouwer, P. Bekaert, Color balance and fusion for underwater image enhancement, IEEE Transactions on Image Processing 27 (1) (2018) 379–393.

[35] A. Shahrizan, A. Ghani, Image contrast enhancement using an integration of recursive-overlapped contrast limited adaptive histogram specification and dual-image wavelet fusion for the high visibility of deep underwater image, Ocean Engineering 162 (2018) 224–238.

[36] X. Zhao, T. Jin, S. Qu, Deriving inherent optical properties from background color and underwater image enhancement, Ocean Engineering 94 (2015) 163–172.

[37] H.-H. Yang, K.-C. Huang, W.-T. Chen, LAFFNet: A lightweight adaptive feature fusion network for underwater image enhancement, in: 2021 IEEE International Conference on Robotics and Automation (ICRA), 2021, pp. 685–692, https://doi.org/10.1109/ICRA48506.2021.9561263.

[38] Y. Zhou, Q. Wu, K. Yan, L. Feng, W. Xiang, Underwater image restoration using color-line model, IEEE Transactions on Circuits and Systems for Video Technology 29 (3) (2019) 907–911.

[39] H. Lu, Y. Li, S. Nakashima, S. Serikawa, Single image dehazing through improved atmospheric light estimation, Multimedia Tools and Applications 75 (24) (2016) 17081–17096.

[40] G. Hou, Z. Pan, B. Huang, G. Wang, X. Luan, Hue preserving-based approach for underwater colour image enhancement, IET Image Processing 12 (2) (2018) 292–298.

[41] P. Zhuang, C. Li, J. Wu, Bayesian retinex underwater image enhancement, Engineering Applications of Artificial Intelligence 101 (2021) 104171.

[42] M. Mathur, N. Goel, Enhancement of nonuniformly illuminated underwater images, International Journal of Pattern Recognition and Artificial Intelligence 35 (03) (2021) 2154008.

[43] M. Mathur, N. Goel, Enhancement algorithm for high visibility of underwater images, IET Image Processing 16 (2022) 1067–1082, https://doi.org/10.1049/ipr2.12210.

[44] S.L. Wong, R. Paramesran, A. Taguchi, Underwater image enhancement by adaptive gray world and differential gray-levels histogram equalization, Advances in Electrical and Computer Engineering 18 (2) (2018) 109–116.

[45] J. Hu, Q. Jiang, R. Cong, W. Gao, F. Shao, Two-branch deep neural network for underwater image enhancement in HSV color space, IEEE Signal Processing Letters (2021) 2152–2156.

[46] Y. Wang, J. Zhang, Y. Cao, Z. Wang, A deep CNN method for underwater image enhancement, in: International Conference on Image Processing, 2017, pp. 1382–1386.

[47] S. Anwar, C. Li, F. Porikli, Deep underwater image enhancement, Journal of Computer Vision and Pattern Recognition 10 (2018) 1–12.

[48] H. Lu, Y. Li, H. Kim, S. Serikawa, Underwater light field depth map restoration using deep convolutional neural fields, Artificial Intelligence and Robotics 752 (2018) 305–312.

[49] C. Li, S. Anwar, F. Porikli, Underwater scene prior inspired deep underwater image and video enhancement, Pattern Recognition 98 (2020) 1–11.

[50] Y. Li, Y. Zhang, X. Xu, L. He, S. Serikawa, H. Kim, Dust removal from high turbid underwater images using convolutional neural networks, in: Special Issue: Optical Imaging for Extreme Environment, Optics and Laser Technology 110 (2019) 2–6.

[51] Y. Hu, K. Wang, X. Zhao, H. Wang, Y. Li, Underwater image restoration based on convolutional neural network, in: 10th Asian Conference on Machine Learning, vol. 95, 2018, pp. 296–311.

[52] Y. Shin, Y. Cho, G. Pandey, A. Kim, Estimation of ambient light and transmission map with common convolutional architecture, in: OCEANS, 2016, pp. 1–7.

[53] C. Li, C. Guo, W. Ren, R. Cong, J. Hou, S. Kwong, D. Tao, An underwater image enhancement benchmark dataset and beyond, IEEE Transactions on Image Processing 29 (2020) 4376–4389.

[54] M.K. Moghimi, F. Mohanna, Real-time underwater image resolution enhancement using super-resolution with deep convolutional neural networks, Journal of Real-Time Image Processing (2020) 1–15.

[55] T. Zhang, Y. Li, S. Takahashi, Underwater image enhancement using improved generative adversarial network, Concurrency and Computation: Practice and Experience 33 (2021) e5841, https://doi.org/10.1002/cpe.5841.

[56] Y. Guo, H. Li, P. Zhuang, Underwater image enhancement using a multiscale dense generative adversarial network, IEEE Journal of Oceanic Engineering 45 (3) (2020) 862–870.

[57] L. Hong, X. Wang, Z. Xiao, G. Zhang, J. Liu, WSUIE: Weakly supervised underwater image enhancement for improved visual perception, IEEE Robotics and Automation Letters 6 (4) (2021) 8237–8244.

[58] P. Hambarde, S. Murala, A. Dhall, UW-GAN: Single-image depth estimation and image enhancement for underwater images, IEEE Transactions on Instrumentation and Measurement 70 (2021) 1–12.

[59] R. Han, Y. Guan, Z. Yu, P. Liu, Y. Zheng, Underwater image enhancement based on a spiral generative adversarial framework, IEEE Access 8 (2020) 218838–218852.

[60] B.J. Boom, P.X. Huang, J. He, R.B. Fisher, Supporting ground-truth annotation of image datasets using clustering, in: 21st International Conference on Pattern Recognition, 2012.

CHAPTER 4

Denoising and enhancement of medical images by statistically modeling wavelet coefficients

Sima Sahu[a], Amit Kumar Singh[b], Amrit Kumar Agrawal[c], and Haoxiang Wang[d]

[a]Department of ECE, Malla Reddy Engineering College, Hyderabad, Telangana, India
[b]Department of Computer Science & Engineering, National Institute of Technology Patna, Patna, India
[c]Department of Computer Science & Engineering, Galgotias College of Engineering & Technology, Greater Noida, Uttar Pradesh, India
[d]Cornell University, Ithaca, NY, United States

4.1 Introduction

Image processing applications in medical science has gained immense attraction due to mass screening, speed, and ease procedure. Medical images carry important information of internal human body parts and play a vital role in disease finding, diagnosis, and treatment [1]. Noise and artifacts are the primary causes of medical image degradation; they generally occur in the acquisition stage. The degraded image leads to incorrect information, and thus disease treatment cannot happen in a fruitful manner. Medical image modalities, such as ultrasound image, MRI image, and OCT image are affected more due to the noise, because of low contrast and small imaging objects. MRI image affected by random noise, OCT, and ultrasound images are affected by speckle noise [2]. For this reason preprocessing step is highly essential for removing the noise and enhancement of the image for further processing [3]. Image denoising methods based on wavelet transform show a remarkable success in removing both additive and multiplicative noises [4,5]. The most important drawback of wavelet transform-based methods is the selection of threshold value, and this can be overcome by modeling and estimating the wavelet coefficient's threshold value from the signal and noise characteristics [6].

Homomorphic filters along with wavelet denoising method are proved to provide better suppression of speckle noise in the case of OCT and ultrasound images. It converts the speckle noise (multiplicative noise) to additive

Digital Image Enhancement and Reconstruction
https://doi.org/10.1016/B978-0-32-398370-9.00011-1
95

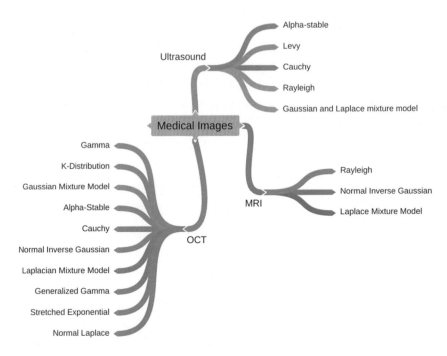

Figure 4.1 Existing probability density functions for medical images.

noise, and multiresolution approach removes the noise by decomposing the image into wavelet coefficients and modeling them statistically with an appropriate probability density function (PDF) [7]. The various PDFs used by authors for modeling wavelet coefficients are discussed in Fig. 4.1.

The rest of the chapter is structured as follows. Section 4.2 discusses the existing denoising schemes. Section 4.3 discusses about homomorphic approach, Haar wavelet transform, MAD estimator, MMSE estimator, and the Gaussian mixture model. The complete methodology is discussed in Section 4.4. Section 4.5 verifies the simulation and results. Section 4.6 concludes the paper.

4.2 Literature survey

In literature many authors concentrated on finding a way to denoise medical images by modeling wavelet coefficients. A probabilistic model for image denoising is always preferable as it provides a descriptive analysis of the noisy image [8].

Normal and generalized extreme value was applied by Kulkarni et al. [9] to model the retinal layer intensity distribution in OCT image. Amini et al. [10] proposed a method that models retinal layer intensities of OCT image by using a normal–Laplace mixture PDF. A stretched exponential distribution was proposed by Grzywacz et al. [11] for modeling the retinal layers intensities in OCT image. Sahu et al. [12] proposed a Cauchy model for modeling the OCT image wavelet coefficients. In literature gamma, K-distribution, Laplace mixture model, Gaussian mixture model, normal inverse Gaussian and alpha–stable have been applied as a probability density function (PDF) to model the OCT image and find the statistical properties of the noise and image [13].

The denoising methods for ultrasound image using statistical modeling methods have been very promising. Rabbani et al. [14] developed a method to despeckle ultrasound image. They used Gaussian and Laplace mixture prior and used MAP and MMSE estimators for removing speckle noise from ultrasound image. Alpha-stable PDF was proposed by Achim et al. [15] for removing speckle noise in SAR images. They implemented MMSE estimator in their proposed method. Bhuiyan et al. [16] proposed a denoising methodology for speckle noise. They used Cauchy prior and MMAE estimator. Sadreazami et al. [17] developed a method for denoising ultrasound image. A Cauchy prior in Contourlet domain was used for modeling. Ranjani et al. [18] proposed Levy distribution. Bibalan et al. [19] proposed a non-Gaussian mixture of Cauchy and Rayleigh mixture model for denoising the ultrasound images. Jafari et al. [20] worked in shearlet transform domain and used MAP estimator for removing noise in ultrasound image.

The main cause of MRI degradation is the random noise that occurs during the acquisition and construction process. Limited acquisition time of MR image reduces the signal-to-noise ratio. Thermal noise is another cause for MRI degradation, which alters the quantitative measurements. Gaussian and Rician noise mostly affect the MR image. In literature statistical methods by modeling the wavelet coefficients were proposed by the author and achieved improved result than the linear and nonlinear filters. A method based on statistical modeling was proposed by Sahu et al. [2]. They applied normal inverse Gaussian (NIG) distribution to model MRI data and remove Gaussian noise. Laplacian mixture model was applied by Rabbani et al. [21] for removing Rayleigh and Gaussian noise from MRI. They proposed Laplacian prior and used Rayleigh distribution to generate a new shrinkage function to remove noise from MRI.

4.3 Background and basic principles

This section gives a brief description of homomorphic model, Gaussian scale mixture (GSM) model, MAD estimator, and Bayesian approached MMSE estimator.

4.3.1 Homomorphic filter

A homomorphic model (H) consists of a linear system, homomorphic, and inverse homomorphic transformation that converts the multiplicative noise into additive noise and works on superposition principle defined as [7]

$$H(Y_1(t)Y_2(t)) = H(Y_1(t)) + H(Y_2(t)). \tag{4.1}$$

H is logarithmic for multiplication operation. Fig. 4.2 shows the block diagram of Homomorphic model.

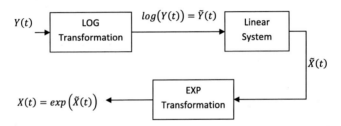

Figure 4.2 Homomorphic approach.

Here, $Y(t)$ is the input function, and the desired output is $\tilde{X}(t)$. After applying the logarithmic transformation the signal $\tilde{Y}(t)$ undergoes through a linear system and the resulted output $\tilde{X}(t)$ converted to the desired output by applying the inverse logarithmic transformation (EXP).

4.3.2 Haar wavelet

Haar wavelet is a simple form of wavelet transform. It preserves the compactness and orthogonality property of wavelet transform. The low-pass transform coefficients h_φ are given by [22]:

$$h_\varphi = \left[\frac{1}{\sqrt{2}} \frac{1}{\sqrt{2}} \right]. \tag{4.2}$$

Wavelet transform decomposes the spatial domain image into time-frequency domain and results in a set of orthogonal wavelets. Important properties of DWT include time-frequency localization, multiresolution, and multiscale. Wavelet decomposition of an image requires application of two-dimensional DWT. Two-dimensional DWT can be obtained by the repeated application of one-dimensional (1D) DWT. For an image, the 1D DWT is applied to all rows, and then to all columns. The diagrammatic representation of wavelet decomposition is shown in Fig. 4.3.

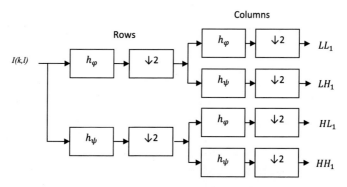

Figure 4.3 Discrete wavelet transform.

Subband representation of wavelet decomposition is shown in the Fig. 4.4. In the first level of decomposition, the image is decomposed into 4 subbands, namely LL (approximation subband), HL (horizontal subband), LH (vertical subband), and HH (detailed subband). In the second level decomposition, the LL is decomposed into four subbands: LL1, LH1, HL1, and HH1. In the third level decomposition, the LL1 is divided into LL2, LH2, HL2, and HH2 subbands. The detailed subband contains the noisy pixels. Approximation subband restores image information. Vertical and horizontal subbands restore vertical and horizontal features, respectively.

In this paper the HH1 subband information is extracted to obtain the noise information. Following Fig. 4.5 shows the first level decomposition of real MR image. It can be noticed that the HH subband contains noise information of the noisy image.

4.3.3 MAD estimator

The HH, diagonal subband consists of image noise information, and a MAD estimator is applied in HH subband to find the Gaussian noise variance [12]. The noise variance $\hat{\sigma}_\eta^2$ is given by

$$\hat{\sigma}_\eta^2 = \left(\frac{median(|HH|)}{0.6745} \right)^2. \tag{4.3}$$

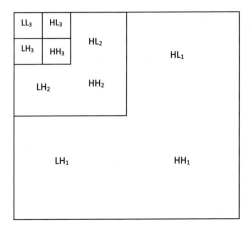

Figure 4.4 Subband decomposition representation of 2D DWT.

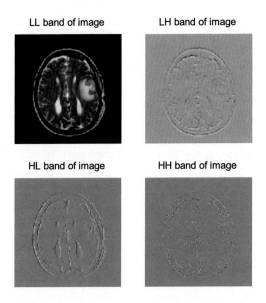

Figure 4.5 First level wavelet decomposition of real MR image.

HH is the first level diagonal subband in finest scale. Discrete wavelet transform (DWT) is a multiresolution and multilevel approach, which converts input image (spatial coordinates) into wavelet coefficients (time frequency domain). Let $g(i,j)$ be the noisy image. Application of wavelet transform decomposes $g(i,j)$ into four subbands (LL, LH, HL, and HH) [22]. These subbands consist of wavelet coefficients. Application of two high-pass filters results in HH subband, also known as diagonal subband, and contains diagonal detailed coefficients, as shown in Fig. 4.7. The noise information about the image can be found from this HH subband. The orthogonality property of DWT says that the wavelet transform of Gaussian noise is also Gaussian in nature. The HH subband wavelet coefficients are modeled using normal PDF.

4.3.4 MMSE estimator

MMSE estimator is based on Baye's rule, defined as [2]

$$f(G \mid W) = \frac{f(W \mid G)f(G)}{f(W)}. \tag{4.4}$$

$f(G \mid W)$ is the posterior of G and can be defined as conditional probability density function of G given W.

$f(W \mid G)$ is the likelihood of the observed signal W or conditional PDF of W given G, $f(G)$ is the prior PDF of G.

$f(W)$ is the PDF of W and known as normalizing factor and gives a normalizing effect. MMSE is a Bayesian estimator, and Bayesian risk function minimization is the main motive of this estimator. Mean square cost function can be minimized to estimate the parameter vector, known as MMSE estimator. It can be defined as

$$\mathcal{R}(\hat{G} \mid W) = E\left[\left((\hat{G} - G)^2 \mid W\right)\right]$$
$$= \int_{-\infty}^{\infty} (\hat{G} - G)^2 f(G \mid W) dG. \tag{4.5}$$

Gradient of the Bayesian risk function is equated with zero to obtain the MMSE estimation. The complete process is discussed as follows.

$$\frac{d\mathcal{R}(\hat{G} \mid W)}{d\hat{P}} = 2\hat{G} \int_{-\infty}^{\infty} f(G \mid W) dG - 2 \int_{-\infty}^{\infty} G f(G \mid W) dG. \tag{4.6}$$

By applying $\int_{-\infty}^{\infty} f(P \mid W) dP = 1$ (property of density function) in Eq. (4.6), it can be written as

$$\frac{d\mathcal{R}(\hat{G} \mid W)}{d\hat{G}} = 2\hat{G} - 2 \int_{-\infty}^{\infty} G f(G \mid W) dG. \tag{4.7}$$

The MMSE estimation of G can be found out by equating Eq. (4.7) to zero.

$$2\hat{G} - 2\int_{-\infty}^{\infty} Gf(G \mid W)dG = 0 \tag{4.8}$$

$$\Rightarrow \hat{G}_{MMSE} = \int_{-\infty}^{\infty} Gf(G \mid W)dG. \tag{4.9}$$

4.3.5 Gaussian scale mixture (GSM) model

In this paper wavelet coefficient modeling is achieved by Gaussian scale mixture (GSM) model because of its robust nature, and it can model, approximately, image wavelet coefficients. In literature GSM model has played a vital role in image quality assessment, denoising, noise estimation, image restoration, and foreground estimation [1]. The GSM model is discussed as follows.

Let X be a d-dimensional random variable. X can be defined as a Gaussian scale mixture for the following condition:

$$X = \sqrt{Z}N. \tag{4.10}$$

Z is a scalar random variable, also called mixing multiplier, and N is the Gaussian random variable of zero mean. The PDF of the GSM random variable X is defined as

$$f_X(x) = \int \frac{1}{(2\pi)^{d/2} \, |ZCov(N)|^{1/2}} \exp\left(\frac{-X^T Cov(N)^{-1} X}{2Z}\right) P(Z)dz. \tag{4.11}$$

X is the random variable used to approximate the subband wavelet coefficients. $Cov(N)$ is the covariance of Gaussian random variable N. The scalar random variable Z can be estimated as

$$\hat{Z} = X^T Cov(N)^{-1} X / d. \tag{4.12}$$

4.4 Methodology

This section discusses about the methodology of the proposed work. MRI, ultrasound image, and OCT image are simulated for additive and multiplicative noise removal. Homomorphic approach is applied on ultrasound and OCT image as both the image suffers from multiplicative noise. The multiplicative (Speckle) noise is converted into additive (Gaussian) noise by applying homomorphic system, which further eases noise removal. The medical image is decomposed using the Haar DWT. Gaussian scale mixture and normal PDF are used for modeling the wavelet coefficients and extract the true signal and noise parameters. Furthermore, a Bayesian estimator is implemented to calculate the threshold value from the signal and noise information and to recover the wavelet coefficients. Next the image is constructed by applying the IDWT to the recovered wavelet coefficients, and then exponential function to obtain the denoised image. The block diagram is given in Fig. 4.6, and the detailed steps are discussed below.

Step 1. Logarithmic transformation (homomorphic approach) of the noisy image.

Step 2. Haar wavelet decomposition of the image resulted from step 1.

Step 3. Modeling of the resulted wavelet coefficients from step 2.

Step 4. Estimation of wavelet threshold value using MMSE estimator.

Step 5. Thresholding the wavelet coefficients and recovering the original image.

4.5 Simulation results

Experimental results and the effectiveness in context to the qualitative and quantitative performance of the proposed method are discussed in this section. The results proved that this method removes the noise and also preserves the edges more efficiently than state-of-the-art methods.

4.5.1 Dataset and experimental settings

Three sets of data, such as those of MRI, ultrasound, and OCT are simulated in MATLAB® environment for noise variances: 0.1, 0.3, and 0.5. The MRI dataset is collected from OSIRIX DIACOM image library [23]. The ultrasound dataset is collected from SP Lab [24]. The OCT dataset is collected from CIRRUS™ HD-OCT (Carl Zeiss Meditec, Inc., SW Ver: "5.1.1.4", Copyright 2010) available at Department of Ophthalmology, Institute of Medical Sciences, Banaras Hindu University (BHU), Varanasi. Simulation work and comparison with existing methods is performed in MATLAB R2019a environment. Haar DWT is used for simulating the proposed scheme.

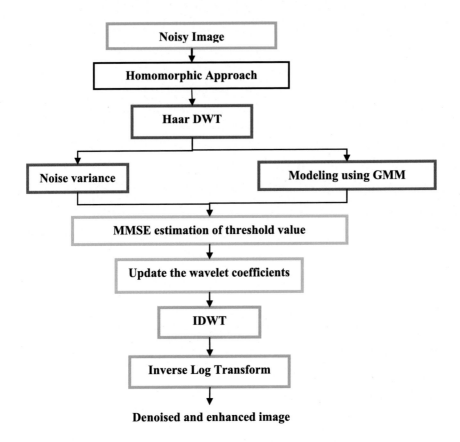

Figure 4.6 Denoising algorithm.

4.5.2 Performance and quality measurement indexes

Quantitative comparison is performed through image quality and performance indexes, such as PSNR, COC, FOM, MSSIM, and EPI [12,25]. The mathematical expressions for the performance indexes are discussed in Table 4.1.

4.5.3 Result discussion

This section discusses about the obtained results and comparison performances after simulation of the proposed filter. The developed scheme is compared with state-of-the-art methods in terms of denoising efficiency and edge preservation. The compared methods are Bayes-shrink [26], Cauchy-shrink [27], and Bayesian estimation method [28]. Extensive ex-

Table 4.1 Description of measurement indexes.

Parameters	Expression
Peak Signal to Noise Ratio (PSNR)	$PSNR = 20 \log_{10} \frac{255}{\sqrt{MSE}}$ $MSE = \frac{1}{P \times Q} \sum_{i=1}^{P \times Q} (x_i - y_i)^2$
Correlation of Coefficient (CoC)	$CoC = \frac{cov(x_i, y_i)}{\sigma_{x_i} \sigma_{y_i}}$
Pratt's Figure of Merit (FOM)	$FOM = (1/\max(N1, N2)) \sum_{j=1}^{N2} \frac{1}{1+\alpha D^2}$
Edge Preservation Index (EPI)	$EPI = \frac{\sum(\Delta x_i - \overline{\Delta x_i})(\Delta y_i - \overline{\Delta y_i})}{\sqrt{\sum(\Delta x_i - \overline{\Delta x_i})^2 \sum(\Delta y_i - \overline{\Delta y_i})^2}}$
Mean Structural Similarity Index (MSSIM)	$MSSIM = \frac{1}{M} \sum_{j=1}^{M} SSIM(x_i, y_j)$ $SSIM$ = Structural Similarity Index and defined as: $SSIM = \frac{(2\overline{x_i y_i} + 2.55)(2\sigma_{x_i y_i} + 7.65)}{(\overline{x_i}^2 + \overline{y_i}^2 + 2.55)(\sigma_{x_i}^2 + \sigma_{y_i}^2 + 7.65)}$

Symbols and description

x_i and y_i = the reference and recovered images, respectively
σ = standard deviation
cov = the covariance operation.
N1 and N2 = the total number of edge points in the image x_i and y_i, respectively.
D = N1-N2
α = the scaling constant (usually taken 1/9)
Δ = Laplacian operator
$(\overline{})$ = Expectation operator
σ^2 = Variance operation
M = the number of local windows and x_i and y_j are the image content for $M = j$.

perimentation is performed on medical images, such as MRI, ultrasound, and OCT images. The qualitative comparisons of the proposed filter and the existing methods are shown in Figs. 4.7, 4.8, and 4.9 for MRI, ultrasound, and OCT images, respectively. It can be seen from the figures that the proposed method achieved better visual quality than the other existing methods.

Tables 4.2–4.8 show the performance parameter comparisons for proposed methods and existing methods. In Table 4.2, the performance is measured in terms of PSNR performance parameter considering ultrasound image for different noise variances (0.1, 0.3, 0.5). The proposed method achieved the following PSNR results: 34.24 dB, 32.11 dB, and 31.69 dB for noise variances 0.1, 0.3, and 0.5, respectively. The best improvement of the proposed scheme is 22% (for $\sigma_n^2 = .1$), 20.7% (for $\sigma_n^2 = 0.2$), and 24.8% (for $\sigma_n^2 = 0.3$) compared to methods [26], [27], and [28].

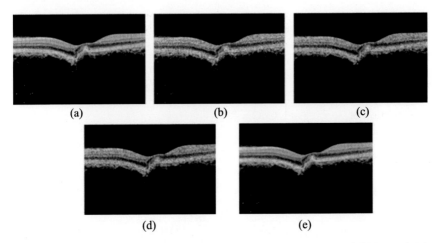

Figure 4.7 Denoising results for different schemes for OCT image. (a) Original, (b) Bayes-shrink [26], (c) Cauchy-shrink [27], (d) Bayesian estimation method [28], (e) proposed method.

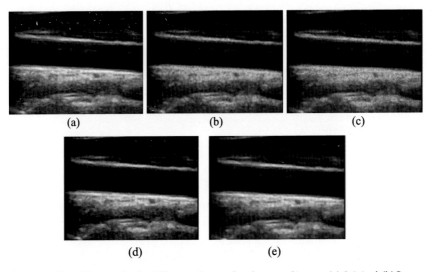

Figure 4.8 Denoising results for different schemes for ultrasound image. (a) Original, (b) Bayes-shrink [26], (c) Cauchy-shrink [27], (d) Bayesian estimation method [28], (e) proposed method.

In Table 4.3, the performance is measured in terms of CoC performance parameter, considering ultrasound image for different noise variances (0.1, 0.3, 0.5). The proposed method achieved the following CoC results: 0.988, 0.964, and 0.953 for noise variances 0.1, 0.3, and 0.5, respectively. The best improvement of the proposed scheme is 18.5% (for $\sigma_n^2 = 0.1$), 28.31%

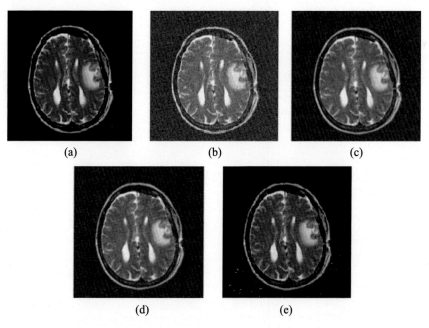

Figure 4.9 Denoising results for different schemes for MRI image. (a) Original, (b) Bayes-shrink [26], (c) Cauchy-shrink [27], (d) Bayesian estimation method [28], (e) proposed method.

Table 4.2 PSNR (dB) values for different techniques.

Techniques	σ_n^2		
	0.1	**0.3**	**0.5**
Noisy	18.25	15.16	10.44
Bayes-shrink [26]	26.39	25.45	23.83
Cauchy-shrink [27]	29.61	28.29	24.31
Bayesian estimation method [28]	30.65	29.32	28.52
Proposed method	34.24	32.11	31.69

Table 4.3 CoC values for different techniques.

Techniques	σ_n^2		
	0.1	**0.3**	**0.5**
Noisy	0.805	0.691	0.623
Bayes-shrink [26]	0.891	0.851	0.848
Cauchy-shrink [27]	0.912	0.902	0.884
Bayesian estimation method [28]	0.965	0.943	0.922
Proposed method	0.988	0.964	0.953

Table 4.4 FOM values for different techniques.

Techniques	σ_n^2		
	0.1	0.3	0.5
Noisy	0.665	0.594	0.563
Bayes-shrink [26]	0.842	0.781	0.717
Cauchy-shrink [27]	0.833	0.826	0.788
Bayesian estimation method [28]	0.951	0.89	0.883
Proposed method	0.952	0.941	0.92

Table 4.5 MSSIM values for different techniques.

Techniques	σ_n^2		
	0.1	0.3	0.5
Noisy	0.561	0.532	0.505
Bayes-shrink [26]	0.798	0.739	0.614
Cauchy-shrink [27]	0.816	0.799	0.732
Bayesian estimation method [28]	0.845	0.832	0.811
Proposed method	0.896	0.863	0.834

Table 4.6 EPI values for different techniques.

Techniques	σ_n^2		
	0.1	0.3	0.5
Noisy	0.343	0.261	0.234
Bayes-shrink [26]	0.603	0.589	0.422
Cauchy-shrink [27]	0.715	0.522	0.436
Bayesian estimation method [28]	0.745	0.674	0.616
Proposed method	0.782	0.693	0.638

(for $\sigma_n^2 = 0.2$), and 11.01% (for $\sigma_n^2 = 0.3$) compared to methods [26], [27], and [28].

In Table 4.4, the performance is measured in terms of FOM performance parameter, considering ultrasound image for different noise variances (0.1, 0.3, 0.5). The proposed method achieved the following FOM results: 0.952, 0.941, and 0.92 for noise variances 0.1, 0.3, and 0.5, respectively. The best improvement of the proposed scheme is 12.5% (for $\sigma_n^2 = 0.1$), 17% (for $\sigma_n^2 = 0.2$), and 22.06% (for $\sigma_n^2 = 0.3$) compared to methods [26], [27], and [28].

In Table 4.5, the performance is measured in terms of MSSIM performance parameter considering Ultrasound image for different noise vari-

Table 4.7 Parameter values for different nonlocal methods for real MR image.

Techniques	Parameters				
	PSNR (dB)	CoC	FOM	MSSIM	EPI
Bayes-shrink [26]	29.67	0.821	0.638	0.852	0.682
Cauchy-shrink [27]	30.59	0.814	0.605	0.813	0.695
Bayesian estimation method [28]	32.43	0.935	0.747	0.905	0.765
Proposed method	34.43	0.946	0.862	0.919	0.786

Table 4.8 Parameter values for different nonlocal methods for OCT image.

Techniques	Parameters				
	PSNR (dB)	CoC	FOM	MSSIM	EPI
Bayes-shrink [26]	24.67	0.828	0.605	0.678	0.589
Cauchy-shrink [27]	28.76	0.865	0.658	0.754	0.667
Bayesian estimation method [28]	29.24	0.933	0.736	0.841	0.733
Proposed method	31.71	0.979	0.788	0.878	0.785

ances (0.1, 0.3, 0.5). The proposed method has achieved the MSSIM results are 0.896, 0.863 and 0.834 for noise variances 0.1, 0.3 and 0.5 respectively. The best improvement of the proposed scheme is 11.9% (for $\sigma_n^2 = 0.1$), 14.36% (for $\sigma_n^2 = 0.2$) and 26.4% (for $\sigma_n^2 = 0.3$) compared to methods [26], [27] and [28].

In Table 4.6, the performance is measured in terms of EPI performance parameter, considering ultrasound image for different noise variances (0.1, 0.3, 0.5). The proposed method achieved the following EPI results: 0.782, 0.693, and 0.638 for noise variances 0.1, 0.3, and 0.5, respectively. The best improvement of the proposed scheme is 22.89% (for $\sigma_n^2 = 0.1$), 24.67% (for $\sigma_n^2 = 0.2$), and 33.85% (for $\sigma_n^2 = 0.3$) compared to methods [26], [27], and [28]. The graphical plots of Tables 4.2–4.6 are shown in Figs. 4.10–4.14, respectively.

In Table 4.7, the performance is measured in terms of EPI performance parameter, considering MRI image for different noise variance 0.3. The improvement is 5.56% in terms of PSNR, 1.16% in terms of CoC, 13.3% in terms of FOM, 1.5% in terms of MSSIM, and 2.67% in terms of EPI than Bayesian estimation method [28], the nest best method.

In Table 4.8, the performance is measured in terms of EPI performance parameter considering OCT image for different noise variance 0.3. The

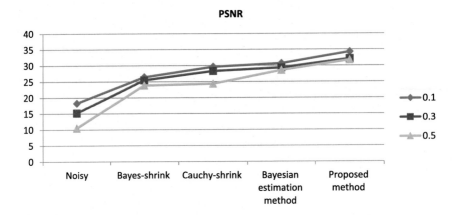

Figure 4.10 Comparison graph for PSNR.

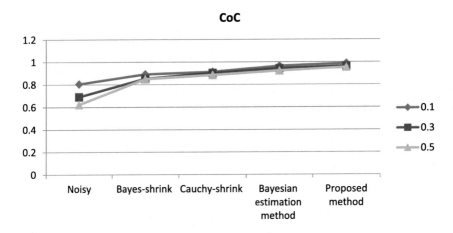

Figure 4.11 Comparison graph for CoC.

improvement is 7.78% in terms of PSNR, 4.69% in terms of CoC, 6.59% in terms of FOM, 4.21% in terms of MSSIM and 6.62% in terms of EPI than Bayesian estimation method [28], one of the three best methods.

4.6 Conclusion

A new statistical modeling-based denoising procedure is presented in this chapter. The wavelet coefficients of the medical images, such as ultrasound image, MRI, and OCT images were modeled using the GSM model, and

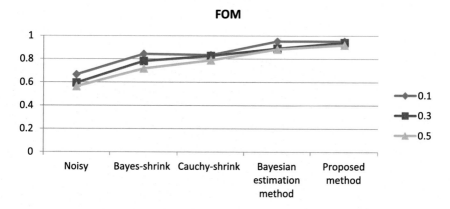

Figure 4.12 Comparison graph for FOM.

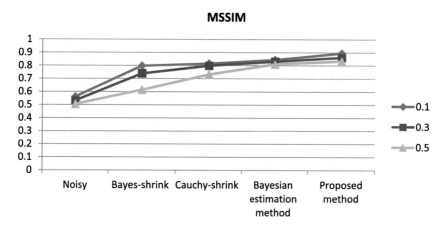

Figure 4.13 Comparison graph for MSSIM.

the signal variances were restored. Median estimator was implemented for effective estimation of noise variance. The original wavelet coefficients were restored using the Bayesian MMSE estimator. Three sets of data were employed for the assessment of the proposed method. Both quantitative and visual output results proved the efficacy of the proposed methodology in terms of denoising performance and edge preservation. This method may be improved by considering improved mixture model distribution in the near future.

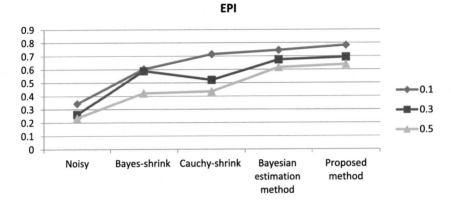

Figure 4.14 Comparison graph for EPI.

References

[1] M. Samieinasab, Z. Amini, H. Rabbani, Multivariate statistical modeling of retinal optical coherence tomography, IEEE Transactions on Medical Imaging 39 (11) (2020) 3475–3487.

[2] S. Sahu, H.V. Singh, B. Kumar, A.K. Singh, A Bayesian multiresolution approach for noise removal in medical magnetic resonance images, Journal of Intelligent Systems 29 (1) (2020) 189–201.

[3] P. Das, C. Pal, A. Chakrabarti, A. Acharyya, S. Basu, Adaptive denoising of 3D volumetric MR images using local variance based estimator, Biomedical Signal Processing and Control 59 (2020) 101901.

[4] S. Kollem, K. Rama Linga Reddy, D. Srinivasa Rao, Modified transform-based gamma correction for MRI tumor image denoising and segmentation by optimized histon-based elephant herding algorithm, International Journal of Imaging Systems and Technology 30 (4) (2020) 1271–1293.

[5] S. Sarkar, P.C. Tripathi, S. Bag, An improved non-local means denoising technique for brain MRI, in: Computational Intelligence in Pattern Recognition, Springer, Singapore, 2020, pp. 765–773.

[6] S. Bharati, T.Z. Khan, P. Podder, N.Q. Hung, A comparative analysis of image denoising problem: noise models, denoising filters and applications, in: Cognitive Internet of Medical Things for Smart Healthcare, Springer, Cham, 2021, pp. 49–66.

[7] H. Yacoub, T.K. Sarkar, A homomorphic approach for through-wall sensing, IEEE Transactions on Geoscience and Remote Sensing 47 (5) (2009) 1318–1327.

[8] S. Sahu, H.V. Singh, A.K. Singh, B. Kumar, MR image denoising using adaptive wavelet soft thresholding, in: Advances in VLSI, Communication, and Signal Processing, Springer, Singapore, 2020, pp. 775–785.

[9] P. Kulkarni, D. Lozano, G. Zouridakis, M. Twa, A statistical model of retinal optical coherence tomography image data, in: 2011 Annual International Conference of the IEEE Engineering in Medicine and Biology Society, IEEE, August 2011, pp. 6127–6130.

[10] Z. Amini, H. Rabbani, Statistical modeling of retinal optical coherence tomography, IEEE Transactions on Medical Imaging 35 (6) (2016) 1544–1554.

[11] N.M. Grzywacz, J. De Juan, C. Ferrone, D. Giannini, D. Huang, G. Koch, et al., Statistics of optical coherence tomography data from human retina, IEEE Transactions on Medical Imaging 29 (6) (2010) 1224–1237.

[12] S. Sahu, H.V. Singh, B. Kumar, A.K. Singh, Statistical modeling and Gaussianization procedure based de-speckling algorithm for retinal OCT images, Journal of Ambient Intelligence and Humanized Computing (2018) 1–14.

[13] S. Sahu, A. Anand, A.K. Singh, A.K. Agrawal, M.P. Singh, MRI de-noising using improved unbiased NLM filter, Journal of Ambient Intelligence and Humanized Computing (2022) 1–12, https://doi.org/10.1007/s12652-021-03681-0.

[14] H. Rabbani, M. Vafadust, S. Gazor, I. Selesnick, Image denoising employing a bivariate cauchy distribution with local variance in complex wavelet domain, in: Proceedings of the 12th-Signal Processing Education Workshop, 4th Digital Signal Processing Workshop, USA, September 24–27, 2006, 2006, pp. 203–208.

[15] A. Achim, A. Bezerianos, P. Tsakalides, Novel Bayesian multiscale method for speckle removal in medical ultrasound images, IEEE Transactions on Medical Imaging 20 (8) (2001) 772–783.

[16] M.I.H. Bhuiyan, M.O. Ahmad, M.N.S. Swamy, Spatially adaptive wavelet-based method using the Cauchy prior for denoising the SAR images, IEEE Transactions on Circuits and Systems for Video Technology 17 (4) (2007) 500–507.

[17] H. Sadreazami, M.O. Ahmad, M.N.S. Swamy, Ultrasound image despeckling in the contourlet domain using the Cauchy prior, in: Proceedings of the IEEE International Symposium on Circuits and Systems (ISCAS), Canada, May 22–25, 2016, 2016, pp. 33–36.

[18] J.J. Ranjani, M.S. Chithra, Bayesian denoising of ultrasound images using heavy-tailed Levy distribution, IET Image Processing 9 (4) (2014) 338–345.

[19] M.H. Bibalan, H. Amindavar, Non-Gaussian amplitude PDF modeling of ultrasound images based on a novel generalized Cauchy-Rayleigh mixture, EURASIP Journal on Image and Video Processing 1 (2016) 48.

[20] S. Jafari, S. Ghofrani, Using heavy-tailed Levy model in nonsubsampled shearlet transform domain for ultrasound image despeckling, Journal of Advances in Computer Research 8 (2) (2017) 53–66.

[21] H. Rabbani, M. Vafadust, P. Abolmaesumi, S. Gazor, Speckle noise reduction of medical ultrasound images in complex wavelet domain using mixture priors, IEEE Transactions on Biomedical Engineering 55 (9) (2008) 2152–2160.

[22] R.C. Gonzalez, R.E. Woods, Digital Image Processing, 2nd ed., Prentice Hall, Upper Saddle River, 2002.

[23] Osirix, OSIRIX DICOM image library, [ONLINE] Available at: http://www.osirix-viewer.com/resources/diacom-image-library/, 2014. (Accessed 14 May 2014).

[24] Ultrasound image database, SP Lab: [online] Available at: http://splab.cz/en/download/database/ultrasound.

[25] B. Kanoun, M. Ambrosanio, F. Baselice, G. Ferraioli, V. Pascazio, L. Gómez, Anisotropic weighted KS-NLM filter for noise reduction in MRI, IEEE Access 8 (2020) 184866–184884.

[26] S.G. Chang, B. Yu, M. Vetterli, Adaptive wavelet thresholding for image denoising and compression, IEEE Transactions on Image Processing 9 (9) (2000) 1532–1546.

[27] S. Sahu, H.V. Singh, B. Kumar, A.K. Singh, De-noising of ultrasound image using Bayesian approached heavy-tailed Cauchy distribution, Multimedia Tools and Applications an International Journal of Springer (2017) 1–18, https://doi.org/10.1007/s11042-017-5221-9.

[28] A. Wong, A. Mishra, K. Bizheva, D.A. Clausi, General Bayesian estimation for speckle noise reduction in optical coherence tomography retinal imagery, Optics Express 18 (8) (2010) 8338–8352.

CHAPTER 5

Medical image denoising using convolutional neural networks

Rini Smita Thakur, Shubhojeet Chatterjee, Ram Narayan Yadav, and Lalita Gupta
Maulana Azad National Institute of Technology, Bhopal, India

5.1 Introduction

Medical imaging plays a vital role in the diagnosis and treatment part of an ailment. The anatomy of different body parts, such as the heart, bones, nerves, brain is being captured by different imaging modalities. The relevant pictorial information is extracted by the interaction of different forms of radiations with the different bodily structures. Mathematical functions can be applied on medical images to predict tumor cells or unhealthy tissues. However, the corruption of medical images with noise and artifacts leads to misinterpretation in diagnosis. It can lead to an incorrect diagnosis of various diseases, and even lead to death in cases where diagnosis or surgical procedures are based on image quality precision. It is a challenging task to prevent pictorial information loss during image acquisition and transmission. The corruption of an image with noise changes the random pixel values and deteriorates image quality. Furthermore, medical images are usually low contrast images, which further reduce the image quality. Therefore image denoising is an indispensable part of the medical images preprocessing stage. The different image modalities are corrupted by different noise types, such as Gaussian noise, Speckle noise, Mixed noise, Rician noise, etc. The most common image modalities are X-ray, magnetic resonance imaging (MRI), computed tomography (CT), and positron emission tomography (PET) [1].

The medical images are susceptible to noise and artifacts. It can be corrupted by random noise, or white noise, or frequency-dependent noise due to the instrument's mechanism or signal processing algorithms. The presence of noise in medical images can lead to an incorrect diagnosis. There are several image processing procedures (image classification, segmentation, super-resolution, and image registration) involved in identification of aliments from medical imaging modalities. The image classification of various

Digital Image Enhancement and Reconstruction
https://doi.org/10.1016/B978-0-32-398370-9.00012-3

115

imaging modalities is crucial for the diagnosis of elements, such as cancer, tumor, Alzheimer, autism spectrum disorder, glaucoma, etc. The basic methodology of image classification comprises image data collection, image preprocessing, feature extraction, feature selection, and classification in chronological order. Image denoising along with resizing and other morphological operations play a noteworthy role as the image pre-processing step for classification problems [2]. Image denoising is also being used as the preprocessing step for the segmentation and extrication of the lesion from the dermoscopic images [3]. Dermoscopic images are prone to be corrupted by Gaussian, speckle, and impulse noise. The other application areas of medical image preprocessing by denoising are segmentation of MRI images for a brain tumor, X-ray images for a lung infection, ultrasound images for fetal development, mammograms for breast cancer detection, etc. [4].

The conventional algorithms of denoising natural images are not applicable in the case of medical images, as its noise nature is signal-dependent [5]. There are different noise removal techniques categorized as spatial domain, transform domain, fuzzy-based, low-rank minimization, and machine learning techniques, which are widely used for medical image denoising [6], [7], [8]. The spatial domain techniques directly apply mathematical operations to the image pixels. The different types of image filters, such as mean filter, Weiner filter, Gaussian filter, bilateral filter, etc., fall in this category. Transform domain techniques apply mathematical operations, such as thresholding on transform domain coefficients for effective image restoration. Wavelet transform is commonly used in multi-resolution image analysis procedure. The image is converted into wavelet domain, followed by the thresholding operation for noise removal on wavelet coefficients, and finally, the application of inverse wavelet transform to restore noise-free image. Fuzzy-based filters are designed based on membership functions that extract spatial, temporal, and color information of an image pixel [9]. The low-rank minimization techniques frame image denoising as nonconvex, nondeterministic polynomial hard problems, which are classified as low-rank matrix minimization and low-rank norm minimization. Since recently, machine learning methods have been used for image restoration problems, whose basic methodology is neural network design and training. There are different neural networks, such as multilayer perceptron, convolutional neural networks, and deep belief networks for image denoising. The networks are trained with the dataset of different biomedical imaging modalities. The development of faster graphical processing units, training algorithms, and open-source datasets has led to the machine learning evolution.

In recent years, convolutional neural networks (CNNs) have excelled in denoising performance as compared to other state-of-the-art methods [10]. It automatically learns features from the image data, unlike its predecessors, which needed hand-crafted features extraction. CNN models do not require manual segmentation of organs by medical experts [11]. The concept of dimensionality reduction and weight sharing reduces the number of parameters, thereby decreasing computational complexity. The key aspects of CNN are local receptive fields, sparse connectivity, subsampling, and parameter sharing, which manifest CNN's invariant to input image data distortions, scaling, and shifting [12]. The concept of sparse connectivity enables easy training by back propagation [13]. The graphical processing units (GPUs) and digital signal processors (DSPs) with higher computational power have been used to train the CNNs. The benchmark datasets of different image restoration tasks are also being made available for the researchers. Moreover, the concept of transfer learning can be applied in CNNs, which facilitates the pretrained network to be reused for a specific application. In this chapter, the denoising of different image modalities using CNNs is discussed in detail.

5.2 Different medical imaging modalities

The imaging modalities utilized in medical and biological science depend on different energy sources, such as electrons, lasers, light waves, X-rays, radionuclides, and nuclear magnetic resonance. The image data is obtained at a different hierarchical level, ranging from molecular, cellular, organ system, and entire body level. The key merits and demerits of imaging modalities are predominantly characterized by the fundamental physics and biological concepts involved in the interaction of energy with scanned body parts. Moreover, modeling of medical applications with advanced engineering also plays a key role in deciding attributes of imaging modalities. The most commonly used medical imaging modalities are magnetic resonance imaging, ultrasound, X-ray, computed tomography, mammography, angiography, etc. MRI extracts both anatomical and physiological information by hydrogen atoms exposure in the presence of magnetic fields and radio waves. Ultrasound images are obtained by the interaction of sound waves with the body, and it gives both anatomical and functional data (heart valve functioning) in real-time via a small portable device. Ultrasonic waves capture soft tissue regions, such as the abdomen, but fail to capture bony and hollow structures. X-ray is high-energy electromagnetic radiation, which is absorbed by different tissues in different amounts according to the radiological intensity of the tissues. The photographic film is on the X-ray detector. X-rays are easily absorbed by high atomic number structures (bone) as compared to low atomic number structures (tissues). Therefore it is extensively used in fracture detection as bony structure provides high contrast in radiograph with respect to tissues. Mammography is the technique that uses X-rays for breast examination by detecting micro-calcification. Computed tomography (CT) utilizes cross-sectional images obtained from multiple X-ray sources and detectors with better resolution and clarity. Although it has adverse effects due to radiation, it can be used in patients with pacemakers and metallic implants. Fluoroscopy uses an X-ray beams and the fluorescent screen to generate the real-time images of the internal body parts. It imitates an X-ray movie, wherein continuous images are displayed on a monitor to assist surgical procedures. The most common application of fluoroscopy is angiography, in which blood vessels are examined by X-ray images using a special kind of dye. Dual energy X-ray absorptiometry (DEXA) scan measures bone density to diagnose osteoporosis. It uses both high-energy and low-energy X-ray beams and measures the X-ray absorption through bone through each of them. The bone density is measured on the basis of the difference in absorption by two beams. Positron emission tomography (PET) uses the radiation linked with altered glucose molecules to form an image on the basis of image uptake. It has a critical role in cancer diagnosis. The combination of CT and PET scans gives both physiological and anatomic images at a time. Table 5.1 gives an overview of the different medical imaging modalities.

5.2.1 Magnetic resonance imaging

It is a noninvasive, nonionizing imaging technique that captures three-dimensional anatomical structures. The MRI images are formed with a magnetic field and its gradient and radio waves. Hydrogen atoms or protons of the human body are forced to align in the direction of the magnetic field. The uniform alignment of protons is then disrupted by the radio frequency wave. When the radio frequency wave is turned off, the energy release phenomenon occurs as protons are realigned. This amount of released energy depends on the chemical and environmental properties of the molecules. The cross-sectional MRI images are created based on the

Table 5.1 Overview of different medical imaging modalities.

Imaging Modality	Noise	Key Features
Magnetic Resonance Images	Rician	• No ionizing radiation • Safe for patients, painless and non-invasive • Better contrast in soft tissues • Strong magnetic fields and gradients, radio waves
Ultrasound Images	Speckle	• Noninvasive and no ionizing radiation • High-frequency sound waves usage • Widely used to check fetal development • Real-time examination
CT Images	Gaussian	• Ionizing radiation • Diagnosis of bone disorders • Provide images of bone, soft-issues, and blood simultaneously • Processes different cross-sectional X-ray images
PET Images	Mixed Gaussian–Poisson	• Shows chemical function of organs and tissues • Usage of radioactive substance • Molecular-level information • Emitted gamma rays are captured to form 3D images

intensity of released signal and time of realignment. Faster realignment of protons produces the brighter image. The raw MRI data is not directly obtained in the image domain; it is complex-valued, which denotes the Fourier transform of magnetization distribution. Image reconstruction steps involve noise prewhitening, interpolation, and raw data filtering [14]. The Fourier transformed raw MRI data is converted into the real and imaginary images, which follow Gaussian distribution with zero mean and uniform variance. Furthermore, magnitude images are formed by non-linear mapping from real and imaginary images. The magnitude of noise distribution is the sum of the squares of two independent Gaussian variables [15]. So, the final MR image follows stationary Rician distribution with constant noise power at each voxel [16]. It is given by

$$Z = \sqrt{(X + N_1)^2 + N_2^2}, \qquad (5.1)$$

where X is noiseless data, N_1 and N_2 are additive Gaussian noise of equal variance. The probability distribution function of MRI noisy image is given by

$$p_Z(X, \sigma_n) = \frac{Z}{\sigma_n^2} e^{\frac{-(Z^2 + X^2)}{2\sigma_n^2}} I_0\left(\frac{XZ}{\sigma_n^2}\right) u(Z), \qquad (5.2)$$

where Z is the observed noisy MR image, X is the clean MRI image, u is the Heaviside function, σ_n^2 is the noise variance, I_0 is Bessel function (0th order). The Rician distribution becomes Gaussian in the high SNR regions, whereas it becomes Rayleigh distribution in the low SNR regions [17].

5.2.2 Computed tomography

Computed tomography (CT) is a noninvasive imaging modality, which uses X-ray images obtained from different machines to create cross-sectional images of muscles, bones, and soft tissues. It is a nondestructive evaluation technique, which captures density, shape, dimensions, and internal defects of an anatomical area with 2-D and 3-D cross-sectional images. However, usage of ionization radiation has adverse effects on patient, but it can be used in the patients with pacemakers or metallic implants, unlike MRI. The tomographic images are formed by applying mathematical algorithms on multiangular X-ray projections. CT imaging involves the application of radon and inverse radon transform on the data received from the X-ray beam [18]. The X-rays are attenuated/absorbed with a different degree, which creates a profile of beams with varying intensities. The detector analyzes this profile and converts it into an image. An absorption process affects CT imaging due to elemental composition differences. Sometimes the contrasting agents of high atomic number are injected or swallowed to provide contrast between blood and muscles.

The major factors that disrupt CT image quality are blurring, field of view, artifacts, and visual noise. The major source noise in CT is random noise, statistical or quanta noise, electronic noise [19]. Random noise occurs in CT due to the detection of finite X-ray quanta in the projection. Statistical or quanta noise occurs fluctuations in quanta detection. The image quality degrades in the case of low-dose CT. The quantum noise is reduced by increasing the number of detected X-ray quanta. Electronic noise is associated with circuits designed for the analog signals reception. The round-off errors occur during the conversion of an analog signal into a digital signal for CT reconstruction. The noise distribution of CT images is Gaussian in nature [20].

5.2.3 Positron emission tomography

Positron emission tomography (PET) is a molecular imaging method that detects radiation from radioactive substances for image formation [21]. Molecular activities of tissues are observed by injecting specific radioactive tracers [22]. These tracers are tagged with short decay time radioactive substances, such as Carbon-11. The PET can be utilized to measure oxygen intake, metabolic functioning of organs and tissues, and blood flow measurements. Detection of gamma rays is done when positron of radioactive substance interacts with electrons in the tissues. It basically shows results at the cellular level, thereby helping in predicting complex systemic diseases. It captures in vivo chemical functioning of organs and tissues, whereas other imaging modalities capture structural details. PET scan can detect the disease at a preliminary stage, unlike CT and MRI because of cellular level diagnosis. It is more expensive than other imaging techniques.

The image quality of PET degrades due to poor signal-to-noise ratio, poor image resolution, and less number of detected protons. The other factor which leads to the noisy image is restraints in the acquisition time and the injection dose particularly in dynamic PET studies [23]. The PET noise is modeled by both Gaussian distribution and mixed Gaussian–Poisson distribution.

5.2.4 Ultrasound

Ultrasound (US) or sonography technique uses differential resistance of high-frequency acoustic waves to capture high-resolution real-time images without ionization radiation [24]. The frequency range is (1–5 MHz). The sound waves are absorbed/attenuated at the tissues boundary and reflected back. The reflected waves are detected by the probe. Distance traveled by the sound waves is calculated using the speed of sound and time required for reflective signal reception. The higher frequencies have shorter wavelengths, thereby making it less penetrating and less used for superficial structures. The lower frequencies are used for deeper penetration. Ultrasound has poor penetration capability for the air-filled and bony structures. In medical imaging, B modes US images are usually used by analyzing the envelope of the back-scattered US acoustic wave during its propagation across an acoustic medium.

The US image is corrupted with speckle-noise, which produces grainy texture in an image. It is multiplicative in nature with non-Gaussian statistics. The cause of speckle noise is an interference of coherent energies (constructive and destructive) of scattered echoes [25]. Speckle noise removal is a tedious task as it is tissue-dependent and nonuniformly modeled. It is dependent on image data and leads to low contrast, blurred, and deteriorated local pseudo features.

5.3 Convolutional neural networks

Convolutional neural networks (CNNs) are prominently used for various image processing applications, such as denoising, segmentation, classification, etc. The key features of CNNs are weight sharing, higher representation capability, reduction in number of trainable entities, preservation of 2-D structural information, and application of transfer learning [10]. The basic building blocks of CNN include the input layer, convolutional layer, activation layer, pooling layer, and the output layer. The image modalities are given directly as input in input layer. Thereafter, the convolutional layer consists of convolution filters or convolutional weights, which extract different features of the image to produce the feature maps. The repeated blocks of convolution, pooling, and activation layer define intermediate layers. The convolutional filter slides on the entire image to get the subsequent output. The activation layer introduces nonlinearity by applying different activation functions, such as sigmoid, rectified linear units (ReLU), tanh, etc. The pooling layer reduces the dimensionality of feature maps by average or maximum pooling. It introduces translational invariance, i.e., resistance toward distortions and shift, and it further decreases the learnable parameters. The commonly used pooling operations are average pooling and maximum pooling. Average pooling calculates an average value of the pixels of the selected window, whereas maximum pooling gives the highest pixel value in the given window. At the final stage, only a convolutional layer or fully connected layer is used to reconstruct the image of the specified dimension. The important aspect of CNN is the feature learning of an image according to a specific restoration application. The basic building block on which many denoising networks are based is convolution+ReLU+batch normalization, as given in Fig. 5.1 [26]. Another DCNND [27] model integrates CNN denoiser with model-based

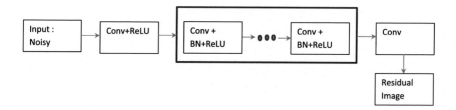

Figure 5.1 Block diagram of benchmark DnCNN Gaussian denoiser.

optimization using residual learning. The basic building block is "dilated convolution+Batch Normalization+ReLU."

Batch normalization normalizes the input of every layer for every mini-match. It is a re-parameterization technique which reduces the effect of internal co-variate shift and enhances the training speed. It reduces the number of epochs, gives some regularization, and reduces the generalization error. The advantages of batch normalization are [28] (a) preventing the vanishing gradient problem, (b) controlling poor weight initialization, (c) reduction in time required for model convergence, (d) reduction in chances of over-fitting.

The training of a CNN is a process of finding the optimum value of learnable parameters, such as weights and biases, which minimize the difference between predicted and actual outputs. The convolutional weights are automatically learned during the training process, whereas hyperparameters, such as stride, padding, number of kernels, and size of kernels are set to particular value before training. The network is trained on the basis of the value of the loss function, i.e., minimization of loss function. The loss function is usually a mean squared error for image denoising applications. The mean square error is given by the following formula:

$$MSE = \frac{1}{P \times Q} \sum_{i=1}^{P} \sum_{j=1}^{Q} \|x(i,j) - \phi(y(i,j))\|_2^2, \tag{5.3}$$

where $P \times Q$ are pixel dimensions, ϕ is the trained model, i and j are pixel indices, y is noisy image, and x is clean image. The supervised training of CNN involves noisy-clean pair of images.

The gradient of the loss function gives the direction of the steepest rate of increase. Weights are updated in the negative direction of the gradient with random step size on the basis of hyperparameter (learning rate). The learnable parameter update equation is given as follows [11]:

$$w = w - \alpha * \frac{\partial L}{\partial w}, \tag{5.4}$$

where L is loss function, α is a learning rate, and w represents each learnable parameter.

The different techniques of gradient-based learning algorithm are batch gradient descent, stochastic gradient descent, and mini-batch gradient descent. In batch gradient descent, the network parameters are updated only once with the calculation of gradient of the whole training set. In stochastic gradient descent, the network parameters are updated at each training sample. This method is both memory-effective and faster as compared to batch gradient descent. In mini-batch gradient descent, training data is divided into several mini-batches. The network parameter updating is done via gradient computation on each mini-batch. It provides steady convergence, enhanced computational efficiency, and memory effectiveness.

The entire image dataset can be divided into three parts: training, validation, and testing dataset. The training dataset is used to train the model that calculates loss function via forward propagation and parameters, are updated by backpropagation. The validation dataset evaluates the network during the training procedure, fine-tunes the hyperparameters, and selects the model. The test dataset finally checks the network performance on different image quality assessment metrics.

The commonly used image quality assessment metrics on denoised images are mean square error, structural similarity index, and peak signal to noise ratio. Their mathematical formulas are given by

$$MSE = \frac{1}{mn} \sum_{i=0}^{m-1} \sum_{j=0}^{n-1} [y(i,j) - x(i,j)]^2, \tag{5.5}$$

$$SSIM = \frac{(2\mu_x\mu_y + C_1)(2\sigma_{yx} + C_2)}{(\mu_y^2 + \mu_x^2 + C_1)(\sigma_y^2 + \sigma_x^2 + C_2)}, \tag{5.6}$$

$$PSNR = 10\log_{10}\left(\frac{MAX^2}{MSE}\right), \tag{5.7}$$

where y and x denote clean and denoised image, respectively, m and n represent image dimensions, i.e., width and height of an image, μ is an average value of an image, σ^2 is variance value of an image, and σ_{xy} is the co-variance of the two compared images. MAX represents the pixel value of an image.

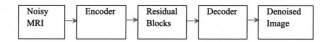

Figure 5.2 CNN-DMRI architecture.

5.4 Review on existing CNN denoisers

5.4.1 CNNs for MR images

CNN-DMRI [29] structure uses residual learning and encoder-decoder structure for extraction of relevant features, as shown in Fig. 5.2. In residual learning, the noisy image is learned by the network, rather than the denoised image. In this network, global and local residual learning is employed to boost up the training process and for the retention of prominent features. The Rician noise is synthetically added on Brainweb, IXI, MS, and prostate datasets. Another MRI denoiser based on encoder-decoder architecture use the standard U-Net [30]. The U-Net is the convolutional autoencoder that tracks high-level image details. Apart from basic conv+batch normalization+activation, it uses transpose convolutional layer for up-sampling and max-pooling layer for down-sampling. 3D-parallel RicianNet [31] is the combination of dilated convolution residual (DCR) module and depthwise separable convolution residual module (DSCR). The usage of dilated convolutions increases the receptive field of the network. DCR module consists of dilated convolution, batch normalization, and leaky rectified linear units. DSCR module reduces the number of parameters and computational complexity.

The benchmark DnCNN [26] and SCNN [32] network for Gaussian noise removal have also been used for MR images. In [33], the comparative analysis of DnCNN and SCNN is done with the proposed dDLR network. The SCNN architecture is almost the same as that of DnCNN with the difference being in the activation. It uses the soft-shrinkage activation function for adaptive noise reduction. The dDLR network [33] is designed with soft shrinkage activation and discrete cosine transform convolution to split the data into the zero-frequency and high- frequency components, as given in Fig. 5.3. The CNN uses residual learning and DnCNN units along with perpetual loss function to preserve structural details [34]. The loss function is the combination of the pixel loss function, feature reconstruction loss, and the total variation regularizer loss. The modified DnCNN is used to denoise diffusion-weighted prostate MR images [35]. It uses a guidance image as additional input apart from the noisy MR image. The low-b value

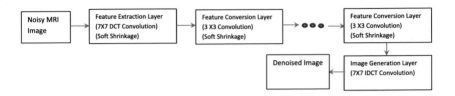

Figure 5.3 dDLR architecture [33].

Table 5.2 Peak signal to noise ratio of different methods on Brainweb dataset.

Methods	1%	3%	5%	7%	9%
NLM	34.1381	32.1259	29.9717	29.4599	27.8319
BM3D	35.3151	33.1937	31.0144	30.4890	28.9093
ODCT3D	48.1295	36.2756	31.5857	30.5124	28.2452
PRI–NLM3D	49.8923	36.8192	31.9597	30.9418	28.5961
CNN-DMRI	47.8125	35.4720	30.8958	29.3533	27.2152
RicianNet	43.4145	37.0095	27.4807	27.6777	28.8616
2D-DCRNet	46.8168	38.6786	34.6277	32.4664	30.5232
2D-Parallel RicianNet	50.9072	41.8099	38.8218	35.9767	34.5207
3D DCRNet	48.5120	39.1336	35.1466	32.7280	31.0916
3D-Parallel RicianNet	**51.7192**	**43.9950**	**40.9218**	**37.6896**	**37.1069**

diffusion-weighted image is used as a guided image. Its basic architecture is the same as that of residual learning-based DnCNN network.

Another network is termed as adaptive sparse reconstruction CNN (AsrCNN) [36] removes Gaussian noise from MR images. It integrates the concept of dictionary learning and a convolutional neural network. The MR images are recovered from the sparse K-space data. The faster training is achieved by training CNN with the image patches to create a dictionary of weights. Table 5.2 gives PSNR values of the Brainweb dataset at different noise levels.

5.4.2 CNNs for CT images

The CT perfusion maps are obtained from the raw CT data. The accuracy of perfusion maps is good for higher radiation dosage. The challenging task is to obtain accurate CT perfusion maps with low radiation dosage. This CT denoiser, given in Fig. 5.4, [37], is based on residual learning based standard DnCNN [26] network with the basic unit of convolution, batch normalization, and rectified linear units activation. Batch normalization nullifies the effect of internal covariant shift. The stochastic gradient

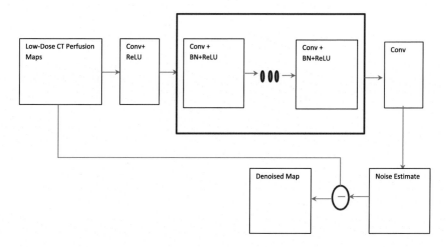

Figure 5.4 Architecture of CNN CT denoiser, given in [37].

descent training involves low–dose cerebral blood flow maps (input) and high-dose cerebral blood flow maps (output). The CNN based on three steps, i.e., patch encoding, nonlinear filtering, and reconstruction, is also being used to convert low-dose CT into normal dose CT [38]. The residual encoder-decoder convolutional neural network (RED-CNN) for low-dose CT denoising consists of autoencoder, deconvolution, and shortcut connections with patch-based end-to-end mapping to map low-dose CT images to normal dose CT [39]. This RED-CNN outperforms DnCNN and BM3D method in terms of PSNR.

ResFCN [40] and ResUNet [40] CNN architectures are also being used for low-dose CT denoising. The Poisson noise is added to CT slices. ResFCN comprises three units of convolutional kernel of size $32 \times 5 \times 5$, followed by batch normalization and ReLU activation, and the last unit is convolution operator. ResUNet comprises of multi-scale fashion arrangement of ten units of convolutional kernel, followed by batch normalization and ReLU activation. The up-sampling and down-sampling operations are also being performed within the network. It uses l_1 norm-based loss function with Adam optimization on XCAT phantom software.

In [41], a library of different networks, such as DnCNN, GAN, U-Net, is designed and analyzed on performance metrics of peak signal-to-noise ratio and structural similarity index. The data inputs, such as training patch size, kernel size, and numeric optimizer inputs (such as batch size, loss function, and learning rate) are tuned for performance metrics. Moreover,

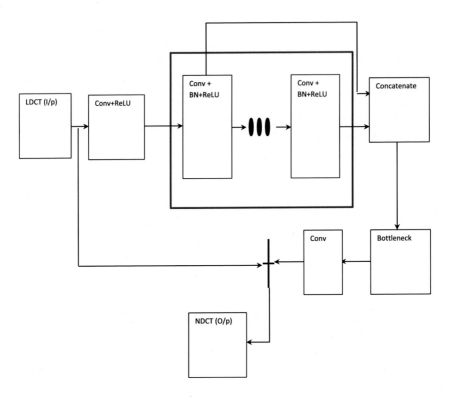

Figure 5.5 DCRN Architecture for CT denoising [42].

CT bench testing metrics, such as noise power spectrum, modular transfer function, and HU accuracy, are applied on network's output.

The densely connected residual network (DCRN) [42] is based on ResNet and DenseNet architectures. It is based on residual learning and batch normalization, which enhance the training efficiency. The densely connected architecture enables access of feature maps of all the preceding layers, unlike other models, which allow access of feature maps of only the previous layer. Therefore it preserves the structural details of low-dose CT on TCIA (The Cancer Archive dataset). Fig. 5.5 depicts block diagram of DCRN.

Two-stage residual CNN (TS-RCNN) [43] denoises the low-dose X-ray CT images. The first stage is for texture denoising, whereas the second stage preserves the structural details. In the first stage, residual CNN with perceptual loss function is applied on high-frequency images. The stationary wavelet transform is used to extract high- frequency images. In the second stage, structural enhancement is done using first stage results.

The inverse stationary wavelet transform yields the final results. This network follows the hybrid methodology of wavelet and CNN denoising. It is designed for Gaussian noise and mixed Gaussian and Poisson noise.

The recent development in the CT image denoising is the usage of complex-valued operators, such as convolution, batch normalization, and rectified linear units [44]. It is based on residual learning, and it is termed as complex-valued medical image denoising network (CVMIDNet). The real-valued image is retrieved at the last stage using the merging layer. The complex-valued CNN has outperformed its real-valued counterpart. It outperforms DnCNN, BM3D, and feature-guided CNN [45].

5.4.3 CNNs for ultrasound images

The speckle noise reduction in ultrasound images is a major concern. The mixed attention-based residual U-Net (MARU) [48] network is being used for real-time speckle noise reduction. The mixed attention mechanism is merged in residual U-Net architecture. It comprises of Leaky ReLU, stacked two residual blocks, and two-stage up-down sampling. The mixed attention block enhances image quality by assigning weights to each pixel in each channel. It is the modified version of the non-local neural network [49] and GCNet [50] architecture. In encoding phase, input images pass through convolution units and mixed attention block. The convolution with stride of two is used instead of pooling layer. The decoding stage comprises of deconvolutional units for upsampling. The feature maps are added using skip connections between encoding and decoding stage. The last layer is convolution to fuse all feature maps into despeckled output. The application framework of noise estimation of MARU is given in Fig. 5.6.

ID-CNN [47] is a speckle noise denoiser with the basic building block of "Convolution+Batch Normalization+ReLU". The end-to-end training is done with component-wise division residual layer and merging of two loss functions, i.e., Euclidean and total variation loss.

The PCANet-based nonlocal means (NLM) technique for removal of speckle noise uses deep learning to extract intrinsic features for nonlocal means despeckling [46]. The hand-crafted features utilized by NLM are not apt for an accurate representation of structural similarity in the ultrasound images. The intrinsic features extracted by PCANet are used for similarity computation of NLM. The improved CNN-based PCANet architecture with parametric linear units and principal component analysis filters. It preserves structural information of ultrasound images. Fig. 5.7 depicts block diagram of PCANet-NLM network.

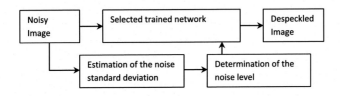

Figure 5.6 Application framework of MARU network.

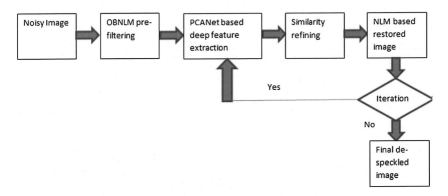

Figure 5.7 Architecture of PCANet-based nonlocal means method.

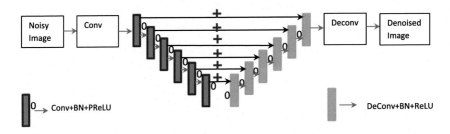

Figure 5.8 USNet architecture.

USNet [51] architecture is specifically designed for ultrasound denoising with six convolution units, six deconvolution units, a single convolution layer as the first layer, and a single deconvolution layer as the second layer, as given in Fig. 5.8. The convolution units comprise of convolution, batch normalization, and rectified linear units. The deconvolution units comprise of deconvolution, batch normalization, and rectified linear units. The hybrid loss function is given by

$$L_{train} = \alpha L_{US} + (1 - \alpha) L_{SSIM}, \tag{5.8}$$

where L_{US} is the loss function designed for ultrasound speckle noise, and L_{SSIM} is the error summation of structural similarity index with respect to the input image and noisy image. L_{US} is given by following equation

$$L_{US} = \frac{1}{2N} \sum_{i=1}^{N} \| \sqrt{F(y_i)} - \sqrt{x_i} \|^2, \qquad (5.9)$$

where N is the total number of images, F is CNN function, y_i is noisy image, and x_i is clean image.

5.4.4 CNNs for positron emission tomography (PET) images

It is a well-known fact that convolutional neural networks (CNNs) demonstrate superior performance in denoising positron emission tomography (PET) images. The procedure can be both supervised and unsupervised. Under supervised denoising methodologies, we have methods that have a heavy processing load. Supervised training of the CNN requires a pair of large, high-quality PET image datasets. Mainly, many low- and high-quality reference PET image pairs are required. This causes researchers to look for dynamic supervised techniques, and some even switch to unsupervised techniques. Deep image prior (DIP) has gained importance in the recent years. It is based on the concept that CNN structures have the intrinsic ability to solve inverse problems, such as denoising without pretraining.

An image denoising problem can be depicted as:

$$min_x E(x; x_0) + R(x), \qquad (5.10)$$

where $E(x; x_0)$ is the data term and $R(x)$ is the image prior. The image prior is captured with the help of a convolutional neural net in a rigorous training process. This gives the equation for the minimizer $\theta^* = argmin_\theta E(f_\theta(z); x_0)$ and the result of the optimization process $x^* = f_{\theta^*}(z)$. The minimizer θ^*, usually gradient descent, starts from randomly initialized parameters and descends into a local best result to yield the x^* restoration function. It works with a single target image. Hashimoto et al. [52] proposed an innovative procedure for the DIP approach with a four-dimensional (4D) branch CNN architecture in end-to-end training to denoise dynamic PET images. Here, dynamic PET images are treated as training labels, and denoised dynamic PET images are obtained from the CNN outputs without any need to prepare high-quality and large patient-related PET images. In Hashimoto et al. [53], dynamic PET images were used as the training labels, and static PET image was used as the network input. The static image acquires all the data from the start to the end of data acquisition. In Onishi et al. [54], a method is proposed that is an unsupervised 3D PET image denoising method based on an anatomical information-guided attention mechanism. The magnetic resonance-guided deep decoder (MR-GDD) utilizes the spatial details and semantic features of MR-guidance image more effectively by introducing encoder-decoder and deep decoder subnetworks. In Gong et al. [22], a deep convolutional neural network was trained to improve PET image quality. Perceptual loss, based on features derived from a pretrained VGG network, was employed as the training loss function, instead of the conventional mean squared error, to preserve image details. The lack of real patient dataset for training is limited; so it proposes to pretrain the network using simulation data and fine-tune the last few layers of the network using real datasets. It can be concluded that unsupervised CNN-based methods using image prior are the mainstream methods used in PET image denoising.

5.5 Result and discussion

In most of the CNN-based medical imaging denoisers, the convolutional layer, batch normalization layer, and rectified linear unit activation are used. The residual learning methodology is widely adapted, in which output is the noise component. The different denoisers are designed with changes in number of layers, loss functions, activation functions, encoder-decoder module, skip connections, etc. The denoising results are evaluated on the basis of image quality assessment metrics, particularly peak signal-to-noise ratio (PSNR) and structural similarity index (SSIM). It has been observed that in case of Gaussian image denoising, there are some benchmark datasets, such as BSD-68 and Set-12, and most of the CNN denoisers have used these for training and testing. The direct comparative analysis is possible as the input dataset and the noise level are same. However, in the case of medical imaging, the direct comparative analysis of all the methods is not possible, as there is lot of variation in the testing datasets and input noise configuration. This is the major issue in the progression of this field.

In the case of MRI image denoising, it has been inferred from Table 5.2 that 3D-parallel RicianNet has outperformed other methods for Rician noise Removal on the Brainweb dataset. It works on both local and global features. It enhances receptive field of the network by a power-

Table 5.3 Comparative analysis of speckle noise reduction on BSD-68 dataset (PSNR/SSIM).

	$\sigma = 2$	$\sigma = 3$	$\sigma = 4$	$\sigma = 5$
PCA-NLM [46]	28.26/0.78	26.79/0.73	25.62/0.69	24.39/0.63
ID-CNN [47]	30.33/0.84	28.01/0.75	25.69/0.63	22.92/0.51
DCNND [27]	30.69/0.86	29.10/0.82	27.87/0.77	27.03/0.74
DnCNN [26]	30.93/0.86	29.26/0.82	27.89/0.77	26.73/0.73
MARU [48]	31.31/0.87	29.40/0.83	28.11/0.79	27.28/0.76

ful convolutional residual module. The other module (depth–wise separable convolution residual) reduces the number of CNN parameters for learning. These two modules are arranged in a parallel fashion.

In the case of the CT image denoising, TS-RCNN, i.e., two-stage residual convolutional neural network outperforms DnCNN, BM3D, and RED-CNN denoisers. This model is trained on LDCT to extract NDCT images. The first stage acts as texture denoiser with the usage of stationary wavelet transform, whereas the second stage acts as a structure enhancer. The final denoised version is obtained by inverse stationary wavelet transform. It is designed for Gaussian and mixture of Gaussian+Poisson noise. The latest development in the CT denoising is the development of the model (CVMIDNet) with complex convolution, complex batch normalization, and complex rectified linear units.

In the case of the ultrasound image denoising, it can be inferred that the mixed attention-based residual UNet is apt for real-time speckle removal. It is designed from nonlocal neural network and GCNet to preserve spatial and channel information. The grading of noise level is done, and it is estimated by an algorithm to deal with complex noise of ultrasound in MARU framework. The MARU network has outperformed other CNN-based denoisers, such as DnCNN, PCA-NLM, IDCNN, DCNND, and PCA-NLM, as given in Table 5.3. The PCA-NLM is another speckle noise denoiser combining the concept of nonlocal means filtering and principal component analysis based CNN for speckle reduction. The PET image denoising is still in the nascent stage. It is based on dynamic PET images and unsupervised learning with image priors.

5.6 Challenges of CNN's denoisers

Although there are numerous research papers in the literature, there are very few manuscripts that give detail description of the network and number of parameters. Therefore reproducibility of results is difficult for smaller research groups, as high computational GPUs are required for large networks. It has been observed that there is stagnation in the peak signal-to-noise ratio after a particular length of network. The designing of network with less number of parameters, optimum length, and computational power is still a challenging problem. Moreover, there are a few problems associated with CNNs: vanishing gradient problem, over-fitting, initialization values, and setting of hyper-parameter values. In the case of medical imaging modalities, the benchmark datasets repository is not widely available for researchers. CNNs mostly rely on supervised training with the availability of clean and noisy pairs of the medical images for denoising. However, the application of CNN in real-time denoising, and in the cases where supervised learning data is not available, is still a challenging problem. In the future, there is a need to model CNNs that can deal with the reconstruction of 3-D images or 3D+time images. But most of the CNN networks solve these problems of multidimensional input by converting them into 2D inputs and outputs. Therefore designing of network with 3-D+time images is need of an hour for future progression in this field. The image restoration method should be evaluated as per the eventual application of the image reconstruction (diagnosis, quantification of the biological process) instead of intermediate metrics, such as structural similarity and peak signal-to-noise ratio. The design of loss functions and image quality metrics is a further open area for research.

5.7 Conclusion

The entire chapter is geared towards highlighting the importance of denoising methodologies in various fields of medical sciences. The work mainly focuses on the modalities like CT, MRI, ultrasound images, and PET images. These images are highly susceptible to additive noises that corrupt the morphological and textural information by creating false artifacts and misleading data discrepancies. To deal with this, it is mandatory to filter out the correct and nondisrupted information from the raw corrected data. The preprocessing image denoising step is inevitable for the accurate diagnosis. Convolutional nets have proved to be very useful in this regard. The CNNs with training-testing module show great denoising results in almost all medical imaging modalities. CNN paves the way for the medical field as it requires no segmentation of organs by medical experts and for the computational viewpoint; it is also not cumbersome due to its inherent nature of reducing the number of parameters. In addition, CNN works well in coordination with training techniques, such as backpropagation. It has been observed that benchmark DnCNN Gaussian denoiser with the basic unit as "Conv+Batch Normalization+ReLU activation" is the reference denoiser for medical imaging. In several methodologies, it has been modified as per noise type and input image. In denoising of MR images, the best CNN models are CNN-DMRI, DnCNN, SCNN, and 3D-parallel RicianNet. For CT images, the CNN models that proved to be beneficial in terms of denoising are TS-RCNN and complex valued convolution-based CVMIDNet. Moreover, DnCNN Gaussian denoiser can be used for CT, MRI, and ultrasound images with some modifications. The MARU and PCA-NLM network is apt for the speckle noise reduction in ultrasound images. For PET images, the most important technique for image denoising is PET denoising with the image prior. This is an unsupervised method of denoising that does not require a huge number of high-quality PET images. Hence this chapter is an attempt to bring out the importance of various CNN-based denoising methods, especially in the field of medical sciences.

References

[1] A. Singha, R.S. Thakur, T. Patel, Deep learning applications in medical image analysis, in: Biomedical Data Mining for Information Retrieval, John Wiley & Sons, Ltd, 2021, pp. 293–350.

[2] R.A. Hazarika, A.K. Maji, S.N. Sur, B.S. Paul, D. Kandar, A survey on classification algorithms of brain images in Alzheimer's disease based on feature extraction techniques, IEEE Access 9 (2021) 58503–58536, https://doi.org/10.1109/ACCESS.2021.3072559.

[3] P. Choudhary, J. Singhai, J.S. Yadav, Curvelet and fast marching method-based technique for efficient artifact detection and removal in dermoscopic images, International Journal of Imaging Systems and Technology (2021), https://doi.org/10.1002/IMA.22633.

[4] P. Kaur, G. Singh, P. Kaur, A review of denoising medical images using machine learning approaches, Current Medical Imaging Reviews 14 (5) (May 2018) 675, https://doi.org/10.2174/1573405613666170428154156.

[5] S.V. Mohd Sagheer, S.N. George, A review on medical image denoising algorithms, Biomedical Signal Processing and Control 61 (Aug. 2020) 102036, https://doi.org/10.1016/J.BSPC.2020.102036.

[6] L. Fan, F. Zhang, H. Fan, C. Zhang, Brief review of image denoising techniques, Visual Computing for Industry, Biomedicine, and Art 2 (1) (2019), https://doi.org/10.1186/s42492-019-0016-7.

[7] R.S. Thakur, S. Chatterjee, R.N. Yadav, L. Gupta, Image de-noising with machine learning: a review, IEEE Access 9 (2021) 93338–93363, https://doi.org/10.1109/ACCESS.2021.3092425.

[8] S. Chatterjee, R.S. Thakur, R.N. Yadav, L. Gupta, D.K. Raghuvanshi, Review of noise removal techniques in ECG signals, IET Signal Processing 14 (9) (Dec. 2020) 569–590, https://doi.org/10.1049/iet-spr.2020.0104.

[9] I. Singh, O.P. Verma, Impulse noise removal in color image sequences using fuzzy logic, Multimedia Tools and Applications 80 (12) (Feb. 2021) 18279–18300, https://doi.org/10.1007/S11042-021-10643-3.

[10] R.S. Thakur, R.N. Yadav, L. Gupta, State-of-art analysis of image denoising methods using convolutional neural networks, IET Image Processing 13 (13) (2019) 2367–2380, https://doi.org/10.1049/iet-ipr.2019.0157.

[11] R. Yamashita, M. Nishio, R.K.G. Do, K. Togashi, Convolutional neural networks: an overview and application in radiology, Insights into Imaging 9 (4) (Jun. 2018) 611–629, https://doi.org/10.1007/S13244-018-0639-9.

[12] A. Mahmood, et al., Deep Learning for Coral Classification, Academic Press, 2017.

[13] R.S. Thakur, R.N. Yadav, L. Gupta, PReLU and edge-aware filter-based image denoiser using convolutional neural network, IET Image Processing 14 (15) (Dec. 2020) 3869–3879, https://doi.org/10.1049/iet-ipr.2020.0717.

[14] M.S. Hansen, P. Kellman, Image reconstruction: an overview for clinicians, Journal of Magnetic Resonance Imaging 41 (3) (Mar. 2015) 573, https://doi.org/10.1002/JMRI.24687.

[15] S. Aja-Fernández, C. Alberola-López, C.F. Westin, Noise and signal estimation in magnitude MRI and Rician distributed images: A LMMSE approach, IEEE Transactions on Image Processing 17 (8) (Aug. 2008) 1383–1398, https://doi.org/10.1109/TIP.2008.925382.

[16] Y. Zeng, et al., Magnetic resonance image denoising algorithm based on cartoon, texture, and residual parts, Computational & Mathematical Methods in Medicine 2020 (2020), https://doi.org/10.1155/2020/1405647.

[17] D. Hong, C. Huang, C. Yang, J. Li, Y. Qian, C. Cai, FFA-DMRI: a network based on feature fusion and attention mechanism for brain MRI denoising, Frontiers in Neuroscience 14 (Sep. 2020) 577937, https://doi.org/10.3389/FNINS.2020.577937.

[18] J. He, Y. Wang, J. Ma, Radon inversion via deep learning, IEEE Transactions on Medical Imaging 39 (6) (Jun. 2020) 2076–2087, https://doi.org/10.1109/TMI.2020.2964266.

[19] M. Diwakar, M. Kumar, A review on CT image noise and its denoising, Biomedical Signal Processing and Control 42 (Apr. 2018) 73–88, https://doi.org/10.1016/j.bspc.2018.01.010, Elsevier Ltd.

[20] S. Hashemi, N.S. Paul, S. Beheshti, R.S.C. Cobbold, Adaptively tuned iterative low dose CT image denoising, Computational & Mathematical Methods in Medicine 2015 (2015), https://doi.org/10.1155/2015/638568.

[21] J.J. Vaquero, P. Kinahan, Positron emission tomography: current challenges and opportunities for technological advances in clinical and preclinical imaging systems, Annual Review of Biomedical Engineering 17 (Dec. 2015) 385, https://doi.org/10.1146/ANNUREV-BIOENG-071114-040723.

[22] K. Gong, J. Guan, C.-C. Liu, J. Qi, PET image denoising using a deep neural network through fine tuning, IEEE Transactions on Radiation and Plasma Medical Sciences 3 (2) (Oct. 2018) 153–161, https://doi.org/10.1109/TRPMS.2018.2877644.

[23] H. Liu, K. Wang, J. Tian, Postreconstruction filtering of 3D PET images by using weighted higher-order singular value decomposition, BioMedical Engineering OnLine 15 (1) (Aug. 2016) 1–20, https://doi.org/10.1186/S12938-016-0221-Y.

[24] Y. Wang, X. Ge, H. Ma, S. Qi, G. Zhang, Y. Yao, Deep learning in medical ultrasound image analysis: a review, IEEE Access 9 (2021) 54310–54324, https://doi.org/10.1109/ACCESS.2021.3071301.

[25] C.A. Duarte-Salazar, E. Castro-Ospina, M.A. Becerra, E. Delgado-Trejos, Speckle noise reduction in ultrasound images for improving the metrological evaluation of biomedical applications: an overview, IEEE Access 8 (2020) 15983–15999, https://doi.org/10.1109/ACCESS.2020.2967178.

[26] K. Zhang, W. Zuo, Y. Chen, D. Meng, L. Zhang, Beyond a Gaussian denoiser: residual learning of deep CNN for image denoising, IEEE Transactions on Image Processing 26 (7) (July 2017) 3142–3155, https://doi.org/10.1109/TIP.2017.2662206.

[27] K. Zhang, W. Zuo, S. Gu, L. Zhang, Learning deep CNN denoiser prior for image restoration, in: Proceedings - 30th IEEE Conference on Computer Vision and Pattern Recognition, CVPR 2017, January 2017, pp. 2808–2817, https://doi.org/10.1109/CVPR.2017.300.

[28] L. Alzubaidi, et al., Review of deep learning: concepts, CNN architectures, challenges, applications, future directions, Journal of Big Data 8 (1) (Mar. 2021) 1–74, https://doi.org/10.1186/S40537-021-00444-8.

[29] P.C. Tripathi, S. Bag, CNN-DMRI: a convolutional neural network for denoising of magnetic resonance images, Pattern Recognition Letters (Apr. 2020), https://doi.org/10.1016/j.patrec.2020.03.036.

[30] D. Eun, R. Jang, W.S. Ha, H. Lee, S.C. Jung, N. Kim, Deep-learning-based image quality enhancement of compressed sensing magnetic resonance imaging of vessel wall: comparison of self-supervised and unsupervised approaches, Scientific Reports 10 (1) (Aug. 2020) 1–17, https://doi.org/10.1038/s41598-020-69932-w.

[31] L. Wu, S. Hu, C. Liu, Denoising of 3D brain MR images with parallel residual learning of convolutional neural network using global and local feature extraction, Computational Intelligence and Neuroscience 2021 (2021), https://doi.org/10.1155/2021/5577956.

[32] K. Isogawa, T. Ida, T. Shiodera, T. Takeguchi, Deep shrinkage convolutional neural network for adaptive noise reduction, IEEE Signal Processing Letters 25 (2) (Feb. 2018) 224–228, https://doi.org/10.1109/LSP.2017.2782270.

[33] M. Kidoh, et al., Deep learning based noise reduction for brain MR imaging: tests on phantoms and healthy volunteers, Magnetic Resonance in Medical Sciences 19 (3) (2020) 195–206, https://doi.org/10.2463/MRMS.MP.2019-0018.

[34] A. Panda, R. Naskar, S. Rajbans, S. Pal, A 3D wide residual network with perceptual loss for brain MRI image denoising, in: 2019 10th Int. Conf. Comput. Commun. Netw. Technol. ICCCNT 2019, Jul. 2019, https://doi.org/10.1109/ICCCNT45670.2019.8944535.

[35] E.A. Kaye, et al., Accelerating prostate diffusion-weighted MRI using a guided denoising convolutional neural network: retrospective feasibility study, Radiology: Artificial Intelligence 2 (5) (Aug. 2020) e200007, https://doi.org/10.1148/RYAI.2020200007.

[36] M.V.R. Manimala, C.D. Naidu, M.N.G. Prasad, Convolutional neural network for sparse reconstruction of MR images interposed with Gaussian noise, Journal of Circuits, Systems, and Computers 29 (7) (Sep. 2020) 2050116, https://doi.org/10.1142/S0218126620501169.

[37] V.S. Kadimesetty, S. Gutta, S. Ganapathy, P.K. Yalavarthy, Convolutional neural network-based robust denoising of low-dose computed tomography perfusion maps, IEEE Transactions on Radiation and Plasma Medical Sciences 3 (2) (Jul. 2018) 137–152, https://doi.org/10.1109/TRPMS.2018.2860788.

[38] H. Chen, et al., Low-dose CT denoising with convolutional neural network, in: Proc. - Int. Symp. Biomed. Imaging, Jun. 2017, pp. 143–146, https://doi.org/10.1109/ISBI.2017.7950488.

[39] H. Chen, et al., Low-dose CT with a residual encoder-decoder convolutional neural network, IEEE Transactions on Medical Imaging 36 (12) (Dec. 2017) 2524–2535, https://doi.org/10.1109/TMI.2017.2715284.

[40] M.P. Heinrich, M. Stille, T.M. Buzug, Residual U-Net convolutional neural network architecture for low-dose CT denoising, Current Directions in Biomedical Engineering 4 (1) (Sep. 2018) 297–300, https://doi.org/10.1515/CDBME-2018-0072.

[41] K.C. Prabhat, R. Zeng, M.M. Farhangi, K.J. Myers, Deep neural networks-based denoising models for CT imaging and their efficacy, in: Medical Imaging 2021: Physics

of Medical Imaging, Proceedings - SPIE 11595 (2021) 115950H, https://doi.org/10.1117/12.2581418.

[42] J. Ming, B. Yi, Y. Zhang, H. Li, Low-dose CT image denoising using classification densely connected residual network, KSII Transactions on Internet and Information Systems 14 (6) (2020), https://doi.org/10.3837/tiis.2020.06.009.

[43] L. Huang, H. Jiang, S. Li, Z. Bai, J. Zhang, Two stage residual CNN for texture denoising and structure enhancement on low dose CT image, Computer Methods and Programs in Biomedicine 184 (Feb. 2020) 105115, https://doi.org/10.1016/J.CMPB.2019.105115.

[44] S. Rawat, K.P.S. Rana, V. Kumar, A novel complex-valued convolutional neural network for medical image denoising, Biomedical Signal Processing and Control 69 (Aug. 2021) 102859, https://doi.org/10.1016/J.BSPC.2021.102859.

[45] G. Dong, Y. Ma, A. Basu, Feature-guided CNN for denoising images from portable ultrasound devices, IEEE Access 9 (2021) 28272–28281, https://doi.org/10.1109/ACCESS.2021.3059003.

[46] H. Yu, M. Ding, X. Zhang, J. Wu, PCANet based nonlocal means method for speckle noise removal in ultrasound images, PLoS ONE (2018), https://doi.org/10.1371/journal.pone.0205390.

[47] P. Wang, H. Zhang, V.M. Patel, SAR image despeckling using a convolutional neural network, IEEE Signal Processing Letters 24 (12) (Dec. 2017) 1763–1767, https://doi.org/10.1109/LSP.2017.2758203.

[48] Y. Lan, X. Zhang, Real-time ultrasound image despeckling using mixed-attention mechanism based residual UNet, IEEE Access 8 (2020) 195327–195340, https://doi.org/10.1109/ACCESS.2020.3034230.

[49] X. Wang, R. Girshick, A. Gupta, K. He, Non-local neural networks, in: Proc. IEEE Comput. Soc. Conf. Comput. Vis. Pattern Recognit, Dec. 2018, pp. 7794–7803, https://doi.org/10.1109/CVPR.2018.00813.

[50] Y. Cao, J. Xu, S. Lin, F. Wei, H. Hu, GCNet: non-local networks meet squeeze-excitation networks and beyond, in: Proc. - 2019 Int. Conf. Comput. Vis. Work. ICCVW 2019, Apr. 2019, pp. 1971–1980.

[51] D. Feng, W. Wu, H. Li, Q. Li, Speckle noise removal in ultrasound images using a deep convolutional neural network and a specially designed loss function, in: Lect. Notes Comput. Sci. (including Subser. Lect. Notes Artif. Intell. Lect. Notes Bioinformatics), vol. 11977, Oct. 2019, pp. 85–92, https://doi.org/10.1007/978-3-030-37969-8_11.

[52] F. Hashimoto, H. Ohba, K. Ote, A. Kakimoto, H. Tsukada, Y. Ouchi, 4D deep image prior: dynamic PET image denoising using an unsupervised four-dimensional branch convolutional neural network, Physics in Medicine and Biology 66 (1) (Jan. 2021), https://doi.org/10.1088/1361-6560/ABCD1A.

[53] F. Hashimoto, H. Ohba, K. Ote, A. Teramoto, H. Tsukada, Dynamic PET image denoising using deep convolutional neural networks without prior training datasets, IEEE Access 7 (2019) 96594–96603, https://doi.org/10.1109/ACCESS.2019.2929230.

[54] Y. Onishi, et al., Anatomical-guided attention enhances unsupervised PET image denoising performance, Medical Image Analysis (Sep. 2021) 102226, https://doi.org/10.1016/J.MEDIA.2021.102226.

CHAPTER 6

Multimodal learning of social image representation

Feiran Huang, Wenxiao Liu, Zhiying Li, and Weichang Huang
Jinan University, Guangzhou, China

6.1 Introduction

With the rapid development of the Internet, social images are increasing on various social networking sites, such as Picasa, Instagram, and Flicker. Social images carry a variety of connections between them, such as textual descriptions and visual content related to social relationships. To analyze and process this kind of data, it is necessary to learn effective representations of social images. The eyes of academia and industry are focusing on how to project the high-dimensional data into low-dimensional vector space, which subsequently poses a great challenge: how to exploit the social relationships between social images to make the learned representation more effective.

Social images not only provide challenges for representational learning, but also provide clues due to their heterogeneity and interconnectedness. First, a social image may contain a variety of representations, such as unique visual content and its related description in text. The multiply modalities usually consist of private and public information. Each data modality can be populated by other types of data modalities. To improve the comprehensiveness and robustness of the learned representations, correlations between different modalities need to be mined, so that both private and common information can be exploited. Second, social images are not independent of each other, and they possess either implicit or explicit relationships. For a better solution, social connections can be used to complement representational learning, for example, two linked images may be more similar in graphical and text content than two unrelated images. Thus two images that are related should generate more similar representations than other two that are not related. However, obtaining the encode relationships for representation learning is also a challenge since links are completely different from content. Third, the number of social images is growing rapidly and

Digital Image Enhancement and Reconstruction
https://doi.org/10.1016/B978-0-32-398370-9.00013-5
139

is showing exponential growth. Therefore to be sufficient to handle such a massive quantity of data, the representation learning method needs to be very effective.

This chapter mainly demonstrates some representative representation learning methods of social images and their related applications.

6.2 Representation learning methods of social media images

Joint modeling of visual content and text has been one of the key research spots in the multimedia field, which supports a variety of applications such as visual question answering and image illustration. There are three main types of existing methods: CCA-based methods, ranking-based methods, and others. Among the evaluation metrics for image-to-text embedding, CCA (canonical correlation analysis) is one of the benchmarks. It maximizes the cross-correlation between the two views and projects the samples in both views into a shared subspace. And the second type of approach is to use neural networks with rank loss SGD to learn matching scores and learn joint embedding spaces for multiview data. As for the other types of methods, there are clustering-based approach, Bayesian-based approach, and knowledge graph-based approach, etc. This section describes three representative methods and some applications.

6.2.1 Multimodal learning of social image representation

Huang et al. [1] proposed a social image representation learning method to make full use of the link information and correlation carried between various modalities. Specifically, they tend to mine the deep associations that exist between multiple modalities to learn embeddings more efficiently. In addition, they leveraged link information for multimodal representation learning. Based on this, they propose a multimodal representation learning method CMVAE-TN (correlated multimodal variation autoencoder via triplet network). In more detail, they adopted CMVAE (correlated multimodal variation autoencoder) to mine deep multimodal intrinsic associations. CMVAE learns a more comprehensive representation by jointly modeling the private and common information in each modal content. Meanwhile, to exploit social connections, they use a triple network structure built upon CMVAE to capture connection information between social images in representation learning. Finally, to unify the two parts for multimodal representation learning, they utilize a deep model for this purpose.

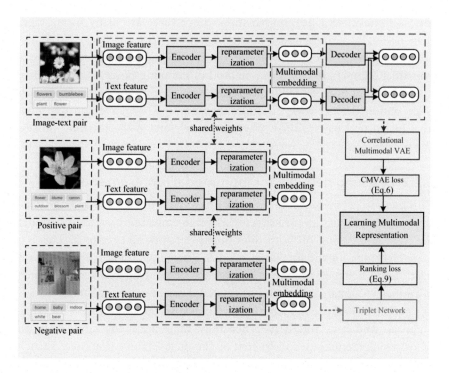

Figure 6.1 The framework of CMVAE-TN.

In addition to this, their proposed method also employs a positive (negative) sampling approach upon the triplet structure to decrease the time of the learning process.

Fig. 6.1 shows the framework of CMVAE-TN. A correlated multimodal variation autoencoder model is utilized to fully explore nonlinear correlations between different modalities to obtain better joint representations to assist multimodal learning. The CMVAE model (red block) builds an associated VAE for each modality, and it attempts to capture these private and common information through reconstructing two modes from each single mode. Next, a triplet network (green block) is used to incorporate the social links between the triplet of an image-text pair, i.e., a given image-text pair, a randomly sampled negative pair unconnected to it, and a randomly sampled positive pair connected to it. It consists of three identical subnetworks that share weight parameters and learn both positive and negative rankings through a hinged rank loss function. A deep model that unifies these two parts is used to optimize them simultaneously to combine multimodal content with link information. Since there are many more edges than nodes in a multimodal network, iterating on all edges within the network to make the objective function optimization could result in exponential complexity. Thus the method of sampling positive and negative needs to be utilized to reduce the complexity of training time. For each node within the network, it randomly samples K negative and one positive image-text pairs; in this way the complexity of the learning process becomes linear.

6.2.2 Learning network for multimodal representation

This method [2] mainly combines the image with the corresponding auxiliary quality information to learn social image embedding, so as to consider the joint embedding on both sides of the network and content. This is a huge challenge for the following reasons. First of all, there is an important relationship between the visual and textual content of social images, such as an image contains a dog and its textual description also contains "dog." For people to find the hidden relationship is easy, but it is difficult for computers to find it by themselves. Secondly, there are many kinds of social links, which are mainly constructed by the metadata in social images (such as users, groups, tags, etc.). Because these links are generally deep nonlinear, it is very important to design effective network embedding methods to combine this kind of information.

The proposed method is denoted as DAMGE, which means deep attentive multimodal graph embedding. This model combines multimodality and social connections to learn the representation of social images more effectively. Specifically, it first constructs a multilevel visual attention network, takes the close relationship between image and text description as learning samples, and deeply excavates samples to learn joint multimodal embedding. Then, the multimodal graph is constructed based on multimodal representation and social links, and the graph convolution network (GCN) is used to obtain deeper node representation. Combined with joint optimizing, these two networks are then integrated into a complete framework to strengthen each other's learning and social image representation. Other than the traditional social image representation methods, DAMGE mainly uses multilevel visual attention networks and graph convolution networks to learn social images from two aspects of the network and content. Moreover, embedding can be combined and mutually promoted.

Fig. 6.2 shows the framework of "DAMGE." Brackets a represent social images, which contain metainformation about social connections and mul-

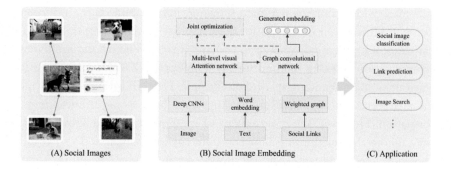

Figure 6.2 The framework of DAMGE.

timodal content. Brackets "b" represent methods for social image representation learning. For each social image and its associated textual description, it first builds a multilevel visual attention model that learns multimodal embeddings by deeply integrating the two models. The model has two types of visual attention: region-level and object-level, which well describe the subtle relationship between images and text. Then, a weighted graph is built using multimodal embeddings and various types of social connections. An unsupervised GCN is used to process weighted graph, while learning graph embeddings by maximizing the mutual information between the patch and entire graph representations. Finally, by integrating attention network and GCN into an overall model, the embedding of social images can be better learned and optimized. Brackets "c" show some applications that employ representation learning.

6.2.3 Multiview-based representation learning

In recent years, with the vigorous development of social platform websites, multiperspective media data in social networking sites appear more and more on many social networking sites. These data can be described with distinct "views" or different sets of features. Text description, network information, and visual content can be seen as different feature sources or different "views." The emergence of multiview data promotes many applications on account of the relationship between different views. Based on the content data, the existing multiview learning methods could be divided into two categories. The first is the method based on canonical correlation analysis (CCA) [3]. The purpose of this method is to maximize the correlation between two views about the projection vector, specifically to find a linear projection. Therefore a three-view embedding method is born from this idea, which aims to integrate semantic information, tags, and visual content. However, it is difficult for these approaches to capture the nonlinear relationship that exists between text and images. The second multiview representation learning method usually employs SGD with ranking loss to learn the joint embedding space. For example, DeViSE [4] map textual and visual features into a shared embedding space by learning a linear transformation. However, the disadvantage of methods described above is that they ignore the relationship between different social images. To solve the above challenges, Huang et al. [5] proposed a three-view model for social image representation learning by exploiting the important link information existing between social networks.

The framework of the model is shown in Fig. 6.3. To effectively encode the information in the social network, Huang et al. [5] changed multilayer relational network into weighted relational network, and realized the non-subtle extension of DeepWalk [6] to learn distributed network representation. The pretrained image features are utilized to represent the visual content, whereas the word vectors represent the textual content. To learn a unified representation for the three views, Huang et al. also proposed a three-branch segmentation encoder with multiple nonlinear layers. Meanwhile, to train deep models, they designed three bidirectional loss functions for cross-learning. In addition, each view uses a split-stack autoencoder (each encoder consists of an encoder and a decoder) and introduces a reconstruction error method in its optimization to maintain the reconfigurability and structure of each view.

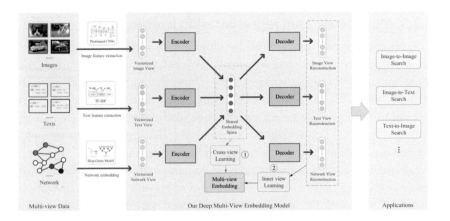

Figure 6.3 An overview of the DMVEM framework for multiview learning.

In addition to text content and vision, there are several other types of relationships in social images. Relationship information is very useful for representation learning. For example, using the network embedding method, the network structure can be transformed into a low-dimensional spatial structure, that is, each node is represented by a vector. This vector is used to retain and capture the structure of network. DeepWalk [6] has been verified to be able to learn the potential representation of unweighted social network nodes through the skip gram language model.

All three views can be represented by eigenvectors. When the relational network model is embedded into the vector representation and input into the DMVEM model, it is used to learn the multiview representation. The DMVEM model consists of two modules: an internal view module and a crossview module. The internal view module ensures that each view is reconstructed as accurately as possible from the latent space to facilitate the learned representations reserving the view's specific functionality. And the crossview module exploits the correlation between different views of the social image to learn the joint representation of the three views. Fig. 6.4 shows the detailed structure diagram of DMVEM.

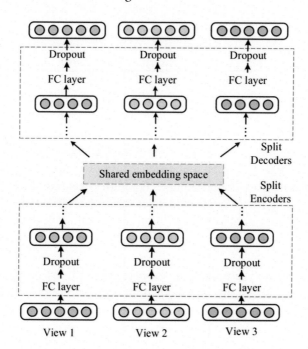

Figure 6.4 The overview of DMVEM structure.

The goal of the crossview module is to learn nonlinear embeddings of the three views, with the help of a deep neural framework. The model structure is shown in Fig. 6.4. The deep model comprises of three branches. In detail, several fully connected hidden layers with weight parameters and some hidden fully connected layers with weight parameters compose each branch. The continuous layer is separated by tanh, which is a nonlinear activation function. Because the function of these fully connected layers is to learn the joint view representation of shared embedded space, these layers are collectively referred to as segmentation encoder.

6.2.4 Applications

Emotions are one of the important factors that affect human behavior. When we need to make a decision, we want to know the views or opinions of others. Many scenes are now using automatic text analysis technology for emotion analysis. Emotion analysis technology has been widely used in various fields, such as the e-commerce industry, the service industry, medical care, and financial services. Traditional emotion analysis methods focus on a single mod. With a large amount of data appearing in different forms on social networks, the traditional methods gradually become ineffective.

Compared with words, the expressiveness of images is more intuitive and vivid, and with the popularity of visual devices, users are more inclined to publish social images on the Internet. Early work directly extracted low-level features of images [7–9]. There is also the use of the support vector machine (SVM) [7] framework for sentiment classification. Li et al. [9] combined SIFT descriptors [10], Gabor textures, and HSV color histograms to generate global embedding vectors that identified the emotions carried by images when accounting for the similarity of two images. Yanulevskaya et al. [11] represent abstract images by extracting LAB [12] and SIFT texture features and using recognition systems to learn emotional patterns. Although it is easier to extract the low-level features, there are emotional differences between the high-level features and the low-level semantics of the image, resulting in insufficient preparation for emotion detection.

Many works now use deep neural networks [13–15] to extract high-level features, thanks to the advancement of deep learning technology. You et al. [14] proposed a progressive algorithm to finetune the CNN structure, which can reduce noise pollution during analysis. Sunet et al. [16] utilized a pretrained and finetuned CNN to calculate sentiment scores and predict sentiment labels. Yang et al. [17] first calculated the emotion scores

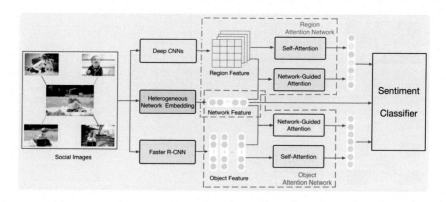

Figure 6.5 Framework of SRGMAN.

of candidate objects, and then found affective regions (ARs) based on the emotion scores and objective scores, and then classified emotions accordingly.

Different from the existing visual sentiment analysis methods, Xu et al. [18] proposed model for social relationship-guided multiple attention networks (SRGMANs). The framework is shown in Fig. 6.5. This method mainly considers the structural network information between social images and has a certain degree of sentiment classification. The approach mainly constructs a heterogeneous network with different types of social relations and introduces a heterogeneous network embedding method to better learn the representation of each image. By designing two visual attention branches (regional attention network and object attention network), more emotion and visual features are extracted, and the attention region and target features learned in the two networks are combined with the network features, which are put into the emotion classifier for the final emotion classification. Through this method, the emotional part of the target image can be fully mined.

At present, although multimodal perception analysis has reached good performance, there are still two main challenges. Firstly, the correlation between image and text should be mined to make up for the heterogeneity between image and text. Secondly, how to use abundant heterogeneous relationship information to promote image emotion classification remains to be solved. This is due to the fact that this complex and highly nonlinear social topological information cannot be derived directly from social relations. To effectively address these two main challenges, Xu et al. [19] proposed an attention-based heterogeneous relation model (AHRM), as

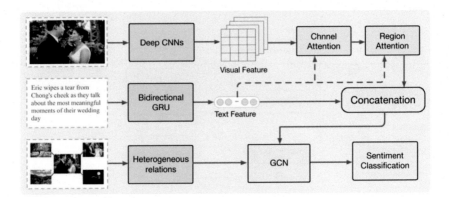

Figure 6.6 Framework of AHRM.

shown in Fig. 6.6, which captures the relationship between images and texts, but only stays at the regional level, ignoring the close connection between channels and semantic information fact. To highlight the channel-level and region-level semantic information, the progressive dual attention mechanism can effectively integrate visual and text features and learn high-quality representation from the perspective of content. To obtain a more comprehensive representation, the complementary information in the social situation is the main body, and the social relationship is the auxiliary.

6.3 Conclusion

This chapter mainly introduces the multimodal learning of social image representations. There is a large amount of social image data in social networks. Using the network information between images and multimodal content information is very useful for applications of social images. At first, we introduce three representative methods on social image representation learning. These three methods make full use of the social link information between social networks and the multimodal content information (e.g., image, tag, description, etc.) carried by social images. Therefore the learned representation is more comprehensive and complementary to be effective for the upper applications. Then, we briefly introduce two representative methods on the application of social image representation learning. These two methods integrate the social feature learning in the task of multimodal sentiment analysis. Social image representation learning is a trending and widely used field, which deserves more scientific and industrial attention.

References

[1] F. Huang, X. Zhang, J. Xu, Z. Zhao, Z. Li, Multimodal learning of social image representation by exploiting social relations, IEEE Transactions on Cybernetics 51 (3) (2019) 1506–1518.

[2] F. Huang, C. Li, B. Gao, Y. Liu, S. Alotaibi, H. Chen, Deep attentive multimodal network representation learning for social media images, ACM Transactions on Internet Technology (TOIT) 21 (3) (2021) 1–17.

[3] Z. Ma, Y. Lu, D. Foster, Finding linear structure in large datasets with scalable canonical correlation analysis, in: International Conference on Machine Learning, in: PMLR, 2015, pp. 169–178.

[4] A. Frome, G.S. Corrado, J. Shlens, S. Bengio, J. Dean, M. Ranzato, T. Mikolov, DeViSE: a deep visual-semantic embedding model, in: Proceedings of the 26th International Conference on Neural Information Processing Systems – Volume 2, 2013, pp. 2121–2129.

[5] F. Huang, X. Zhang, Z. Zhao, Z. Li, Y. He, Deep multi-view representation learning for social images, Applied Soft Computing 73 (2018) 106–118.

[6] B. Perozzi, R. Al-Rfou, S. Skiena, DeepWalk: online learning of social representations, in: Proceedings of the 20th ACM SIGKDD International Conference on Knowledge Discovery and Data Mining, 2014, pp. 701–710.

[7] V. Yanulevskaya, J.C. van Gemert, K. Roth, A.-K. Herbold, N. Sebe, J.-M. Geusebroek, Emotional valence categorization using holistic image features, in: 2008 15th IEEE International Conference on Image Processing, IEEE, 2008, pp. 101–104.

[8] J. Machajdik, A. Hanbury, Affective image classification using features inspired by psychology and art theory, in: Proceedings of the 18th ACM International Conference on Multimedia, 2010, pp. 83–92.

[9] B. Li, S. Feng, W. Xiong, W. Hu, Scaring or pleasing: exploit emotional impact of an image, in: Proceedings of the 20th ACM International Conference on Multimedia, 2012, pp. 1365–1366.

[10] D.G. Lowe, Distinctive image features from scale-invariant keypoints, International Journal of Computer Vision 60 (2) (2004) 91–110.

[11] V. Yanulevskaya, J. Uijlings, E. Bruni, A. Sartori, E. Zamboni, F. Bacci, D. Melcher, N. Sebe, In the eye of the beholder: employing statistical analysis and eye tracking for analyzing abstract paintings, in: Proceedings of the 20th ACM International Conference on Multimedia, 2012, pp. 349–358.

[12] R. Szeliski, Computer Vision: Algorithms and Applications, Texts in Computer Science, Springer, London, U.K., 2011, pp. 1–398.

[13] Q. You, J. Luo, H. Jin, J. Yang, Cross-modality consistent regression for joint visual-textual sentiment analysis of social multimedia, in: Proceedings of the Ninth ACM International Conference on Web Search and Data Mining, 2016, pp. 13–22.

[14] Q. You, J. Luo, H. Jin, J. Yang, Robust image sentiment analysis using progressively trained and domain transferred deep networks, in: Twenty-Ninth AAAI Conference on Artificial Intelligence, 2015.

[15] J. Yang, D. She, M. Sun, Joint image emotion classification and distribution learning via deep convolutional neural network, in: IJCAI, 2017, pp. 3266–3272.

[16] M. Sun, J. Yang, K. Wang, H. Shen, Discovering affective regions in deep convolutional neural networks for visual sentiment prediction, in: 2016 IEEE International Conference on Multimedia and Expo (ICME), IEEE, 2016, pp. 1–6.

[17] J. Yang, D. She, M. Sun, M.-M. Cheng, P.L. Rosin, L. Wang, Visual sentiment prediction based on automatic discovery of affective regions, IEEE Transactions on Multimedia 20 (9) (2018) 2513–2525.

[18] J. Xu, Z. Li, F. Huang, C. Li, S.Y. Philip, Visual sentiment analysis with social relations-guided multiattention networks, IEEE Transactions on Cybernetics (2020) 1–13.

[19] J. Xu, Z. Li, F. Huang, C. Li, S.Y. Philip, Social image sentiment analysis by exploiting multimodal content and heterogeneous relations, IEEE Transactions on Industrial Informatics 17 (4) (2020) 2974–2982.

CHAPTER 7

Underwater image enhancement: past, present, and future

Surendra Nagar[a,c], Ankush Jain[b], and Pramod Kumar Singh[a]

[a]CIDMR Laboratory, ABV-Indian Institute of Information Technology & Management, Gwalior, India
[b]School of Computer Science Engineering & Technology (SCSET), Bennett University, Greater Noida, India
[c]Department of Computer Science & Engineering, ASET, Amity University, Gwalior, India

List of abbreviations

UI	Underwater image
PDF	Polarization difference imaging
DCP	Dark channel prior
UDCP	Underwater DCP
IFM	Image formation model
CNN	Convolutional neural network
GAN	Generative adversarial network
IQA	Image quality assessment
FR	Full reference
NR	Nonreference
MSE	Mean square error
PSNR	Peak signal-to-noise ratio
SSIM	Structural similarity index measure
PCQI	Patch-based contrast quality index
UCIQE	Underwater color image quality evaluation
UIQM	UI quality measure
HVS	Human visual system
UICM	UI colorfulness measure
UISM	UI sharpness measure
UIConM	UI contrast measure

7.1 Introduction

In recent years, exploration and exploitation of underwater resources have become a sought-after area in the world of water (e.g., oceans, seas, and rivers) [58,28,19]. A broad investigation of underwater imaging has revealed multiple opportunities to exploit the sea resources under various applications, e.g., naval operations, deep-sea installations and monitoring,

Digital Image Enhancement and Reconstruction
https://doi.org/10.1016/B978-0-32-398370-9.00014-7
151

marine ecological analysis [70,46], fisheries, petroleum, and natural gas exploration [21]. Furthermore, millions of known and unknown underwater sea resources exist that are highly significant to human beings. In this regard, researchers have developed various autonomous devices, i.e., automatic underwater vehicles and remote-operated underwater machines equipped with high-quality imaging sensors to analyze the underwater ecosystem more precisely [37,7]. To collect detailed information on the sea resources, at present, most of the researchers and scientists rely upon the recorded underwater images with low quality. However, the complex marine environment with unfavorable lighting situations makes enhancing such low-quality images highly challenging. Generally, UIs are degraded through wavelength-bound absorption and scattering problem (i.e., forward and backward scattering) [35,32,10,8]. Moreover, oceanic snow brings a noise effect that severely magnifies the scattering problem. These undesirable effects decrease the contrast and visibility inside the water. They are responsible for the color casts effect too, which restricts the practical applicability of underwater images in marine ecology [60], marine archaeology and biology [47], and other applications [70]. For ensuring the usability of underwater images in any real-world application, it is required to enhance their quality in real-time. UI enhancement technique improves the visual quality of the images/videos recorded under the water environment. In the past decade, several methods have been proposed to address the enhancement/restoration problem of underwater imaging. Based on the working principle, existing methods are classified into four categories: (a) supplementary information-based, (b) nonphysical model-based, (c) physical model-based, and (d) data-driven (deep-learning based) methods. This is depicted in Fig. 7.1. In the upcoming sections, we present the underwater imaging model. A detailed description of recent UI enhancement methods falls under the aforementioned categories.

The rest of the chapter is summarized in the following manner. Section 7.2 summarizes the underwater environment with a typical underwater imaging model and underwater scattering effect. A detailed description of several recent UI enhancement methods is presented in Section 7.3. Section 7.4 presents the description of a few benchmark datasets used in the recent UI enhancement methods. Section 7.5 describes and formulates significant image quality assessment measures used in the state-of-the-art UI processing methods. The primary challenges in UI enhancement and some future research recommendations are highlighted in Section 7.6. Finally, Section 7.7 concludes this chapter.

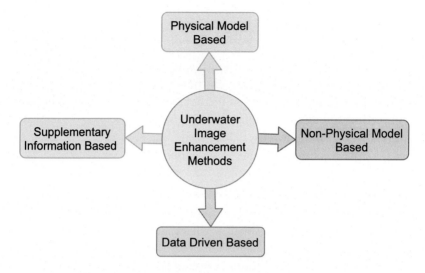

Figure 7.1 Categorization of existing UI enhancement methods based on their working model.

7.2 Underwater environment

The underwater environment is the entire observable area inside a natural or artificial water origin, e.g., ocean, sea, lake, and river. It plays an indispensable role in serving the habitat and food to the millions of organisms and species belonging to the water source. The underwater environment is also crucial from a human point of view; it offers unlimited research possibilities for minerals, food, and other creative activities within the deepwater zone. Therefore it is desirable to understand the fundamental underwater imaging model before switching to a detailed description of various UI enhancement methods.

7.2.1 Underwater imaging model

Literature shows that the physical model-based mechanisms have been widely adopted to develop UI enhancement methods. The Jaffe–McGlamery's model [48,35] is a well-known and widely used physical model in several UI restoration methods [58,64]. In this model, the camera's irradiance E_T consists of the three major components: (a) direct component E_d, (b) forward-scattered component E_f, and (c) backscatter component E_b (nontarget reflected light). The following expression represents the total irradiance E_T:

$$E_T = E_d + E_f + E_b. \tag{7.1}$$

Here, E_T is the light received by the camera; E_d represents direct light arriving at the camera reflected through the object without being scattered; forward scatter E_f introduces when the light reflected from the object scatters in the forward direction, before arriving at the camera; and backscatter E_b occurs when the light reflected from the object directly reaches at the camera, before reaching the scene to be illuminated.

7.2.2 Underwater scattering effect

In the underwater environment, the primary factors for light scattering include the presence of several small particles and dust in the water. For a normal imaging medium, the light reflected from an object is directly received by the camera; however, the reflected light encounters several dirty particles that lead to forming the scattering effect for an underwater imaging medium.

Mainly, two types of scattering effects impact underwater imaging: (a) forward scattering and (b) backward scattering [70]. The forward scattering occurs by the divergence of light reflected from an object to the camera, leading to the blurred image outcome. In contrast, the backward scattering is introduced by the reflection of a segment of light through the tiny particles that lead to the various unpleasant effects, e.g., poor contrast and haze in the outcome image [70,46,12]. An illustration of the scattering effect in underwater imaging is depicted in Fig. 7.2.

7.3 Underwater image enhancement methods

In recent years, the underwater environment attracted the research community's great attention concerning exploring novel marine resources [58,28,19]. UI enhancement methods deal with the improvement of the visual quality of degraded underwater recorded images. UI enhancement methods acquire the detailed information of concerned images without considering much prior knowledge of the underwater environment. Hence these methods possess more generality as compared to the image restoration approaches. In the past decade, several methods have been evolved for UI processing and UI analysis; most of them are derived from the existing methods adopted for the general image processing [38,64]. These UI enhancement methods can be grouped into different classes based on

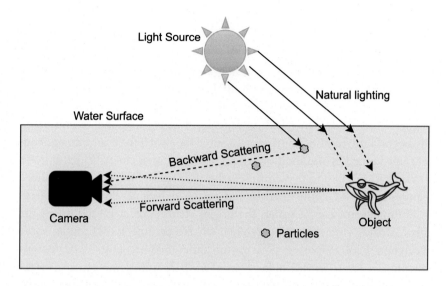

Figure 7.2 Illustration of forward and backward scattering in the underwater imaging.

the approach they apply to the degraded underwater images, e.g., contrast stretch, noise elimination, color correction, fusion-based enhancement, and deep-learning based methods.

This section reviews different UI enhancement methods based on the approach applied, i.e., supplementary information-based, nonphysical model-based, physical model-based, and data-driven (deep-learning based) methods.

7.3.1 Supplementary information and hardware-based UI enhancement methods

Supplementary information-based methods were used in the earlier stage of UI enhancement techniques. For improving the visibility of UIs, these methods depend on the auxiliary information obtained from various available images [51] or utilize some hardware-based methods (e.g., fluorescence imaging [63,50], range-gated imaging [61,43], polarization filtering [59,56,57], and stereo imaging [46]). The fluorescence imaging approach is employed to capture the coral reefs' microorganisms. Range-gated imaging is an effective approach in underwater imaging and is actively used for turbid water systems. Polarization filtering is a passive approach for image enhancement used to significantly alleviate images' noise effect and capture the images straightway. Stereo imaging employs some real-time algorithms for its system designing and is primarily used in autonomous underwater vehicles. These methods aim to estimate the coefficient of visibility for enhancing the UIs.

Under range-gated imaging, Chen and Yang [16] proposed a UI enhancement super-resolution method that uses a maximum-a-posteriori-based framework regularized through a point spread function (PSF) to detect UIs. It shows that PSF is capable of enhancing the resolution of UIs beyond the limit of hardware. To solve the problem of inhomogeneous light introduced by the additional light sources, Chen et al. [17] presented a UI restoration method that considers the ambient lights' region-specialized changes for color compensating and image dehazing. However, it faces some limitations, e.g., it makes the bright channel prior invalid under the spread shadows or the high presence of darker objects. Recently, some researchers have employed polarization difference imaging (PDI) for enhancing the UIs. For example, Tian et al. [62] utilize the Strokes vector scheme to implement a simple PDI that provides an enhanced and consistent contrast for UIs. This method appropriately works for the detection of mobile objects by incorporating polarimetry imaging. However, in some cases, it shows invalid results; thus it is needed to investigate the incorporation of PDI with a suitable contrast enhancement technology. These methods encounter some limitations under challenging conditions, such as dynamic scene problems, where single UI enhancement-based methods have proven more suitability [40].

7.3.2 Nonphysical model-based UI enhancement methods

Nonphysical model-based methods target manipulating images' spatial pixel intensity through color correction techniques to restore the visual quality of degraded UIs. Iqbal et al. [33] developed a UI enhancement method that applied different stretching, i.e., brightness and saturation into HSI space and contrast into RGB color space. It shows significant visual improvement; however, the authors did not present the same through any quantitative analysis. Ghani and Isa [24,25] extended the work of [33] and proposed a UI enhancement scheme that deals with poor contrast and noise problems in UIs by employing the Rayleigh stretching-based color correction approach. It unified a modified image histogram into RGB and HSV color models, where the blue color histogram of the RGB model was stretched to the lower gray level, whereas the red color histogram of the RGB model was stretched to the higher gray level. Finally, the image was transformed into the HSV color model. The method shows a significant contrast enhancement and blue–green effect minimization in the outcome images. Furthermore, Sankpal and Deshpande [55] proposed a separate color channel's Rayleigh stretching-based contrast improvement method that incorporates maximum–likelihood estimation for degraded UIs.

Ancuti et al. [11] developed a UI enhancement model incorporating the color-corrected and the contrast-enhanced images under a multiscale blending scheme. Recently, Fu et al. [22] proposed an image enhancement framework to address the contrast degradation and color shift problems. It is composed of two subsolutions, where the first one employs piecewise linear conversion for color correction, whereas the second one introduces an optimal contrast enhancement scheme to deal with low contrast problems. The method claims that it significantly enhances the UIs' contrast, color, and object prominence with its real-time applicability.

Many researchers focused their attention on the Retinex model too for developing the techniques for UI enhancement. Fu et al. [23] employed the Retinex model for UI enhancement. It consists of the visual quality enhancement, layer decomposition, and color correction schemes to improve the visual quality of UIs. Recently, inspired by the Retinex model, Zhang et al. [72] proposed a UI enhancement method, namely LAB-MSR. It mimics the human visual system and employs a joint (bilateral and trilateral) filter scheme on the three channels of the images under the CIELAB color space. The method shows competitive performance improvement and also eliminates the halo artifacts problem of the traditional Retinex model. However, it faces some limitations, e.g., defogging effect and contrast enhancement in the case of turbid water.

7.3.3 Physical model-based UI enhancement methods

Physical model-based methods aim to enhance the UIs by forming an image model as an inverse problem, where the model's parameters are estimated using the available degraded image. These methods first build a physical degradation model, then estimate the model's unknown parameters, and finally, utilize the estimated parameters to recover the enhanced image [40].

Under this category, many authors utilized a compelling image prior, i.e., dark channel prior (DCP), to enhance the UIs. DCP is a statistical property implied in the haze-free outdoor images, where the local patches of at least one color channel comprise some low-intensity pixels. He et al. [30] employed the DCP to design a single image haze removal model that obtains haze-free images by estimating the haze density. Chiang et al. [18] proposed a UI enhancement method that uses the DCP scheme and jointly performs image dehazing and wavelength compensation on degraded images. However, here, DCP causes some compensation errors due to the scene depth estimation. Though DCP is an intuitive approach, it encounters a standard limitation: higher absorption of the red channel inside the underwater environment. To address this problem, Drews et al. [21] presented a light propagation physical model-based method that considers some significant degradation factors, i.e., scattering, absorption, and backscattering. Additionally, it employs underwater DCP (UDCP) to enhance the visual quality of UIs. Though UDCP shows promising results, it lacks performance in terms of robustness and reliability due to the restrictions that arose from different assumptions. Furthermore, unlike existing DCP-based methods, Li et al. [42] use a random forest-based regression to estimate underwater object's devolution to enhance the visual quality. In [53], the authors proposed a UI enhancement method that employs depth-dependent color conversion for estimating the ambient light and estimates the scene transmission. Moreover, the method combines adaptive color correction with an image formation model (IFM) to alleviate the color cast.

Many researchers also exploit the underwater optical characteristics of UIs. In [15], the authors employed the idea that the attenuation in the red channel is quicker than the green and the blue channels in the underwater environment. They estimated underwater scene transmission through a prior that exploits the attenuation difference in the three channels under the RGB space. Zhao et al. [73] proposed a UI enhancement method that exploits the latent optical characteristics from the background color of underwater images. For underwater scenes, Peng et al. [54] presented a depth prediction model-based on light absorption and image blurriness and used it in the IFM to enhance the contrast and color distortion of UIs. Wang et al. [66] incorporated the underwater light dispersion properties with the nonlocal adaptive attenuation curve prior. It predicts each pixel's transmission based on the curves' distributions and estimates the attenuation factor to compensate for the transmission. Recently, Akkaynak and Treibitz [9] developed a UI color correction model that employs a revised underwater IFM physical model. The method shows significant performance improvement for the degraded UIs. Unlike [9], most of the available physical model-based methods employ the simplified IFMs that work on the assumption that water holds the attenuation coefficients characteristics only and are identical across the color channels' scene. This assumption leads to a problem of visually unpleasing and unstable results [8,9].

7.3.4 Data-driven (deep-learning-based) UI enhancement methods

In the past decade, deep-learning techniques have gained significant achievements to solve various low-level vision problems in different image processing and computer vision applications, e.g., image denoising [74] and image super-resolution [26]. These methods aim to design a convolutional neural network (CNN) or generative adversarial network (GAN) and train it through the huge amount of synthetic training pairs (i.e., low-quality images and high-quality counterpart images). However, the UI image formation models directly rely on different effects, e.g., scene, lighting conditions, turbidity, temperature. Thus it is very challenging to avail realistic UIs for training the CNNs or the GANs. Though many researchers have proposed various deep-learning-based UI enhancement methods, they are unable to match the desired performance level of other deep-learning-based low-level vision solutions [12].

Recently, Hou et al. [31] proposed a deep-learning-based UI enhancement framework that jointly performs residual learning on image and transmission domains. For investigating the distribution of UIs, it estimates transmission maps by aggregating prior knowledge. The method claims that it effectively enhances the contrast and removes the haze effect of degraded UIs. In [44], the authors proposed a GAN-based underwater scene enhancement method, namely WaterGAN. For realistic UIs, WaterGAN simulates the underwater scenes from depth pairings and in-air images in an unsupervised scheme. Using the generated data, the authors trained a two-stage network that restores the UIs and addresses the color cast problem. Inspired by cycle-consistent GANs [74], Li et al. [41] presented a weakly supervised model to improve the color distributions. For network training, the model does not require paired UIs; instead, it provides the flexibility to utilize the UIs collected from unknown locations. Though the model is highly flexible, it suffers from inconsistent results due to several possible outcomes for some cases. Furthermore, Guo et al. [27] developed a multiscale dense GAN for UI restoration that combines the nonsaturated GAN loss with gradient loss and l_1 loss for learning the distribution of realistic images in the future domain. However, this method also suffers from the problem of multiple possible results in GANs. More recently, Li et al. [39] proposed a scene prior-based CNN model for UI enhancement named UWCNN. It exploits the underwater scene prior for synthesizing the UI training data and trains the lightweight CNN model to enhance UIs. Though researchers are continuously working on deep-learning-based UI enhancement techniques, it is still challenging to meet conventional state-of-the-art methods' performance.

Concluding remarks: The supplementary information-based methods [16,17] improve the visual quality by utilizing the auxiliary details obtained from multiple images. Though the performance of these methods is acceptable under favorable conditions (e.g., a proper combination of color and contrast, static objects), they encounter low performance problem under undesirable conditions (e.g., dynamic scene problems). The nonphysical model-based methods aim to enhance the visual quality of UIs by incorporating color correction techniques. These methods [72,55] have shown significant visual improvement (e.g., enhancement of contrast, color, object prominence, and noise effect) to the degraded UIs. However, in some cases, like turbid water, it seems challenging for these methods to address the low-contrast and defogging effects. The physical model-based methods aim to design an image degradation model and estimate its unknown parameters. For doing so, they consider several degradation factors. Though these methods [54,66] show significant improvement in the visual quality of degraded UIs, they encounter unstable and unpleasing results due to the various assumptions taken in their image formation model. The deep-learning-based methods have shown promising performance in addressing several low-level vision problems, e.g., image denoising and image super-resolution. However, due to the lack of appropriate real-world underwater images' training datasets, their performance still lags behind the conventional UI enhancement techniques.

7.4 Underwater image datasets

Investigation of UI datasets is an essential concern as they play a vital role in the evolution of UI enhancement techniques. This section summarizes artificial and real-world UI datasets utilized by the researchers for UI enhancement and restoration methods in the past decade, as presented in Table 7.1. Few sample images of these UI datasets are shown in Fig. 7.3. However, these datasets encounter several challenges, e.g., limited scenes, single target object, lesser degradation parameters, few categories, and insufficient labeling data. Moreover, due to the diverse water and lighting conditions, it is challenging to simultaneously capture the underwater image and its corresponding ground-truth image of an identical scene. These problems create multiple barriers in developing a desirable, intelligent UI processing mechanism for addressing the concerned real-world issues.

Table 7.1 Underwater image datasets crawled between years 2010–2020.

Dataset	Year	# Images	Objects	Annotations	Resolution	Origin
Fish4Knowledge [14]	2010	27370 images segregated into 23 clusters	Marine ecosystem and creatures	No	Variable	The Fish4Knowledge team
Wild Fish Marker dataset [20]	2015	1934 in positive image set, 3167 in negative image set, and 2061 fish images	Fishes and other species near the sea level	Yes	Variable	NOAA Fisheries
Port Royal UI Database [44]	2015	18091	Artificial and natural structures' components	No	1360 × 1024	Real scientific surveys in Port Royal
OUCVISION UI dataset [36]	2017	4400	Artificial structures and rocks	Yes	2592 × 1944	Ocean Univ. of China
Underwater Rock Image Database [44]	2018	15057	Rocks structures	No	1360 × 1024	Univ. of Michigan
RGBD UI dataset [9,13]	2018	1100	Waterproof color charts	No	1369 × 914	Tel Aviv Univ.
HabCam UI dataset [4,2,3]	2019	10465	Rocks, sand dollars, scollop, and fishes	Yes	2720 × 1024	Integrated and provided by CVPR AAMVEM Workshop

continued on next page

Table 7.1 (*continued*)

Dataset	Year	# Images	Objects	Annotations	Resolution	Origin
AFSC UI dataset [2,3]	2019	571	Fishes and other creatures	Yes	2112 × 2816	Integrated and provided by CVPR AAMVEM Workshop
MOUSS UI dataset [2,3]	2019	159	Fishes	Yes	968 × 728	Integrated and provided by CVPR AAMVEM Workshop
NWFSC UI dataset [2,3]	2019	123	Fishes and other species near the sea level	Yes	2448 × 2050	Integrated and provided by CVPR AAMVEM Workshop
MBARI underwater image dataset [2,3,6]	2019	666	Fishes	Yes	1920 × 1080	Monterey Bay Aquarium Research Institute
RUIE dataset [45,1]	2019	Nearly 4000	Sea cucumbers, Scollop, and sea urchins	Partially	400 × 300	Dalian Univ. of Technology
UI Enhancement Benchmark (UIEB) [40]	2019	950	Diverse species	Partially	Variable	Li et al. "An UI enhancement benchmark dataset and beyond"
EUVP UI dataset [34,5]	2020	12000 paired and 8000 unpaired	Separate sets of paired and unpaired image samples	No	Variable	University of Minnesota

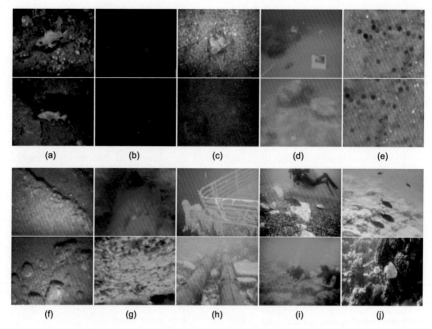

Figure 7.3 Sample images from different underwater image datasets [70,40]: (a) Wild fish marker, (b) Port Royal, (c) OUCVISION, (d) RGBD, (e) HabCam, (f) NWFSC, (g) RUIE, and (h)–(j) UIEB.

7.5 Underwater image quality assessment

The image quality assessment (IQA) of enhanced/restored images of the corresponding degraded underwater images plays a significant role in designing an accurate UI enhancement system [69]. In literature, various IQA metrics have been employed to evaluate the quality of images automatically and accurately. These IQA approaches are categorized into two groups: (a) objective IQA and (b) subjective IQA [49]. As the subjective IQA methods are pretty time-consuming and costly, they are less preferable in real-time applications. Objective IQA methods are widely adopted as they employ several statistical models based on the human visual system (HVS) to estimate the image quality automatically. Based on the availability of reference images, objective IQAs are further classified into two classes: (a) full-reference (FR) IQA and (b) nonreference (NR) IQA. As the name suggests, FR approaches are utilized when a reference image is available, whereas NR approaches are considered when the reference image is unavailable. Generally, the automatic IQAs are carried out using the widely adopted metrics, i.e., mean square error (MSE), peak signal-to-noise ratio (PSNR), structure similarity index measure (SSIM) [67], and patch-based contrast quality index (PCQI) [65]. In addition, two IQAs, i.e., UCIQE [71] and UIQM [52], are widely used to evaluate the quality of images in UI enhancement techniques. A detailed description of all the mentioned IQAs is given in what follows; their reliability and limitations are also presented.

- *Mean square error (MSE):* MSE provides the cumulative squared error between a given original image and an estimated recovered image. Mathematically, MSE is expressed as

$$MSE = \frac{1}{MN} \sum_{i=1}^{M} \sum_{j=1}^{N} \left\{ O(i,j) - E(i,j) \right\}. \tag{7.2}$$

Here, $M \times N$ is the image size and $O(i,j)$ and $E(i,j)$ represent the original and estimated images' pixels at $(i,j)^{th}$ location, respectively.

- *Peak signal-to-noise ratio (PSNR):* It is the ratio between highest intensity value in the image and the MSE. PSNR is expressed as

$$PSNR = 20\log_{10} \frac{I_{max}^2}{MSE}. \tag{7.3}$$

Here, I_{max} is the maximum pixel intensity in the image, i.e., 255 for gray level image.

MSE and PSNR are widely adopted IQAs due to their several usage advantages, e.g., simple computation, explicit physical meaning; all norms are good distance metrics, and both are feasible in the context of optimization.

The abovementioned IQAs presume that the signal fidelity do not rely on the relationship among (i) actual signal, (ii) signs of the erroneous signal, and (iii) corrupted and actual signal. However, none of them even roughly holds in the context of measuring the visual perception of image fidelity.

- *Structure similarity index measure (SSIM) [68]:* SSIM is another most widely used IQA metric that aims to provide the similarity between two image patches. SSIM is composed of three primary components, i.e., luminance, contrast, and local structure. Mathematically, it is given as

$$SSIM = l(x, y) \cdot c(x, y) \cdot s(x, y). \tag{7.4}$$

Here, $l(x, y)$, $c(x, y)$, and $s(x, y)$ are defined as

$$l(x, y) = \left\{ \frac{2\mu_x\mu_y + C_1}{\mu_x^2 + \mu_y^2 + C_1} \right\}, \quad c(x, y) = \left\{ \frac{2\sigma_x\sigma_y + C_2}{\sigma_x^2 + \sigma_y^2 + C_2} \right\}, \quad \text{and}$$

$$s(x, y) = \left\{ \frac{\sigma_{xy} + C_3}{\sigma_x + \sigma_y + C_3} \right\}. \tag{7.5}$$

Here, μ_x and μ_y denote the mean values, whereas σ_x and σ_y represent the standard deviation of image patches x and y, respectively. σ_{xy} is the covariance between x and y. The constants C_1, C_2, and C_3 are used to avoid near-zero divisions and ensure the stability for image regions, where the local standard deviation or mean is near to zero. Hence small nonnegative values should be assigned to these constants. The default values of these constants are used as $C_1 = (0.01 * L)^2$, $C_2 = (0.03 * L)^2$, and $C_3 = C_2/2$, where L is the dynamic range of the input image.

- *Patch-based contrast quality index (PCQI) [65]:* PCQI aims to compute the similarity between original image patch and estimated image patch. For doing so, it takes three independent measures of an image patch into account, i.e., signal strength, mean, and local structure. Mathematically, PCQI is expressed as

$$PCQI = p_i(x, y) \cdot p_c(x, y) \cdot p_s(x, y). \tag{7.6}$$

Here, $p_i(\cdot)$, $p_c(\cdot)$, and $p_s(\cdot)$ represent the comparison of mean intensity, contrast change, and structural distortion, respectively (refer to [65] for the detailed description and formulation of $p_i(x, y)$, $p_c(x, y)$, and $p_s(x, y)$). Compared to other IQAs, PCQI is computationally more expensive.

Next, two more IQAs are discussed that are specifically developed for UI enhancement methods.

- *Underwater color image quality evaluation (UCIQE) [71]:* UCIQE was specially developed to measure the effect of contrast, chroma, and saturation that affect underwater images. For an image in CIELab space, UCIQE is defined as

$$UCIQE = C_1 \times \sigma_{chr} + C_2 \times \sigma_{con_l} + C_3 \times \sigma_{\mu_{sat}}. \tag{7.7}$$

Here, σ_{chr}, σ_{con_l}, and $\sigma_{\mu_{sat}}$ denote the standard deviation of chroma, the contrast of luminance, and the mean of saturation, respectively (refer to [29] for the detailed description and formulation of σ_{chr}, σ_{con_l}, and $\sigma_{\mu_{sat}}$).

C_1, C_2, and C_3 are the weighted coefficients. It should be noted that variance of chroma shows higher correlation with the human perception.

- *Underwater image quality measure (UIQM) [52]:* UIQM employs the human visual system (HVS) model, only without the requirement of any reference image. It is composed of three primary measures of UI: (i) UI colorfulness measure (UICM), (ii) UI sharpness measure (UISM), and (iii) UI contrast measure (UIConM). Mathematically, UIQM is expressed as

$$UIQM = w_1 \times UICM + w_2 \times UISM + w_3 \times UIConM. \qquad (7.8)$$

Here, w_1, w_2, and w_3 are the three coefficients that should be chosen based on the application, e.g., higher weight to be assigned to w_1 for color correction in UI, whereas w_2 and w_3 are more significant to enhance the visibility of the UI scene. Panetta et al. [52] empirically fixed these coefficients values as $w_1 = 0.0282$, $w_2 = 0.2953$, and $w_3 = 0.0339$ in their work. For the detailed description and formulation of $UICM$, $UISM$, and $UIConM$, one can refer to [52].

7.6 Challenges and future recommendations

The primary aim of this chapter is to provide a summary of the state-of-the-art UI enhancement methods, identify the significant challenges encountered in underwater scene enhancement, and then draw some ideas and recommendations for the potential future directions. Some open issues, challenges, and possible future research recommendations are listed below that can be considered before developing novel UI enhancement methodologies.

- Variable and random illumination conditions of the underwater environment, poor contrast of objects, and complex blurred seabed scenes jointly lead to blurry images with unrealistic color details. For such circumstances, it is very challenging to enhance the degraded images for object and scene recognition.
- In the underwater environment, light scattering, light absorption, and refraction are the primary factors that impact the visual quality of UIs. Additionally, the underwater turbidity effect is also a significant issue for degrading the images' quality. The existing UI enhancement models have considered only a single degradation factor; however, it will

be more beneficial to incorporate multiple degradation factors, while building a UI enhancement model.

- Presently, the deep-learning-based UI enhancement techniques are in the emerging stage, and there is a great scope to improve their performance over the conventional state-of-the-art methods. The existing UI databases for deep-learning techniques are not adequate to achieve the desired performance. Therefore creating a large UI dataset with labeled and realistic images will be highly advantageous in improving the performance of such learning models.

- In deep-learning-based approaches, to address the limited data problem, a potential direction could be the development of specific unsupervised learning mechanisms that may improve the performance of deep-learning-based UI enhancement algorithms.

- The existing methods primarily utilize the objective functions commonly used in conventional image enhancement methods. Though these functions obtain desirable outcomes in some specific cases, they encounter restricted performance due to the absence of underwater physical models' characteristics. Therefore more suitable objective functions are needed to empower the research of UIs enhancement.

- The prior knowledge is highly beneficial to improve the performance of low-level vision imaging. As humans also use their domain knowledge to precept any unknown environmental scene, it could be more beneficial to enhance the performance of UI enhancement methods by incorporating prior auxiliary knowledge, e.g., attribute guidance and annotations.

- The existing UI enhancement quality assessment measures, i.e., UCIQE and UIQM, primarily depend upon the human visual perception that may lead to inconsistent results in some cases. Therefore, in the future, one can work on developing more consistent and effective measures for assessing the enhancement quality of UIs.

7.7 Conclusion

This chapter presents the mathematical formulation of the UI model and underwater scattering effect, a brief review of recent state-of-the-art UI enhancement methods, and widely used benchmark datasets and performance measures for evaluating these methods' performances. It describes the existing UI enhancement methods under four categories, i.e., supplementary information-based, nonphysical model-based, physical model-based, and data-driven (deep-learning-based) methods and also summarizes common limitations associated with these categories. The major findings of this chapter are summarized as follows:

- The UIs are degraded with multiple degradation factors, e.g., low-contrast, illumination variations, light scattering, noise, turbidity, simultaneously; however, the existing UI enhancement methods consider single or few degradation factors.
- The lack of suitable real-world UI images' datasets to train the deep-learning-based UI enhancement methods restricts their generalization and robustness concerning to the conventional state-of-the-art UI enhancement methods.
- Both the UI evaluation measures, UCIQE and UIQM, depend on the human visual perception, which could not ensure the consistent performance as humans have not evolved to see in aquatic habitats. Therefore these measures may fail to obtain appropriate results under some specific cases.

Finally, we analyze the significant challenges that impact the performance of existing UI enhancement methods, and then furnish some potential future directions for the design and development of the UI enhancement methods.

References

[1] [Online]. Available: https://github.com/dlut-dimt/Realworld-Underwater-Image-Enhancement-RUIE-Benchmark.

[2] CVPR 2018 Workshop and Challenge (AAMVEM), [Online]. Available: http://www.viametoolkit.org/.

[3] CVPR 2019 Workshop and Challenge (AAMVEM), [Online]. Available: https://sites.google.com/view/aamvem/data-challenge.

[4] HabCam: Habitat Mapping Camera System, [Online]. Available: https://habcam.whoi.edu/.

[5] IRVLAB: Interactive Robotics and Vision Lab, [Online]. Available: http://irvlab.cs.umn.edu/resources/euvp-dataset.

[6] MBARI: Monterey Bay Aquarium Research Institute, [Online]. Available: https://www.mbari.org.

[7] J. Ahn, S. Yasukawa, T. Sonoda, T. Ura, K. Ishii, Enhancement of deep-sea floor images obtained by an underwater vehicle and its evaluation by crab recognition, Journal of Marine Science and Technology 22 (4) (2017) 758–770.

[8] D. Akkaynak, T. Treibitz, A revised underwater image formation model, in: Proceedings of the IEEE Conference on Computer Vision and Pattern Recognition, 2018, pp. 6723–6732.

[9] D. Akkaynak, T. Treibitz, Sea-Thru: A method for removing water from underwater images, in: 2019 IEEE/CVF Conference on Computer Vision and Pattern Recognition (CVPR), 2019, pp. 1682–1691.

[10] D. Akkaynak, T. Treibitz, T. Shlesinger, Y. Loya, R. Tamir, D. Iluz, What is the space of attenuation coefficients in underwater computer vision?, in: Proceedings of the IEEE Conference on Computer Vision and Pattern Recognition, 2017, pp. 4931–4940.

[11] C. Ancuti, C.O. Ancuti, T. Haber, P. Bekaert, Enhancing underwater images and videos by fusion, in: 2012 IEEE Conference on Computer Vision and Pattern Recognition, IEEE, 2012, pp. 81–88.

[12] S. Anwar, C. Li, Diving deeper into underwater image enhancement: A survey, Signal Processing: Image Communication 89 (2020) 115978, [Online]. Available: https://www.sciencedirect.com/science/article/pii/S0923596520301478.

[13] D. Berman, D. Levy, S. Avidan, T. Treibitz, Underwater single image color restoration using haze-lines and a new quantitative dataset, IEEE Transactions on Pattern Analysis and Machine Intelligence 43 (08) (Aug 2021) 2822–2837.

[14] B.J. Boom, J. He, S. Palazzo, P.X. Huang, C. Beyan, H.-M. Chou, F.-P. Lin, C. Spampinato, R.B. Fisher, A research tool for long-term and continuous analysis of fish assemblage in coral-reefs using underwater camera footage, Ecological Informatics 23 (2014) 83–97.

[15] N. Carlevaris-Bianco, A. Mohan, R.M. Eustice, Initial results in underwater single image dehazing, in: Oceans 2010 Mts/IEEE Seattle, IEEE, 2010, pp. 1–8.

[16] Y. Chen, K. Yang, Map-regularized robust reconstruction for underwater imaging detection, Optik 124 (20) (2013) 4514–4518.

[17] Z. Chen, H. Wang, J. Shen, X. Li, L. Xu, Region-specialized underwater image restoration in inhomogeneous optical environments, Optik 125 (9) (2014) 2090–2098.

[18] J.Y. Chiang, Y.-C. Chen, Underwater image enhancement by wavelength compensation and dehazing, IEEE Transactions on Image Processing 21 (4) (2012) 1756–1769.

[19] R. Cui, L. Chen, C. Yang, M. Chen, Extended state observer-based integral sliding mode control for an underwater robot with unknown disturbances and uncertain nonlinearities, IEEE Transactions on Industrial Electronics 64 (8) (2017) 6785–6795.

[20] G. Cutter, K. Stierhoff, J. Zeng, Automated detection of rockfish in unconstrained underwater videos using Haar cascades and a new image dataset: labeled fishes in the wild, in: 2015 IEEE Winter Applications and Computer Vision Workshops, IEEE, 2015, pp. 57–62.

[21] P.L. Drews, E.R. Nascimento, S.S. Botelho, M.F. Montenegro Campos, Underwater depth estimation and image restoration based on single images, IEEE Computer Graphics and Applications 36 (2) (2016) 24–35.

[22] X. Fu, Z. Fan, M. Ling, Y. Huang, X. Ding, Two-step approach for single underwater image enhancement, in: 2017 International Symposium on Intelligent Signal Processing and Communication Systems (ISPACS), IEEE, 2017, pp. 789–794.

[23] X. Fu, P. Zhuang, Y. Huang, Y. Liao, X.-P. Zhang, X. Ding, A retinex-based enhancing approach for single underwater image, in: 2014 IEEE International Conference on Image Processing (ICIP), IEEE, 2014, pp. 4572–4576.

[24] A.S.A. Ghani, N.A.M. Isa, Underwater image quality enhancement through composition of dual-intensity images and Rayleigh-stretching, SpringerPlus 3 (1) (2014) 1–14.

[25] A.S.A. Ghani, N.A.M. Isa, Underwater image quality enhancement through integrated color model with Rayleigh distribution, Applied Soft Computing 27 (2015) 219–230.

[26] C. Guo, C. Li, J. Guo, R. Cong, H. Fu, P. Han, Hierarchical features driven residual learning for depth map super-resolution, IEEE Transactions on Image Processing 28 (5) (2018) 2545–2557.

[27] Y. Guo, H. Li, P. Zhuang, Underwater image enhancement using a multiscale dense generative adversarial network, IEEE Journal of Oceanic Engineering 45 (3) (2019) 862–870.

[28] M. Han, Z. Lyu, T. Qiu, M. Xu, A review on intelligence dehazing and color restoration for underwater images, IEEE Transactions on Systems, Man, and Cybernetics: Systems 50 (5) (2020) 1820–1832.

[29] D. Hasler, S.E. Suesstrunk, Measuring colorfulness in natural images, in: Human Vision and Electronic Imaging VIII, vol. 5007, International Society for Optics and Photonics, 2003, pp. 87–95.

[30] K. He, J. Sun, X. Tang, Single image haze removal using dark channel prior, IEEE Transactions on Pattern Analysis and Machine Intelligence 33 (12) (2011) 2341–2353.

[31] M. Hou, R. Liu, X. Fan, Z. Luo, Joint residual learning for underwater image enhancement, in: 2018 25th IEEE International Conference on Image Processing (ICIP), IEEE, 2018, pp. 4043–4047.

[32] W. Hou, S. Woods, E. Jarosz, W. Goode, A. Weidemann, Optical turbulence on underwater image degradation in natural environments, Applied Optics 51 (14) (2012) 2678–2686.

[33] K. Iqbal, R.A. Salam, A. Osman, A.Z. Talib, Underwater image enhancement using an integrated colour model, IAENG International Journal of Computer Science 34 (2) (2007).

[34] M.J. Islam, Y. Xia, J. Sattar, Fast underwater image enhancement for improved visual perception, IEEE Robotics and Automation Letters 5 (2) (2020) 3227–3234.

[35] J. Jaffe, Computer modeling and the design of optimal underwater imaging systems, IEEE Journal of Oceanic Engineering 15 (2) (1990) 101–111.

[36] M. Jian, Q. Qi, J. Dong, Y. Yin, W. Zhang, K.-M. Lam, The OUC-vision large-scale underwater image database, in: 2017 IEEE International Conference on Multimedia and Expo (ICME), 2017, pp. 1297–1302.

[37] G. Johnsen, M. Ludvigsen, A. Sørensen, L.M. Sandvik Aas, The use of underwater hyperspectral imaging deployed on remotely operated vehicles - methods and applications, in: 10th IFAC Conference on Control Applications in Marine Systems (CAMS 2016), IFAC-PapersOnLine 49 (23) (2016) 476–481, [Online]. Available: https://www.sciencedirect.com/science/article/pii/S2405896316320390.

[38] R. Kumar Rai, P. Gour, B. Singh, Underwater image segmentation using CLAHE enhancement and thresholding, International Journal of Emerging Technology and Advanced Engineering 2 (1) (2012) 118–123.

[39] C. Li, S. Anwar, F. Porikli, Underwater scene prior inspired deep underwater image and video enhancement, Pattern Recognition 98 (2020) 107038.

[40] C. Li, C. Guo, W. Ren, R. Cong, J. Hou, S. Kwong, D. Tao, An underwater image enhancement benchmark dataset and beyond, IEEE Transactions on Image Processing 29 (2019) 4376–4389.

[41] C. Li, J. Guo, C. Guo, Emerging from water: Underwater image color correction based on weakly supervised color transfer, IEEE Signal Processing Letters 25 (3) (2018) 323–327.

[42] C. Li, J. Guo, C. Guo, R. Cong, J. Gong, A hybrid method for underwater image correction, Pattern Recognition Letters 94 (2017) 62–67.

[43] H. Li, X. Wang, T. Bai, W. Jin, Y. Huang, K. Ding, Speckle noise suppression of range gated underwater imaging system, in: Applications of Digital Image Processing XXXII, vol. 7443, International Society for Optics and Photonics, 2009, p. 74432A.

[44] J. Li, K.A. Skinner, R.M. Eustice, M. Johnson-Roberson, WaterGAN: Unsupervised generative network to enable real-time color correction of monocular underwater images, IEEE Robotics and Automation Letters 3 (1) (2018) 387–394.

[45] R. Liu, X. Fan, M. Zhu, M. Hou, Z. Luo, Real-world underwater enhancement: challenges, benchmarks, and solutions, arXiv preprint, arXiv:1901.05320, 2019.

[46] H. Lu, Y. Li, Y. Zhang, M. Chen, S. Serikawa, H. Kim, Underwater optical image processing: a comprehensive review, Mobile Networks and Applications 22 (6) (2017) 1204–1211, https://doi.org/10.1007/s11036-017-0863-4.

[47] M. Ludvigsen, B. Sortland, G. Johnsen, H. Singh, Applications of geo-referenced underwater photo mosaics in marine biology and archaeology, Oceanography 20 (4) (2007) 140–149.

[48] B.L. McGlamery, A computer model for underwater camera systems, in: S.Q. Duntley (Ed.), Ocean Optics VI, vol. 0208, International Society for Optics and Photonics, SPIE, 1980, pp. 221–231, [Online]. Available: https://doi.org/10.1117/12.958279.

[49] P. Mohammadi, A. Ebrahimi-Moghadam, S. Shirani, Subjective and objective quality assessment of image: A survey, Majlesi Journal of Electrical Engineering 9 (1) (Dec. 2014) 55–83, [Online]. Available: http://mjee.iaumajlesi.ac.ir/index/index.php/ee/article/view/1376.

[50] Z. Murez, T. Treibitz, R. Ramamoorthi, D. Kriegman, Photometric stereo in a scattering medium, in: Proceedings of the IEEE International Conference on Computer Vision, 2015, pp. 3415–3423.

[51] S.G. Narasimhan, S.K. Nayar, Contrast restoration of weather degraded images, IEEE Transactions on Pattern Analysis and Machine Intelligence 25 (6) (2003) 713–724.

[52] K. Panetta, C. Gao, S. Agaian, Human-visual-system-inspired underwater image quality measures, IEEE Journal of Oceanic Engineering 41 (3) (2016) 541–551.

[53] Y.-T. Peng, K. Cao, P.C. Cosman, Generalization of the dark channel prior for single image restoration, IEEE Transactions on Image Processing 27 (6) (2018) 2856–2868.

[54] Y.-T. Peng, P.C. Cosman, Underwater image restoration based on image blurriness and light absorption, IEEE Transactions on Image Processing 26 (4) (2017) 1579–1594.

[55] S. Sankpal, S. Deshpande, Underwater image enhancement by Rayleigh stretching with adaptive scale parameter and energy correction, in: Computing, Communication and Signal Processing, Springer, 2019, pp. 935–947.

[56] Y.Y. Schechner, N. Karpel, Clear underwater vision, in: Proceedings of the 2004 IEEE Computer Society Conference on Computer Vision and Pattern Recognition, 2004, CVPR 2004, vol. 1, IEEE, 2004, pp. I–I.

[57] Y.Y. Schechner, N. Karpel, Recovery of underwater visibility and structure by polarization analysis, IEEE Journal of Oceanic Engineering 30 (3) (2005) 570–587.

[58] R. Schettini, S. Corchs, Underwater image processing: State of the art of restoration and image enhancement methods, EURASIP Journal on Advances in Signal Processing 2010 (1) (2010) 746052, https://doi.org/10.1155/2010/746052.

[59] N. Shashar, R.T. Hanlon, A.d. Petz, Polarization vision helps detect transparent prey, Nature 393 (6682) (1998) 222–223.

[60] N. Strachan, Recognition of fish species by colour and shape, Image and Vision Computing 11 (1) (1993) 2–10, [Online]. Available: https://www.sciencedirect.com/science/article/pii/026288569390027E.

[61] C. Tan, G. Seet, A. Sluzek, D. He, A novel application of range-gated underwater laser imaging system (ULIS) in near-target turbid medium, Optics and Lasers in Engineering 43 (9) (2005) 995–1009.

[62] H. Tian, J. Zhu, S. Tan, Y. Zhang, Y. Zhang, Y. Li, X. Hou, Rapid underwater target enhancement method based on polarimetric imaging, Optics and Laser Technology 108 (2018) 515–520.

[63] T. Treibitz, Y.Y. Schechner, Turbid scene enhancement using multi-directional illumination fusion, IEEE Transactions on Image Processing 21 (11) (2012) 4662–4667.

[64] S. Vasamsetti, N. Mittal, B.C. Neelapu, H.K. Sardana, Wavelet based perspective on variational enhancement technique for underwater imagery, Ocean Engineering 141 (2017) 88–100, [Online]. Available: https://www.sciencedirect.com/science/article/pii/S0029801817303074.

[65] S. Wang, K. Ma, H. Yeganeh, Z. Wang, W. Lin, A patch-structure representation method for quality assessment of contrast changed images, IEEE Signal Processing Letters 22 (12) (2015) 2387–2390.

[66] Y. Wang, H. Liu, L.-P. Chau, Single underwater image restoration using adaptive attenuation-curve prior, IEEE Transactions on Circuits and Systems I: Regular Papers 65 (3) (2017) 992–1002.

[67] Z. Wang, E. Simoncelli, A. Bovik, Multiscale structural similarity for image quality assessment, in: The Thirty-Seventh Asilomar Conference on Signals, Systems Computers, 2003, vol. 2, 2003, pp. 1398–1402.

[68] Z. Wang, A. Bovik, H. Sheikh, E. Simoncelli, Image quality assessment: from error visibility to structural similarity, IEEE Transactions on Image Processing 13 (4) (2004) 600–612.

[69] Q. Xu, Q. Huang, Y. Yao, Online crowdsourcing subjective image quality assessment, in: Proceedings of the 20th ACM International Conference on Multimedia, 2012, pp. 359–368.

[70] M. Yang, J. Hu, C. Li, G. Rohde, Y. Du, K. Hu, An in-depth survey of underwater image enhancement and restoration, IEEE Access 7 (2019) 123638–123657.

[71] M. Yang, A. Sowmya, An underwater color image quality evaluation metric, IEEE Transactions on Image Processing 24 (12) (2015) 6062–6071.

[72] S. Zhang, T. Wang, J. Dong, H. Yu, Underwater image enhancement via extended multi-scale retinex, Neurocomputing 245 (2017) 1–9.

[73] X. Zhao, T. Jin, S. Qu, Deriving inherent optical properties from background color and underwater image enhancement, Ocean Engineering 94 (2015) 163–172.

[74] J.-Y. Zhu, T. Park, P. Isola, A.A. Efros, Unpaired image-to-image translation using cycle-consistent adversarial networks, in: Proceedings of the IEEE International Conference on Computer Vision, 2017, pp. 2223–2232.

CHAPTER 8

A comparative analysis of image restoration techniques

Srishty Dwivedi, Ram Narayan Yadav, and Lalita Gupta
Maulana Azad National Institute of Technology, Bhopal, India

8.1 Introduction

An image consists of many information and facts, but due to imperfection during capturing and recording, the image's quality degrades and minimizes the content of knowledge present in it [1,2]. This gives rise to the concept of image restoration. The method of restoration enhances the image's quality. The two significant sources of degradation are noise and blur. As a result, the primary goal of this procedure is to return the detected image to its original state. This process finds application in many areas, such as security and surveillance [3], medical imaging [4,5], remote sensing [6,7], digital media restoration, law enforcement, modular spectroscopy, etc. Each point of the original moment is spread throughout numerous points of the picture and blended during the capture of the image; as a result of this propagation, the image gets blurred. Therefore, the image restoration works to model the function of noise and blur, and then implements the denoise and deblurred model to the inverse model. So, to reconstruct the image, two types of models can be employed. These are (a) the degradation model and (b) the restoration model.

The mathematical model of the degraded image $g(x, y)$ is represented by

$$g(x, y) = f(x, y) * h(x, y) + n(x, y) \qquad (8.1)$$

where $h(x, y)$ represents a point spread function that degrades the original image $f(x, y)$, and then the noise is added, which is characterized by $n(x, y)$. The problem of restoring f from g is referred to as linear image restoration. $h(x, y)$ should follow specific properties:

a) Linearity,
b) Space invariance.

Image restoration and enhancement [8] are entirely different processes since restoration is more rational and practical, whereas it is more subjective for

Digital Image Enhancement and Reconstruction
https://doi.org/10.1016/B978-0-32-398370-9.00015-9

image enhancement. The mathematical function does not accurately reflect image enhancement, whereas image restoration is related to removing features from the imperfect image. The degraded image is interfered with by enhancement, the image contrast is increased, and the visual quality can be improved.

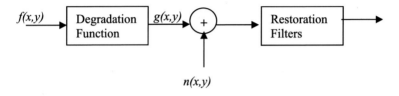

Figure 8.1 Image degradation and restoration model [9].

Fig. 8.1 represents a degradation and restoration model for the image. The blur function H is convolved with the actual picture $f(x, y)$. Then additional noise $n(x, y)$ is added as result the function is degraded $g(x, y)$; after that by applying some restoration technique the desired image will be obtained. The restoration method can be classified as supervised and unsupervised/blind methods

8.2 Reasons for degradation in image

There are many reasons for an image to degrade. Such include camera motion of relative objects, sudden atmospheric turbulence, poor camera focus, etc. Transmission of image and image acquisition are the two main situations where the image degrades [3].

8.2.1 Blurring model

Blurring is a type of bandwidth reduction caused by an inaccurate picture creation method [9]. An imperfect image generation process causes blurring, which is a sort of bandwidth reduction. It is caused by the camera's and the target's relative motion or an optical feature that is focused on when the image is taken. Sometimes photographer intentionally tries to blur the image for its effectiveness, but unintentional blur will reduce the clarity of the picture. The image gets blurred due to many kinds of blur. Fig. 8.2 shows the types of blur models that are typically used in literature.

- Gaussian blur: A Gaussian blur filter combines a set pixel count sequentially according to a bell-shaped curve. The blurring is thicker in the middle and gradually fades outward.

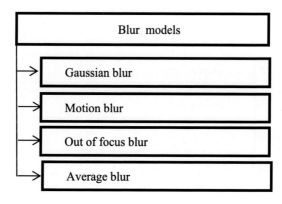

Figure 8.2 Types of blur models.

- Motion blur: The relative motion between the object and camera image gets blurred while capturing an image. This type of blurring is called motion blur.
- Out of focus blur: In the real scenario when the camera captures a 3D image to a 2D image, some parts of the scene get out of focus. This type of blurring is called out-of-focus blur.
- Average blur: Average blurring can be spread horizontally and vertically. It can be calculated by finding radius R, which is given by

$$R = \sqrt{g^2 + f^2} \tag{8.2}$$

8.2.2 Noise model

It is an unwanted effect that hides the essential details. Images get noisy during image acquisition and transmission. As shown in Fig. 8.3, different types of noises that are present in images are discussed below [10,11,91]:

- Gaussian noise: Gaussian noise [12] can occur in images during the acquisition. A spatial filter can be used to minimize the Gaussian noise. However, this filter can produce undesirable results, because it blurs fine-scaled edges and information due to its high-frequency blockage power.
- Periodic noise: Periodic noise occurs in the image because of electromechanical or electrical interference.
- Uniform noise: The pixels of the detected image were quantized into many distinct ranges during uniform noise. It is also known as quantization noise.

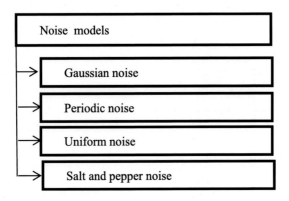

Figure 8.3 Types of the noise model.

- Salt and pepper noise: Another name for this noise is impulsive noise [13]. It causes bright pixels to appear randomly in dark areas and dark pixels to appear randomly in bright areas in an image.

8.3 Image restoration techniques

8.3.1 Direct inverse filtering

Direct inverse filtering is the simplest method of image restoration can be defined as in Eq. (8.3):

$$\hat{f}(u, v) = \frac{G(u, v)}{H(u, v)} \tag{8.3}$$

where $G(u, v)$ is the Fourier transform of the degraded image, and $H(u, v)$ is the Fourier transform of the degradation function [14]. The main advantage of this filtering is that only the point spread function is required as a priori knowledge. This approach is usually used where no additive noise is present in the degraded image signal. That's where we can describe the image in the following format:

$$g(x, y) = f(x, y) * h(x, y) \tag{8.4}$$

If we add noise to a damaged image, then this filtering results in very bad performance.

$$\hat{F}(u, v) = F(u, v) + N(u, v)H(u, v) \tag{8.5}$$

From Eqs. (8.4) and (8.5), it is clear that this method fails in the presence of additive noise. Because the noise is random, it is difficult to find noise spectrum $N(u, v)$.

8.3.2 Wiener filter algorithm

Wiener filter [14–16] is a typical approach to image restoration suggested by N. Wiener in 1942, which combines all degradation functions and statistical characteristics of noise. It is not a blind restoration of the image; that is why the reference picture and point spread function needed to be restored. It eliminates additive noise and also inverts the blur as discussed in Algorithm 8.1. The formula of this filter is represented by Eq. (8.6):

$$F(u, v) = \left[\frac{1}{H(u, v)} \times \frac{|H(u, v)|^2}{[H(u, v)]^2 + S_\eta(u, v)/S_f(u, v)} \right] \qquad (8.6)$$

where, $[H(u, v)]^2$ = complex conjugate of $H(u, v)$, $H(u, v)$ = degradation function, the power spectrum of noise is denoted by S_η, and the power spectrum of the original image is denoted by S_f.

1: Find out the degradation function and, accordingly, get its Fourier transform $H(u, v)$.
2: Calculate $G(u, v)$
3: Apply Wiener filtering and find $F(u, v)$.
4: At last, find out the Fourier transform of $\hat{F}(u, v)$ to get the restored image

---

Algorithm 8.1: Wiener filtering [17].

This technique aims to discover an approximation of the actual image to reduce the MSE between the two. Suppose that the noise is estimated to zero, so the spectrum of noise power therefore also becomes zero, thereby limiting the Wiener filter to the inverse filter. The block diagram of the Wiener filter is shown in Fig. 8.4.

8.3.3 Richardson–Lucy filter algorithm [18]

If the point spread function is known, the restoration technique used is called a nonblind deconvolution method. In the 1970s, Richardson and Lucy derived this method from Bayes' theorem. This algorithm became popular in the fields of medical imaging and astronomy. This algorithm is

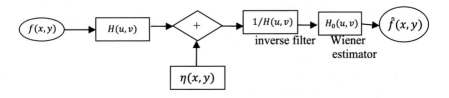

Figure 8.4 Block diagram of Wiener filter [16].

so popular because of the maximum likelihood method implementation, and it produces a restored image of good quality, even when high noise is present.

1: Read the input image
2: Simulating noise and blur
3: Recover the noisy and blurred image
4: Iterate to discover the image reconstruction
5: Regulation of the amplification of noise by damping
6: Form sample image
7: Simulating blur
8: Give the WEIGHT array
9: Give the finer-sampled point spread function

Algorithm 8.2: Richardson–Lucy filter [16].

We noted that in Algorithm 8.2 the iterative methodology, which is nonlinear, is better than a linear one. As we cannot predict the nonlinear behavior, it also needed computing resources. As the number of iterations grows, the image we acquire gets nearer to the ideal original image, lowering MSE. When the obtained mean square error becomes constant, the operation of this program is ended.

8.3.4 Regularization filter algorithm

Regularized filtering [16] is best used when adding smoothness as one of the constraints to the recovered image, and we have very little knowledge about the additive noise. We can restore the noisy and blurred image by using a technique called a regularized filter algorithm. The result of the regularization filter and Wiener filtering result is almost the same, but the point of difference in both filtering techniques is their view. In this filtering, there is less requirement for earlier information. A linear degradation model is given by

$$u_0 = Ku + n \tag{8.7}$$

where u_0 is the observed image, K is the blur operator, u is the original image, and n is noise.

The regularized solution is defined as the solution of the following problem:

$$\min L_\alpha(u) = \min\{\alpha R(u) + \|u_0 - Ku\|_2^2\} \tag{8.8}$$

where $R(u)$ is a regularization function, α is the regularization parameter $\| \ \|_2$ = Euclidean norm in the equation. If we do not have enough information, we assume smoothness as a natural assumption. We can write the regularization functional as

$$R(u) = \|Su\|_2^2 \tag{8.9}$$

In Eq. (8.9), S is the smoothing operator.

8.3.5 Model selection criterion

In this technique, the image restoration problem is handled as a learning system. In this method, the model is selected, and we estimate the parameters. We can easily obtain the parameters corresponding to the restored image. Additionally, the right choice of the regularization parameter will decide the accuracy of the restored image. Many approaches have been developed for estimating the regularization parameter (λ). Among them, we have equivalent degrees of freedom (EDF) [19], i.e., equivalent degrees of freedom method, then we have the Chi-squared method (CHI) and mean square error (MSE). In the mean square error method, knowledge of noise variance (σ_w^2) and original image (f) is required, that is, we need a priori knowledge, whereas in the EDF method and Chi-squared method the only requirement is the knowledge of σ_w^2. However, practically in σ_w^2 the noise variance is not known; therefore we generally don't use these methods. Cross-validation and maximum likelihood are the two methods that allow us to select λ, even when we have no idea of σ_w^2. These algorithms depend upon the datasets and no requirement of a priori is required. ML method is used to produce oversmoothed solutions [20], whereas if we consider cross-validation, it can fail in some circumstances where the smoothening parameter is not positive. Model selection criterion turns out to be a very powerful tool for image restoration. Based on the theoretical arguments

[21] Akaike information criterion (AIC) was the very first criterion that became popular for model selection. In [22], another model selection criterion, based on Bayesian arguments, is called Bayesian information criterion (BIC). The various model selection criteria are the following.

8.3.5.1 Akaike information criterion (AIC) [23]

Let y = set of data observed, $y = (y_1, \ldots, y_n)$ is sampled from $G(y)$, which is an unknown distribution, and its density function is given by $g(y)$. $g(y)$ can be estimated by the set of candidate models $M_1, \ldots, M_k$, whose probability densities are $f(y \mid \theta_k)$, $k = 1, 2, \ldots, K$. One of the members of the approximating family is g, which is also a generating density model. Let $\hat{\theta}(y)$ be a vector of the predicted parameters determined by maximizing the chances or likelihood $f(y/\theta_k)$ above θ_k and assume $f(y/\hat{\theta}_k)$ represents the fitted model. To determine which density model accurately depicts the unknown model $g(y)$, we need to have a metric that reflects the separation between $g(y)$ and an approximated model $f(y/\hat{\theta}_k)$. The Kullback–Leibler divergence is sometimes referred to as the cross-entropy. The Kullback–Leibler divergence between $f(y/\theta_k)$ and $g(y)$ can be defined as

$$I_n(g(.).f(./\hat{\theta}_k)) = E_g \left\{ 2\ln \frac{g(y)}{f(y/\hat{\theta}_k)} \right\} \tag{8.10}$$

$$= E_g \left\{ -2\ln f(y/\hat{\theta}_k) \right\} - E_g \left\{ -2\ln g(y) \right\} \tag{8.11}$$

$$= d_n(g.f_k) - d_n(g.g) \tag{8.12}$$

Here, f is the original image; g is the observed image; k = number of model parameters; $d_n(g.f_k) = E_g\{-2\ln f(y/\hat{\theta}_k)\}$; the expectation with respect to $g(y)$ is represented by $E_g\{.\}$. After the observed data is broken into multiple samples, Eq. (8.10)–(8.12) reduces to

$$d_n(g.f_k) = \frac{1}{k} \sum_{i=1}^{k} -2\ln f(y^{(i)} \mid \hat{\theta}_k(y^{(i)})) \tag{8.13}$$

The ranking of models according to $I_n(g(.).f(./\hat{\theta}_k))$ will be the same, doing ranking according to $d_n(g.f_k)$. Therefore the above formula can be formulated as in Eqs. (8.14) and (8.15):

$$d_n(g.f_k) = E_g \left\{ -2\ln f(y/\hat{\theta}_k) \right\} \tag{8.14}$$

$$= -2\ln f(y/\hat{\theta}_k) + E_g \left\{ -2\ln f(y/\hat{\theta}_k) \right\} - \left\{ -2\ln f(y/\hat{\theta}_k) \right\} \tag{8.15}$$

The above equation will give a proper estimate of Kullback–Leibler divergence. Still evaluation of $d_n(g.f_k)$ is difficult, because to evaluate this, we require the knowledge of $g(\gamma)$. If we prefer proper regularity condition, then the bias adjustment

$$E_g\left\{E_g\left\{-2\ln f(\gamma/\hat{\theta}_k)\right\}\right\} - E_g\left\{-2\ln f(\gamma/\hat{\theta}_k)\right\} \tag{8.16}$$

can be equated by $2k$. Based on this, Eq. (8.16) reduces to

$$AIC = -2\ln f(\gamma/\hat{\theta}_k) + 2k \tag{8.17}$$

If we consider

$$\Delta_n(k,g) = E_g\left\{d_n(g.f_k)\right\} \tag{8.18}$$

Then Eq. (8.18) holds [21].

$$\Delta_n(k,g) = E_g\left\{AIC\right\} + o(1) \tag{8.19}$$

In Eq. (8.19), AIC, the penalty term is very simple. As such, there is no certainty that a bias correction would return a fair Kullback–Leibler divergence approximation. In reality, autoregressive time-series and parametric linear regression conditions the corrected bias of the AIC can be represented in Eq. (8.20):

$$AIC = -2\ln f(\gamma.\hat{\theta}_k(\gamma)) + 2\frac{(k+1)q}{q-k-2} \tag{8.20}$$

where k is the number of model parameters and q is the sample size.

8.3.5.2 Improved AIC for the regularized choice of parameter

This part presents an information-based approach to choosing regularization parameters for the image restoration issue. Provided a family of probability densities $p(g\,|\,f,\lambda)$, which is defined by parameter vector f, the value of λ, corresponding to the density function that matches with unknown density $p(g)$, will be selected. Whenever we try to estimate the image, different choices of λ will give some different approximating density $p(g\,|\,\hat{f}_\lambda,\lambda)$. λ, which is the regularization parameter, can be determined to be the minimizer of the Kullback–Leibler divergence as

$$\hat{\lambda} = \arg\min_{\lambda} I(p(g), p(g \mid \hat{f}_{\lambda}, \lambda)) \tag{8.21}$$

As $p(g)$ is not known, so $\log p(g \mid \hat{f}_{\lambda}, \lambda)/n$ empirical distribution should be used and the average log-likelihood will be estimated by the expected log-likelihood in Eq. (8.21). This can be shown in Eqs. (8.22) and (8.23):

$$AIC_{\lambda} = -\frac{2}{n}\left\{\log p(g \mid \hat{f}_{\lambda}.\lambda)\right\} + \frac{2}{n}tr\left[H(H^{T}H + \lambda Q^{T}Q)^{-1}H^{T}\right] \tag{8.22}$$

where H is the known distortion blurring matrix.

$$\hat{\lambda}_{AIC} = \arg\min AIC_{\lambda} \tag{8.23}$$

For proof, refer to [23].

8.3.5.3 The Bayesian approach

Through Bayes theorem, the posterior probability of kth family with models for candidates is usually described by

$$p(M_k \mid y) = \frac{p(y \mid M_k)p(M_k)}{p(Y)} \tag{8.24}$$

The marginal density of any data is provided by $p(y \mid M_k)$, as shown in Eq. (8.24); the prior probability of the model M_k is given by $p(M_k)$. The marginal density of the data is given by Eq. (8.25):

$$p(y) = \sum_{k=1}^{K} p(y \mid M_k)p(M_k) \tag{8.25}$$

To determine the better candidate model's family, $p(M_k \mid y)$ is assessed for the values of $k = 1, 2, \ldots, K$. Selection of the model will be done based on a maximum value of $p(M_k \mid y)$. This density can be assessed by

$$p(y \mid M_k) = \int p(y \mid \theta_k.M_k)p(\theta_k \mid M_k)d\theta_k. \tag{8.26}$$

Based on M_k the likelihood is represented by $p(\gamma \mid \theta_k . M_k)$; prior on the parameter vector θ_k. is given by $p(\theta_k \mid M_k)$. Under certain regularity conditions [92], the Laplace transform of Eq. (8.26) can be given by

$$p(\gamma \mid M_k) = \frac{(2\pi)^{\frac{k}{2}}}{n^{k/2} Q(\theta_k.)^{\frac{1}{2}}} \exp \left\{ p\left((\gamma \mid \theta_k . M_k)\right) \right\} (1 + O_p(n^{-1})) \qquad (8.27)$$

After the calculation of Eq. (8.27), BIC can be given by

$$BIC = -2 \ln p M_k \qquad (8.28)$$

Ignoring higher-order terms, BIC in Eq. (8.28), results in Eq. (8.29):

$$BIC = -2 \ln p(\gamma \mid \hat{\theta}_k, M_k) + k \ln(n) \qquad (8.29)$$

But Eq. (8.29) cannot be used directly for the choice of λ. So BIC is extended [23] so that value of λ can be chosen in a way that it can be applied in image restoration problems.

8.3.6 Discrete wavelet transformation (DWT)

During the capture of the image, every point of the original scene stretches across several points of the image and blends together. Due to the spread, we get a blurred image. We can find out this spread with the help of function (PSF) also called as point spread function, and it is often called "Blur kernel" when restoring a blurred image. DWT is renowned for its multiresolution capabilities and can be used for image processing to detect edges and lower the effects of noise contained by the image. The use of the wavelet filter can remove the defects contained by the image. The image can be transformed into various frequency components and varying resolution scales. This transition takes place by considering very small waves called wavelets. Several wavelet decomposition filters are available to decompose the image. Among them, the popular filter is the Haar wavelet filter.

8.3.6.1 Haar wavelet

This transform was titled after Alfred Haar who was a mathematician. The function of this wavelet can be represented as $I(\frac{d^l}{d^l})$ [24], where there is a d^l states, the approximate image, and the d^n states the missing accurate details of the image; l is the number of decomposition levels. The main advantage of wavelet transform over Fourier transforms is its time resolution; that is, wavelet transform can capture both frequencies and information of position (location in time). To eliminate the aliasing effect from the blurred edges of the image, the padding of the image is done. Padding is added to both the blurred image and in real image with the scale same as that of the real image.

8.3.6.2 Methodology

Since the primary cause of degradation is blur and noise, to minimize or eradicate the consequences of these degradations, the used approach incorporates the principle of padding and kernel. The approach is known as hybrid kernel padding since the method of restoring the image uses both the padding and the kernel after the image is degraded, and is padded with the size of the image of the kernel. This method can be explained by the two processes, which are described by the following procedures:

1. Degrading the image

   During the process of image degradation, the image gets noisy and blurred. The procedures for degrading the image include the following:

   (a) Creation of kernel: The values of the mean (m) and variance (σ^2) is set to generate the kernel for blur by using the following formulas:

$$Kernel = \frac{1}{2\pi\sigma^2} e^{\left[\frac{-(X-m)^2+(Y-m)^2}{2\times\sigma^2}\right]}$$

(8.30)

   Here variance is denoted by σ^2, the mean is denoted by m, the distance from the horizontal axis is denoted by X, and the distance from the vertical axis is denoted by Y. From Eq. (8.30), it can be seen that the blur is inversely proportional to variance. Therefore the mean must be selected so that it becomes the center of the representation of the kernel. The amount and position of the blur in the image can be decided by the kernel.

   (b) Addition of noise: Noise is applied so that the image becomes noisy. For this purpose, salt and pepper noise is used. For blurring the image, DWT is applied to the noisy image and to the kernel. Before that, the kernel must be put in an image and it should be of the same size as that of the original image. The location of the kernel does not matter, and it can be put anywhere within the image. Once the kernel is placed in a new image, 2-D DWT of the noisy and kernel image are taken. The kernel of DWT should be modified such that no zero values are in the kernel. This is not critical, because kernel multiplication is going on with the DWT, but after some time, when it will be broken down, to divide, it will trigger a warning if any zero value is present in the DWT of the kernel. The first extraction of zero values from the kernel DWT guarantees that the operation is symmetrical. After zeros have been extracted from the kernel DWT, the DWT multiplication of the noisy image is performed. The above method is known as point-to-point multiplication, after which a blurred image is obtained.

2. Padding

After degradation of the image, padding is added to reduce the blurring effect in the image, resulting in an image with the size of the original one. With the aid of the Wiener filter, noise is reduced before the padding process. This helps to minimize both blur and noise degrades. The next inverse DWT is performed on the image so that the deblurred image can be obtained as summarized in Algorithm 8.3.

1: Upload an original 'I' file.
2: Set the variance and mean.
3: img1 = add salt and pepper noise in real image.
4: img2 = blur kernel
5: nd = dwt(img1, haar)
6: gd = dwt(img2, haar)
7: d = nd×gd where d = degraded image
8: pad the degraded image as 'Pad' = pad_image(d, real image size)
9: Deblur the image as 'di' = idwt(p, haar)

Algorithm 8.3: Algorithm of DWT [24].

8.3.7 Iterative denoising and backward projections

Most of the algorithms which are present in literature for image degradation specifically work on a particular task, such as image denoising [25–27], super-resolution [28,29], painting [30–32], and deblurring [33–35]. In this process, the image is reconstructed from a deteriorated image, blurry, noisy, or even both. The plug-and-play (P&P) method [36] provides an ideal solution for decoupling the measurement model. This method benefits software integration and makes it easier to use state-of-the-art denoising approaches that are not specifically formulated as optimization problems. The plug-and-play approach directly applies the alternating direction method of multipliers (ADMM), the alternating directions method of multipliers.

There is also no need to state the prior, because it is implied by the selection of the denoiser. Applications of the P&P process are post-processing of compressed images [37], electron tomography of bright light [38], and Poisson denoising [39]. However, parameter tuning is sometimes needed for the P&P [40,41] to achieve good quality results. In addition, since it is an iterative process, further iterations are required. An alternative method of plug and play requires fewer iterations and less parameter tuning. In this algorithm, firstly, a cost function is transformed into a novel optimization problem; thereafter, an effective minimization scheme is used. At last, an automatic tuning mechanism is provided so that the parameter of the method can be set. The most attractive property of the suggested technique is its minimal parameter tuning.

8.3.7.1 Problem formulation

The best part of this method is that its parameter tuning is minimum.

$$y = Hx + e \qquad (8.31)$$

where $y \in R^m$ represents the observations, $x \in R^n$ represents the unknown original image, $e \in R^m$ is a vector of independent and identical distributed Gaussian random variables having a mean equal to zero and standard deviation of σ_e and H is the degradation matrix, which is equal to $m \times n$. Almost every approach to x recovery requires the formulation of a cost function, consisting of terms such as penalties and fidelity, and minimizes the expected output. The principle of fidelity guarantees that the solution is consistent with the results and also stems from the negative log-likelihood function. Through the prior image model, the penalty term regularizes the problem of optimization. The cost function can be formulated in Eq. (8.32) as

$$f(\tilde{x}) = \frac{1}{2\sigma_e^2} \|y - H\|_2^2 + s(\tilde{x}) \qquad (8.32)$$

Here $s(x)$ represents the prior image model; the optimization variable is denoted by $\tilde{x}$ and the Euclidean norm is denoted by $\|.\|_2$.

8.3.7.2 Plug-and-play method

Instead of searching for different methods to solve $\min f(\tilde{x})$, a general method for recovery has been suggested in [42], popularly known as the plug-and-play approach. The plug-and-play method reestablishes the minimization problem as

$$\min_{\tilde{x},\tilde{v}} l(\tilde{x}) + \beta s(\tilde{v}) \quad \text{s.t.} \quad \tilde{x} = \tilde{v} \tag{8.33}$$

Here $l(\tilde{x})$ is the fidelity term and β is the positive parameter that will bring versatility to the cost function. The plug-and-play approach is presented in Algorithm 8.4.

Input: y, H, σ_e, denoising operator $D(.; \sigma)$, stop the criterion. $y = Hx + e$, such that it is
$e \sim N(0, \sigma_e^2 I_m)$ and an unknown signal is denoted by x and its prior model is be given by $D(.; \sigma)$.
Output: $\hat{x}$ an estimate of x is given by $\hat{x}$.
Initialize: $\check{v}_0 =$ initialize, $\hat{u}_0 = 0$, and $k = 0$,
    And do some initialization for β and λ
while unfulfilled stopping criterion **do**
    $k = k + 1$;
    $\hat{x}_k = (H^T H + \lambda \sigma_e^2 I_n)^{-1} \times (H^T y + \lambda \sigma_e^2 (\hat{v}_{k-1} - \hat{u}_{k-1}))$;
    $\hat{v}_k = D(\hat{x}_k + \hat{u}_{k-1}; \sqrt{\beta/\lambda})$;
    $\hat{u}_k = \hat{u}_{k-1} + (\hat{x}_k - \hat{v}_k)$;
end
    $\hat{x} = \hat{x}_k$;

Algorithm 8.4: Plug and play (P&P) [42].

Here, u is the dual variable, $\tilde{u}$ is the scaled dual variable, and λ is the alternating direction method of multipliers (ADMM) penalty parameter. ADMM can overcome the cost function issue. Based on ADMM theory, global convergence, i.e., objectively reaches its optimal value, and iterations approach feasibility only if $s(x)$ and $l(x)$ are accurate, closed, convex, and the unenhanced Lagrangian has a saddle point and still, the instantaneous effect of the result on the plug-and-play approach is minimal because the prior functions linked with it are sometimes are either not very clear or non-convex. Fixed point convergence is another form that ensures that an iterative algorithm achieves an asymptotically steady state. Such convergence shall be ensured in an updated version of the plug-and-play approach, where λ, which is the ADMM parameter, increases between iterations. Under some moderate conditions on the denoiser. Everything has its pros and cons, and so with the plug-and-play approach. The main disadvantage of this approach is that a significant proportion of iterations is often needed to lead to a suitable method. In Eq. (8.33) the specification of β and λ is chosen for a design that is often not explicit, and these parameters significantly affect the performance.

8.3.7.3 Iterative denoising and backward projection approach

Here to solve inverse problems using denoising algorithms another strategy is presented. Starting with formulating the cost function shown in Eq. (8.34) and (8.35):

$$f(\tilde{x}) = \frac{1}{2\sigma_e^2} \|y - H\|_2^2 + s(\tilde{x}) \tag{8.34}$$

$$= \frac{1}{2\sigma_e^2} \|H^\dagger y - \tilde{x}\|_{H^T H}^2 + s(\tilde{x}) \tag{8.35}$$

where $H^\dagger$ is the pseudo inverse of full row rank matrix H, $s(x)$ is the prior image model, and $\tilde{x}$ is the optimization parameter

$$H^\dagger = H^T (HH^T)^{-1} \tag{8.36}$$

Input: y, H, σ_e, denoising operator $D(.; \sigma)$,
    Stop the criterion. $y = Hx + e$, such that it is $e \sim N(0, \sigma_e^2 I_m)$ and an unknown signal is denoted by x and its prior model is be given by $D(.; \sigma)$.
Output: $\hat{x}$ is an estimate of x which is given by $\hat{x}$.
Initialize: $\tilde{y}_0 =$ initialization, $k = 0$, *approximate* δ
While unfulfilled stopping criterion **do**
    $k = k + 1$;
    $\hat{x}_k = D(\tilde{y}_{k-1}; \sigma_e + \delta)$;
    $\hat{y}_k = H^\dagger y + (I_n - H^\dagger H)\hat{x}_k$;
end
    $\hat{x} = \hat{x}_k$;

Algorithm 8.5: Algorithm of iterative denoising and backward projection [42].

where σ_e is the noise variance, δ is the design parameter, and $D(.; \sigma)$ is the denoising operator

The iterative denoising and backward projection approach are summarized in Algorithm 8.5. As the null space of $H^T H$ is nontrivial, to get the meaningful solution the priors ($\tilde{x}$) is important. The optimization problem

$\min f(\tilde{x})$ is given by

$$\min(\tilde{x}, \tilde{y}) \frac{1}{2\sigma_e^2} \left\| \tilde{y} - \tilde{x}, \right\|_{H^T H}^2 + s(\tilde{x}) \quad \text{s.t.} \quad \tilde{y} = H^\dagger y \qquad (8.37)$$

In Eq. (8.37), the variable $\hat{y}_k$ is supposed to be similar to x the real signal, and y which is the raw observations. To obtain better estimation, this method oscillates between the estimation of the signal and using this estimation the solution of $\tilde{y}$ trivial $\tilde{y} = H^\dagger y$ because of the degenerate constraint. To facilitate the estimation of x, it is necessary to lose the variable $\tilde{y}$ in a restricted manner. In this approach, firstly by using constraint $H\tilde{y} = y$ instead of $\tilde{y} = H^\dagger y$, a few degrees of freedom are provided to $\tilde{y}$. But these components are not easy to control, therefore they may disagree very strongly with the $s(\tilde{x})$ prior and also makes difficult the optimization with respect to $\tilde{x}$. To deal with this problem the optimization issue can be mathematically represented by Eqs. (8.39)–(8.41):

$$\min(\tilde{x}, \tilde{y}) \frac{1}{2(\sigma_e + \delta)^2} \left\| \tilde{y} - \tilde{x} \right\|_2^2 + s(\tilde{x}) \quad \text{s.t.} \quad H\tilde{y} = y \qquad (8.38)$$

$\hat{x}_k$ can be estimated by solving

$$\min(\tilde{x}, \tilde{y}) \frac{1}{2(\sigma_e + \delta)^2} \left\| \tilde{y} - \tilde{x} \right\|_2^2 + s(\tilde{x}) \quad \text{s.t.} \quad H\tilde{y} = y \qquad (8.39)$$

$$\hat{x}_k = \arg\min \frac{1}{2(\sigma_e + \delta)^2} \left\| \tilde{y}_{k-1} - \tilde{x} \right\|_2^2 + s(\tilde{x}) \qquad (8.40)$$

and $\hat{y}_k$ is estimated by solving

$$\hat{y}_k = \arg\min \left\| \tilde{y} - \hat{x}_k \right\|_2^2) \quad \text{s.t.} \quad \tilde{H}y = y \qquad (8.41)$$

We noted that Algorithm 8.6 gives the auto-tuned IDBP for deblurring of images.

8.3.8 Fast and adaptive boosting techniques for variational based image restoration

Variational problems are a significant class of problems and provide the potential for development in processing an image [43]. In this section, four image restoration techniques are discussed. To remove noise and retain edges of the image in image restoration, various algorithms and energy regularization–based variational models have already been established. A total variation (TV) method [44] is amongst the most pioneering methods of

---

Input: y, h, σ_e, denoising operator $D(.; \sigma)$, stopping criterion. $y = x \times h + e$, such that it is

$e \sim N(0; \sigma_e^2 I_n)$ and an unknown signal is denoted by x and its prior model is be given by $D(.; \sigma)$.

Output: $\hat{x}$ is an estimate of x which is given by $\hat{x}$.

Parameters: $\tilde{y}_0 = $ initialization, $k = 0$, moderate defined value is given by δ, initial minimal value is defined as ϵ

the little increment is given by $\Delta\epsilon$, confidence margin is given by τ and it is greater than 1.

Default init.: $\tilde{y}_0 = y$, $\Delta\epsilon = 1e\text{-}4$, $\delta = 5$, $\epsilon = 5e\text{-}4$, $\tilde{y}_0 = y$, $\tau = 3$.

While unfulfilled stopping criterion **do**

    $k = k + 1$;

    $\hat{x}_k = D(\tilde{y}_{k-1}; \sigma_e + \delta)$;

Calculate $\hat{y}_k$;

Calculate η_L and η_R;

If $k > 1$ and $\eta_L / \eta_R < \tau$

then

    $\epsilon = \epsilon + \Delta\epsilon$;

Process restart: $k = 0$;

end

    $\hat{x} = \hat{x}_k$;

Algorithm 8.6: Algorithm of auto-tuned IDBP for deblurring [42].

regularization. It has many advantages in digital image processing, such as retaining the edges of the image and eliminating noise. Total variation is used extensively for many applications, for example [45–56]. It has been upgraded to derivative models, which are of a higher order, such as total generalized variation (TGV), Hessian model and vectorial models [57–63] for color and for grayscale image restoration purposes. Considering the considerable success of the following algorithms and methods, image efficiency can be improved during the reconstruction process by using boosting techniques. "Boosting" is a term borrowed from the field of machine learning, which means making a powerful learner from a combination of weak learners, as in [64] for more information. However, in this section, boosting refers to iteratively increasing the efficiency of the restoration process, in that we use these variational approaches as the "Black Box" (tool). The boosting approach is an algorithm, in which the results of an actual image can be enhanced by iteratively solving the existing model. The key principle of boosting is to use the output. Tukey proposed [71] the very first boosting technique. This technique was used to boost the low- and high-pass filters [65], respectively. One fascinating iteration method has been suggested in [66], where the writers have formed a variational method for image decomposition. The iterative method in [66] hierarchically produces a set that converges with the image observed. An iterative approach is suggested, based on regularization, in that the residual was added to the input signal again [67]. The latest boosting approach is called the strengthening operating subtraction (SOS) boosting technique [68]. The effect is achieved by upgrading three measures: (a) enhancing the image, (b) executing the noise reduction algorithm, and (c) simply removing from the earlier image that which was restored from the result. Almost all of the boosting algorithms that have been discussed above were found to have constant regularization parameters. Fortunately, an adaptive detected signal can be strengthened by these algorithms.

8.3.8.1 Variational modeling

Mathematically, for the machine vision system, the linear model can be represented as

$$h = \Phi g + n \tag{8.42}$$

In Eq. (8.42), h is the image, which we observe; n is a noise, which can be random Gaussian noise or salt and pepper noise; Φ is bounded operator, and g is the output that needs to be estimated [69]. A very basic procedure for optimization that is based on energy regularization can be given as

$$\hat{g} = \arg\min_g R(g, h) \tag{8.43}$$

In Eq. (8.43), R describes a functional energy restoration. Some examples of this are when

$$R(g, h) = U(g) + \alpha V(g, h) \tag{8.44}$$

where $U(g)$ is the variational regularization term and α is a positive parameter in Eq. (8.44). Various methods and algorithms for restoration have been studied [70–77] to find $\hat{g}$ of the original image g. Different restoration methods with regularization terms are provided in Table 8.1. The results of these methods and algorithms can be strengthened by boosting techniques.

Table 8.1 Regularization methods [78].

Restoration method	Regularization term
Total variation (TV)	$\|\nabla g\|_1$
Total generalized variation (TGV)	$\lambda_1\|\nabla g - v\|_1 + \lambda_0\|c(v)\|$. Here complex vector is represented by v and $c(v) = \frac{1}{2}\left(\nabla v + \nabla v^T\right)$
Hessian	$\|\nabla g\|_1$
Chambolle–Lions (CL)	$\|\nabla g_1\|_1 + \lambda\|\nabla(\nabla g_2)\|_1$. Here $g = g_1 + g_2$
Chan–Esedoglu–Park (CEP)	$\|\nabla g_1\|_1 + \lambda\|(\Delta g_2)\|_1$
Euler's Elastica	$\left(a + b\left(\nabla.\frac{\nabla g}{|\nabla g|}\right)^2\right)\|\nabla g\|_1$, where a and b are positive constants

8.3.8.2 Description of boosting techniques

Osher et al. [79] upgraded the estimation function according to the following procedure:

---

1. Firstly initialize $v_0 = 0$ and $\hat{g} = 0$.
2. In the case of $k = 0, 1, 2, \ldots$:
  Calculate $\hat{g}_{k+1}$ as the denoising model minimizer, i.e.,
$$\hat{g}_{k+1/\alpha} = \arg\min_g \left\{ U(g) + \alpha\left\|h + v_k - g\right\|_2^2 \right\}$$
3. Update
$$v_{k+1} = v_k + h - \hat{g}_{k+1}$$

Algorithm 8.7: Algorithm for boosting technique [78].

Here, v is residual. If we analyze the above algorithm, we will see that $h - \hat{g}_k$ is again added to h, which is nothing but the noisy image. The basic principle here is to make the residual signal more effective than the noisy signal. The method is being used for image denoising. Using Tukey's method [62], we can write the estimation function as

$$\hat{g}_{k+1/\alpha} = \hat{g}_k + \arg\min_g \left\{ U(g) + \alpha\left\|h + v_k - \hat{g}_k\right\|_2^2 \right\} \tag{8.45}$$

Without using adaptive regularization parameters, we can state the boosting technique as

$$\hat{g}_{k+1/\alpha} = \arg\min_g \left\{ U(g) + \alpha\left\|\left(\frac{h + \hat{g}_k}{2}\right) - g\right\|_2^2 \right\} \tag{8.46}$$

The primary disadvantage of all the above recursive methods is their poor convergence. However, these methods can be improved further by applying the choice of adaptive parameters and also using the alternating direction method of multipliers.

8.3.8.3 Adaptive boosting techniques

$\varepsilon(.)$ denotes the methods of adaptive boosting, and the boosting parameter is η. The algorithm for the adaptive boosting method is:

---

1. Firstly initialize $g_0 = 0$, $h_0 = h$, and $\alpha_0 = \alpha$
2. In the case of $k = 0, 1, 2, \ldots,$
3. Then update α_k as $\alpha_k = \eta^k \alpha_0$
4. Now calculate:
$$\hat{g}_{k+1/\alpha} = \varepsilon(h_0, \hat{g}_k, \alpha_k, R)$$

Algorithm 8.8: Algorithm for adaptive technique [78].

where $\hat{g}_k$ is the restored signal, α_k is the adaptive parameter at k^{th} iteration, and h_0 is the initial input image are used in Algorithm 8.8. Restoration algorithm $R(.)$ is applied iteratively and α is the parameter that changes each time, i.e., $\alpha_{new} \leftarrow \alpha_{old}$. Finally, the improved result can be obtained by outputting the sequence $(\hat{g}_{k+1/\alpha})$ after k steps.

8.3.8.4 ADMM method used for image restoration model

The ADMM is an algorithm that breaks the convex optimization problems into smaller pieces, thus it becomes easy to handle. The model for restoration can be stated as follows:

$$\min_g \left\{ E(g) = G(Wg) + H(\Phi g, h) \right\} \tag{8.47}$$

Here, E is the energy, Φ and W are linear and bounded operators, and $G(Wg) = \| Wg \|_p$. Now, this model is solved by the ADMM.

The stopping criterion that is used in Eq. (8.47) is

$$\frac{\left\| \hat{g}_{k+1} - \hat{g}_k \right\|}{\left\| \hat{g}_k \right\|} \leq \epsilon \tag{8.48}$$

Here, for the Algorithm 8.8 stopping threshold, ε is fixed to 10^{-4}.

---

1. Firstly initialize multiplier $\lambda_0^1 \lambda_0^2$ and also the variables g_0, q_0, z_0;

2. Calculate g_m, q_m, z_m and update λ_m^2, λ_m^1

In the case of $m = 1, 2, \ldots$

    Step 1: Calculate

    $g_m = \arg\min_g \mathcal{L}\left(g, q_{m-1}, z_{m-1}; \lambda_{m-1}^2, \lambda_{m-1}^1\right);$

    Step 2: Calculate

    $q_m = \arg\min_q \mathcal{L}\left(g_m, q, z; \lambda_{m-1}^2, \lambda_{m-1}^1\right);$

    Step 3: Calculate

    $z_m = \arg\min_z \mathcal{L}\left(g_m, q_m, z; \lambda_{m-1}^2, \lambda_{m-1}^1\right);$

    Step 4: Update

    $\lambda_m^1 = \lambda_{m-1}^1 + \gamma^1 (q_m - Wg_m);$

    $\lambda_m^2 = \lambda_{m-1}^2 + \gamma^2 (q_m - Wg_m);$

3. End using any stopping criterion calculate an output g_m as restored image.

Algorithm 8.9: ADMM for image restoration model [78].

Here, $q = \nabla g$, $z = \Phi g$, λ^1 and λ^2 are Lagrangian multipliers f, and γ^1 and γ^2 are positive parameters. For computation purposes, fast Fourier transform (FFT) is used. TV - boosting algorithm is summarized in Algorithm 8.9 and α_0 given by Eq. (8.49):

$$\alpha_0 = 4.82 \times \frac{TV(h) \times \tau}{M \times N} + 0.09 \times \left(\frac{TV(h) \times \tau}{M \times N}\right)^2 - 0.72110 \qquad (8.49)$$

For the TGV boosting algorithm α_0 is given by

$$\alpha_0 = 3.422 \times \frac{TV(h) \times \tau}{M \times N} + 1.64 * \left(\frac{TV(h) \times \tau}{M \times N}\right)^2 + 0.8911 \qquad (8.50)$$

where $M \times N$ shows the dimension of the image and τ is a small positive integer.

8.3.9 Image restoration using DWT in a tile-based manner

The suggested method decomposes the image into four tiles and removes noise from each one separately. Since localized parameters can be set for various regions of an image based on the amount of deterioration each region has experienced, this approach has proven to be more accurate. The

---

1. Firstly initialize:
Parameter $\alpha_0 = \alpha$, $h_0 = h$, and $\hat{g}_0 = 0$;
2. In the case of $k = 0, 1, 2, \ldots$:
Calculate $\hat{g}_k$ from Algorithm 8.7;
Update adaptive parameter α_k as:
$$\alpha_k = \eta^k \alpha_0$$
Then calculate $\hat{g}_{k+1/\alpha}$
3. End by using any stopping criterion calculates the output $\hat{g}_{k+1}$.

Algorithm 8.10: Algorithm for boosting technique [78].

denoising technique would be forced to use the same parameters for all regions if the image is considered as a whole. This can cause unnecessary blurring in areas of the picture where the degree of deterioration is minimal in comparison to other areas.

8.3.9.1 Detailed design

Based on the degree of damage, various restoration procedures can be applied individually to the partitioned image. The partitioning mechanism is depicted in Fig. 8.5. In Fig. 8.6, decomposition of DWT is shown.

After partitioning, noise is eliminated from each tile using the wavelet-based method. Each of the individual denoised tiles will be rejoined to get the entire denoised image.

The DWT generates the first degree of hierarchy by decomposing the input image high-pass and low-pass components using high-pass filter (HPF) and low-pass filter (LPF). This method is iterated to achieve several hierarchies, as shown in Fig. 8.6. First, the input image is divided into four subbands: LL, LH, HL, and HH. The LL subband, which is the top left subband, is further decomposed into four subbands, as shown in Fig. 8.7. As a result, an image of size N × N is divided into four N/2 × N/2 subbands. The noise reduction algorithm that follows is applied to each of the four tiles.

8.3.9.2 Noise removal algorithm

Step 1: Using the technique shown in Fig. 8.7, the image is converted into a 2D signal, which is then decomposed up to the desired degree (say N). This stage yields two vectors: a C vector and an L vector. The vector (C) is ordered as A(N), H(N), V(N), D(N), H(N-1), V(N-1), D(N-1), H(1),

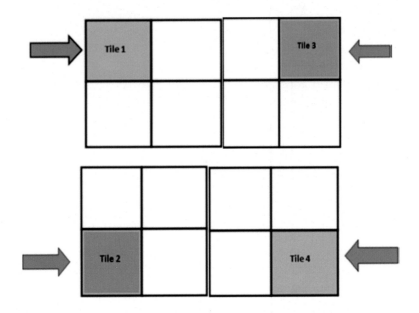

Figure 8.5 Image is partitioned to form tiles [80].

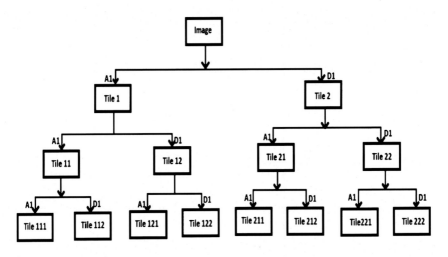

Figure 8.6 DWT Decomposition [80].

V(1), D(1), where A contains the approximation coefficients; H contains the horizontal detail coefficients; V contains the vertical detail coefficients; and D contains the diagonal detail coefficients. The length of each component is determined by the vector (L).

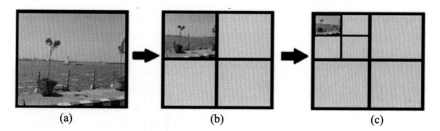

Figure 8.7 DWT decomposition: (a) Input image; (b) 2D decomposition after one level; (c) 2D decomposition after the two-level [80].

Step 2: All components of N-level approximation and first N levels of detail coefficients are the coefficients of an N-level decomposition of the signal.

Step 3: Threshold selection is critical since a small threshold requires more coefficients, resulting in a lower smoothed quality, whereas a high threshold induces oversmoothing because of the removal of more coefficients.

Step 4: Based on the wavelet decomposition structure, a multilevel wavelet reconstruction of the image matrix is performed.

After that, the restored tiles are rejoined to complete the image [80].

8.3.10 Hybrid sparsity learning

Sparse coding and its variations are expected to be among the highest researched in the literature regarding model-based techniques [81–87]. Sparse representations are possible for natural photos in a transformed space, which is the basic concept behind sparse coding. The characterization of transient events in seismic images was the objective of initial sparse coding research. A basis function with decent localization properties in frequency and spatial domain can be achieved by mathematical design. After, a series of simultaneous sparse codings, such as block matching 3D (BM3D) and nonlocal sparsity-dependent image restoration, recognized the significance of utilizing nonlocal similarity in natural photos. Nonlocal sparsity has recently been linked to the Gaussian scalar mixture (GSM) model, resulting in state-of-the-art performance in this technique.

Dictionary learning, in which a trained pair of low-resolution (LR) and high-resolution (HR) dictionaries were used to define provided LR images and recreate HR images with the HR dictionary and the corresponding representation codes concerning LR images, was an early work in learning-based method. Stacks of collaborative auto-encoders are used to layer by layer recover an HR image. Multiple convolutional neural networks have been presented for directly learning the nonlinear mapping between LR and HR images. A multistage trainable nonlinear reaction-diffusion network for image restoration has also been presented. In general, a deeper neural network improves SR efficiency. It is suggested that a residual dense block incorporates the skip and dense connections to remove features for image restorations, which were then fused in subsequent layers, resulting in a state-of-the-art image restoration technique. For image super-resolution, the deep residual channel attention network (RCAN) was proposed. Remember that the DNN method still performs poorly on certain sample images. A fundamental flaw of all learning-based methods is the discrepancy between training and testing results.

To overcome the above limitation, a hybrid strategy combining the strengths of both worlds has been proposed.

8.3.10.1 Prior prelearning from the training dataset

Synthesis sparse model-dependent image restoration is represented by Eq. (8.51):

$$(x, \alpha_i) = \arg\min\nolimits_{x,\alpha_i} \left\| y - Hx \right\|_2^2 + \eta \sum_i \left\{ \left\| R_i x - D\alpha_i \right\|_2^2 + \lambda \left\| \alpha_i \right\|_1 \right\} \quad (8.51)$$

Here D represents the dictionary and R represents the matrix attracting patches. If the patches are extracted from the image, then the transformation of every patch can be implemented by convolution with w_k filters.

$$(x, z_k) = \arg\min\nolimits_{x,\alpha_i} \left\| y - Hx \right\|_2^2 + \eta \sum_{k=1}^{K} \left\{ \left\| W_k * x - z_k \right\|_2^2 + \lambda \left\| z_k \right\|_1 \right\} \quad (8.52)$$

Corresponding to W_k filter in Eq. (8.52), z_k represents a sparse feature map. It aims to learn the feature maps z_k of a desired restored image x with respect to filters W_k for a given image y. The learning feature may be defined as follows without compromising the generality:

$$\hat{Z} = G(y; \Theta) \quad (8.53)$$

where $G(.)$ denotes the learning function in Eq. (8.53). It has been observed that learning a series of feature maps z_k *regarding* W_k is unstable; rather, it is recommended to learn the desired restored image x first, and then compute the feature maps. Algorithm 8.11 summarizes the overall structured analysis sparse coding (SASC) model for image restoration. It should be noted that Algorithm 8.11 usually takes hundreds of iterations to reach a satisfactory result. As a result, the proposed SASC model has a high computational cost; however, the research filters W_k used in Algorithm 8.11 are fixed.

---

1. Initialization:
    (a) Assign the parameters η and λ;
    (b) Calculate the initial estimate $\hat{x}^{(0)}$ by the CNN;
    (c) Group a set of related patches G_i for each patch $\hat{x}_i$ using $\hat{x}^{(0)}$;
    (d) Determine the prior feature maps μ_k;
2. Outer loop: Iteration over $t = 1, 2, \ldots, T$
    (a) Determine feature maps $z_k^{(t)}$, $k = 1, \ldots, K$;
    (b) Then update the HR image $\hat{x}^{(t)}$;
    (c) Update μ_k;
3. Output: $x(t)$.

Algorithm 8.11: Image restoration with ASC (SASC) [88].

Here, μ_k is the new nonlocal prior, z_k represents sparse feature map.

8.3.10.2 From structured analysis sparsity coding (SASC) to structured analysis sparsity learning (SASL)

The main architecture for SASL network implementation is shown in Fig. 8.8, which expands the iterative phases of Algorithm 8.11 into several stages and easily trained implementation. The degraded picture y is first passed via the CNN to generate a preliminary approximation of the desired image, which is then utilized to form similar group patches and compute hybrid prior feature maps. The degraded picture y is processed first by a convolution layer for sparse feature maps, which are then anticipated by learned initial feature maps. The residuals of the anticipated function mappings are subjected to a nonlinear soft-thresholding layer. After the soft-thresholding layer, the trained prior function maps k are applied to the performance of the soft-thresholding layer. The revised function mappings are then transmitted via a reconstruction layer with a set of 2D convolution filters. The reconstruction layer's final output is combined with the preprocessed degraded signal.

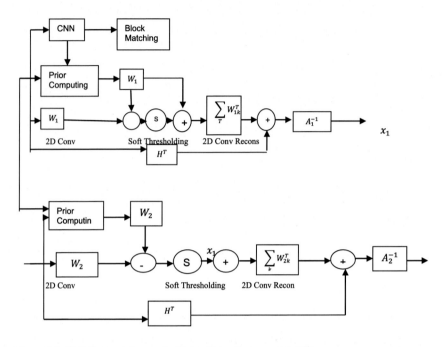

Figure 8.8 SASL Network for a trainable and iterative approach [88].

8.4 Performance analysis of image restoration

In this chapter, several image restoration techniques have been compared to get a greater understanding of their efficacy in removing noise and blur [78,89–91]. The two evaluation parameters that are taken to analyze the restoration technique are PSNR, i.e., peak signal-to-noise ratio and MSE, i.e., mean square. PSNR is defined as the ratio of the maximum possible signal power and the corrupting noise power. Mathematically, PSNR is given by Eq. (8.54), and MSE is given by Eq. (8.55). Mean square error (MSE) is the average and the difference between the one which is estimated and the real or original image. The higher value of PSNR implies the better quality of the reconstructed image, and the lower the value of MSE implies the lower error.

$$PSNR = 10\log\left(\frac{MAX_i^2}{MSE}\right) \qquad (8.54)$$

Table 8.2 Comparison of various techniques in the presence of blur [89].

Image	Wiener Filter		Regularization Filter		Lucy–Richardson Filter	
	PSNR	MSE	PSNR	MSE	PSNR	MSE
Cameraman	22.18	98.67	24.45	244.17	29.58	71.58
Lena	27.45	113.42	22.75	324.4	30.71	54.2

Here, MAX_i^2 is the maximum possible pixel value of the image, and MSE is the mean square error.

$$MSE = \frac{1}{M.N} \sum_{i=0}^{N-1} \sum_{i=0}^{M-1} \left| f(i,j) - \hat{f}(i,j) \right|^2 \qquad (8.55)$$

Here, M and N are the number of rows and columns in input images.

8.5 Performance analysis

A quantitative analysis is shown in Table 8.2, 8.11. In Table 8.2 Wiener filter, Lucy–Richardson filter, and regularization filter are compared in the presence of blur for the cameraman and Lena. It can be seen from this table that the highest PSNR and lowest MSE are achieved through the Lucy–Richardson filter for both images. Table 8.3 discusses the restoration performance on cameraman images for two different sizes. For image size 256×256 and noise variance 0.05, it is observed that the highest PSNR and lowest MSE are achieved through the Richardson–Lucy filter. The quality of the image becomes better when the number of iterations increases. When noise variance is 0.007, the PSNR of Lucy–Richardson is even better. In Table 8.4, in the presence of only the blur cameraman and Lena, both the images are restored well in the Lucy–Richardson filter. If both blur and noise are present, the Lucy–Richardson filter performs better, and the Wiener filter provides a better result than the regularization filter. From Tables 8.2–8.5, it is clear that Lucy–Richardson performs better if filtering techniques are compared in every situation. Table 8.6 compares the findings of model selection approaches for estimating the regularization parameter in image restoration in terms of peak signal-to-noise ratio (PSNR) and improvement in signal-to-noise-ratio (ISNR). This table shows that the highest value of regularization parameter, that is, lambda, is yielded by ML technique irrespective of the noise variance, which oversmooth the re-

Table 8.3 Comparison of various techniques on cameraman images [90].

Image size	256 × 256				512 × 512			
Noise variance	0.05		0.007		0.05		0.007	
	MSE	PSNR	MSE	PSNR	MSE	PSNR	MSE	PSNR
Inverse Filter	0.0262	15.8123	0.0068	21.7024	0.0042	22.7645	0.0083	20.7954
Wiener Filter	0.0138	18.5958	0.0061	22.1819	0.0020	27.0082	0.0028	25.5632
RL Filter — Iteration 1	0.0680	11.6762	0.0654	11.8434	0.0210	16.7799	0.0440	13.5639
Iteration 10	0.0268	15.7245	0.0245	16.1020	0.0019	27.1238	0.0064	21.9615
Iteration 20	0.0112	19.5254	0.0071	21.5087	0.0011	29.6501	0.0022	26.6454
Iteration 30	0.0070	21.5233	0.0035	24.6023	$8.9311e^{-0.04}$	30.4910	0.0018	27.4981

Table 8.4 Comparison of various techniques in the presence of Gaussian blur [16].
Gaussian function Matrix size = $[21 \times 21]$

Image	Wiener Filter			Regularization Filter			Lucy–Richardson Filter		
	PSNR	SSIM	MSE	PSNR	SSIM	MSE	PSNR	SSIM	MSE
Camer-aman	28.18	0.88	98.87	24.45	0.78	233.61	29.60	0.92	71.28
Lena	27.58	0.88	113.55	22.89	0.78	334.17	30.76	0.91	54.56

Table 8.5 Comparison of various techniques in the presence of Gaussian blur and noise [16].
Gaussian function Matrix size = $[21 \times 21]$, standard deviation = 1.2

Image	Wiener Filter			Regularization Filter			Lucy–Richardson Filter		
	PSNR	SSIM	MSE	PSNR	SSIM	MSE	PSNR	SSIM	MSE
Camer-aman	20.23	0.48	616.95	11.99	0.20	4107.89	25.98	0.78	163.94
Lena	19.66	0.47	703.23	11.73	0.19	4364.09	26.33	0.78	151.45

Table 8.6 Comparison of various techniques in the presence of noise [23].

Noise variance	10			100			150		
Method-ologies	λ	ISNR	PSNR	λ	ISNR	PSNR	λ	ISNR	PSNR
λ_{BIC}	0.07	0.92	15.82	0.30	1.74	15.42	0.35	2.53	14.95
λ_{AIC}	0.23	0.67	15.59	0.57	1.49	15.13	0.72	2.25	14.47
λ_{ML}	0.29	0.60	15.52	0.77	1.47	15.04	0.83	2.18	14.36
λ_{CV}	0.08	0.78	15.63	0.18	1.58	15.27	0.27	2.47	14.83

stored image. The regularization parameter of AIC is also significant when compared with BIC; hence AIC also tends to oversmooth.

In contrast to the other completely data-based approaches used in this case, the restoration obtained from BIC generates the maximum ISNR and PSNR, as seen in Table 8.6; it can thus be favored in applications. Table 8.7 shows that Iterative Denoising and Backward Projections (IDBP) give better performance than other techniques in the noisy case and require less parameter tuning and iterations. Table 8.8 discusses TV (total variation), TGV (total generalized variation), TV boosting, and TGV boosting methods for Lena image with Lagrange multipliers $\gamma = 2$. It is clear from this table that the SNR and SSIM of the image are larger in boosting techniques than TV and TGV methods. Table 8.9 shows the average PSNR effects on the dataset [12] for the possible denoising method versions. Table 8.9 shows that the SASC approach surpasses the original ASC method

Table 8.7 Comparison of various techniques in the presence of noise [42].

Variance	2		8		Computational complexity
Methodologies	SNR	SSIM	SNR	SSIM	No of iterations
IDD-BM3D	8.86	0.886	7.12	0.856	200
P&P-BM3D	8.03	0.883	6.06	0.842	50
IRCNN	9.08	0.894	7.33	0.867	30
IDBP-BM3D	8.51	0.893	6.61	0.858	30
Auto-tuned IDBP-BM3D	8.40	0.890	6.56	0.858	30
IDBP-CNN	9.08	0.897	7.28	0.866	30
Auto-Tuned IDBP-CNN	9.07	0.897	7.23	0.864	

Table 8.8 Comparison of various techniques in the presence of noise [78].

	Image - Lena and parameter $\gamma = 2$							
σ	TV		TV - Boosting		TGV		TGV - Boosting	
	SNR	SSIM	SNR	SSIM	SNR	SSIM	SNR	SSIM
0	18.2713	0.8524	19.6355	0.8863	18.7876	0.8840	19.8850	0.9339
15	16.6871	0.8017	17.7462	0.8355	16.9216	0.8153	18.0566	0.8471
20	15.4702	0.7883	16.53858	0.8009	15.6412	0.7951	16.6822	0.8166
25	14.5243	0.7533	15.5640	0.7852	14.9013	0.7762	15.7738	0.8072
30	13.6975	0.7120	14.8166	0.7338	14.2983	0.7225	14.9382	0.7594

Table 8.9 Comparison of various techniques in the presence of noise on Dataset 12 [88].

	$\sigma = 15$	$\sigma = 25$	$\sigma = 50$
ASC	32.60	30.30	27.01
SASC	32.98	30.57	27.35
CNN	32.85	30.38	27.24
SASL	33.32	30.99	27.69

Table 8.10 Comparison of various techniques in the presence of blur on Dataset 12 [88].

Methods	Kernel 1 (19×19)			Kernel 2 (17×17)		
	$\sigma = 2$	$\sigma = 2.55$	$\sigma = 7.65$	$\sigma = 2$	$\sigma = 2.55$	$\sigma = 7.6$
ASC	33.04	32.40	28.70	32.96	32.29	28.49
SASC	33.35	32.67	29.02	32.58	32.58	28.61
CNN	33.22	32.72	28.87	32.63	32.63	28.55
SASL	34.05	33.17	29.16	32.94	32.94	28.74

by integrating the internal nonlocal self-similarity prior. CNN network can be viewed as an implementation of DnCNN, which relies on the integra-

Table 8.11 PSNR results of different denoising techniques on Dataset 12.

Image	C.Man	House	Peppers	Starfish	Monar	Airpl	Parrot	Lena	Barb	Boat	Man	Coup	Avg
Noise level $\sigma = 15$													
BM3D [11]	31.92	34.94	32.70	31.15	31.86	31.08	31.38	34.27	33.11	32.14	31.93	32.11	32.38
WNNM [27]	32.18	35.15	32.97	31.83	32.72	31.40	31.61	34.38	33.61	32.12	32.12	32.18	32.70
EPLL [40]	31.82	34.14	32.58	31.08	32.03	31.16	31.40	33.87	31.34	31.97	31.97	31.90	32.10
TNRD [43]	32.19	34.55	33.03	31.76	32.57	31.47	31.63	34.25	32.14	32.24	32.24	32.11	32.51
DnCNN-S [69]	32.62	35.00	33.29	32.23	33.10	31.70	31.84	34.63	32.65	32.47	32.47	32.47	32.87
Hybrid Sparsity [88]	32.16	35.51	33.87	32.67	33.30	31.98	32.21	35.19	33.92	32.93	32.93	33.08	33.31
Noise level $\sigma = 25$													
BM3D [11]	29.45	32.86	30.16	28.56	29.25	28.43	28.93	32.08	30.72	29.91	29.62	29.72	29.98
WNNM [27]	29.64	33.23	30.40	29.03	29.85	28.69	29.12	32.24	31.24	30.03	29.77	29.82	30.26
EPLL [40]	29.24	32.04	30.07	28.43	29.30	28.56	28.91	31.62	28.55	29.69	29.63	29.48	29.63
TNRD [43]	29.71	32.54	30.55	29.02	29.86	28.89	29.18	32.00	29.41	29.92	29.88	29.71	30.06
DnCNN-S [69]	30.19	33.09	30.85	29.40	30.23	29.13	29.42	32.45	30.01	30.22	30.11	30.12	30.43
Hybrid Sparsity [88]	29.82	33.82	31.47	30.10	30.67	29.50	29.87	33.09	31.32	30.86	30.64	30.77	30.99
Noise level $\sigma = 50$													
BM3D [11]	26.13	29.69	26.68	25.04	25.82	25.10	25.90	29.05	27.23	26.78	26.81	26.46	26.73
WNNM [27]	26.42	30.33	26.91	25.43	26.32	25.42	26.09	29.25	27.79	26.97	26.94	26.64	27.04
EPLL [40]	26.02	28.76	26.63	25.04	25.78	25.24	25.84	28.43	24.82	26.65	26.72	26.24	26.35
TNRD [43]	26.62	29.48	27.10	25.42	26.31	25.59	26.16	28.93	5.70	26.94	26.98	26.50	26.81
DnCNN-S [69]	27.00	30.02	27.29	25.70	26.77	25.87	26.48	29.37	26.23	27.19	27.24	26.90	27.17
Hybrid Sparsity [88]	26.90	30.50	27.89	26.46	27.37	26.35	26.96	29.87	27.17	27.74	27.67	27.41	27.69

tion of external priors. The suggested structured analysis sparsity learning (SASL) approach increases denoising efficiency by including both external and internal priors. Table 8.10 reveals that two different blur kernels among the proposed deblurring method's variants produce similar effects. Three model-based denoising methods (BM3D, EPLL, and WNNM) and two deep learning-based methods (TNRD and DnCNN-S), and the hybrid sparsity approach, are compared. On Dataset 12, the PSNR comparison results of different techniques are seen in Table 8.11. The hybrid sparsity approach surpasses all other competing approaches, such as BM3D [11], EPLL [27], WNNM [40], and two deep learning methods DnCNN-S [43] and TNRD [69]. Specifically, this process outperforms the previous state-of-the-art DnCNN-S by 0.56 dB on average.

8.6 Conclusion

In this chapter, various image restoration techniques have been discussed. After the analysis, it has been observed that the hybrid sparsity learning technique performs better than the other state-of-the-art techniques. In this technique, the concept of joint optimization of trainable layers is used to learn the structured sparse priors iteratively. The experimental table of this method shows that the iterative and trainable SASL significantly improves image restoration in terms of both subjective and objective performances.

References

[1] Xiao-jun Bi, Ting Wang, Adaptive blind image restoration algorithm of degraded image, in: IEEE Proceedings of the 2008 Congress on Image and Signal Processing, vol. 3, 2008, pp. 536–540.

[2] Y. Pei, Y. Huang, Q. Zou, X. Zhang, S. Wang, Effects of image degradation and degradation removal to CNN-based image classification, IEEE Transactions on Pattern Analysis and Machine Intelligence 43 (4) (2021) 1239–1253, https://doi.org/10.1109/TPAMI.2019.2950923.

[3] W.W.W. Zou, P.C. Yuen, Very low-resolution face recognition problem, IEEE Transactions on Image Processing 21 (1) (January 2012) 327–340.

[4] S. Li, H. Yin, L. Fang, Group-sparse representation with dictionary learning for medical image denoising and fusion, IEEE Transactions on Biomedical Engineering 59 (12) (2012) 3450–3459.

[5] Y. Chang, L. Yan, M. Chen, H. Fang, S. Zhong, Two-stage convolutional neural network for medical noise removal via image decomposition, IEEE Transactions on Instrumentation and Measurement 69 (6) (2020) 2707–2721.

[6] H. Fan, Y. Chen, Y. Guo, H. Zhang, G. Kuang, Hyperspectral image restoration using low-rank tensor recovery, IEEE Journal of Selected Topics in Applied Earth Observations and Remote Sensing (ISSN 1939-1404) 10 (2017) 4589–4604.

[7] Y. Chang, L. Yan, M. Chen, H. Fang, S. Zhong, W. Liao, HIS-DeNet: Hyperspectral image restoration via convolutional neural network, IEEE Transactions on Geoscience and Remote Sensing 57 (2) (2019) 667–682.

[8] M. Awad, A. Elliethy, H.A. Aly, Adaptive near-infrared and visible fusion for fast image enhancement, IEEE Transactions on Computational Imaging (ISSN 2573-0436) 6 (2020) 408–418, https://doi.org/10.1109/TCI.2019.2956873.

[9] C. Gu, X. Lu, Y. He, C. Zhang, Blur removal via blurred-noisy image pair, IEEE Transactions on Image Processing (ISSN 1057-7149) 30 (2021) 345–359, https://doi.org/10.1109/TIP.2020.3036745.

[10] Prabhishek Singh, Raj Shree, A comparative study to noise models and image restoration techniques, International Journal of Computer Applications 149 (1) (September 2016) 18–27.

[11] Rini Smita Thakur, R.N. Yadav, Lalita Gupta, State-of-art analysis of image denoising methods using convolutional neural networks, IET Image Processing 13 (2019) 2367–2380, https://doi.org/10.1049/iet-ipr.2019.0157.

[12] A. Foi, M. Trimeche, V. Katkovnik, K. Egiazarian, Practical Poissonian-Gaussian noise modeling and fitting for single-image raw-data, IEEE Transactions on Image Processing 17 (10) (2008) 1737–1754, https://doi.org/10.1109/TIP.2008.2001399.

[13] R.H. Chan, Chung-Wa Ho, M. Nikolova, Salt and pepper noise removal by median type noise detectors and detail-preserving regularization, IEEE Transactions on Image Processing 14 (10) (2005) 1479–1485.

[14] Shuo Sun, Application of fuzzy image restoration in criminal investigation, Journal of Visual Communication and Image Representation (ISSN 1047-3203) 71 (2020).

[15] A. Maurya, R. Tiwari, A novel method of image restoration by using different types of filtering techniques, International Journal of Engineering Science and Innovative Technology (IJESIT) 3 (4) (2014) 124–129.

[16] Muhammad Rifki Kurniawan, Apriani Kusumawardhani, Analysis and comparison of image restoration algorithms using MATLAB, https://doi.org/10.13140/RG.2.2.22236.90246, 2017.

[17] Anita Thakur, Adiba Kausar, Ariz Iqbae, Comparison efficacy of restoration method for space-variant motion-blurred images using Kalman and Wiener filter, in: 6th International Conference - Cloud System and Big Data Engineering, vol. 8, Amity University, Noida, India, Jan. 2016, pp. 508–512.

[18] Monika Maru, M.C. Parukh, Image restoration techniques: a survey, International Journal of Computer Applications 160 (6) (2017) 0975.

[19] A.M. Thompson, J.C. Brown, J.W. Kay, D.M. Titterington, A study of methods of choosing the smoothing parameter in image restoration by regularization, IEEE Transactions on Pattern Analysis and Machine Intelligence 13 (4) (1991) 326–339.

[20] N. Fortier, G. Demoment, Y. Goussard, GCV and ML methods of determining parameters in image restoration by regularization: Fast computation in the spatial domain and experimental comparison, Journal of Visual Communication and Image Representation 4 (1993) 157–170.

[21] H. Akaike, A new look at the statistical model identification, IEEE Transactions on Automatic Control AC-19 (6) (1974) 716–723.

[22] G. Schwarz, Estimating the dimension of a model, Institute of Mathematical Statistics 6 (2) (1978) 461–464.

[23] Abd-Krim Seghouane, Model selection criteria for image restoration, IEEE Transactions on Neural Networks 20 (8) (2009) 1357–1363.

[24] Rohina Ansari, Himanshu Yadav, Anurag Jain, Restoration of blur & noisy images using hybrid kernel-padding algorithm with transformation technique, in: 4th International Conference on Computer and Communication Technology (ICCCT), MNNIT Allahabad, India, Sep 2013, pp. 66–71.

[25] K. Dabov, A. Foi, V. Katkovnik, K. Egiazarian, Image denoising by sparse 3-D transform-domain collaborative filtering, IEEE Transactions on Image Processing 16 (8) (2007) 2080–2095.

[26] M. Elad, M. Aharon, Image denoising via sparse and redundant representations over learned dictionaries, IEEE Transactions on Image Processing 15 (12) (2006) 3736–3745.

[27] S. Gu, L. Zhang, W. Zuo, X. Feng, Weighted nuclear norm minimization with application to image denoising, in: Proc. of the IEEE CVPR, 2014, pp. 2862–2869.

[28] J. Kim, J. Kwon Lee, K. Mu Lee, Accurate image super-resolution using very deep convolutional networks, in: Proceedings of the IEEE Conference on Computer Vision and Pattern Recognition, Las Vegas, USA, June 2016, pp. 1646–1654.

[29] Y. Romano, J. Isidoro, P. Milanfar, RAISR: Rapid and accurate image super-resolution, IEEE Transactions on Computational Imaging 3 (1) (2017) 110–125.

[30] M. Bertalmio, G. Sapiro, V. Caselles, C. Ballester, Image inpainting, in: Proceedings of the 27th Annual Conference on Computer Graphics and Interactive Techniques, ACM Press/Addison-Wesley Publishing Co., 2000, pp. 417–424.

[31] A. Criminisi, P. Pérez, K. Toyama, Region filling and object removal by exemplar-based image inpainting, IEEE Transactions on Image Processing (ISSN 1057-7149) 13 (9) (2004) 1200–1212.

[32] M. Elad, J.-L. Starck, P. Querre, D.L. Donoho, Simultaneous cartoon and texture image inpainting using morphological component analysis (MCA), Applied and Computational Harmonic Analysis 19 (3) (2005) 340–358.

[33] M. Delbracio, G. Sapiro, Burst deblurring: Removing camera shake through Fourier burst accumulation, in: Proceedings of the IEEE Conference on Computer Vision and Pattern Recognition, Boston, Massachusetts, June 2015, pp. 2385–2393.

[34] J.A. Guerrero-Colón, L. Mancera, J. Portilla, Image restoration using space-variant Gaussian scale mixtures in overcomplete pyramids, IEEE Transactions on Image Processing 17 (1) (2008) 27–41.

[35] A. Danielyan, V. Katkovnik, K. Egiazarian, BM3D frames and variational image deblurring, IEEE Transactions on Image Processing 21 (4) (2012) 1715–1728.

[36] S.V. Venkatakrishnan, C.A. Bouman, B. Wohlberg, Plug-and-play priors for model-based reconstruction, in: Global Conference on Signal and Information Processing (GlobalSIP), IEEE, 2013, pp. 945–948.

[37] Y. Dar, A.M. Bruckstein, M. Elad, R. Giryes, Postprocessing of compressed images via sequential denoising, IEEE Transactions on Image Processing 25 (7) (2016) 3044–3058.

[38] S. Sreehari, S.V. Venkatakrishnan, B. Wohlberg, G.T. Buzzard, L.F. Drummy, J.P. Simmons, C.A. Bouman, Plug-and-play priors for bright field electron tomography and sparse interpolation, IEEE Transactions on Computational Imaging 2 (4) (2016) 408–423.

[39] A. Rond, R. Giryes, M. Elad, Poisson inverse problems by the plug-and-play scheme, Journal of Visual Communication and Image Representation (ISSN 1047-3203) 41 (2016) 96–108.

[40] D. Zoran, Y. Weiss, From learning models of natural image patches to whole image restoration, in: Proc. of the IEEE Int. Conf. Comput. Vis., 2011, pp. 479–486, https://doi.org/10.1109/iccv.2011.6126278.

[41] S.H. Chan, X. Wang, O.A. Elgendy, Plug-and-play ADMM for image restoration: Fixed-point convergence and applications, IEEE Transactions on Computational Imaging 3 (1) (2017) 84–98.

[42] Tom Tirer, Raja Giryes, Image restoration by iterative denoising and backward projections, IEEE Transactions on Image Processing 28 (3) (2019) 1220–1234.

[43] Y. Chen, T. Pock, Trainable nonlinear reaction-diffusion: a flexible framework for fast and effective image restoration, IEEE Transactions on Pattern Analysis and Machine Intelligence 39 (6) (2017) 1256–1272.

[44] L.I. Rudin, S. Osher, E. Fatemi, Nonlinear total variation based noise removal algorithms, Physica D, Nonlinear Phenomena 60 (1–4) (1992) 259–268.

[45] C. Wu, X.-C. Tai, Augmented Lagrangian method, dual methods, and split Bregman iteration for ROF, vectorial TV, and high order models, SIAM Journal on Imaging Sciences 3 (3) (2010) 300–339.

[46] T. Goldstein, S. Osher, The split Bregman method for L1-regularized problems, SIAM Journal on Imaging Sciences 2 (2) (2009) 323–343.

[47] J. Yang, Y. Zhang, W. Yin, An efficient TVL1 algorithm for deblurring multichannel images corrupted by impulsive noise, SIAM Journal on Scientific Computing 31 (4) (2009) 2842–2865.

[48] V. Grimm, R.I. McLachlan, D.I. McLaren, G. Quispel, C. Schönlieb, Discrete gradient methods for solving variational image regularisation models, Journal of Physics. A, Mathematical and General 50 (29) (2017) 295201.

[49] V.B.S. Prasath, D. Vorotnikov, R. Pelapur, S. Jose, G. Seetharaman, K. Palaniappan, Multiscale Tikhonov-total variation image restoration using spatially varying edge coherence exponent, IEEE Transactions on Image Processing 24 (12) (2015) 5220–5235.

[50] U. Erkan, D.N.H. Thanh, L.M. Hieu, S. Engínoğlu, An iterative mean filter for image denoising, IEEE Access 7 (2019) 167847–167859.

[51] S.H. Chan, R. Khoshabeh, K.B. Gibson, P.E. Gill, T.Q. Nguyen, An augmented Lagrangian method for total variation video restoration, IEEE Transactions on Image Processing 20 (11) (2011) 3097–3111.

[52] D.N. Thanh, V.S. Prasath, L.M. Hieu, A review on CT and X-ray images denoising methods, Informatica 43 (2) (2019) 151–159.

[53] J.-F. Aujol, Some first-order algorithms for total variation based image restoration, Journal of Mathematical Imaging and Vision 34 (3) (2009) 307–327.

[54] J. Shen, T.F. Chan, Mathematical models for local nontexture in paintings, SIAM Journal on Applied Mathematics 62 (3) (2002) 1019–1043.

[55] O. Scherzer, M. Grasmair, H. Grossauer, M. Haltmeier, F. Lenzen, Variational Methods in Imaging, vol. 320, 1st ed., Springer, 2009.

[56] Z. Zhang, Y. Xu, J. Yang, X. Li, D. Zhang, A survey of sparse representation: Algorithms and applications, IEEE Access 3 (1) (2015) 490–530.

[57] R.H. Chan, H. Liang, S. Wei, M. Nikolova, X.-C. Tai, High-order total variation regularization approach for axially symmetric object tomography from a single radiograph, Inverse Problems and Imaging 9 (1) (2015) 55–77.

[58] T. Sanders, R.B. Platte, Multiscale higher-order TV operators for L1 regularization, Advanced Structural and Chemical Imaging 4 (1) (2018) 12.

[59] L. Sun, K. Chen, A new iterative algorithm for mean curvature-based variational image denoising, BIT Numerical Mathematics 54 (2) (2014) 523–553.

[60] J. Zhang, K. Chen, A total fractional-order variation model for image restoration with nonhomogeneous boundary conditions and its numerical solution, SIAM Journal on Imaging Sciences 8 (4) (2015) 2487–2518.

[61] S. Wali, A. Shakoor, A. Basit, L. Xie, C. Huang, C. Li, An efficient method for Euler's elastica based image deconvolution, IEEE Access 7 (2019) 61226–61239.

[62] Z. Liu, S. Wali, Y. Duan, H. Chang, C. Wu, X.-C. Tai, Proximal ADMM for Euler's elastica based image decomposition model, Numerical Mathematics: Theory, Methods and Applications 12 (2) (2018) 370–402.

[63] W. Lu, J. Duan, Z. Qiu, Z. Pan, R.W. Liu, L. Bai, Implementation of high-order variational models made easy for image processing, Mathematical Methods in the Applied Sciences 39 (14) (2016) 4208–4233.

[64] Y. Freund, R.E. Schapire, A decision-theoretic generalization of on-line learning and an application to boosting, Journal of Computer and System Sciences 55 (1) (1997) 119–139.

[65] J. Kaiser, R. Hamming, Sharpening the response of asymmetric non-recursive filter by multiple use of the same filter, IEEE Transactions on Acoustics, Speech, and Signal Processing 25 (5) (1977) 415–422.

[66] E. Tadmor, S. Nezzar, L. Vese, A multiscale image representation using hierarchical (BV, L2) decompositions, Multiscale Modeling & Simulation 2 (4) (2004) 554–579.

[67] Rini Smita Thakur, R.N. Yadav, Lalita Gupta, PReLU and edge-aware filter-based image denoiser using convolutional neural network, IET Image Processing 14 (15) (2020) 3869–3879.

[68] Y. Romano, M. Elad, Boosting of image denoising algorithms, SIAM Journal on Imaging Sciences 8 (2) (2015) 1187–1219.

[69] K. Zhang, W. Zuo, Y. Chen, D. Meng, L. Zhang, Beyond a Gaussian denoiser: Residual learning of deep CNN for image denoising, IEEE Transactions on Image Processing 26 (7) (2017) 3142–3155.

[70] A. Effland, E. Kobler, K. Kunisch, T. Pock, An optimal control approach to early stopping variational methods for image restoration, arXiv:1907.08488, 2019, pp. 1–32.

[71] J.H. Friedman, J.W. Tukey, A projection pursuit algorithm for exploratory data analysis, IEEE Transactions on Computers C-23 (9) (1974) 881–890.

[72] S. Basalamah, S.D. Khan, H. Ullah, Scale driven convolutional neural network model for people counting and localization in crowd scenes, IEEE Access 7 (2019) 71576–71584.

[73] H. Ullah, M. Uzair, M. Ullah, A. Khan, A. Ahmad, W. Khan, Density independent hydrodynamics model for crowd coherency detection, Neurocomputing 242 (2017) 28–39, https://doi.org/10.1016/j.neucom.2017.02.023.

[74] P. Rota, H. Ullah, N. Conci, N. Sebe, F.G. De Natale, Particles cross-influence for entity grouping, in: Proc. 21st Eur. Signal Process. Conf. (EUSIPCO), 2013, pp. 1–5.

[75] M. Ullah, F.A. Cheikh, Deep feature based end-to-end transportation network for multi-target tracking, in: Proc. 25th IEEE Int. Conf. Image Process. (ICIP), 2018, pp. 3738–3742.

[76] F. Ahmad, A. Khan, I.U. Islam, M. Uzair, H. Ullah, Illumination normalization using independent component analysis and filtering, The Imaging Science Journal 65 (5) (2017) 308–313.

[77] E. Bratsolis, M. Sigelle, A spatial regularization method preserving local photometry for Richardson–Lucy restoration, Astronomy & Astrophysics 375 (3) (2001) 1120–1128.

[78] Samad Wali, Chunming Li, Abdul Basit, Abdul Shakoor, Raheel Ahmed Memon, Sabit Rahim, Samina Samina, Fast and adaptive boosting techniques for variational based image restoration, IEEE Access 7 (2019) 181491–181504, https://doi.org/10.1109/ACCESS.2019.2959003.

[79] S. Osher, M. Burger, D. Goldfarb, J. Xu, W. Yin, An iterative regularization method for total variation based image restoration, Multiscale Modeling & Simulation 4 (2) (2005) 460–489.

[80] J. Ghosh Dastidar, S. Dutta, S. Bhattacharya, A. Jaiswal, Image restoration using DWT in a tile-based manner, International Journal for Research in Engineering Application & Management 4 (5) (2018) 413–418.

[81] W. Dong, L. Zhang, G. Shi, X. Li, Nonlocally centralized sparse representation for image restoration, IEEE Transactions on Image Processing 22 (4) (2013) 1620–1630.

[82] R. Timofte, V. De Smet, L. Van Gool, A+: adjusted anchored neighbourhood regression for fast super-resolution, in: Asian Conference on Computer Vision, in: Lecture Notes in Computer Science, ISSN 0302-9743, vol. 9006, Springer, Singapore, Nov. 2014.

[83] R. Timofte, R. Rothe, L. Van Gool, Seven ways to improve example-based single-image super-resolution, in: Proceedings of the IEEE Conference on Computer Vision and Pattern Recognition, 2016, pp. 1865–1873.
[84] C. Dong, C.C. Loy, K. He, X. Tang, Image super-resolution using deep convolutional networks, IEEE Transactions on Pattern Analysis and Machine Intelligence 38 (2016) 295–307.
[85] C. Osendorfer, H. Soyer, P. Van Der Smagt, Image super-resolution with fast approximate convolutional sparse coding, in: International Conference on Neural Information Processing, Springer, Kuching, Malaysia, November 2014, pp. 250–257.
[86] Z. Wang, D. Liu, J. Yang, W. Han, T. Huang, Deep networks for image super-resolution with sparse prior, in: Proceedings of the IEEE International Conference on Computer Vision, Santiago, Chile, Dec 2015, pp. 370–378.
[87] Shubhojeet Chatterjee, Rini Thakur, R.N. Yadav, Lalita Gupta, Sparsity-based modified wavelet de-noising autoencoder for ECG signals, Signal Processing 198 (September 2022) 108605, https://doi.org/10.1016/j.sigpro.2022.108605, Elsevier.
[88] Fangfang Wu, Weisheng Dong, Tao Huang, Guangming Shi, Shaoyuan Cheng, Xin Li, Hybrid sparsity learning for image restoration: An iterative and trainable approach, Signal Processing 178 (2021) 1–13.
[89] Reeturaj Mishra, Neetu Mittal, Sunil Kumar Khatri, Digital image restoration using image filtering techniques, in: International Conference on Automation, Computational and Technology Management (ICACTM), Amity University, India, April 2019, pp. 268–272.
[90] Madri Thakur, Shilpa Datar, Image restoration based on deconvolution by Richardson–Lucy algorithm, International Journal of Engineering Trends and Technology 14 (4) (2014).
[91] R.S. Thakur, S. Chatterjee, R.N. Yadav, L. Gupta, Image de-noising with machine learning: a review, IEEE Access (ISSN 2169-3536) 9 (2021) 93338–93363, https://doi.org/10.1109/ACCESS.2021.3092425.
[92] A.A. Neath, J.E. Cavanaugh, Regression and time series model selection using variants of the Schwartz information criterion, Communications in Statistics 26 (1997) 559–580.

CHAPTER 9

Comprehensive survey of face super-resolution techniques

Anurag Singh Tomar[a]**, K.V. Arya**[a]**, Shyam Singh Rajput**[b]**, and Ciro R. Rodriguez**[c]

[a]Multimedia and Information Security Research Group, ABV-Indian Institute of Information Technology and Management, Gwalior, India
[b]Department of Computer Science and Engineering, National Institute of Technology Patna, Patna, India
[c]Dept of Software Engineering, Universidad National Mayor de San Marcos, UNMSM, Lima, Peru

9.1 Introduction

Image super-resolution is the technique to reconstruct the high-resolution (HR) image, which contains the high-frequency component, sharper visual details, and larger spatial dimension from low-resolution (LR) image. Classification of image super-resolution methods [1] is based on (i) number of input low-resolution images, such as single or multiple images, (ii) type of input image, such as generic or domain specific image, and (iii) domain of operating the image, for example, spatial or frequency domain. The classification of existing image super-resolution methods is depicted in Fig. 9.1. Single LR image is given as input for single image super-resolution, whereas the multiple LR images for multiple image super-resolution. In many real-life scenarios single LR image is available. Due to that researchers are more attracted towards the single-image super-resolution. In the spatial domain, pixel manipulation is directly implemented, whereas in the frequency domain, firstly image is transformed into frequency domain, and then the super-resolution process is implemented; after that, inverse transformation takes place to convert the image into spatial domain. Domain-specific image super-resolution corresponds to face, biometric, or text widely used for different applications.

Researchers are more attracted to face super-resolution due to its applicability in the field of face recognition system. The structure and components of facial parts are more prominently visible in super-resolution facial image than its counterpart, low-resolution, and hence can be used in the face recognition system, given the availability of discriminating features. Existing face recognition system [26] may not be able to recognize

Digital Image Enhancement and Reconstruction
https://doi.org/10.1016/B978-0-32-398370-9.00016-0

213

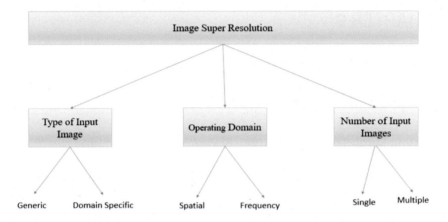

Figure 9.1 Classification of image super-resolution.

the blur, downsampled, and noisy facial images. Therefore identity preserving face super-resolution systems are required, which will preserve the identity of the super-resolved face images. The LR and HR face images are subdivided into overlapped patches, and corresponding to each LR patch, high-resolution face patch is reconstructed with the help of a super-resolution algorithm. Furthermore, all HR reconstructed face patches are integrated to construct the global HR face image, which smoothens the overlapped region by taking the average of pixel values.

9.2 Face image degradation model

Face super-resolution algorithm required the dataset that contains the pair of LR and HR facial images. Practically HR facial images are available; hence, the degradation process needs to be implemented on HR face images to get the corresponding LR image. Mathematical modeling of the degradation process helps in representing the relationship between HR and the obtained LR facial image during the acquisition process. A degraded version of HR face image is generally obtained due to misalignment of cameras, motion, downsampling, system and environmental noise, etc. To obtain the LR face images [1] few operations, such as a blur, downsample, and addition of noise have to be performed over the HR face image. The degradation model, shown in Fig. 9.2, represents the process of degrading the high-resolution image to obtain the low-resolution image.

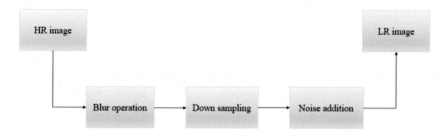

Figure 9.2 Face image degradation model.

The mathematical model to implement the degradation over the HR face image is represented in the form of Eq. (9.1):

$$(HR \circledast B) \downarrow s + n = LR \tag{9.1}$$

where B is blur kernel, $\circledast$ denotes convolution operation, $\downarrow s$ represents downsampling by a factor of s, HR is high-resolution image, n is noise, and LR is low-resolution image. In many super-resolution methods to increase the spatial dimension, interpolation is applied on the LR image to make it same size as HR Image.

9.3 Classification of face hallucination methods

Face hallucination is one of the domains of image super-resolution, where input face images are often blurry, noisy, and smaller. Fig. 9.3 depicts the classification of available face hallucination methods: interpolation-based, reconstruction, and learning-based approaches. Interpolation-based approaches, such as the nearest neighbor, bilinear, and bicubic, upsample the LR image and estimate the unknown pixel value based on available pixel values. It is very simple to use, but not effective, and the resultant image may be blurred. Reconstruction-based approaches estimate the high-resolution image from the sequence of blur and downsampled LR images. Although it is not very popular due to unavailability of multiple LR images of the same image, for the purpose of research, different manipulation operations are performed to generate the multiple LR images. Learning-based approach uses the learning phase to learn the mapping relationship between a pair of LR and HR image patch through the training set, and inference phase estimates the HR patch corresponding to LR patch. Learning-based methods achieve a high visual quality facial image as

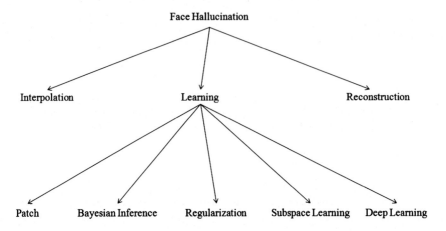

Figure 9.3 Classification of face hallucination methods.

compared to the reconstruction-based approach. Model parameters learned from the training pairs are used to map the input LR into the HR facial image. Although various super-resolution images may exist corresponding to a single LR image, therefore methods like facial structure prior, and identity prior are used to get more accurate and unique super-resolved facial image.

Learning-based methods of face hallucination [21] are generally categorized as patch-based, Bayesian inference regularization, subspace learning, and deep learning-based methods. Learning-based face hallucination methods are discussed below in more detailed manner.

9.3.1 Patch-based method

Patch-based face super-resolution methods subdivide the face images into the small overlapped patches, then reconstruct each patch separately. These methods are helpful to preserve the fine detail of facial image. Although these methods are computationally expensive and time-consuming, they super-resolved the face images in an accurate way. Patch-based methods are further classified as position patch-based method and neighbor patch-based methods.

9.3.1.1 Position patch-based methods

They are very popular methods in face super-resolution as they reconstruct the input image patch using the same position patches [2,9,31,33,37,38] of the training set. We need to learn the representation coefficient corresponding to the individual training position patches to reconstruct the input image patch. High–resolution face image patches are reconstructed using the same representation coefficients.

9.3.1.2 Neighbor patch-based methods

These methods reconstruct the input image patch by using similar training image patches [1] instead of the same position–based patches. Similarity among the input and training patch is computed by using the pixel-wise Euclidean distance and/or some other methods, such as feature similarity. However, this method is more popular in generic image super-resolution.

9.3.2 Bayesian inference

Bayesian inference is a statistical method, in which the Bayes theorem [3] is used to estimate the unknown variable or parameter. Bayes theorem is used in Bayesian inference to estimate the probabilistic high-resolution face, whereas low-resolution image is given. The Bayesian inference framework, shown in Fig. 9.4, is used to best estimate the high-resolution of a face image by using the maximum a posteriori (MAP) rule in Bayesian statistics [4] for face hallucination is represented in the form of Eqs. (9.2) and (9.3):

$$\hat{I}_h = argmax \, P(I_h \mid I_l) \tag{9.2}$$

$$\hat{I}_h = argmax \, P(I_l \mid I_h) P(I_h) \tag{9.3}$$

where I_h and I_l correspond to high- and low-resolution face image, $P(I_l \mid I_h)$ is the likelihood and can also be taken as Gaussian form, $P(I_h)$ is the prior, $P(I_l)$ is constant as I_l is given as input. The Bayesian inference-based approach is used in gradient prior and Markov random field.

9.3.2.1 Markov random field

Markov random field [5] is an undirected graphical model that models the dependency relationship among the random variables and helps to compute the joint probability distribution of variables. Each node in the graph represents the random variable, and edges represent the dependency relationship among the nodes. Markov random field [6,7] represents the face image patches as nodes, LR–HR pair as vertical edges, and HR neighbor patches by horizontal edges as shown in Fig. 9.4.

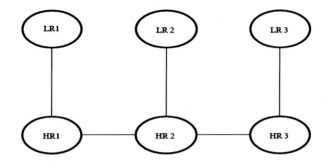

Figure 9.4 Markov random field.

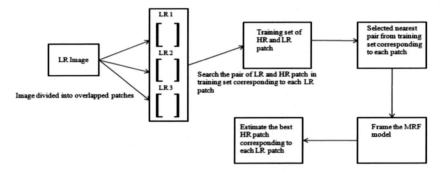

Figure 9.5 Face super-resolution process using Markov random field.

In face hallucination, a pair of HR and LR face images are collected, and each image is divided into overlapped patches to build the training set. For each input, LR patch, firstly, the K nearest pair of LR and HR patch is selected from the training set to build the compatibility matrix and neighbor relationship or smoothness constraint among the neighboring high-resolution face images. The process of face super-resolution through Markov random field is shown in Fig. 9.5.

Framing of MRF model, as shown in Fig. 9.6, involves estimating the best HR face image corresponding to each LR patch such that HR patch best explains the LR patch and compatible to neighbor HR patch or similar intensity value in the overlapped region in neighboring HR patch. In this way, we try to balance the data fidelity and smoothness prior of an face image so that the super-resolution face image would be less blur, smooth, and closer to the HR version of the face image. Compatibility matrix $\Phi(\mathrm{HR}_k, \mathrm{LR}_k)$ describes the relationship between k^{th} HR and LR patches, and $\Psi(\mathrm{HR}_k, \mathrm{HR}_{k+1})$ describes the neighborhood relationship among the

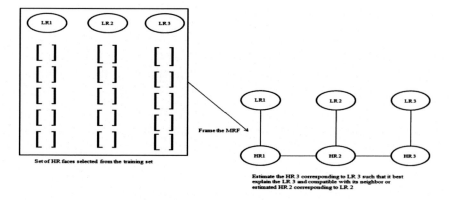

Figure 9.6 Framing of MRF model.

adjacent HR patches. The joint probability over a HR image I_h and its LR image I_l can be written in the form of below equation (9.4):

$$P(I_h, I_l) = P(I_{h1}, I_{h2}, I_{hk}, I_{l1}, I_{l2}, I_{lk})$$
$$= \Psi(I_{h1}, I_{h2})\Psi(I_{h2}, I_{hk})\Phi(I_{h1}, I_{l1})\Phi(I_{h2}, I_{l2})\Phi(I_{hk}, I_{lk}) \qquad (9.4)$$

Compatibility function Ψ and Φ are computed with the help of training samples and represented by Eqs. (9.5) and (9.6), respectively:

$$\Psi(I_{h1}^l, I_{h2}^m) = e^{-1/2\sigma_c^{2(I_{h1}^l - I_{h2}^m)^2}} \qquad (9.5)$$

$$\Phi(I_{h1}^l, I_{l1}) = e^{-1/2\sigma_n^{2(I_{l1}^l - I_{l1})^2}} \qquad (9.6)$$

where σ_c, σ_s are the predefined parameters; I_{h1}^l, I_{h2}^m are l^{th}, m^{th} possible face image patch corresponding to I_{h1}, I_{h2}, which overlapped with each other, and I_{l1}^l is the lth nearest neighbor of I_{l1} patch. Probabilistic super-resolution face is computed by Eqs. (9.7) and (9.8).

$$I_h^* = argmax\, P(I_{h1}, I_{h2}, I_{hk}, I_{l1}, I_{l2}, I_{lk}) \qquad (9.7)$$

$$I_h^* = argmax \prod \Psi(I_{h1}, I_{h2})\Psi(I_{h2}, I_{hk}) \prod \Phi(I_{h1}, I_{l1})\Phi(I_{h2}, I_{l2})\phi(I_{hk}, I_{lk}) \quad (9.8)$$

Here, I_h^* is the super-resolved image corresponding to I_l, which is obtained by integrating overlapped super-resolved patches I_{h1}, I_{h2}, I_{hk} and take the average of the intensity in the overlapped region.

9.3.3 Regularization methods

Regularization methods can improve the conditioning of the undetermined problem to get the unique and stable solution. These methods are helpful to handle the effect of noise and outlier during the reconstruction of super-resolution facial images. Variety of facial prior is used in the field of super-resolution, such as smoothness, structural feature, edge, facial components, etc., to generate a good quality facial image. Few of popular regularization methods [8] are discussed below.

9.3.3.1 Sparse representation

In the last few years sparse coding [25] became popular in signal and image processing due to its simplicity and lot of application in different fields. A signal can be represented as linear combination of few atoms of dictionary, and dictionary contains the K atoms or columns, which contains the basis of discrete cosine transform, discrete wavelet transform, etc. Once you obtained the dictionary by either of the methods, the objective is then to find out the sparse few nonzero coefficient corresponding to dictionary to represent the signal or image. Sparse representation also has application in image super-resolution, where the task is to find out the sparse few nonzero coefficients to represent the high- and low-resolution images. Face hallucination using the sparse representation is to recover the high-frequency information from the low-resolution facial image. Firstly, the LR and HR facial images are divided into overlapped patches and represent each patch in vector form. The LR and HR dictionaries are prepared by arranging the individual patches in form of columns or atoms into matrix. For each input LR patch sparse representation coefficient is computed with the help of the LR dictionary and the same representation coefficient is used with corresponding HR image patches to compute the super-resolution facial image. Sparse representation coefficient of LR patch y can be computed by Eq. (9.9):

$$\min \|\alpha\|_0 \quad \text{s.t.} \quad \|D_L \alpha - y\|_2^2 \leq \epsilon \tag{9.9}$$

L_0 norm can be replaced with L_1 norm to efficiently solve the optimization problem.

The sparse representation problem can be reformulated using the L_1 norm, as shown in Eq. (9.10):

$$\min \|\alpha\|_1 \quad \text{s.t.} \quad \|D_L \alpha - y\|_2^2 \leq \epsilon \tag{9.10}$$

The sparse representation problem reformulated using the Lagrange multipliers is shown in Eqs. (9.11) and (9.12):

$$\min \|D_L \alpha - \gamma\|_2^2 + \lambda \|\alpha\|_1 \tag{9.11}$$

$$x = D_H \alpha \tag{9.12}$$

where D_L, D_H, α, γ, x, λ represent the LR dictionary, HR dictionary, sparse coefficient, LR patch, HR patch, and trade-off parameter to balance the reconstruction error and regularization term, respectively.

9.3.3.2 L_p norm

It is the generalized form of norm, where $p = 1, 2$ are corresponding to L_1, L_2 norm, and for $p > 2$, L_p norm is defined by Eqs. (9.13) and (9.14):

$$\|\alpha\|_p = \sum (\alpha_i^p)^{1/p} \tag{9.13}$$

as the p approaches infinity, called infinity or maximum norm, where the maximum element of vector or cost function is affected. Infinity norm is defined as

$$\|\alpha\|_{inf} = \max |\alpha_i| \tag{9.14}$$

Face super-resolution optimization problem consists of data fidelity or reconstruction error and prior term. In the infinity norm, we are trying to penalize those coefficients, i.e., α corresponding to LR face patches which results the higher reconstruction error.

9.3.3.3 Locality-constrained

Sparse representation methods are based on strong sparsity of representation coefficient, leading to ignorance of locality constrained. Locality constrained is more important to preserve the true geometry of the face image patches. Locality constraint [10] assigns the higher weights to more relevant patch, hence helps to preserve the true geometry of patches. Face super-resolution problem using locality constrained is defined by Eq. (9.15):

$$\min \|D_L \alpha - \gamma\|_2^2 + \lambda R(\alpha) \tag{9.15}$$

where D_L, α, γ, λ, $R(\alpha)$ represent the low-resolution dictionary, representation coefficient, LR face image patch, regularization parameter, and locality-constrained, respectively.

9.3.3.4 Tikhonov regularization

Locality constrained reconstruct the input image patch by using the entire training position patches with different degrees of freedom, which may cause facial discrimination loss. Tikhonov regularized face super-resolution method [11] uses only the K similar training faces in the training set, which helps to maintain the facial discrimination. Tikhonov regularized neighbor representation used the Tikhonov matrix to assign the different degree of freedom, which helped to get a unique and stable solution. Tikhonov regularization term is defined by Eqs. (9.16) and (9.17):

$$R(\alpha) = \|L\alpha\|_2^2 \qquad (9.16)$$

where $L = \beta I$ is multiple of identity matrix I, β is the distance matrix of LR face image patch to its nearest neighbor LR training patches, and L is called Tikhonov matrix super-resolution problem. The Tikhonov regularization can be defined as

$$\min \|D_L\alpha - y\|_2^2 + \lambda R(\alpha) \qquad (9.17)$$

where D_L, α, y, λ, $R(\alpha)$ represent the low-resolution dictionary, representation coefficient, LR face image patch, regularization parameter, and Tikhonov regularization, respectively.

9.3.3.5 Total variation regularization

Total variation is the gradient or discrete differentiation-based regularization technique to preserve the sharp edges of image. Furthermore, it is used as a prior in face super-resolution optimization problem to enhance the solution. Total variation regularization term is defined by Eqs. (9.18) and (9.19):

$$R(\alpha) = \|L\alpha\|_1 = \sqrt{\left(\frac{d}{dx}\alpha\right)^2 + \left(\frac{d}{dy}\alpha\right)^2} \qquad (9.18)$$

where L is discrete differentiation operator or first-order derivate. Total variation using the first-order gradient in the direction of x and y, so it is highly sensitive towards the noise, and suffer from staircase artifact and produce the blurry edges. Face super-resolution problem using the total variation regularization can be defined as

$$\min \|D_L\alpha - y\|_2^2 + \lambda R(\alpha) \qquad (9.19)$$

where D_L, α, γ, λ, $R(\alpha)$ represent the low-resolution dictionary, representation coefficient, LR face image patch, regularization parameter, and total variation regularization, respectively.

9.3.4 Subspace learning

It is a method to learn the low-dimensional subspace embedded in high-dimensional space. Learning subspace includes finding a projection matrix from the training samples, which can project high to low dimensions. In the linear subspace learning [12], problem can be formulated as generalized eigenvalue decomposition, which is defined as $Au_i = \lambda_i B u_i$ where A, B are matrix, u_i is the eigenvector corresponding to eigenvalue λ_i. The given face image vector can be easily projected into linear subspace with the help of projection matrix constructed with the engagement of eigenvectors. The eigenvectors with maximum variance are selected to preserve maximum information. A similar idea can be extended for nonlinear subspace or non-linear manifold learning. In manifold learning, the local neighborhood of pixel or patch structure is explored to learn the relationship between the LR and HR face image patches. Subspace learning approach assumes that the weight learned for reconstructing LR patches or pixels through the local neighborhood is also used to construct the HR patches. Generally, learning of subspace includes the learning of weights through the local neighborhood in training samples, and the same weights are used to reconstruct high-resolution face images. The framework of learning subspace is shown in Fig. 9.7.

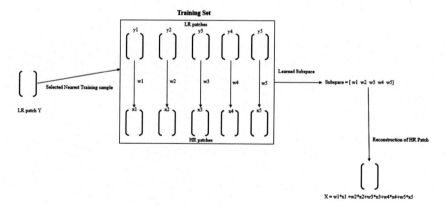

Figure 9.7 Framework of subspace learning.

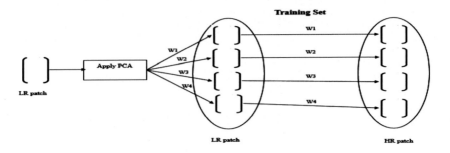

Figure 9.8 PCA-based subspace learning.

9.3.4.1 Linear subspace learning

It is a method of learning the weights from the training set to reconstruct the high-resolution face images. The generalized eigen decomposition method is used to find the eigenvectors from the training set, and the given low-resolution input face image is transformed into the subspace. Principal component analysis (PCA) is the one of the methods used in the linear subspace learning approach to learn the weight vector.

PCA-based subspace learning method [12,13], as shown in Fig. 9.8, is discussed below.

1. The given low-resolution facial image is subdivided into the overlapped patches. Each patch is represented in vector form. For each patch find the k similar pair of LR and HR patches from the training set.
2. Make the matrix of k a similar LR face image and find the eigenvector using the standard eigen decomposition method.
3. Project the given LR patch in subspace using the projection matrix, and it will act as a weight vector for the reconstruction of given LR face image patch.
4. The same weight vector can be used to reconstruct the face image patch corresponding to HR training samples.

9.3.4.2 Nonlinear manifold-based learning

Manifold learning acts like a nonlinear version of PCA, where we are projecting the data points over nonlinear subspace. PCA projects the points over low-dimensional space, whose surface is linear; in some cases, the best representation of points may not lie in linear subspace or may lie in nonlinear subspace, so in that case, manifold learning is valuable. Manifold is an essential aspect in mathematics that describes the surface of any shape, so we can project the points or represent the points in nonlinear subspace.

Face super-resolution uses manifold-based learning [14] to get the optimum weight vector for reconstructing LR face images. The same weight vector can be used to get the HR face image through the local neighborhood structure. Local linear embedding (LLE) is a method of manifold-based learning used for super-resolution.

9.3.5 Deep learning

Deep learning-based methods have become more prevalent in face super-resolution due to their representation ability and learning relationship of input and output. Deep learning-based methods extract, enhance, and up-sample the features to generate the super-resolution image. Generally, face super-resolution methods [22,23] are based on convolution neural network (CNN), generative adversarial network (GAN) [15], residual network, and dense network. Convolution neural network is the basic building block to design the network due to its ability to extract the features. Cascaded CNN blocks are used with skip connections to build the residual-based network, which helps in sharing the features and provides the alternate path for the flow of gradient. Dense connection is another way to reuse the features from all the previous layers, but this way of reusing the features is more complex than residual connections. Generative adversarial network has the generator to generate the super-resolution image and discriminator to distinguish between high-resolution and super-resolution face images. The attention-based deep learning method [16] has become more popular as it reweights the features at every block of the feature extractor to prioritize essential features, which will further help to improve the quality of super-resolution images. Identity prior-based deep learning methods [17] attracted the researcher due to their ability to increase face recognition accuracy [26,29,30,34–36] or preserve identity in super-resolution face images. Generated super-resolution images are passed through the face recognition network to learn the embedding of face images and update the weights of the super-resolution model accordingly.

The author presented the face super-resolution model using generative adversarial network, which can ultra-resolve a low-resolution facial image [18] to a larger spatial dimension. The discriminator network learns the essential components of facial images, whereas the generator network blends these components to reconstruct the high-resolution image. The generator model is trained with pixel-wise L2 regularization and exploits the feedback of the discriminative network to reconstruct the more realistic super-resolution image. Ultra-resolving face images by discriminative generative networks super-resolved the low-resolution face images, regardless of pose and facial expression variations.

Early face super-resolution techniques used the face images with minor variations, but later super-resolution algorithms used the face images with different poses and variations. Facial prior knowledge could be helpful to improve the quality of super-resolution images. Face super-resolution technique uses various priors, such as geometrical, facial landmark, and parsing maps to super-resolved the low-resolution facial images. In a novel deep end-to-end trainable face super-resolution network (FSRNet) [27], first construct a coarse super-resolution image. The coarse super-resolution image is sent to the super-resolution encoder module and prior estimation network to extract the features and prior, respectively. The super-resolution decoder uses the extracted features and prior to reconstruct the high-resolution image.

Generative adversarial network architectures having the generator module, which uses the residual blocks to super-resolved the facial images, usually have undesirable artifacts. To improve the visual quality of super-resolution facial images [15], the generator network uses dense convolutional blocks, instead of residual blocks that connect each layer to every other layer in a feed-forward fashion and help in sharing the previous layer features. Discriminator network acts as a classifier to distinguish the high-resolution and super-resolution facial images. Generator learns from the feedback of the discriminator to preserve the essential features of facial images.

Wasserstein GAN (WGAN) has overcome the classical generative adversarial network issues, which uses the KL and JS divergence. In contrast, the WGAN uses the Wasserstein distance metric to measure the distance between the generated face image and high-resolution face image distribution. Classical GAN becomes highly unstable when the distribution does not overlap, while WGAN can correctly measure the distance in such a case. The adversarial loss with several variations is used in face super-resolution techniques to generate realistic super-resolution facial images. Face super-resolution using Wasserstein GAN (WGAN) [19] used various architectures, such as deep convolution generative adversarial network (DCGAN) and residual network. Generator network uses the deconvolution layers to upsample the low-resolution image, whereas the discriminator network uses the convolution layers to discriminate the facial images.

Recently, researchers have been attracted more towards the attention-based mechanisms in face super-resolution. The key idea is to reweight the features using a score map to highlight key facial features and suppress less useful ones. The researcher used the face attention unit [16], in which the attention module is used with a feature extractor block to focus on key face structure. Novel spatial attention residual network (SPARNet) architecture focuses on a high- and low-level view of the face to learn global and local details of facial features. SPARNet uses the multiple face attention unit to focus on individual facial components, and later upsamples these key facial components to reconstruct the high-resolution facial images.

Face super-resolution techniques focus on improving the visual quality of super-resolution images without considering the facial identity, which causes poor accuracy in the face recognition system. An identity-preservation-based deep learning method [28] is proposed to address these problems for super-resolving blurry face images. It consists of restoration and recognition modules trained separately with mean absolute error and softmax loss function, respectively. Later both the modules are trained together with the combined loss function to backpropagate the weights from recognition to restoration module.

9.4 Assessment criteria of face super-resolution algorithm

Super-resolution facial image quality is evaluated by visual attributes and the perception of the human observer. However, super-resolution algorithm performance is evaluated by using subjective and objective methods. The subjective method includes the human perception about the quality of an image. Hence the number of observers observed the super-resolution image and evaluated the quality in terms of mean opinion and variance score. The objective method computes the parameter [23], such as mean square error (MSE), peak signal-to-noise ratio (PSNR) to evaluate the quality of super-resolution facial images. However, these methods fail to capture human visual perception; furthermore, objective-based methods are classified as full and reduced references. In the full reference method, super-resolved image is compared with full reference image, whereas in reduced reference compared with extracted features. Few face image quality assessment methods are discussed below.

9.4.1 Mean opinion score

It is an easy and most common method used to assess the quality of super-resolution facial images. Based on their visual perception, several human observers were asked to rate the quality of facial images on some predefined scale and compute the mean opinion score by taking the average of all the ratings assigned to the image. However, it suffered from the bias and variance of rating parameters. It is a method to measure perceptual quality accurately.

9.4.2 Mean square error

It is defined as the pixel–wise sum of the square of the difference between the high–resolution and the reconstructed super-resolved facial image. It concerns only corresponding pixel values, not the perceptual quality. Mean square error (MSE) is defined as

$$MSE = \frac{1}{N} \sum (I(i) - \hat{I}(i))^2 \tag{9.20}$$

where I and $\hat{I}$ represent the high-resolution and reconstructed super-resolution face image, respectively.

9.4.3 Peak signal-to-noise ratio

It is defined as the ratio of the square of the largest possible pixel value and root mean square error. Given the high-resolution face image I and reconstructed $\hat{I}$ with N pixel value, the peak signal-to-noise ratio (PSNR) is computed as

$$PSNR = 10 \log_{10} \frac{L^2}{\frac{1}{N} \sum (I(i) - \hat{I}(i))^2} \tag{9.21}$$

where L is the highest possible pixel value. It behaves badly in the context of human perception.

9.4.4 Structural similarity index measure

It is highly sensitive towards image structure and measures its similarity. It is better in the context of the human visual system, which extracts the structure of an image. Image is compared in terms of luminance, contrast, and structure. Both luminance and contrast are estimated as mean and standard deviation and denoted by μ_I and σ_I, respectively. Given high-resolution face image I with n pixels, the mean and standard deviation is computed as $\mu_I = \frac{1}{N}\sum I(i)$ and $\sigma_I = \sqrt{\frac{1}{N-1}\sum(I(i) - \mu_I)^2}$.

To compare the luminance, contrast, and structure similarity between two face images, the following equations are used: (9.22), (9.23) and (9.24), respectively:

$$C_L = \frac{2\mu_I\mu_{\hat{I}} + C_1}{\mu_{\hat{I}}^2 + \mu_{\hat{I}}^2 + C_1} \tag{9.22}$$

$$C_c = \frac{2\sigma_I\sigma_{\hat{I}} + C_2}{\sigma_I^2 + \sigma_{\hat{I}}^2 + C_2} \tag{9.23}$$

$$C_s = \frac{\sigma_{I\hat{I}} + C_3}{\sigma_I\sigma_{\hat{I}} + C_3} \tag{9.24}$$

$\sigma_{I\hat{I}}$ is covariance between high-resolution and super-resolved facial image; C_1, C_2, and C_3 are stability constants. $C_1 = (k_1 L)^2$, $C_2 = (k_2 L)^2$, $C_3 = (k_3 L)^2$ where k_1, k_2, and $k_3 \ll 1$. Therefore structural similarity index measure (SSIM) is defined between the high-resolution I and super-resolved facial image $\hat{I}$ by Eq. (9.25):

$$SSIM(I, \hat{I}) = (C_L)^a(C_c)^b(C_s)^c \tag{9.25}$$

where a, b, c are tuning parameters to adjust each term's important.

9.5 Issues and challenges

Face super-resolution has become more popular due to its broad applicability or application in different fields. Although various learning-based face super-resolution methods, such as sparse representation, Bayesian inference, subspace learning, regularization techniques, and deep learning methods are used to improve the quality of the facial images, still some challenges exist for the face hallucination. Choosing the appropriate learning method with prior, selection of regularization parameter, the trade-off in data fidelity and a regularization term, learning of dictionary in sparse representation, and solving the optimization problem are significant challenges in most cases. These challenges are discussed in detail below.

1. Traditional face super-resolution algorithms use a pixel value as a single feature to represent the face image patch, which does not efficiently represent the face image patch. Therefore we need to apply the feature extraction algorithm to extract the image patch feature and represent it

by multiple features to compute the representation coefficients, while reconstructing the input face images.

2. In sparse representation, dictionary learning plays a crucial role to reconstruct the super-resolved face images. However, a dictionary can be initialized randomly by selecting the random training face image patches or constructed using the discrete cosine transform (DCT), discrete Fourier transform (DFT), and wavelet transform. Hence there is a need to develop a novel mechanism to get the optimum dictionary.

3. Face super-resolution algorithms learn the representation coefficients or weights using the traditional optimization methods to reconstruct the input face images. These weights may not be unique or optimum, which causes the construction of poor quality super-resolution face images. Regularized swarm-based optimization techniques [20,32] can be used to learn the optimum representation coefficients.

4. In several real-world scenarios, captured face images often suffer from noise, occlusion, etc., due to various reasons, such as low-resolution imaging system, motion between object and imaging sensor, and the far distance of an object from the camera. Traditional face super-resolution algorithm cannot properly handle noisy facial images or it may recover the poor quality super-resolution face images, so there is a need to explore the noise-robust face super-resolution algorithm [24] that can recover the high-quality super-resolved face images.

5. Traditional face super-resolution techniques work with frontal facial images, but are not efficient for different poses and facial expressions images. Hence we can use the deep learning-based methods for super-resolution of face images with different poses and expressions.

The researcher can propose different variations in face super-resolution algorithms to overcome the existing problems. Prior knowledge, flexible prior or automatic selection of prior can be helpful for the reconstruction of face images. Deep-learning-based methods can super-resolve the noisy low-resolution face images with different poses and expressions. To improve the face recognition system's performance, identity prior needs to be included with deep-learning-based face super-resolution methods.

9.6 Conclusion

This chapter provides a comprehensive survey of learning-based face super-resolution methods and their performance. This comprehensive survey differs from earlier published chapters because of the focus on learning-based approaches, future research direction, and the issues and challenges of the existing face super-resolution techniques. We briefly discussed the classification of face super-resolution techniques and various learning-based approaches, such as patch-based methods, Bayesian inference, regularization, subspace learning, and deep-learning-based methods. This survey highlights the various challenges, for example, efficient representation of face image patches, developing the noise-robust, different poses and facial expression preserving super-resolution methods, learning of optimum dictionary, and representation coefficients.

References

[1] Kamal Nasrollahi, Thomas B. Moeslund, Super-resolution: a comprehensive survey, Machine Vision and Applications 25 (6) (2014) 1423–1468.

[2] X. Ma, J. Zhang, C. Qi, Hallucinating face by position-patch, Pattern Recognition 43 (6) (2010) 2224–2236.

[3] X. Tang, X. Wang, Face sketch recognition, IEEE Transactions on Circuits and Systems for Video Technology 14 (1) (2004) 1–7.

[4] M. Tanveer, N. Iqbal, A Bayesian approach to face hallucination using DLPP and KRR, in: 20th International Conference on Pattern Recognition, 2010, pp. 2154–2157.

[5] S. Li, Markov Random Field Modeling in Image Analysis, Springer, Berlin, 2010.

[6] W. Freeman, E. Pasztor, O. Carmichael, Learning low-level vision, International Journal of Computer Vision 40 (1) (2000) 25–47.

[7] W. Freeman, T. Jones, E. Pasztor, Example-based super resolution, IEEE Computer Graphics and Applications 22 (2) (2002) 56–65.

[8] J. Shi, X. Liu, Y. Zong, C. Qi, G. Zhao, Hallucinating face image by regularization models in high-resolution feature space, IEEE Transactions on Image Processing 27 (6) (2018) 2980–2995.

[9] C. Jung, L. Jiao, B. Liu, M. Gong, Position-patch based face hallucination using convex optimization, IEEE Signal Processing Letters 18 (6) (2011) 367–370.

[10] J. Jiang, R. Hu, Z. Wang, Z. Han, Noise robust face hallucination via locality constrained representation, IEEE Transactions on Multimedia 16 (5) (2014) 1268–1281.

[11] J. Jiang, C. Chen, K. Huang, Z. Cai, R. Hu, Noise robust position-patch based face super-resolution via Tikhonov regularized neighbor representation, Information Sciences 367 (2016) 354–372.

[12] A. Chakrabarti, A.N. Rajagopalan, R. Chellappa, Super-resolution of face images using kernel PCA-based prior, IEEE Transactions on Multimedia 9 (4) (2007) 888–892.

[13] C. Hsu, C. Lin, H. Liao, Cooperative face hallucination using multiple references, in: Proceedings of IEEE International Conference on Multimedia & Expo, 2009, pp. 818–821.

[14] S. Roweis, L. Saul, Nonlinear dimensionality reduction by locally linear embedding, Science 290 (5500) (2000) 2323–2326.

[15] M. Wang, Z. Chen, Q.J. Wu, M. Jian, Improved face super-resolution generative adversarial networks, Machine Vision and Applications 31 (4) (2020) 1–12.

[16] C. Chen, D. Gong, H. Wang, Z. Li, K.-Y.K. Wong, Learning spatial attention for face super-resolution, IEEE Transactions on Image Processing 30 (2020) 1219–1231.

[17] K. Grm, W.J. Scheirer, V. Štruc, Face hallucination using cascaded super resolution and identity priors, IEEE Transactions on Image Processing 29 (2019) 2150–2165.

[18] X. Yu, F. Porikli, Ultra-resolving face images by discriminative generative networks, in: European Conference on Computer Vision, Springer, Cham, 2016, pp. 318–333.

[19] Z. Chen, Y. Tong, Face super-resolution through Wasserstein GANs, arXiv preprint, arXiv:1705.02438, 2017.

[20] S.S. Rajput, V.K. Bohat, K.V. Arya, Grey wolf optimization algorithm for facial image super-resolution, Applied Intelligence 49 (4) (2019) 1324–1338.

[21] Nannan Wang, Dacheng Tao, Xinbo Gao, Xuelong Li, Jie Li, A comprehensive survey to face hallucination, International Journal of Computer Vision 106 (1) (2014) 9–30.

[22] Junjun Jiang, Chenyang Wang, Xianming Liu, Jiayi Ma, Deep learning-based face super-resolution: A survey, arXiv preprint, arXiv:2101.03749, 2021.

[23] Zhihao Wang, Jian Chen, Steven C.H. Hoi, Deep learning for image super-resolution: A survey, IEEE Transactions on Pattern Analysis and Machine Intelligence 43 (10) (2020) 3365–3387.

[24] S.S. Rajput, K.V. Arya, Noise robust face hallucination via outlier regularized least square and neighbor representation, IEEE Transactions on Biometrics, Behavior, and Identity Science 1 (4) (2019) 252–263.

[25] J. Yang, J. Wright, T.S. Huang, Y. Ma, Image super-resolution via sparse representation, IEEE Transactions on Image Processing 19 (11) (2010) 2861–2873.

[26] K.V. Arya, S.S. Rajput, Recognition of facial images via self-organizing landmark location with approximate graph matching, in: Recent Trends in Electronics and Communication, in: Lecture Notes in Electrical Engineering, vol. 777, Springer, Singapore, 2022, pp. 1043–1055.

[27] Y. Chen, Y. Tai, X. Liu, C. Shen, J. Yang, FSRNet: End-to-end learning face super-resolution with facial priors, in: Proceedings of the IEEE Conference on Computer Vision and Pattern Recognition, 2018, pp. 2492–2501.

[28] Y. Xu, H. Zou, Y. Huang, L. Jin, H. Ling, Super-resolving blurry face images with identity preservation, Pattern Recognition Letters 146 (2021) 158–164.

[29] S.S. Rajput, K.V. Arya, A robust face super-resolution algorithm and its application in low-resolution face recognition system, Multimedia Tools and Applications 79 (2020) 23909–23934, https://doi.org/10.1007/s11042-020-09072-5.

[30] S.S. Rajput, K.V. Arya, CNN classifier based low-resolution face recognition algorithm, in: 2020 International Conference on Emerging Frontiers in Electrical and Electronic Technologies (ICEFEET), 2020, pp. 1–4, https://doi.org/10.1109/ICEFEET49149.2020.9187001.

[31] S.S. Rajput, K.V. Arya, A robust facial image super-resolution model via mirror-patch based neighbor representation, Multimedia Tools and Applications 78 (2019) 25407–25426, https://doi.org/10.1007/s11042-019-07791-y.

[32] S.S. Rajput, K.V. Arya, V.K. Bohat, Face image super-resolution using differential evolutionary algorithm, in: N. Verma, A. Ghosh (Eds.), Computational Intelligence: Theories, Applications and Future Directions - Volume II, in: Advances in Intelligent Systems and Computing, vol. 799, Springer, Singapore, 2019, https://doi.org/10.1007/978-981-13-1135-2_48.

[33] S.S. Rajput, K.V. Arya, V. Singh, V.K. Bohat, Face hallucination techniques: a survey, in: 2018 Conference on Information and Communication Technology (CICT), 2018, pp. 1–6, https://doi.org/10.1109/INFOCOMTECH.2018.8722416.

[34] K.V. Arya, S.S. Rajput, S. Upadhyay, Noise-robust low-resolution face recognition using SIFT features, in: N. Verma, A. Ghosh (Eds.), Computational Intelligence: Theories, Applications and Future Directions - Volume II, in: Advances in Intelligent Systems and Computing, vol. 799, Springer, Singapore, 2019, https://doi.org/10.1007/978-981-13-1135-2_49.

[35] Y.K. Mydam, S. Singh Rajput, P. Chanak, Low rank representation based discriminative multi manifold analysis for low-resolution face recognition, in: 2018 Conference

on Information and Communication Technology (CICT), 2018, pp. 1–5, https://doi.org/10.1109/INFOCOMTECH.2018.8722393.

[36] K.V. Arya, A. Rajawat, M.K. Pandey, S.S. Rajput, Very low resolution face recognition using fused visual and texture features, in: 2017 Conference on Information and Communication Technology (CICT), 2017, pp. 1–5, https://doi.org/10.1109/INFOCOMTECH.2017.8340642.

[37] Shyam Singh Rajput, K.V. Arya, Vinay Singh, Robust face super-resolution via iterative sparsity and locality-constrained representation, Information Sciences 463–464 (2018) 227–244, https://doi.org/10.1016/j.ins.2018.06.050.

[38] Shyam Singh Rajput, Ankur Singh, K.V. Arya, Junjun Jiang, Noise robust face hallucination algorithm using local content prior based error shrunk nearest neighbors representation, Signal Processing 147 (2018) 233–246, https://doi.org/10.1016/j.sigpro.2018.01.030.

CHAPTER 10

Fusion-based backlit image enhancement and analysis of results using contrast measure and SSIM

Gaurav Yadav[a]**, Dilip Kumar Yadav**[a]**, and P.V.S.S.R. Chandra Mouli**[b]

[a]Department of Computer Science and Engineering, National Institute of Technology, Jamshedpur, India
[b]Department of Computer Science, Central University of Tamil Nadu, Thiruvarur, India

10.1 Introduction

The backlit image contains both very dark and very bright regions together. The human visual system, to some extent, can discriminate between the contents that lie in the dark and low-contrast regions. With nonuniform lighting, the images seem quite dark, and backlighting visualization of the contents of the image becomes more difficult. Backlit images also provide inadequate boundary and textural information about the objects as compared to ordinary visual images. Apart from the low-contrast images, very low- and high-intensity regions simultaneously result in a backlit image. To increase visual perception, enhancing the ROI in backlit images is essential to better visualize dark and low-contrast regions. Because the objects of interest are often dark and not visible, the challenge is important to overcome. This happens due to the domination caused by the backlighting conditions during the generation of the image. So, to improve the visual perception and understanding of the objects, to improve different recognition and detection processes, backlit image enhancement finds its applicability.

A substantial number of methods for improving uniform or nonuniform illumination are available in the literature. These approaches include spatial domain enhancement based on neighborhood pixels, providing better performance. Such studies, however, find a trade-off in the form of halos or enhanced noise and image artifacts during enhancement. There has been a vast amount of literature about image enhancement through the years. Based on multiple feature enhancement and fusion techniques, the best results are obtained for backlit images.

Digital Image Enhancement and Reconstruction
https://doi.org/10.1016/B978-0-32-398370-9.00017-2
235

Pizer et al. [21] developed a histogram equalization-based approach for studying undesired lighting. Equalization approaches based on histograms [34] presume that perhaps the histogram is distributed equally. Rajput et al. [22] proposed a novel hallucination algorithm based on error shrunk nearest neighbors representation (ESNNR). Wang et al. [36] presented a comprehensive observational study assessment of the most extensively utilized low-light picture enhancing techniques. For low-light gray images, a global and adaptive contrast improvement method minimizes uneven lighting and low overall gray image contrast [9]. In [40], the camera response models are also investigated for low-light image improvement. The natural preservation of low-light image enhancement was addressed in the Retinex model. Ren et al. [23] investigated the retinex model for low-light scene enhancement that preserves naturalness. In [3], a novel illumination boost methodology is proposed for nighttime image development. This approach necessitates the use of fundamental exponential, logarithmic, and linear scaling functions, among other things. Using the response characteristics of cameras to improve low-light images [11], Wang et al. [37] proposed a new absorption of light-scattering-based model (ALSM) to improve low-light pictures by using camera response characteristics. After getting an underexposed and an overexposed version of the original low-light image, [16] showed a pair of complementary gamma functions (PCGF). A spatial contextual similarity histogram (SCSH) was proposed by Srinivas et al. [29], which is based on spatial contextual similarity among neighboring pixels.

To increase image quality, several ways to dealing with undesirable illuminations have been investigated and proposed in the literature. We went through some of the most important approaches for improving unfavorable lighting circumstances, and their drawbacks. Pizer et al. [21] suggested a histogram equalization-based approach for studying unwanted light. A novel lighting increase technique is provided [3] as part of research for nighttime image creation. This approach necessitates the use of fundamental exponential, logarithmic, and linear scaling functions, among other things.

The use of spatial information of pixels to increase visual contrast is being researched in the literature. To accomplish contrast enhancement for low-contrast pictures, the discrete entropy metrics are discussed in [5]. These methods use spatial-based pixel treatment; they integrate image restoration preprocessing with the algorithm to make it more efficient. This is especially true when, like with most contrast enhancement methods based on histograms, before and after enhancement, the histogram intensity values of some images are the same. Niu et al. [20] developed a unique strategy based on identifying the potential of tone-preserving dis-crete entropy maximization. To make their technique more robust, they incorporated image restoration pretreatment with it. For low-illumination gray pictures, Li et al. [15] suggested a global and adaptive contrast aug-mentation technique that eliminates uneven lighting and reduces the gray image's overall contrast. The effects of histogram triple partitioning and the effects of histogram clipping on the enhancement ratio were also stud-ied. To monitor the enhancement ratio, the histogram's triple partitioning and histogram clipping have been investigated. Shin et al. [25] suggested a method for increasing the visibility of still pictures automatically. By eval-uating the image information alone, there is no threshold or magic value in this approach. Mertens et al. [18] suggest fusing photos using a brack-eted exposure sequence to generate a high-quality image. In this work, the blending of several exposures guided by contrast and saturation is rec-ommended. A bracketed exposure series is also used to obtain a superior image utilizing the fusion-based image technique. Because exposure merg-ing has various drawbacks [7], this study involves several exposures driven by contrast and saturation. However, as stated in [10], exposure fusion has several limits. The obtained results are a consequence of combining all of these processing steps with an image exposure fusion method. Fusion of the generated inputs with their respective weight maps in a multiscale model improves the backlit image enhancement process. A multi-exposure-based picture enhancement strategy is employed to maintain information based on tone mapping curves and exposed areas. Tone mapping curves and ex-posed zones are used in the multi-exposure image enhancement approach to preserve detail. By keeping the information in the image, simple gra-dient domain-based analysis may eliminate the influence of nonuniform illumination. Singh et al. [26] employed nonlinear translation-variant fil-ters and exposure fusion to enhance detail. Contrast enhancement and naturalness preservation were combined. Wang et al. [33] investigated the multilayer lightness statistics of high-quality outdoor images. To some ex-tent, to resolve this issue, high-quality outdoor images having multilayer lightness statistics with contrast enhancement and naturalness preservation combination should resolve this issue. Sinha et al. [27] proposed a mod-ified fuzzy-based decision algorithm for removing impulse noise in the image enhancement process. Also, partial unsharp masking and conserva-tive smoothing-based study is done by Uddin et al. [30]. Fourier techniques in image enhancement were studied by Sinha et al. [28]. A novel method proposed by Jha et al. [14] using discrete cosine transform (DCT) dynamic stochastic resonance. In the discrete cosine transform (DCT) domain, Jha et al. introduced a unique approach based on dynamic stochastic resonance. A research on noise enhanced iterative processing was given by Chouhan et al. [6]. Iterative scaling of DCT coefficients is used to improve low-contrast photographs utilizing Fourier coefficients. By undertaking noise-enhanced iterative processing experiments based on Fourier coefficients, iterative scaling can also improve low-contrast images. By decomposing image patches using DCT transformation, a unique multi-exposure fusion approach was proposed. Curved Gabor filters are also investigated, focusing on ridge frequency estimation for curved regions and image enhancement [5]. Morel et al. [19] suggested a simple gradient-domain approach for removing the influence of nonuniform lighting, while keeping picture features. Huang et al. suggested the CNN-based unit model [12] and showed how to improve low-illumination photos using mix loss functions. Using these methods, the contrast and brightness are greatly boosted. Enhancing a backlit image in the final phases necessitates numerous shots with differing exposure information.

As mentioned in [24], content-aware algorithms improve dark photos by sharpening edges, while simultaneously disclosing information in textured parts and maintaining the smoothness of flat sections. These algorithms improve dark images, sharpen the edges by revealing information hidden in textured regions simultaneously, and preserve smoothness in regions. Buades et al. [4] suggested a technique for enhancing the contrast of backlit images by employing various tone mappings and adjusting different parts of the picture. All of these processing and picture fusion methods are combined in the final output. Dhara et al. [7] investigated the backlit image restoration technique. This method uses a multiscale synthesis of several pseudo-exposed pictures and information for backlighting restoration, and the human visual system's (HVS) sensitivity-based approach. Yadav et al. [38,39] proposed a multiple-input-based enhancement technique for ROI of backlit images. The method selects an ROI of the image into channels and performs the enhancement processes.

For dark foreground extraction in backlit situations, Zhao [41] presented a K closest neighbors (KNN)-based matting approach, and a logarithmic change to enhance the backlit region. To improve the foreground region, this approach merely uses a logarithmic transform. Akai et al. and Ueda et al. [2,31] proposed a simple backlit picture improvement solution based on intensity conversion with color and saturation preservation. As multistep solutions for enhancing backlit images, transmission coefficients computation, multiple exposures generation based on transmission coefficients, and picture fusion are all examined by [13]. Multiple tone mapping functions strengthen contrast and process different image regions. Multistep approaches for improving backlit images have been developed based on a transmission coefficient, and multiple exposure development depends on transmission coefficients and image fusion. Fu et al. [8] devised a multiscale fusion of derived inputs with matching weights to enhance the input. Wang et al. [32] proposed a novel multiscale-based fusion approach for enhancing single backlit images. One of the acceptable factors for the validation of the acquired findings is the contrast measure (CM) [4]. CM is dependent on the image's local variance. The SSIM [1,35] is another metric used in the literature to observe structural changes in images. The SSIM computation accurately represents the shift in contrast and exposes the augmented image's improved textural richness. In the enhanced image, the SSIM computation accurately represents the change in contrast and indicates the improvement in textural content.

As many of the outcomes show, there is always a trade-off between image detail enhancement, local contrast, and naturalness. This study proposes an improved strategy for improving the region of interest in backlit pictures, with an emphasis on improving the properties of ROI in backlit visuals. As a result of the preceding considerations, it is necessary to overcome the limits of existing backlit image enhancement approaches. This chapter focuses on a method for improving the ROI of backlit images by focusing on the various inputs. In this chapter, an approach is investigated for enhancing the ROI in backlit images. Fig. 10.1 (a), (b), (c), (d), and (e) represents a set of five backlit images from Wang et al. [32]; in Fig. 10.3, all images represent the selected ROI, respectively, from Fig. 10.1. This study demonstrates ROI contrast enhancement in single backlit images. This is achieved by concentrating on the ROI, i.e., region under dark and low contrast section. It is possible to monitor the contrast enhancement stage of the local ROI.

The chapter is organized as follows: Section 10.2 details the basic HVS characteristics, Section 10.3 presents the methodology, Section 10.4 discusses the result discussion, and Section 10.5 presents the summary.

10.2 Basic HVS characteristics

The HVS is a complicated system. It is hard to offer even an approximate description of the human visual system, therefore gaining a thorough com-

(a)   (b)   (c)

(d)   (e)

Figure 10.1 The Original backlit images from Wang et al. [32].

prehension remains a struggle. The four basic phenomenological processes of color perception are discussed here. Perceptual functionals are chosen via these techniques.

10.2.1 Contrast enhancement at the local level

Not only does the HVS improve edge perception, but it also uses local contrast augmentation. Visual phenomena, such as simultaneous contrast and Mach bands have verified this. The margins hold a significant portion of the visual information. As a result, it's no surprise that the HVS has devised a method for improving perception. The most crucial feature highlighted is that edge enhancement is local, subject to the local light intensity distribution around every point.

10.2.2 Average luminance level adaptation

A photon reaching the eyes and striking the retina is the main event that allows vision. A photoreceptor might absorb the photon. The photon energy's intensity and spectrum composition determine whether of the (L, M, S) three cones or a rod is used. The photochemical transfer from the photon's electromagnetic energy to the photoreceptor's difference in electric potential is activated by absorption. When a photoreceptor receives a bright photon, its membrane's electric potential changes according to Michaelis–

Menten's equation (also known as Naka–Rushton equation when the value is unitary).

In a certain waveband, all sorts of cones are particularly responsive. The absorbed amount of light in any specific waveband determines the semisaturation value. It does not belong to the overall luminosity of light sources. The level of adaptation is also associated with the semisaturation level.

The sigmoid-based transformation explanation is as follows:

(i) Photoreceptors have a threshold of intensity beyond which they do not respond. They then reply in a very linear manner.

(ii) Finally, when we approach high brightness levels, the response saturates.

(iii) The semisaturation value LS is at the "heart" of this behavior. The retinal cells "adjust" to the average luminance of each scene in this fashion, allowing people to perceive light intensity modulations around LS.

(iv) This retinal cell flexibility is crucial for human vision; without it, we would be unable to see when moving from a poorly light to a brightly illuminated environment, and vice versa.

10.2.3 Consistency in color

The capacity of the HVS to adjust to changing light intensities is known as light adaptation. At first look, color constancy refers to the capacity to adjust to various spectral content of light. While the lighting changes, it's important to maintain the colors as consistent as possible.

This trait is deeply ingrained in our visual system, and we frequently take it for granted. To obtain two photos with differing illuminations that give identical color perceptions, we execute a careful white balancing. The intricacies of color constancy are outside the scope of this work.

10.2.4 Weber's law

E. Weber, a German scientist, conducted a series of psychophysical experiments to examine contrast perception in the eighteenth century. A dark-adapted human observer was put in a dimly lit room in front of a white display with a focused light beam projected in the center of its field of vision. According to Weber's law, when background light rises, the difference must increase in proportion to be considered different from background light. This explains why people are more sensitive to noise in visual situations with dark areas. As a result, in some circumstances, doing denoising processes in dark regions is sometimes advantageous.

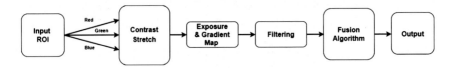

Figure 10.2 Block diagram based representation of the method.

10.2.5 Fusion

Image fusion [17] collects pertinent information from two or more channels and combines it into a single picture. Multiple channels of the same image or photos captured at varying moments in the same channel are used to collect data. The merged image can be examined or utilized for further processing.

10.3 Methodology

The absence of brightness and decreased contrast are the two most essential backlit images inside exposed zones. The proposed methodology, as shown in Fig. 10.2, performs the contrast stretch using the global tone mapping functions. First, exposure maps are carried out, followed by feature improvement operations, and then all the features are combined. Basic essential features of backlit images in underexposed regions [25] include a loss of brightness and poor contrast. By improving luminance and contrast, retaining boundaries, and fusing information based on all aspects, this methodology addresses the issues associated with backlit images. The input color image is segregated for separate treatment into the corresponding three-channel images (R, G, B), accompanied by specific feature enhancement-based operations. Corresponding images of three channels act as inputs and work in layers. Exposure maps are created, and then combined information into a single image. Finally, all of the component outputs are merged using fusion to create an enhanced version of the image ROI. In the backlit images, extremely low- and high-intensity zones enable low luminance regions to be handled.

10.3.1 Contrast stretch

The input single backlit picture is first divided into three corresponding channel images. To achieve the improved contrast, global tone mapping procedures based on log transform and gamma correction are applied. For contrast enhancement, global tone mapping methods are commonly utilized. Overall the separated channel images, tone mappings functions, log transformation, and gamma correction were applied. Logarithmic transformation is given in Eq. (10.1), and gamma correction is shown in Eq. (10.2):

$$L(\alpha) = \frac{255 \times \log(\alpha I + 1)}{\log(255\alpha + 1)} \tag{10.1}$$

$$G(\gamma) = 255 \times (I/255)^{\gamma} \tag{10.2}$$

I represents the image, γ stand for the adaptation factor, α stand for the brightness factor. γ can be calculated for a range of values, based on which the contrast in the image varies. Buades et al. [4], has taken the values of the γ as $\{0.4, 0.6, 0.8, 1, 2, 3\}$ and for obtaining the logarithmic tone map coefficients values as $\{0.1, 0.2, 0.3, 0.4, 0.5\}$ to obtain a better contrast measure. The values for adaption factor in the study is $\{0.4, 0.6, 0.8\}$, and brightness factor is $\{0.1, 0.3, 0.5\}$, respectively.

10.3.2 Exposure and gradient maps

The directional shift and edge details, as defined in the equation, are obtained by the gradient map (10.3). The gradient map is used to produce the edge details available in the channel images. The intensity change of a specific location in a specific direction is represented by every pixel in the original channel image. The gradient magnitude and gradient map for all the three corresponding channel images is shown in Fig. 10.2 for the ROI of the giraffe image. The gradient information is obtained as magnitude, representing the edge information and direction map in the vector form. In the 3-by-3 neighborhood, the gradient of a pixel is a weighted pixel sum.

$$\nabla t = \left[\binom{k_m}{k_n} \right] = \left[\binom{\partial t/\partial n}{\partial t/\partial n} \right], \tag{10.3}$$

$\partial t/\partial m$ denotes the derivative of m, and $\partial t/\partial n$ denotes the derivative of n.

10.3.3 Filtering

Similarly, statistics filtering is used over the image to obtain a smoothened image. Median filtering is operated for this purpose, as defined in Eq. (10.4). Every entry is replaced with the median values of neighbor pixels. To generate a smoothed version of the image median filtering is used.

$$y[m, n] = median\left\{x[i, j], (i, j) \in w\right\} \tag{10.4}$$

where w denotes the local neighborhood centered on the image's position $[m, n]$. The size of the window selected in this investigation is 5×5 based on the experimental results obtained.

The exposure measure determines a closeness dependent on the Gaussian curve [18] to the mid–intensity values, as given in Eq. (10.5), where σ_i is a parameter set to 0.2 by the authors.

$$wt(I) = \exp - \left(\frac{\left(\frac{I}{255} - 0.5 \right)^2}{2\sigma_i^2} \right) \qquad (10.5)$$

10.3.4 Fusion

Image fusion approach [18] is used to merge the results of tone mappings of color channel images, exposure, filtering, and gradient, among other parameters, obtained by applying (10.1), (10.2), (10.3), (10.4), and (10.5). As shown in Eq. (10.6), they devised an approach to blend various feature inputs from processed pictures.

$$I'(x) = \sum_{k=1}^{N} wt_k(x) I_k(x) \qquad (10.6)$$

where the weight map is defined by $wt_k(x)$, the exposure map is based on Eq. (10.3), and the various feature inputs of the image generated in the procedure are represented by $I_j(x)$.

10.4 Result discussion

To evaluate the methodology, the outcomes of the stated approach were compared to the results obtained from Wang et al. [32]'s fusion–based method for single backlit (FMSB) image enhancement. For the assessment, many reference images from [32]'s backlit image database were utilized. The results were obtained on an 8 GB RAM Intel i5-3230 CPU 3.20 GHz unit system. Fig. 10.3, Fig. 10.4, and Fig. 10.5 represent the subjective appraisal of standard evaluations of ROI images and their results. It can be found that FMSB is not sufficiently able to improve the ROI of images. Also, FMSB findings are influenced by certain undesired artifacts. Compared with FMSB, the discussed approach, which is specifically recommended for backlit image ROI enhancement, is superior in terms of the backlighting component of the images' exposure. Fig. 10.3 shows the actual ROI extracted from the original images presented in Fig. 10.1. Fig. 10.4 shows

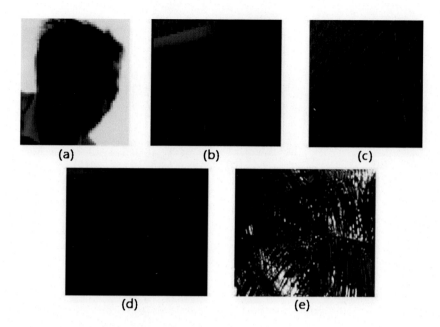

(a)   (b)   (c)

(d)   (e)

Figure 10.3 Selected ROI from backlit images given in Fig. 10.1.

the enhanced ROI result using the FMSB method. Fig. 10.5 shows the enhanced ROI result using the proposed method. The same can be observed
quantitatively in Table 10.1 and Table 10.2 for all images as presented in
Fig. 10.6 and Fig. 10.7.

   To evaluate the degree of enhancement in results, we consider the contrast measure [4] and SSIM [35] for the quantitative evaluation. ROI's results
are validated after primarily focusing on two different assessment criteria.
The contrast measure (CM) [4], as discussed in Eq. (10.7), is used to determine how well the image's contrast has improved.

$$CM = \frac{1}{T} \sum_{k=1}^{T} \frac{Var_k(processed)}{Var_k(original)} \qquad (10.7)$$

where Var_k represents the variance of a 16×16 size patch. The variance estimated on the original and processed images is represented by $Var_k(original)$
and $Var_k(processed)$. The total number of patches is denoted by T.

   The structural similarity index measure (SSIM) [35] is the next metric to
determine the proposed system's structural similarity. The lower the value
of the SSIM index, the better the perceptual quality in the case of enhanced

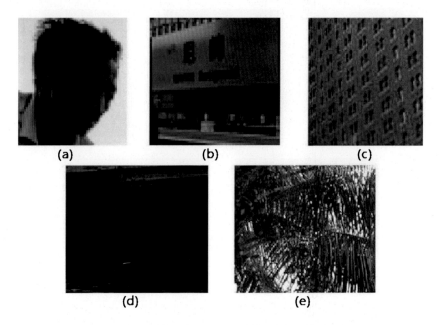

Figure 10.4 Represents the enhanced ROI using method [32].

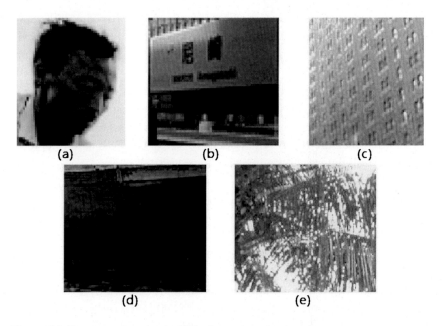

Figure 10.5 Represents the enhanced ROI using proposed approach.

Table 10.1 Comparison based on contrast measure.

Image	Contrast measure	
	FMSB [32]	Proposed
Face	0.66	**1.67**
Sea	8.96	**15.489**
Sign	5.898	**10.811**
Leaf	1.247	**2.692**
Building	3.105	**4.861**

Table 10.2 Comparison based on SSIM index.

Image	SSIM	
	FMSB [32]	Proposed
Face	0.782	**0.452**
Sea	0.314	**0.124**
Sign	0.294	**0.173**
Leaf	0.607	**0.250**
Building	0.451	**0.189**

ROI of backlit images. This measure is appropriate, because it ensures the structural similarity of the improved version concerning the actual ROI.

Table 10.1 and Table 10.2 provide the reference and proposed results analysis based on the assessment. The proposed method's acquired findings are matched with the exact location ROI of Wang et al.'s [32] reference results. Tables 10.1 and 10.2 show the contrast measure and SSIM index of the reference and discussed result images, respectively. It reveals that the discussed methodology has a higher contrast measure and a lower SSIM of the enhanced ROI, which implies an improvement in brightness and changes in the structural similarity of ROI images.

A comparative representation of contrast measure and SSIM index between the FMSB [32] and the proposed method is provided in Fig. 10.6 and Fig. 10.7. The analyzed images are shown in the subfigures of Fig. 10.3, Fig. 10.4, and Fig. 10.5 in two rows. Fig. 10.3 shows the ROI of the original image in two rows. The ROI results using the FMSB [32] method approach are shown in Fig. 10.4, respectively. Finally, the images in Fig. 10.5 depict the results of the presented methodology in this chapter.

The figures in Fig. 10.5 results appear brighter than the ROI image and reference output, as shown in Fig. 10.3 and Fig. 10.4, respectively. Also, the output images in Fig. 10.5 emerge adequately in terms of contrast and color representation. The dark and low-contrast regions of the image are

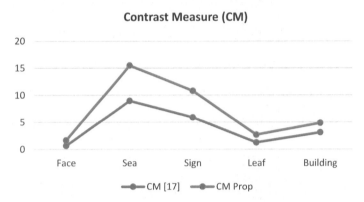

Figure 10.6 Comparative representation of contrast measure between the FMSB [32] and proposed method.

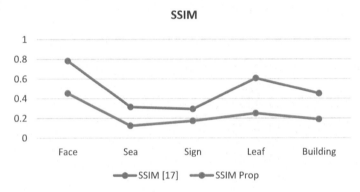

Figure 10.7 Comparative representation of SSIM index between the FMSB [32] and proposed method.

processed. More enhancement is obtained by the discussed method, which makes the visualization of the ROI suitable for human perception. Both contrast measure and SSIM index are given in Table 10.1 and Table 10.2 of the proposed method; they represent an overall contrast enhancement and structural change. Although the SSIM index of sea and sign are nearby, the better perceptual quality can be observed qualitatively for the two images in Fig. 10.4 and Fig. 10.5. A minimal change in the SSIM index is observed for the proposed results. It is observed that with higher contrast measure values, beyond some extent, the trade-off in detail and naturalness of the image starts to get compromised. For the selected values of the coefficients, the proposed method gives satisfactory results. Face, Sign, Building, Sea, and Leaf images in Fig. 10.3, Fig. 10.4, and Fig. 10.5 represent the ROI images obtained from the original backlit image, the FMSB method, and the proposed method. All lines in Fig. 10.4 represent the reference results obtained using the method proposed in FMSB [32]. The described method's results with increased contrast and color information by structural modification in the ROI images are shown in Fig. 10.5. As indicated in Fig. 10.6 and Table 10.1, all the presented results have higher CM values, evidenced from the output, as shown in Fig. 10.4 and Fig. 10.5. A small amount of artifacts is observed in some cases as the other details, including contrast, are enhanced significantly. The change in SSIM can be seen in Fig. 10.7, and the results in Table 10.2 show an overall improvement of the outcome of the method with enhanced contrast measure.

10.5 Summary

This chapter investigates a unique method for enhancing a single backlit image's dark and low-contrast ROI. Contrast stretching based on gamma and logarithmic tone mappings improves the low-contrast regions. In the resulting image, the textural and edge information of the selected region is well preserved; noise is to some extent eliminated. Whereas, under the over-exposed areas, we observed some artifacts that indicate the trade-off that persists when enhancing the color information and sharpness. The validation of the proposed approach is performed based on the contrast measure and, as discussed, the SSIM values of all the images. In a future research, it may be able to assess the analysis by minimizing the trade-off in developing color knowledge in overexposed areas.

References

[1] M. Abdoli, F. Nasiri, P. Brault, M. Ghanbari, A quality assessment tool for performance measurement of image contrast enhancement methods, IET Image Processing 13 (5) (2019) 833–842.
[2] M. Akai, Y. Ueda, T. Koga, N. Suetake, A single backlit image enhancement method for improvement of visibility of dark part, in: 2021 IEEE International Conference on Image Processing (ICIP), IEEE, 2021, pp. 1659–1663.
[3] Z. Al-Ameen, Nighttime image enhancement using a new illumination boost algorithm, IET Image Processing 13 (8) (2019) 1314–1320.
[4] A. Buades, J.L. Lisani, A.B. Petro, C. Sbert, Backlit images enhancement using global tone mappings and image fusion, IET Image Processing 14 (2) (2019) 211–219.
[5] T. Celik, Spatial mutual information and PageRank-based contrast enhancement and quality-aware relative contrast measure, IEEE Transactions on Image Processing 25 (10) (2016) 4719–4728.

[6] R. Chouhan, P.K. Biswas, R.K. Jha, Enhancement of low-contrast images by internal noise-induced Fourier coefficient rooting, Signal, Image and Video Processing 9 (1) (2015) 255–263.

[7] S.K. Dhara, D. Sen, Exposure correction and local enhancement for backlit image restoration, in: Pacific-Rim Symposium on Image and Video Technology, Springer, 2019, pp. 170–183.

[8] X. Fu, D. Zeng, Y. Huang, Y. Liao, X. Ding, J. Paisley, A fusion-based enhancing method for weakly illuminated images, Signal Processing 129 (2016) 82–96.

[9] R.C. Gonzalez, R.E. Woods, Digital Image Processing, Prentice-Hall, Upper Saddle River, 2002.

[10] C. Hessel, An implementation of the exposure fusion algorithm, Image Processing On Line 8 (2018) 369–387.

[11] S.C. Hsia, C.J. Chen, W.C. Yang, Improvement of face recognition using light compensation technique on real-time imaging, The Imaging Science Journal 64 (6) (2016) 334–340.

[12] H. Huang, H. Tao, H. Wang, A convolutional neural network-based method for low-illumination image enhancement, in: Proceedings of the 2nd International Conference on Artificial Intelligence and Pattern Recognition, 2019, pp. 72–77.

[13] J. Im, I. Yoon, M.H. Hayes, J. Paik, Dark channel prior-based spatially adaptive contrast enhancement for backlighting compensation, in: 2013 IEEE International Conference on Acoustics, Speech and Signal Processing, IEEE, 2013, pp. 2464–2468.

[14] R.K. Jha, R. Chouhan, K. Aizawa, P.K. Biswas, Dark and low contrast image enhancement using dynamic stochastic resonance in the discrete cosine transform domain, APSIPA Transactions on Signal and Information Processing 2 (2013).

[15] C. Li, J. Liu, A. Liu, Q. Wu, L. Bi, Global and adaptive contrast enhancement for low illumination gray images, IEEE Access 7 (2019) 163395–163411.

[16] C. Li, S. Tang, J. Yan, T. Zhou, Low-light image enhancement via pair of complementary gamma functions by fusion, IEEE Access 8 (2020) 169887–169896.

[17] C. Ma, S. Zeng, D. Li, A new algorithm for backlight image enhancement, in: 2020 International Conference on Intelligent Transportation, Big Data & Smart City (ICITBS), IEEE, 2020, pp. 840–844.

[18] T. Mertens, J. Kautz, F. Van Reeth, Exposure fusion: a simple and practical alternative to high dynamic range photography, Computer Graphics Forum 28 (2009) 161–171, Wiley Online Library.

[19] J.M. Morel, A.B. Petro, C. Sbert, Screened Poisson equation for image contrast enhancement, Image Processing On Line 4 (2014) 16–29.

[20] Y. Niu, X. Wu, G. Shi, Image enhancement by entropy maximization and quantization resolution upconversion, IEEE Transactions on Image Processing 25 (10) (2016) 4815–4828.

[21] S.M. Pizer, E.P. Amburn, J.D. Austin, R. Cromartie, A. Geselowitz, T. Greer, B. ter Haar Romeny, J.B. Zimmerman, K. Zuiderveld, Adaptive histogram equalization and its variations, Computer Vision, Graphics, and Image Processing 39 (3) (1987) 355–368.

[22] S.S. Rajput, A. Singh, K.V. Arya, J. Jiang, Noise robust face hallucination algorithm using local content prior based error shrunk nearest neighbors representation, Signal Processing 147 (2018) 233–246.

[23] Y. Ren, Z. Ying, T.H. Li, G. Li, LECARM: low-light image enhancement using the camera response model, IEEE Transactions on Circuits and Systems for Video Technology 29 (4) (2018) 968–981.

[24] A.R. Rivera, B. Ryu, O. Chae, Content-aware dark image enhancement through channel division, IEEE Transactions on Image Processing 21 (9) (2012) 3967–3980.

[25] J. Shin, H. Oh, K. Kim, K. Kang, Automatic image enhancement for under-exposed, over-exposed, or backlit images, Electronic Imaging 2019 (14) (2019) 088-1–088-5.

[26] H. Singh, V. Kumar, S. Bhooshan, A novel approach for detail-enhanced exposure fusion using the guided filter, The Scientific World Journal 2014 (2014).

[27] G.R. Sinha, N. Agrawal, Fuzzy based image enhancement method, International Journal of Computer Applications 975 (2015) 8887.

[28] G.R. Sinha, D.R. Hardaha, Fourier techniques in image enhancement, in: Proc. ICNFT, SAASTRA, 2004, pp. 1–6.

[29] K. Srinivas, A.K. Bhandari, A. Singh, Low-contrast image enhancement using spatial contextual similarity histogram computation and color reconstruction, Journal of the Franklin Institute 357 (18) (2020) 13941–13963.

[30] N. Uddin Khan, K.V. Arya, M. Pattanaik, An efficient image noise removal and enhancement method, in: 2010 IEEE International Conference on Systems, Man and Cybernetics, IEEE, 2010, pp. 3735–3740.

[31] Y. Ueda, D. Moriyama, T. Koga, N. Suetake, Histogram specification-based image enhancement for the backlit image, in: 2020 IEEE International Conference on Image Processing (ICIP), IEEE, 2020, pp. 958–962.

[32] Q. Wang, X. Fu, X.P. Zhang, X. Ding, A fusion-based method for single backlit image enhancement, in: 2016 IEEE International Conference on Image Processing (ICIP), IEEE, 2016, pp. 4077–4081.

[33] S. Wang, G. Luo, Naturalness preserved image enhancement using a priori multi-layer lightness statistics, IEEE Transactions on Image Processing 27 (2) (2017) 938–948.

[34] Y. Wang, Q. Chen, B. Zhang, Image enhancement based on equal area dualistic sub-image histogram equalization method, IEEE Transactions on Consumer Electronics 45 (1) (1999) 68–75.

[35] Z. Wang, A.C. Bovik, H.R. Sheikh, E.P. Simoncelli, Image quality assessment: from error visibility to structural similarity, IEEE Transactions on Image Processing 13 (4) (2004) 600–612.

[36] W. Wang, X. Wu, X. Yuan, Z. Gao, An experiment-based review of low-light image enhancement methods, IEEE Access 8 (2020) 87884–87917.

[37] Y.F. Wang, H.M. Liu, Z.W. Fu, Low-light image enhancement via the absorption light scattering model, IEEE Transactions on Image Processing 28 (11) (2019) 5679–5690.

[38] G. Yadav, D.K. Yadav, Multiple feature-based contrast enhancement of ROI of backlit images, Machine Vision and Applications 33 (1) (2022) 1–12.

[39] G. Yadav, D.K. Yadav, P.C. Mouli, Enhancement of region of interest from a single backlit image with multiple features, in: International Conference on Computer Vision and Image Processing, Springer, Singapore, 2020, pp. 467–476.

[40] Z. Ying, G. Li, Y. Ren, R. Wang, W. Wang, A new low-light image enhancement algorithm using camera response model, in: Proceedings of the IEEE International Conference on Computer Vision Workshops, 2017, pp. 3015–3022.

[41] M. Zhao, D. Cheng, L. Wang, Backlit image enhancement based on foreground extraction, in: 12th International Conference on Graphics and Image Processing (ICGIP 2020), vol. 11720, International Society for Optics and Photonics, 2021, p. 1172019.

CHAPTER 11

Recent techniques for hyperspectral image enhancement

Abhishek Singh[a], K.V. Arya[b], Vineet Kansal[a], and Manish Gaur[a]

[a]Department of Computer Science and Engineering, Institute of Engineering and Technology Lucknow, Dr. A.P.J. Abdul Kalam Technical University, Lucknow, India
[b]Department of ICT, ABV-Indian Institute of Information Technology and Management, Gwalior, India

11.1 Introduction

Hyperspectral imaging (HSI) is the capturing and processing of an image at a very large number of wavelengths. Whereas multispectral imaging might evaluate an image in three or four colors (red, green, blue, and near-infrared, for example), hyperspectral imaging breaks down the image into tens or hundreds of colors, as shown in Fig. 11.1. In the recent few decades, hyperspectral image processing has been recognized as an emerging field because of its application in various fields, for example, agriculture [1], biotechnology [2], atmospheric science [3], forensic science [4], medical imaging [5], medical science [6], planetary science [7], surface examination [8], security and safeguard administrations [9], municipality arranging [10], confirmation of records or endorsements [11], climate change [12], and so on.

Hyperspectral images with hundreds of contiguous spectral bands provide large signal information for some specific applications, such as itemized planning, object recognizable proof, and mineral investigation; hyperspectral detecting is the main means of information gathering herein as an ordinary multispectral methodology has been verified as inadequate.

Hyperspectral image sensors collect data from contiguous bands of wavelength, ranging from 350 to 2200 nm. Each band has the same number of pixels and a fixed spectral resolution dependent on the capability of sensors. Each pixel has some spatial resolution that defines an area of the surface covered in a pixel. It collects the reflectance value of an area for different wavelengths in different bands, forming a data cube that is beneficial in many applications

Digital Image Enhancement and Reconstruction
https://doi.org/10.1016/B978-0-32-398370-9.00018-4

253

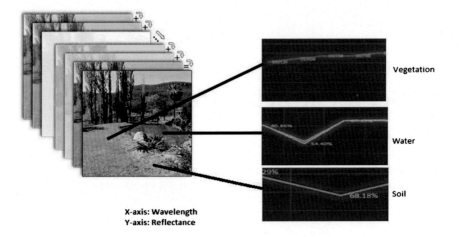

Figure 11.1 Basic concept of hyperspectral imaging.

Along with benefits, HSIs have some limitations that give rise to the concept of compression. The need for HSI compression is as follows:

- The size of the HSI acquired by the sensors is in hundreds and thousands of megabytes. For example, an infrared imaging spectrometer (AVIRIS) sensor captures 224 spectral bands with 614×500 pixels in each band, where each pixel takes 16 bits. The size of an image from such a sensor is $224 \times 614 \times 500 \times 16 = 131.17$ MB, hence storage of this large size data is an issue.
- Limited transmission channel bandwidth: HSIs have to be transmitted from one place to another, and large size of data requires high bandwidth, which is a costly resource.
- Limited data transmission time: At sensors, HSIs are captured very frequently that needs processing at a high rate, which is very complex at capturing device.

Researchers have proposed a large number of HSI compression methods, which can be roughly split into two categories: lossless and lossy compression schemes, depending on the data loss during the compression process. Two types of redundancies exist in any HSI image: spatial redundancy and spectral redundancy [13]. Spatial redundancy is the statistical dependencies among pixels of a single frame of HS images, whereas spectral redundancy is a redundancy corresponding to pixels with the same spatial locations in adjacent frames of HSI images.

The major attributes of hyperspectral datasets are diverse, and should be fundamentally handled under explicit numerical formalisms, such as classification and clustering. For example, a few artificial intelligence and image handling strategies have been applied to separate significant data from hyperspectral information during the last decade [14]. Scientific categorizations of remote detecting information handling calculations (hyperspectral analysis strategies) have been created in the literature [15]. It is identified, that most accessible hyperspectral information handling strategies focused on investigating the information without consolidating data on the spatially adjacent information, i.e., hyperspectral information are typically not treated as pictures, but as an unordered listing of estimations with no specific plan [20]. Because of the fewer number of preparing tests and the big number of components accessible in remote applications, reliable assessment of measurable class boundaries is another difficult objective.

Accordingly, with a limited dataset, grouping exactness will, in general, diminish as the quantity of components increments. A few artificial intelligence and image handling methods have been applied to separate extracted data from hyperspectral information. In any case, the most accessible hyperspectral information handling strategies zeroed in on breaking down the information without joining data on the spatially contiguous information, i.e., hyperspectral information is normally not treated as pictures. Hyperspectral image information is extremely large, so its compression is needed [52,53].

This chapter is organized as follows: Section 11.2 presents objective of hyperspectral image enhancement; Section 11.3 explains the various recently used techniques for hyperspectral image enhancement; Section 11.4 addresses advantages of hyperspectral image enhancement, and Section 11.5 presents the application of hyperspectral image, and the conclusions are presented in Section 11.6.

11.2 The major objective of hyperspectral image enhancement

The major objectives of hyperspectral image enhancement are the following:

i) Hyperspectral image improvement is important on the basis of data gathering, because a very huge amount of information is stored in HSI images. Overall, a solitary HS image has a size of around 200 MB. Along with these, on normal 6 to 7 HS images can be stored in an average memory of 1 GB. To save memory and processing time, the HSI image compress turns into an important stage. The memory prerequisite of wavelet (change) based HS image compression plan require the coding memory for encoding and interpreting DWT coefficient. Currently, machines create an enormous volume of data (11.2 exabyte in 2017 and 49.25 exabyte in 2021). As a result, information pressure is currently a fundamental challenge, and it is one of the developing areas of exploration for the improvement of the application-based compress calculations. The proficient hyperspectral image compression scheme (HSICS) reduces the information, decreases information handling time, and brings down the force utilization for information handling.

ii) To get the right significance of hyperspectral data gathered imagery into distinct material constituents pertinent to specific applications and produce classified maps that show where the constituents are available. Such data items can incorporate land cover maps for ecological remote sensing, surface mineral guides for geographical applications and valuable mineral investigation, vegetation species for rural or other geology contemplates, or synthetic materials for metropolitan mapping. Processing time brings down the force utilization for information handling.

iii) Hyperspectral image (HSI) enhancement is to deal with the visibility of image features for examination. The improvement connection doesn't construct the characteristic information content, but basically underlines specific predetermined image characteristics. Hyperspectral image improvement techniques join distinction and edge redesign, jumble isolating, pseudo-coloring, sharping, and enhancing.

iv) In hyperspectral imaging, sensors regularly gather data all at once, so the hyperspectral images can precisely describe distinctive landcover types with plentiful otherworldly data. In any case, these weird clusters additionally contain repetitive data that should be taken out. Band choice is perhaps the most generally utilized strategy to eliminate noise or repetitive bands.

On the basis of the above objective, in recent years, researchers developed many methods, for example, 3D-Embedded Zero tree Wavelet (3D-EZW) [21], 3D-Set Partitioning In Hierarchical Trees (3D-SPIHT) [22], 3D-Set Partitioning Embedded Block (3D-SPECK) [23], 3D-Set Partitioned Embedded Zero Block Coding (3D-SPEZBC) [24], F. Zhao's calculation [25], 3D-wavelet texture [50], JPEG-2000 for HS picture pressure [26], simple square-based between band straight expectation followed by a square-based discrete cosine change (DCT) [27], and many other also help a wide range of hyperspectral image enhancement functionalities.

However, some algorithms have made a significant effort in reducing the coding memory 3D-SPECK [23], and 3D-SPIHT [22] is the state-of-the-art wavelet-based HS image compression scheme that exploits the energy compaction property of wavelet transform by arranging the insignificant elements in zero block cube [28] or zero trees [22] or zero block cube tree [29].

11.3 Recent techniques in hyperspectral image enhancement by compressing the image

Majority of the techniques uses the images compression method for enhancement of hyperspectral image. HS image compression can also be categorized into four different categories, namely predictive coding [16], vector quantization [17], hybrid [18], and transform-based HSI image compression schemes [19], as shown in Fig. 11.2.

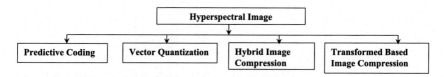

Figure 11.2 Various hyperspectral image compression methods.

Various parameters are used for calculating and identifying the compression of hyperspectral images (HSI). The coding efficiency is the measure of the rate-distortion (RD) performance of any HS image compression scheme. It is calculated mathematically in terms of peak signal-to-noise ratio (PSNR) [45]:

$$PSNR = 10 \log \frac{Maximal\ signal\ power}{Mean\ square\ error\ (MSE)}. \qquad (11.1)$$

Mean square error (MSE) [46] is the reconstructed HS image with the original HS image, which is calculated with Eq. (11.2):

$$MSE = 1/N \sum_{k=0}^{n} [f(x, y, z) - g(x, y, z)]^2. \qquad (11.2)$$

The compression ratio (CR) is the ratio between the bits used in the original HS image to the bits used in the reconstructed HS image [47]. Mathematically, it is formulated as Eq. (11.3):

$$CR = \frac{original\ image\ size\ in\ bits}{Decode\ image\ size\ in\ bits}.$$ (11.3)

The mathematical relationship between the compression ratio and bit rate (bpppb) [48] is defined by Eq. (11.4):

$$Bitrate(bpppb) = \frac{Pixel\ depth * Row * Column * Wavelength}{Compression\ ratio}.$$ (11.4)

The structural similarity (SSIM) index can be viewed as a quality measure of the original HS images being compared, provided the reconstructed HS image is regarded as of perfect quality [49]. It is another parameter that observed the quality of the reconstructed HS image. SSIM is calculated with Eq. (11.5):

$$SSIM = \frac{(2\mu_x\mu_y + C_1)(2\sigma_{xy} + C_2)}{(\mu_x^2 + \mu_y^2 + C_1)(\sigma_x^2 + \sigma_y^2 + C_2)}.$$ (11.5)

The complexity of any HSICS has been measured in terms of encoding and decoding time. The encoding time is the time required to convert the transform HS image to the encoded embedded bitstream, whereas the decoding process is the time required to reconstruct the HS image from the received bitstream. It has been observed that the decoding time is always less than the encoding time for any compression scheme. If any compression scheme is complex in nature, the encoding or recording time will increase rapidly, because for the generation of the output-based bitstream, the compression scheme will require more time.

On the basis of the compression ratio of an image, the compression efficiency (CR) of any HSICS is defined in terms of bits per pixel per band (bpppb). In the predictive coding of HS images, the future worth of the pixel is determined with the assistance of the difference between the current pixel and the previous pixel. The predictive coding ideas are applied to the HS image in the spatial domain. The differential pulse-code modulation (DPCM) is one particular example of predictive coding [51]. The coding complexity is of listless compression schemes, which is always less than the compression scheme, having lists for tracking the significance

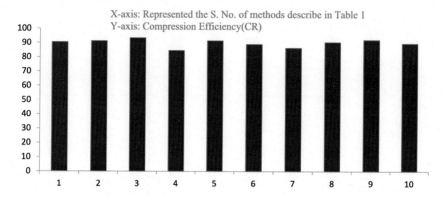

Figure 11.3 Compression efficiency (CR) of various techniques presented in Table 11.1.

or insignificance of sets or coefficients, because listless compression schemes have no multiple memory access operations (access the lists).

Vector quantization is based on dictionary-based HS image compression that divides the HS image into the various blocks, it is based on the Euclidean distance that take the approximate guess and produces the particular image or codewords for each block.

The hybrid compression method uses the neural network with predictive coding or vector quantization for the lossless HS image compression. The neural networks are trained with the assistance of machine learning method (counting deep neural network and recurrence neural network). Before the beginning of the compression, the training of the neural network is performed with the machine learning algorithm.

Transform-based HS image compression is the subcategory that utilizes the mathematical transform to change over the image into the other area and packs the energy into the couple of coefficients. These compression plans are important when the high correlation exists in the image [39]. The transform-based coding plans convert the HS images of exceptionally associated outlines into the energy concentrated by a few uncorrelated transform coefficients.

In Table 11.1 some recently used techniques for enhancement of hyperspectral images are classified into four compression techniques (discussed above) and their compression efficiency are described in Fig. 11.3.

In low-memory obstructed memory [29] proposed wavelet-based 3D-LMBTC is a novel hyperspectral lazy block shape tree-based technique, which accomplishes inter- and intra-subband connections in the 3D wavelet change. It diminishes a little fixed size static memory to moni-

Table 11.1 Recent techniques for hyperspectral image enhancement by using compression.

S. No.	Techniques	Year	Classification	Compression Efficiency (CR)
1.	Low memory block tree coding [29]	2019	Transform based HS Compression	90.54
2.	A low complexity hyperspectral image compression through 3D set partitioned embedded zero block coding [38]	2021	Transform based HS Compression	91.32
3.	Low complexity regression wavelet analysis [30]	2018	Transform based HS Compression	93.46
4.	Hyperspectral Remote Sensing Images and Supervised Feature Extraction [31]	2019	Hybrid Compression	84.56
5.	Spatially and Spectrally Concatenated Neural Networks for Efficient Lossless Compression of Hyperspectral Imagery [32]	2020	Hybrid Compression	91.45
6.	Support Vector Machine Accuracy Assessment for Extracting Green Urban Areas in Towns [33]	2019	Vector Quantization	89.00
7.	The linear prediction vector quantization for hyperspectral image compression [34]	2019	Vector Quantization	86.32
8.	Hyperspectral image compression using hybrid transform with different wavelet-based transform coding [35]	2020	Transform based HS Compression	90.47
9.	Hyperspectral image denoising using SURE-based unsupervised convolutional neural networks [36]	2020	Hybrid compression Technique	92.07
10.	Lossy Hyperspectral Image Compression on a Reconfigurable and Fault-Tolerant FPGA-Based Adaptive Computing Platform [37]	2020	Predictive based Compression	89.56

tor block set/tree packages and coding of wavelet. Algorithm proposed in 3D-ZM-SPECK is less perplexing [38], while protecting coding productivity. The wavelet change-based hyperspectral compression plans are basic (simple to execute with less hardware interest), quick (less disconcerting with other image compression unite), and implanted (decoded at the less bit rate than the encoding rate) in nature. In Routing Wavelength Assignment (RWA) spectral change [30], acquainting novel variations that lead with a further developed lossless coding execution. An extensive correlation with the best in class remote-detecting data compression procedures shows the aggressive conduct of RWA as far as lossless coding execution (yielding lower bit rates), computational intricacy (mentioning lower execution time). In mixture remote detecting strategy [35], HSI is decayed into 1D and it is grouped and tiled. Each group is applied with integer Karhunen–Loeve transform (IKLT), and, as such, it is applied for the entire picture to get IKLT groups in unearthly measurement. Then, at that point, IKLT groups are applied with integer wavelet transform (IDWT) to decorrelate the spatial information in spatial measurement. The mix of IKLT and IDWT is known as hybrid change.

Noval algorithm is used for proposed neural network, subsequently wiping out the requirement for pre-preparing utilizing decompressed data [32]. With the assistance of a support vector machine (SVM), this paper intends to give a combination of boundaries to extract green metropolitan regions with the most significant level of accuracy, to accelerate metropolitan arranging and at last develop town conditions [33]. An efficient calculation for hyperspectral image compression, which comprises of three principle methodology: creating the reference groups by K-implies, foreseeing every one of the groups by direct band forecast, and encoding the expectation lingering by VQ [34]. In this paper, administered highlight extraction procedures for hyperspectral pictures, i.e., prototype space feature extraction (PSFE), modified Fisher's linear discriminant analysis (MFLDA), maximum margin criteria-based (MMC-based), and partitioned MMC-based techniques are explained [31].

An efficient algorithm of compression is proposed, the HSI denoising method, called Stein's unbiased risk estimate-convolutional neural network (SURE-CNN). The method is based on an unsupervised CNN and SURE [36]. Algorithm for lossy multispectral and hyperspectral image compressor for on-board operation in space missions. The compression algorithm is a lossy extension of the Consultative Committee for Space Data Systems (CCSDS) [37].

11.4 Advantages of hyperspectral imaging over multispectral imaging

Hyperspectral imaging offers various advantages; however, it requires handling of data acquired to have a reasonable vision of the spectroscopic class that may be covered inside an immense measure of data. The significant advantages during the upgrade of hyperspectral image are as follows:

- Hyperspectral imaging sensor data has a larger number of benefits than multispectral data for the distinguishing proof and segregation of target components or items. They give detailed data about any article due to narrowband data gaining. Hyperspectral sensors have a fine spectral goal. Hyperspectral data is frequently acquired in a certain distant reach.
- Hyperspectral imaging is indisputably more valuable than multispectral imaging since bands of hyperspectral information are adjacent and overlapped, making them helpful to identify all fundamental data. The continuous range helps environmental windows to be perceived for expulsion from the brilliance signal, which isn't material for multispectral sensors.
- The signal-to-noise ratio cannot be reduced in multispectral data, because of the number of discontinuous bands.
- The problem of mixed spectra can be solved by directly deriving the relative abundance of materials.
- The objects or classes of a hyperspectral image can be derived from various spaces, such as the spectral space, image space, and character space.

11.5 Application of hyperspectral image

Hyperspectral images have various applications in the past but it has some latest applications in various fields, such as agriculture, environment, and earth surface. But his section presents its latest application, in fields such as medical science [5], remote sensing, plant disease, and vehicle tracking.

Hyperspectral imaging is an emerging region in remote sensing. Remote sensing satellites furnish a variety of information with remarkable and various attributes in panchromatic, multispectral, and hyperspectral optical locales [40]. Hyperspectral sensors gain in excess of 100 contiguous bands with a limited transfer bandwidth (5–10 nm) in a wavelength locale, somewhere in the range of 500 and 2500 nm [54]. Hyperspectral sensors are currently being generally utilized for planning land assets as multispectral datasets have basic information of data hyperspectral imaging sensors, with a large number of contiguous bands, carry valuable diagnostic information about the earth's surface, and have improved the feasibility of unambiguously identifying numerous soil and plant absorption features, related to mineralogy, liquid water, chlorophyll, cellulose, and lignin content.

The most investigated and applied hyperspectral imaging spectroradiometers are airborne sensors. These studies are led at the territorial level. Countless explorations have been done and approved for airborne sensors; nonetheless, there are as yet many fields to disclose. The continuous and impending space-borne missions have a huge ability for the checking and evaluation of different wetland environments at the worldwide level. There is a need to have a spectral library of various wetland life forms, such as lowered green growth, organisms, microorganisms, no rooted drifting vegetation, rambling, coastline vegetation, sedges, grasses, sea-going weeds and organisms in hydric soils, which are the essential purchasers of wetland food networks [41]. Because wetlands differ in their inclination in term of geological area, and climatic circumstances, their soil and water properties also alter with the seasons. The checking and evaluation of their physicochemical boundaries will give additional data about their trophic status, turbidity level, contamination, and tainting specialists alongside intrusive species. This will therefore be utilized to anticipate soil, water, and biomass efficiency levels and to appraise carbon and nitrogen pools.

Hyperspectral images arrangements are considered for the recognition and tracking of vehicles, acknowledging low-rate video hyperspectral imaging frameworks [43]. The vehicles are thought to be passing through the parking garage and passing behind different impediments inside the scene, such as trees behind the scenes and left vehicles, at a predetermined greatest speed. The set-up incorporates a combination of high-rate information obtaining hyperspectral line scanner with a high-velocity sea container slant unit that contains position and pointing data. Then, at that point, the acknowledgment of digital elevation models (DEM) is concocted: HSI time series symbolism after reconciliation onto an adjustable shaft framework from various vantage focuses, sound system hyperspectral sees, and the meaning of bidirectional reflectance appropriation capacity would all be able to be inferred.

Hyperspectral images examine the medical results of the recovering of diabetic foot ulcers by an HSI instrument [42]. Such a tool is introduced as profoundly accommodating on the grounds that foot ulcers are without a doubt a significant confusion of diabetes.

Hyperspectral images address the issue of interpretation of plant disease [44]. A strategy is introduced to spatially reference the time series of short contiguity of hyperspectral images, defeating the ineffectiveness of past studies of expressions over the long haul to identify beginning phases of sickness when they are as yet invisible.

11.6 Conclusion

In this chapter, we include the development of recent techniques used for hyperspectral imaging enhancement by compressing the image and how much these algorithms are efficient. We also present advantages of hyperspectral imaging enhancement over multispectral imaging. This article also gives the application of hyperspectral imaging enhancement in various fields, such as hyperspectral imaging (which is a growing area in remote sensing), hyperspectral remote sensing in precision agriculture, hyperspectral imaging in environmental monitoring, to detect plant disease, vehicle tracking.

In the future, the abovementioned techniques can be tried to solve the image super-resolution problem [55–64].

References

[1] P. Singh, P.C. Pandey, G.P. Petropoulos, A. Pavlides, P.K. Srivastava, N. Koutsias, K.A.K. Deng, Y. Bao, Hyperspectral remote sensing in precision agriculture: present status, challenges, and future trends, in: Hyperspectral Remote Sensing, 2020, pp. 121–146, https://doi.org/10.1016/B978-0-08-102894-0.00009-7.

[2] S. Arrigoni, G. Turra, A. Signoroni, Hyperspectral image analysis for rapid and accurate discrimination of bacterial infections: a benchmark study, Computers in Biology and Medicine 88 (2017) 60–71, https://doi.org/10.1016/j.compbiomed.2017.06.018.

[3] A. Rangnekar, N. Mokashi, E.J. Ientilucci, C. Kanan, M.J. Hoffman, AeroRIT: a new scene for hyperspectral image analysis, IEEE Transactions on Geoscience and Remote Sensing (2020), https://doi.org/10.1109/TGRS.2020.2987199.

[4] C. Malegori, E. Alladio, P. Oliveri, C. Manis, M. Vincenti, P. Garofano, F. Barni, A. Berti, Identification of invisible biological traces in forensic evidences by hyperspectral NIR imaging combined with chemometrics, Talanta 215 (2020) 120911, https://doi.org/10.1016/j.talanta.2020.120911.

[5] K. Nageswaran, K. Nagarajan, R. Bandiya, A novel algorithm for hyperspectral image denoising in medical application, Journal of Medical Systems 43 (9) (2019) 291, https://doi.org/10.1007/s10916-019-1403-5.

[6] S.W. Song, J. Kim, C. Eum, Y. Cho, C.R. Park, Y.-A. Woo, H.M. Kim, H. Chung, Hyperspectral Raman line mapping as an effective tool to monitor the coating thickness of pharmaceutical tablets, Analytical Chemistry 91 (9) (2019) 5810–5816.

[7] P.R. Kumaresan, J. Saravanavel, K. Palanivel, Lithological mapping of Eratosthenes crater region using Moon Mineralogy Mapper of Chandrayaan-1, Planetary and Space Science 182 (2020) 104817, https://doi.org/10.1016/j.pss.2019.104817.

[8] R. Anand, S. Veni, J. Aravinth, Big data challenges in airborne hyperspectral image for urban landuse classification, in: 2017 International Conference on Advances in Computing, Communications and Informatics (ICACCI), 2017, pp. 1808–1814, https://doi.org/10.1109/ICACCI.2017.8126107.

[9] M. Shimoni, R. Haelterman, C. Perneel, Hyperspectral imaging for military and security applications: combining myriad processing and sensing techniques, IEEE Geoscience and Remote Sensing Magazine 7 (2) (2019) 101–117, https://ieeexplore.ieee.org/document/8738016.

[10] N. Kranjčić, D. Medak, R. Župan, M. Rezo, Support vector machine accuracy assessment for extracting green urban areas in towns, Remote Sensing 11 (6) (2019) 655, https://doi.org/10.3390/rs11060655.

[11] R. Qureshi, M. Uzair, K. Khurshid, H. Yan, Hyperspectral document image processing: applications, challenges and future prospects, Pattern Recognition 90 (2019) 12–22, https://doi.org/10.1016/j.patcog.2019.01.026.

[12] K.V. Subrahmanyam, K.K. Kumar, N.N. Reddy, New insights into the convective system characteristics over the Indian summer monsoon region using space-based passive and active remote sensing techniques, IETE Technical Review 37 (2) (2019) 211–219, https://doi.org/10.1080/02564602.2019.1593890.

[13] E. Christophe, C. Mailhes, P. Duhamel, Hyperspectral image compression: adapting SPIHT and EZW to anisotropic 3-D wavelet coding, IEEE Transactions on Image Processing 17 (12) (2008) 2334–2346, https://doi.org/10.1109/TIP.2008.2005824.

[14] P.K. Varshney, M.K. Arora (Eds.), Advanced Image Processing Techniques for Remotely Sensed Hyperspectral Data, Springer Verlag, 2004.

[15] R.L. King, Putting information into the service of decision making: the role of remote sensing analysis, in: IEEE Workshop on Advances in Techniques for Analysis of Remotely Sensed Data, 2003, pp. 25–29.

[16] N. Keshava, J.F. Mustard, Spectral unmixing, IEEE Signal Processing Magazine 19 (2002) 44–57.

[17] R. Li, Z. Pan, Y. Wang, The linear prediction vector quantization for hyperspectral image compression, Multimedia Tools and Applications 78 (9) (2019) 11701–11718, https://doi.org/10.1007/s11042-018-6724-8.

[18] X. Wang, J. Tao, Y. Shen, M. Qin, C. Song, Distributed source coding of hyperspectral images based on three-dimensional wavelet, Journal of the Indian Society of Remote Sensing 46 (4) (2018) 667–673, https://doi.org/10.1007/s12524-017-0735-1.

[19] B. Sujitha, V.S. Parvathy, E. Laxmi Lydia, P. Rani, Z. Polkowski, K. Shankar, Optimal deep learning based image compression technique for data transmission on industrial Internet of things applications, Transactions on Emerging Telecommunications Technologies 32 (7) (2020), https://doi.org/10.1002/ett.3976.

[20] X. Tang, S. Cho, W.A. Pearlman, 3D set partitioning coding methods in hyperspectral image compression, in: IEEE International Conference on Image Processing (Cat. No. 03CH37429), vol. 2, Barcelona, Spain, 2003, pp. 239–242, https://doi.org/10.1109/ICIP.2003.1246661.

[21] E. Christophe, C. Mailhes, D. Leger, Quality criteria benchmark for hyperspectral imagery, IEEE Transactions on Geoscience and Remote Sensing 43 (9) (2005) 2103–2114, https://doi.org/10.1109/TGRS.2005.853931.

[22] X. Tang, W.A. Pearlman, Three-dimensional wavelet-based compression of hyperspectral images, in: Hyperspectral Data Compression, Springer, Boston, 2006, pp. 273–308, https://doi.org/10.1007/0-387-28600-4_10.

[23] X. Tang, W.A. Pearlman, Lossy-to-lossless block-based compression of hyperspectral volumetric data, in: IEEE International Conference on Image Processing, vol. 5, Singapore, 2004, pp. 3283–3286, https://doi.org/10.1109/ICIP.2004.1421815.

[24] J. Wu, Z. Wu, C. Wu, Lossy to lossless compressions of hyperspectral images using three-dimensional set partitioning algorithm, Optical Engineering 45 (2) (2006) 027005, https://doi.org/10.1117/1.2173996.

[25] F. Zhao, G. Liu, X. Wang, An efficient macroblock-based diverse and flexible prediction modes selection for hyperspectral images coding, Signal Processing. Image Communication 25 (9) (2010) 697–708, https://doi.org/10.1016/j.image.2010.07.003.

[26] H.S. Lee, N.H. Younan, R.L. King, Hyperspectral image cube compression combining JPEG-2000 and spectral decorrelation, in: IEEE International Geoscience and Remote Sensing Symposium 2002, vol. 6, 2002, pp. 3317–3319, https://doi.org/10.1109/IGARSS.2002.1027168.

[27] A.K. Rao, S. Bhargava, Multispectral data compression using bidirectional interband prediction, IEEE Transactions on Geoscience and Remote Sensing 34 (2) (1996) 385–397, https://doi.org/10.1109/36.485116.

[28] B. Beong-Jo, W.A. Pearlman, An embedded wavelet video coder using three-dimensional set partitioning in hierarchical trees (SPIHT), in: IEEE Data Compression Conference DCC '97, 1997, pp. 251–260, https://doi.org/10.1109/DCC.1997.582048.

[29] S. Bajpai, N.R. Kidwai, H.V. Singh, A.K. Singh, Low memory block tree coding for hyperspectral images, Multimedia Tools and Applications 78 (19) (2019) 27193–27209, https://doi.org/10.1007/s11042-019-07797-6.

[30] S. Álvarez-Cortés, N. Amrani, J. Serra-Sagristà, Low complexity regression wavelet analysis variants for hyperspectral data lossless compression, International Journal of Remote Sensing 39 (7) (2018) 1971–2000, https://doi.org/10.1080/01431161.2017.1375617.

[31] A. Datta, S. Ghosh, A. Ghosh, Hyperspectral remote sensing images and supervised feature extraction, in: Cloud Computing for Geospatial Big Data Analytics, vol. 49, Springer, Cham, 2019, pp. 265–289, https://doi.org/10.1007/978-3-030-03359-0_13.

[32] Z. Jiang, W.D. Pan, H. Shen, Spatially and spectrally concatenated neural networks for efficient lossless compression of hyperspectral imagery, Journal of Imaging 6 (6) (2020) 38, https://doi.org/10.3390/jimaging6060038.

[33] M. Dennis, D. Barlow, G. Cavan, P. Cook, A. Gilchrist, J. Handlay, P. James, J. Thompson, K. Tzoulas, C. Wheather, S. Lindley, Mapping urban green infrastructure: A novel landscape-based approach to incorporating land use and land cover in the mapping of human-dominated systems, Land 7 (1) (2018) 655, https://doi.org/10.3390/land7010017.

[34] M. Ding, G. Fan, Multilayer joint gait-pose manifolds for human gait motion modeling, IEEE Transactions on Cybernetics 45 (11) (2015) 2314–2424, https://doi.org/10.1109/TCYB.2014.2373393.

[35] R. Nagendran, A. Vasuki, Hyperspectral image compression using hybrid transform with different wavelet-based transform coding, International Journal of Wavelets, Multiresolution and Information Processing 18 (01) (2020) 1941008, https://doi.org/10.1142/S021969131941008X.

[36] Han V. Nguyen, M.O. Ulfarsson, J.R. Sveinsson, Hyperspectral image denoising using SURE-based unsupervised convolutional neural networks, IEEE Transactions on Geoscience and Remote Sensing (2020), https://doi.org/10.1109/TGRS.2020.3008844.

[37] Yubal Barrios, Alfonso Rodríguez, Antonio Sánchez, Arturo Pérez, Sebastián López, Andrés Otero, Eduardo de la Torre, Roberto Sarmiento, Lossy hyperspectral image compression on a reconfigurable and fault-tolerant FPGA-based adaptive computing platform, Electronics 9 (10) (2020) 1576, https://doi.org/10.3390/electronics9101576.

[38] S. Bajpai, N.R. Kidwai, H.V. Singh, et al., A low complexity hyperspectral image compression through 3D set partitioned embedded zero block coding, Multimedia Tools and Applications (2021), https://doi.org/10.1007/s11042-021-11456-0.

[39] J.E. Fowler, J.T. Rucker, Three-dimensional wavelet-based compression of hyperspectral imagery, in: Hyperspectral Data Exploitation: Theory and Applications, Springer, 2007, pp. 379–407, https://doi.org/10.1007/0-387-28600-4_10.

[40] P.C. Pandey, H. Blazter, G.P. Petropoulos, P.K. Srivastava, B. Bhattacharya (Eds.), Hyperspectral Remote Sensing Theory and Applications: A Volume in Earth Observation, Elsevier, ISBN 978-0-08-102894-0, 2020, https://doi.org/10.1016/C2018-0-01850-2.

[41] C. Malegori, E. Alladio, P. Oliveri, M. Casale, G. Pastorini, An in-depth study of cheese ripening by means of NIR hyperspectral imaging: Spatial mapping of dehydration, proteolysis and lipolysis, Food Chemistry 343 (2021) 128547, https://doi.org/10.1016/j.foodchem.2020.128547.

[42] Q. Yang, S. Sun, W.J. Jeffcoate, D.J. Clark, A. Musgove, F.L. Game, S.P. Morgan, Investigation of the performance of hyperspectral imaging by principal component analysis in the prediction of healing of diabetic foot ulcers, Journal of Imaging 4 (12) (2018) 144, https://doi.org/10.3390/jimaging4120144.

[43] Burak Uzkent, Aneesh Rangnekar, Matthew J. Hoffman, Aerial vehicle tracking by adaptive fusion of hyperspectral likelihood maps, https://arxiv.org/pdf/1707.03553.pdf, 2017.

[44] Anne-Katrin Mahlein, Matheus Kuska, Stefan Thomas, David Bohnenkamp, Elias Alisaac, Jan Behmann, Mirwaes Wahabzada, K. Kersting, Plant disease detection by hyperspectral imaging: from the lab to the field, Advances in Animal Biosciences 8 (2017) 238–243, https://doi.org/10.1017/S2040470017001248.

[45] R. Bhardwaj, Enhanced encrypted reversible data hiding algorithm with minimum distortion through homomorphic encryption, Journal of Electronic Imaging 27 (2) (2018) 023017, https://doi.org/10.1117/1.JEI.27.2.023017.

[46] N.R. Kidwai, E. Khan, M. Reisslein, ZM-SPECK: a fast and memoryless image coder for multimedia sensor networks, IEEE Sensors Journal 16 (8) (2016) 2575–2587, https://doi.org/10.1109/JSEN.2016.2519600.

[47] M. Tausif, N.R. Kidwai, E. Khan, M. Reisslein, FrWF-based LMBTC: memory-efficient image coding for visual sensors, IEEE Sensors Journal 15 (11) (2015) 6218–6226, https://doi.org/10.1109/JSEN.2015.2456332.

[48] Y. Dua, V. Kumar, R.S. Singh, Comprehensive review of hyperspectral image compression algorithms, Optical Engineering 59 (9) (2020) 090902, https://doi.org/10.1117/1.OE.59.9.090902.

[49] B. Penna, T. Tillo, E. Magli, G. Olmo, Transform coding techniques for lossy hyperspectral data compression, IEEE Transactions on Geoscience and Remote Sensing 45 (5) (2007) 1408–1421, https://doi.org/10.1109/TGRS.2007.894565.

[50] N. Zikiou, M. Lahdir, D. Helbert, Support vector regression-based 3D-wavelet texture learning for hyperspectral image compression, The Visual Computer 36 (7) (2019) 1473–1490, https://doi.org/10.1007/s00371-019-01753-z.

[51] R. Li, Z. Pan, Y. Wang, The linear prediction vector quantization for hyperspectral image compression, Multimedia Tools and Applications 78 (9) (2019) 11701–11718, https://doi.org/10.1007/s11042-018-6724-8.

[52] S. Lim, K. Sohn, C. Lee, Compression for hyperspectral images using three dimensional wavelet transform. Scanning the present and resolving the future, in: Proceedings IEEE International Geoscience and Remote Sensing Symposium (Cat. No. 01CH37217), Sydney, NSW, Australia, 2001, pp. 109–111, https://doi.org/10.1109/IGARSS.2001.976072.

[53] A. Anastasia, G. Tsagkatakis, T. Panagiotis, Tensor decomposition learning for compression of multidimensional signals, IEEE Journal of Selected Topics in Signal Processing 15 (3) (2021) 476–490, https://doi.org/10.1109/JSTSP.2021.3054314.

[54] M. Picollo, C. Cucci, A. Casini, L. Stefani, Hyper-spectral imaging technique in the cultural heritage field: new possible scenarios, Sensors 20 (10) (2020) 2843, https://www.mdpi.com/1424-8220/20/10/2843.

[55] S.S. Rajput, K.V. Arya, A robust face super-resolution algorithm and its application in low-resolution face recognition system, Multimedia Tools and Applications 79 (2020) 23909–23934, https://doi.org/10.1007/s11042-020-09072-5.

[56] S.S. Rajput, K.V. Arya, CNN classifier based low-resolution face recognition algorithm, in: 2020 International Conference on Emerging Frontiers in Electrical and Electronic Technologies (ICEFEET), 2020, pp. 1–4, https://doi.org/10.1109/ICEFEET49149.2020.9187001.

[57] S.S. Rajput, K.V. Arya, A robust facial image super-resolution model via mirror-patch based neighbor representation, Multimedia Tools and Applications 78 (2019) 25407–25426, https://doi.org/10.1007/s11042-019-07791-y.

[58] S.S. Rajput, K.V. Arya, V.K. Bohat, Face image super-resolution using differential evolutionary algorithm, in: N. Verma, A. Ghosh (Eds.), Computational Intelligence: Theories, Applications and Future Directions - Volume II, in: Advances in Intelligent Systems and Computing, vol. 799, Springer, Singapore, 2019, https://doi.org/10.1007/978-981-13-1135-2_48.

[59] S.S. Rajput, K.V. Arya, V. Singh, V.K. Bohat, Face hallucination techniques: a survey, in: 2018 Conference on Information and Communication Technology (CICT), 2018, pp. 1–6, https://doi.org/10.1109/INFOCOMTECH.2018.8722416.

[60] K.V. Arya, S.S. Rajput, S. Upadhyay, Noise-robust low-resolution face recognition using SIFT features, in: N. Verma, A. Ghosh (Eds.), Computational Intelligence: Theories, Applications and Future Directions - Volume II, in: Advances in Intelligent Systems and Computing, vol. 799, Springer, Singapore, 2019, https://doi.org/10.1007/978-981-13-1135-2_49.

[61] Y.K. Mydam, S. Singh Rajput, P. Chanak, Low rank representation based discriminative multi manifold analysis for low-resolution face recognition, in: 2018 Conference on Information and Communication Technology (CICT), 2018, pp. 1–5, https://doi.org/10.1109/INFOCOMTECH.2018.8722393.

[62] K.V. Arya, A. Rajawat, M.K. Pandey, S.S. Rajput, Very low resolution face recognition using fused visual and texture features, in: 2017 Conference on Information and Communication Technology (CICT), 2017, pp. 1–5, https://doi.org/10.1109/INFOCOMTECH.2017.8340642.

[63] Shyam Singh Rajput, K.V. Arya, Vinay Singh, Robust face super-resolution via iterative sparsity and locality-constrained representation, Information Sciences 463–464 (2018) 227–244, https://doi.org/10.1016/j.ins.2018.06.050.

[64] Shyam Singh Rajput, Ankur Singh, K.V. Arya, Junjun Jiang, Noise robust face hallucination algorithm using local content prior based error shrunk nearest neighbors representation, Signal Processing 147 (2018) 233–246, https://doi.org/10.1016/j.sigpro.2018.01.030.

CHAPTER 12

Classification of COVID-19 and non-COVID-19 lung computed tomography images using machine learning

Khin Wee Lai, Cai Yee Chang, and Wei Kit Loo
Department of Biomedical Engineering, Faculty of Engineering, Universiti Malaya, Kuala Lumpur, Malaysia

12.1 Introduction

In late December 2019, an unprecedented outbreak of unknown respiratory disease was identified and reported in Wuhan City, Hubei Province, China. The first case was reported to the World Health Organization (WHO) on December 31, 2019. A new type of coronavirus currently designated as severe acute respiratory syndrome coronavirus 2 (SARS-CoV2) was then identified as the main causative pathogen. Coronaviruses are single-stranded ribonucleic acid (RNA) viruses, having genome sizes from 26 to 32 kilobases in length. They fall under *Coronaviridae* family, *Coronavirinae* subfamily and *Nidovirales* order [1]. From the view of the electron microscope of a coronavirus, spike-like shapes are covering the outer surface of the virus; it looks like a corona is surrounding the virion. Corona is the crown-like appearance spiking on the surface of the virus.

On 11 March 2020, it was declared as a global pandemic by WHO in the effort to provide more insights on this newly emerged coronavirus disease (COVID-19) [17]. Till 23 August 2021, a total of more than 211 million cases of COVID-19 were reported to World Health Organization (WHO) worldwide, with a total of more than 4.4 million of deaths [12]. The sudden emergence of COVID-19 had caused overburdens to the medical systems across the world, particularly the pandemic areas.

In terms of clinical manifestations, the onset symptoms of COVID-19 cases are not specific, especially those with mild nonrespiratory symptoms. A wide range of symptoms had been identified with COVID-19 patients, ranging from mild to severe. These clinical symptoms include fever or chills,

Digital Image Enhancement and Reconstruction
https://doi.org/10.1016/B978-0-32-398370-9.00019-6

cough, breathing difficulty, fatigue, muscle aches, headache, loss of taste or smell, sore throat, diarrhea, and nausea [11]. There are no specific symptoms that applied to all and are multicomprehensive. These cases tend to be missed out easily without genetic-related laboratory tests, contributing to further infections. Thus, as of now, the viral nucleic acid or antigen test is the key diagnosis method for SARS-CoV-2 detection. Through reverse transcription polymerase chain reaction (RT-PCR) test, respiratory samples, such as nasal or oral swabs, are collected to identify the presence of SARS-CoV-2 in both symptomatic and asymptomatic people. The tests require at least 24 hours to get the results. Apart from RT-PCR, the collected samples can be tested using isothermal amplification assay; it is a rapid method, as the result can be obtained in 5 minutes. However, it has a lower accuracy than RT-PCR tests [3].

Recent studies reported that different imaging tools, such as chest radiography and computed tomography (CT) scan can also be used as diagnostic tools for COVID-19. The most common and economical medical imaging technique is chest radiography. However, a chest X-ray is not recommended in this case due to the lack of visual features evidence. In a chest X-ray, the features are not easily accessible, as the ribs and soft tissues appear to be overlapped, thus providing low sensitivity and low contrast [6]. On the other hand, a lung CT scan is identified to be a more practical approach in the diagnosis and treatment of COVID-19. This is because the CT scan of COVID-19 positive patients had presented characteristic features, and these can help in accessing the severity of the disease.

CT scan, especially high-resolution CT does not have a structural overlapping issue and provides clear insights into the lungs, allowing detection of small lesions early. Its key value in COVID-19 diagnosis is that it can detect lesions in the lungs, visualize the inflammations to the radiologists, thus providing important warning signals to the patients, who tested negative with nucleic acid or antigen tests. Apart from this, it plays a crucial role in the quantification assessment of COVID-19 and helps to monitor the outcomes of the treatments, including the progression, stability, and absorption of the lungs during the treatment stage.

The radiological manifestations showed in CT scans can be divided into 5 stages: ultra-early stage, early stage, rapid progression stage, consolidation stage, and dissipation stage. The ultra-early stage is the first stage, in which the patients do not show any clinical symptoms, but tested positive in the throat swab test for COVID-19. The imaging manifestation showed single or double ground-glass opacity (GGO). The second stage, early-stage refers to 1 to 3 days after symptoms, such as fever or dry cough. This stage showed multiple patchy GGO that are scattered and separated by thickened interlobular septa. The third stage is the rapid progression stage, which refers to 3–7 days after the clinical symptoms. The CT scan demonstrated light consolidation with air-bronchogram features. Next, the fourth stage is the consolidation stage, which refers to 7–14 days after symptoms appeared. The CT scan showed multiple smaller and denser consolidations than the third stage. The final stage is known as the dissipation stage, 2 to 3 weeks after the clinical symptoms. In this stage, CT scan manifested patchy consolidations, strip-like opacity, interlobular thickening, and the bronchial wall with strip-like twists [7].

COVID-19 CT scan manifested a few notable features in the early stage of the infection. The features on the images represent the inflammatory conditions of lung tissue exudation, proliferation, and metamorphism [2]. GGO is characterized by regions with slightly higher density, which are white in color under the pleura, however, the blood vessels are still visible. Consolidations happen as the inflammation progresses and characterized by increased opacity in the lungs without margins of vessels. Next, paving stones are characterized by the superimposition of lobular interval thickening and interlobular interval line shadows on GGO. The thickened vessels can appear at the edge of lesions; lesions appeared due to the inflammations. Halo signs are characterized as lesions that have a higher density at the center and lower around the edges. The word "halo" refers to the thin cloud-like glass shadow circles surrounding the lesions [2]. Apart from this, air bubbles are also observed as small air-containing spaces in the lung of COVID-19 patients.

Though CT imaging can serve as a reliable alternative for the RT-PCR test for COVID-19 detection and disease monitoring, the diagnosis results need to be accurate. Along with the advancement of sophisticated technology, various image processing techniques have been applied in health care, including medical image segmentation, image enhancement, classification, and tumor detection. On top of that, the rapid growth of deep learning (DL) approaches in artificial intelligence (AI), such as artificial neural network (ANN), have been utilized extensively in medical image processing. These approaches have demonstrated very promising performances, particularly the powerful prediction capabilities and were able to achieve similar results as radiologists [9]. This study presents an automated method to differentiate the COVID-19 CT images from the non-COVID-19 images using different convolutional neural networks (CNN).

Table 12.1 The details of COVID-19 and non-COVID-19 images.

Category	COVID-19	Non-COVID-19
Image File Format	PNG	JPG, PNG
Size	No Standard Size	
Number of Patients	216	92
Total Images	349	397

12.2 Methodology

Classification model to classify the input CT images into binary classes of COVID-19 and non-COVID-19 were built. The methodology were separated into several phases: data acquisition, data preprocessing, image augmentation, and classification using convolutional neural network (CNN) and localization of abnormalities.

The dataset had a total of 746 CT images, in which 349 images from 216 patients who tested positive for COVID-19 and 397 non-COVID-19 images, as shown in Table 12.1.

The images were extracted from COVID-19–related research papers from medRxiv, bioRxiv, NEJM, and Lancet from 19th January to 25th March 2020 using PyMuPDF. It was used to extract the images' low-level structures and the localization of all embedded figures. The meta-information, including the patients' gender, age, medical information, COVID-19 severity, scanning time, and COVID-19 abnormalities were also manually recorded. From the 349 COVID-19 CT images, there were 169 images with known age, whereas 137 images with known gender. The number of male patients was more than female, 86 and 51, respectively.

In CT scan images, lung tissue density was presented in Hounsfield units (HU). This was defined as the HU of air is -1000, whereas water is 0 HU. A window could be adjusted to focus on issues of interest. In this dataset, the lung window (axial slice) was used to view lung parenchyma (500 HU). A sample of lung window is shown in Fig. 12.1.

It appeared as gray as it is within the range, whereas air pockets (-1000 HU) that were not within the range appeared as black in color. This provided a clear differentiation between the lung parenchyma and air pockets.

Only two standard preprocessing techniques were employed, which were resizing and intensity normalization to optimize the training process. This study avoided extensive preprocessing processes to ensure that the model was more robust to noise, artifacts, and capable to handle different

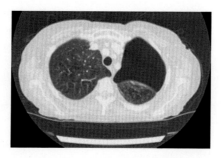

Figure 12.1 Lung window on chest CT (axial slice).

Table 12.2 The splitting of the dataset into 3 sets: training, validation, and testing.

Classes	Selected Dataset (images)	Testing Set (images)	Training & Validation Sets (images)
COVID-19	325	33	292
Non-COVID-19	334	34	300

input variations, especially at the feature extraction phase. Apart from this, the dataset also presented the scans with soft tissues window, which were not suitable for training, as the lung density appeared as completely black. Hence these images were removed from the original dataset; the remaining dataset is shown in Table 12.2.

Before image augmentation, the dataset was split into three parts: training data, validation data, and testing data with the ratio of 8:1:1. The augmentation was only applied to training and validation data, whereas the test data remained as raw data without augmentation. In this work, four augmentation techniques were applied, they were rotations ($-40°$ to $40°$), horizontal flips, vertical flips, translations in x and y axis. These transformations preserved the details of the image and did not distract the radiologists from accessing and interpreting the images. Apart from the 4 techniques, random scaling was applied and transformed randomly on the fly before training to ensure variability of the dataset. Fig. 12.2 shows the image augmentation techniques used. The total number of images available after the data augmentation is shown in Table 12.3.

The dataset was ready to be fitted to the CNN networks for training after preprocessing and augmentation were carried out. In this phase, transfer learning-based techniques were implemented, which pretrained models that had been trained on large dataset had been used, and the network were fine-tuned with our dataset to give better performance. In this study, the

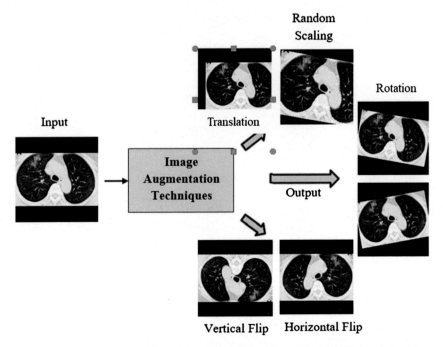

Figure 12.2 The 5 image augmentation techniques: Rotations (−40° to 40°), translations in *x* and *y* directions, random scaling, horizontal and vertical flips.

Table 12.3 Dataset after image augmentation.

Classes	Training & Validation Sets (images)	Training (80%)	Validation (10%)	Testing (10%)
COVID-19	1138	1012	126	33
Non-COVID-19	1144	1017	127	34
Total	**2282**	**2029**	**253**	**67**

pretrained models had been trained on the ImageNet dataset. This means that the models were able to filter the low-level features, and even higher features, as a result of the previous learning. By utilizing the pretrained models, they acted as the feature extractors, and the networks could learn faster during the training process rather than training from scratch.

Different DL pretrained models were used in this study with PyTorch frameworks, namely, ResNets, DenseNets, VGGs, AlexNet, GoogleNet, SqueezeNet, and ResNeXt. The models' selection criteria were based on the error rate achieved on image large-scale visual recognition competition (ILSVRC) and the models' architecture.

Appropriate hyperparameters played an integral role in determining the success of the training. Generally, large neural networks required a longer time to train, so appropriate hyperparameters settings helped to reduce the training time, while giving great accuracy. The learning rate was set at 0.001; this small learning rate required longer training time, but it helped to converge smoothly. Next, to prevent oscillations, momentum was set at 0.9. It helped the network to know the next step with the knowledge from previous learning, controlling the networks' learning speed during training. The batch size was set at 64; it was the number of subsamples fitted to the network every epoch. The number of epochs was set at 300 epochs; there was also an early stopping setting, which helped to stop the training once the validation loss values showed no improvements within 10 epochs compared to minimum loss values.

Moreover, during training, backpropagation was used to calculate the gradients, while the optimizer performed learning using this gradient [10]. SGD optimizer was implemented in the network training to minimize the loss function. It updated the model's parameters based on the computed gradients on each training example at a time. Then, cross-entropy loss was applied in the training. It was suitable to measure the model's performance, whose model output was a probability value between 0 and 1. It took the logits as inputs and performed "log_softmax" internally to ensure numerical stability. Cross-entropy loss increased as the predicted probability diverged from the actual labels. It was used when adjusting model weights during training. The aim was to reduce the loss; the smaller the loss, the better the training. After setting up all the training algorithms, the networks were trained by loading the preprocessed and augmented data into the pretrain networks.

Model evaluation metrics were needed to quantify the models' performances, particularly classification metrics. To access the ability of our trained model, a confusion matrix was used to test on the testing set, which represented the unseen data by the model, as shown in Fig. 12.3.

Four classification metrics were being calculated, representing which classes were being predicted correctly and incorrectly, and the type of errors made by the classifier when applying on the testing set. True Positive (TP) indicated True: the model prediction was "Non-COVID-19," and it matched the actual class, which was also "Non-COVID-19." False Positive (FP) indicated False: the model prediction was "COVID-19," and it did not match the actual class, which was "Non-COVID-19." False Negative (FN) indicated False: the model prediction was "Non-COVID-19," whereas the

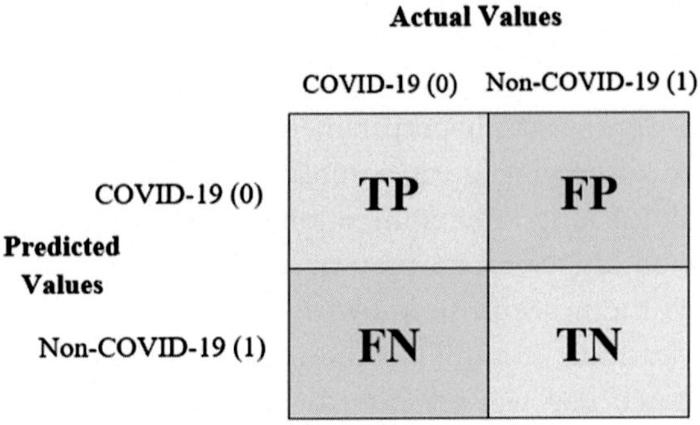

Actual Values

COVID-19 (0)   Non-COVID-19 (1)

	COVID-19 (0)	Non-COVID-19 (1)
COVID-19 (0)	**TP**	**FP**
Non-COVID-19 (1)	**FN**	**TN**

Predicted Values

Figure 12.3 The 2 × 2 confusion matrix of binary classifier of COVID-19 and non-COVID-19.

actual class is "COVID-19." Lastly, True Negative (TN) indicated True: the model predicted "Non-COVID-19," whereas the actual class was also "Non-COVID-19."

Though classification accuracy alone was not able to quantify whether the models performed well, the performance indicators were used to compute the evaluation metrics in a more detailed form, which are accuracy, sensitivity, specificity, positive predictive value (PPV), negative predictive value (NPV), and F1 score. Apart from computing the confusion matrix to access the model on the testing set, to know the predictions indicated by these values on both classes, the confidence levels of the model on both classes on one testing image were calculated and visualized, as shown in Fig. 12.4.

To gain more insights into the trained model, CAM was used to visualize the models' predictions. It used the gradients of the targeted class passing to the last convolutional layer to produce the localization mapping with the highlighted region of interest that was responsible for the predictions [16]. Hence it was applied to visualize which regions the model had paid attention to in predicting the output as COVID-19 or non-COVID-19. This enabled us to analyze if the model predictions were reasonable and to identify the failure modes of the models.

12.3 Results

The dataset was trained with seven different pretrained architectures: ResNets, VGGs, DenseNet, AlexNet, GoogleNet, ResNeXt, and Squeeze-Net. For ResNet architecture, three sets of training were done with the different number of layers: ResNet50 with 50 layers, ResNet101 with

99.9989% Covid, 0.0011% NonCovid   99.9991% Covid, 0.0009% NonCovid

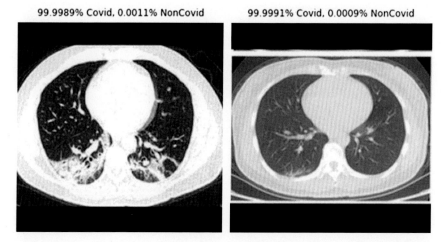

Figure 12.4 The confidence levels of the ResNet101 model predictions on 2 testing images. The model predicted that both images were COVID-19 with 99.99% confidence level.

101 layers, and ResNet152 with 152 layers. For VGG architecture, two sets of training were done on 16 layers and 19 layers of VGG networks. Then, the training was done once for DenseNet201, AlexNet, GoogleNet, SqueezeNet, and ResNeXt, respectively.

For each epoch, after the training loop ended, the validation loop started to evaluate the trained model, and this step was repeated until the maximum number of epochs. The training and validation losses and the accuracy of the transfer learning models are shown in Fig. 12.5 and Fig. 12.6.

Table 12.4 and Fig. 12.7 show the training parameters of all the transfer learning models and the training time per epoch. In every epoch, the total number of images loaded into the networks was 2029, with a batch size of 64. Thereafter, the training and validation were completed. The trained transfer learning models were tested on the testing dataset, which was unseen by the networks. The accuracy, sensitivity, specificity, PPV, NPV, and F1-score of the testing are recorded in Table 12.5.

The confusion matrixes of the testing set on different transfer learning models are shown in Fig. 12.8, Fig. 12.9, Fig. 12.10, Fig. 12.11, and Fig. 12.12. Class 0 represents COVID-19, whereas Class 1 represents non-COVID-19.

To gain more insights on the network, gradient descent class activation mapping (GradCAM) visualization was applied to ResNet152 and ResNeXt to understand the region of interest that the network had paid attention to, as shown in Table 12.6.

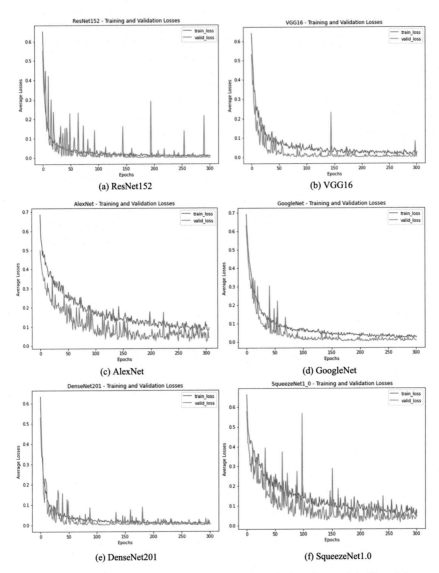

Figure 12.5 The training and validation losses of the transfer learning models. The minimum number of epochs set was 300 epochs and early stop triggered if there was no improvement in validation loss for 10 epochs continuously. The blue line represents training loss, and the orange line represents the validation loss.

12.4 Discussions

From Fig. 12.5, the transfer learning models were trained for 300 epochs and early stopping was triggered if the number of epochs with no im-

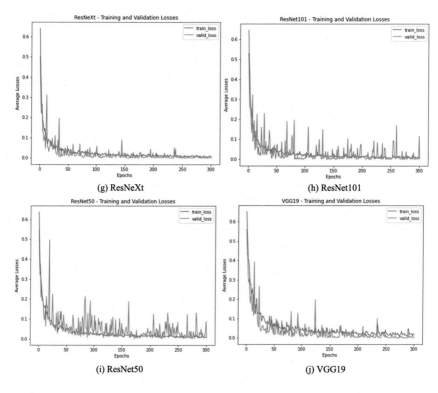

(g) ResNeXt

(h) ResNet101

(i) ResNet50

(j) VGG19

Figure 12.5 (*continued*)

Table 12.4 The total training parameters for all transfer learning models and computation time for one epoch with the same batch size, 64.

Models	Training Parameters	One epoch (seconds)
ResNet50	23,512,130	32.06
ResNet101	42,504,258	30.50
ResNet152	58,147,906	63.66
DenseNet201	18,096,770	43.82
VGG16	5,601,954	44.15
VGG19	139,578,434	52.68
AlexNet	57,012,034	17.78
GoogleNet	5,601,954	18.09
SqueezeNet	**736,450**	**15.85**
ResNeXt	22,984,002	41.08

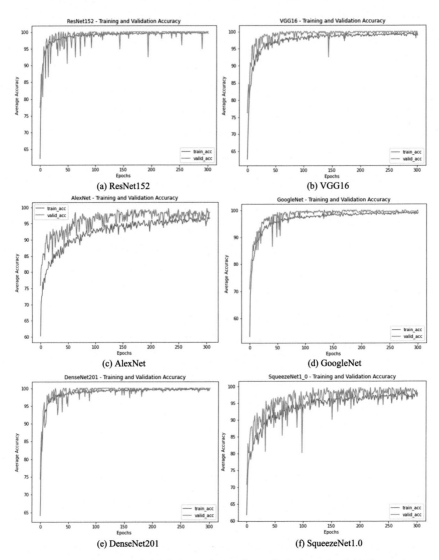

Figure 12.6 The training and validation accuracy of transfer learning models. The minimum number of epochs set was 300 epochs and early stop triggered if there was no improvement in validation loss for 10 epochs continuously. The blue line represents training accuracy, and the orange line represents the validation accuracy.

provement was equal to 10 epochs continuously after 300 epochs. From the plots, the blue line represented the training losses, whereas the orange line represented the validation losses. It was shown that the training and validation losses decreased drastically from the beginning, continued to go

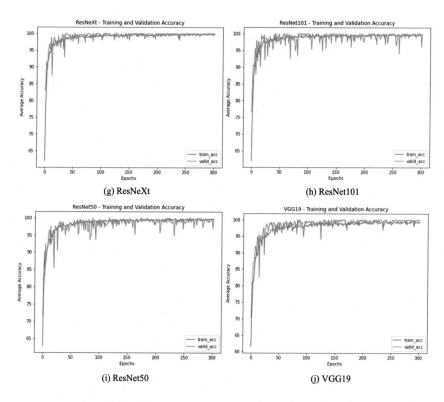

Figure 12.6 (*continued*)

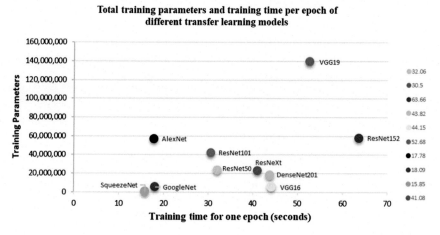

Figure 12.7 The training parameters and computation time for one epoch for different transfer learning models. The batch size is 64.

Table 12.5 The performance metrics of transfer learning models on the testing set.

Pretrained models	Performance metrics (%)					
	Specificity (%)	Sensitivity (%)	NPV (%)	PPV (%)	Accuracy (%)	F1 score
ResNet50	91.18	100.00	100.00	91.67	95.52	0.9538
ResNet101	91.18	100.00	100.00	91.67	95.52	0.9538
ResNet152	97.06	100.00	100.00	97.06	**98.51**	0.9851
DenseNet201	97.06	100.00	100.00	97.06	**98.51**	0.9851
VGG16	94.12	100.00	100.00	94.29	97.01	0.9697
VGG19	94.12	96.97	96.97	94.12	95.52	0.9552
AlexNet	88.24	96.97	96.97	88.89	92.54	0.9231
GoogleNet	97.06	100.00	100.00	97.06	**98.51**	0.9851
SqueezeNet	100.00	93.94	94.44	100.00	97.01	0.9714
ResNeXt	100.00	96.97	97.14	100.00	**98.51**	0.9855

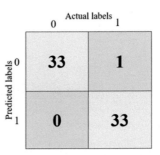

Figure 12.8 The confusion matrixes of DenseNet201 (Left) and ResNet152 (Right) have TP of 33 images and TN of 33 images out of the total 33 COVID-19 images and 34 non-COVID-19 images.

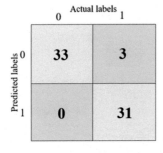 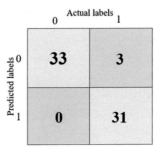

Figure 12.9 The confusion matrix of ResNet101(Left) and ResNet50 (Right) with TP of 33 images and TN of 31 images out of the total 33 COVID-19 images and 34 non-COVID-19 images.

down and reached almost zero after 75 epochs for ResNet152, ResNet101, ResNet50, VGG16, GoogleNet, DenseNet201, ResNeXt, and VGG19.

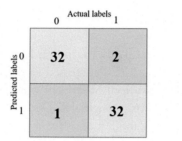
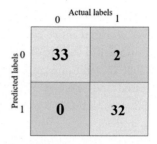

Figure 12.10 The confusion matrix of VGG19 (left) were having TP and TN of 32 images out of the total 33 COVID-19 images and 34 non-COVID-19 images. The VGG16 (right) were having TP of 33 images and TN of 32 images out of the total 33 COVID-19 images and 34 non-COVID-19 images.

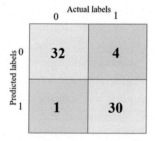
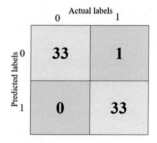

Figure 12.11 The confusion matrix of AlexNet (left) with TP of 32 images and TN of 30 images out of the total 33 COVID-19 images and 34 non-COVID-19 images. The confusion matrix of GoogleNet (right) with TP and TN of 33 each.

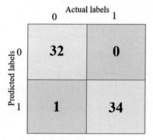
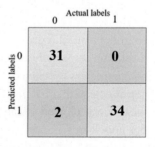

Figure 12.12 The confusion matrix of ResNeXt (left) with TP of 32 images and TN of 34 images out of the total 33 COVID-19 images and 34 non-COVID-19 images. The confusion matrix of SqueezeNet (right) with TP of 31 images and TN of 34 images.

This was normal, as the model was trained to fit the train data as well as possible. However, the training and validation losses of AlexNet and SqueezeNet continued to go down and reached almost zero around 200 epochs, which were slower than the other models. Both AlexNet and SqueezeNet required more epochs to converge.

The training and validation accuracy were plotted as in Fig. 12.6. It was observed that the training and validation accuracy increased as the training progressed and reached 95%, and above from 50 epochs onwards for ResNet152, ResNet101, ResNet50, VGG16, GoogleNet, DenseNet201, ResNeXt, and VGG19. However, AlexNet and SqueezeNet required 150 epochs to reach 95% accuracy. Apart from this, from Figs. 12.5 and 12.6, the validation losses and accuracy represented by the orange color lines showed noisy movements around the training loss, fluctuating in a larger amplitude than the training losses and accuracy. These were due to the stochastic gradient descent (SGD) optimizers used in the training. Since the SGD updated the model parameters more frequently compared to other gradient descents, there were high variances and fluctuations in the loss functions compared to other optimizers [15]. Apart from the optimizer, the insufficient validation dataset also contributed to the noisy movements; the validation set was not providing enough information compared to the training set. Also, there was no overfitting found as the training and validation losses were decreased simultaneously and fluctuated in the same range, starting from 250 epochs. This showed that a larger epoch allowed the networks to train longer, thus the networks learned more and converged better and smoother.

In CNN training, the execution time for overall training can be used to compute the training cost and also allows us to predict the hyperparameter settings to improve the training performance [8]. Thus it is of utmost importance to understand the time taken and predict the computation cost for the overall training, especially before the deployment. Table 12.4 recorded the training parameters for each of the models and the corresponding training time per epoch with a batch size fixed at 64. The comparison between different models was plotted in Fig. 12.7. The x-axis represented the training time per epoch in seconds, whereas the y-axis represented the training parameters of the models. It showed that the SqueezeNet model had the lowest number of parameters, 736,450, and the training time per epoch was the shortest; it took 15.85 seconds only for one epoch. This was then followed by AlexNet with 57,012,034 training parameters and 17.78 seconds per epoch, GoogleNet, ResNet101, ResNet50, ResNeXt, DenseNet201, and VGG16. The VGG19 had the largest amount of training parameters, 139,578,434 and the training time per epoch was 52.68 seconds. However, the ResNet152 which had a smaller number of training parameters than

Table 12.6 The GradCAM visualizations of ResNet152 and ResNeXt models. Class 0 denoted COVID-19, Class 1 denoted non-COVID-19. The third column represents the original CT scan images with the expected ROI labeled with red arrows, whereas the last column represents the class activation maps of the models. The red region after GradCAM visualization shows the highest score for the class of interest.

Models	Classes scores [Class 0, Class 1]	Original Image	After GradCAM
ResNet152	[0.99998, 0.00002]	(a)	(a)
	[0.9588, 0.0412]	(b)	(b)
ResNeXt	[0.99983, 0.17370]	(c)	(c)
	[0.8665, 0.1335]	(d)	(d)

VGG19 required the longest training time per epoch, 63.66 seconds. The training time for one epoch involved the time taken for the single forward and backward propagation of all the training dataset. However, the training time was different with different hardware and hyperparameter tunings. By computing the execution time per epoch, the computation cost can be predicted and the strategy can be planned to reduce the cost and time needed for deployment.

After the training and validation were completed, it came to the most important step to evaluate how well the trained models generalized and performed on the unseen testing dataset. The confusion matrix for the binary classification by each of the trained models was plotted, as in Fig. 12.9, until Fig. 12.12. Class 0 denoted the class "COVID-19" with a total of 33 testing images and Class 1 denoted the class "Non-COVID-19" with a total of 34 testing images. All the testing images were classified into 4 parts based on the ground truth labels and the prediction results: TP, TN, FP, and FN [4]. The diagonal cells with dark blue color represented the number of testing images that were correctly classified. On the other hand, the off-diagonal cells with light blue color represented the number of testing images that were incorrectly classified. The results demonstrated that the DenseNet201, ResNet152, GoogleNet, and ResNeXt had only one image that was misclassified. This was followed by VGG16 with 2 images having been wrongly classified; the VGG19, ResNet101, ResNet50 had 3 images classified wrongly. The AlexNet had the most images incorrectly classified, 5 in total.

Then, the confusion matrix was used to compute the performance metrics of all the models. Table 12.5 showed the sensitivity, specificity, PPV, NPV, accuracy, and F1 score on the testing dataset. Accuracy is the number of cases that are classified correctly divided by the total number of images; it represented the overall performance of the training [5]. ResNeXt, GoogleNet, ResNet152, and DenseNet201 had achieved the highest accuracy of 98.51%. The latter models were able to classify all the testing images correctly with only one misclassified image. Meanwhile, the AlexNet had the lowest accuracy, which was only 92.54%; its overall performance was lower compared to other networks.

The sensitivity, specificity, PPV, and NPV evaluated the models' performance by class. To access the model's ability in classifying COVID-19 images, sensitivity and PPV were the main focus. Sensitivity was the percentage of COVID-19 images that were classified correctly out of the total number of COVID-19 images. From Table 12.5, ResNet50, ResNet101,

ResNet152, DenseNet201, VGG16, and GoogleNet achieved sensitivity of 100% with no misclassified COVID-19 images. VGG19, AlexNet and ResNeXt misclassified one COVID-19 image with a sensitivity of 96.97%, and, lastly, SqueezeNet misclassified 2 COVID-19 images with a sensitivity of 93.94% only. Moreover, the PPV can also be referred to as the precision value, indicating the true COVID-19 frequency among whole COVID-19 outputs (TP+FP). The models would not be considered as performing well if the precision value were not good, despite the accuracy being very high.

Only SqueezeNet and ResNeXt had achieved 100% PPV; ResNet152, DenseNet201, and GoogleNet had PPV of 97.06% with one non–COVID-19 image misclassified as COVID-19. VGG16 and VGG19 had PPV of 94.29% and 94.12%, respectively, with 2 images misclassified as COVID-19. AlexNet had the least PPV of 88.89%, with 4 non–COVID-19 images misclassified as COVID-19.

On the other hand, specificity represented the ability of the models in recognizing non–COVID-19 images correctly. Out of 34 negative images in testing data, only SqueezeNet and ResNeXt were able to classify all the non–COVID-19 images correctly. The opposite of the PPV was the NPV, which represented the performance of the model in detecting negative images [18]. NPV is also known as recall. The results showed that ResNet50, ResNet101, ResNet152, DenseNet201, VGG16, and GoogleNet had achieved recall of 100%; ResNeXt with 97.14%; VGG19 with 96.97%; AlexNet with 96.77%, and, lastly, SqueezeNet with 94.44%.

In overall, ResNet50, ResNet101, VGG16, and AlexNet performed better in classifying COVID-19 images. ResNet152, DenseNet201, VGG19, and GoogleNet showed the same performance for both classes, and, lastly, SqueezeNet and ResNeXt performed better in classifying non–COVID-19 images.

To make the CNN training more transparent and have a better understanding of how the models made decisions, GradCAM visualizations were performed [14]. Table 12.6 showed the GradCAM visualization of ResNeXt and ResNet152 on the same images to visualize the models' region of interest. The first column, starting from the left side showed the models used to visualize; the second column showed prediction scores for each class; the third column was the original images, whereas the last column showed the heatmaps on the images. The high-intensity regions, which were blue and red in color, showed the region of interest to the models. The red color represented the highest score for the class of interest [13].

The results showed that different models had a different region of interest, despite both models having the same overall accuracy of 98.51%. Both ResNeXt and ResNet152 had different prediction scores for each image, and the region of interest for class COVID-19, showed in red color, were also different. For example, in image b, the ResNet152 model showed the prediction score of 0.9588, and the region of interest was at the left bottom side, in which the consolidation was located. However, in ResNeXt, the model's region of interest was at the middle of the left side, which was different from the ResNet152. This region did not provide any features that would probably contribute to the decision as COVID-19 class. This showed that the model was still not confident enough in detecting the COVID-19 region of interest, and that further training was needed. Steps, such as increasing the dataset and finetuning, can be carried out to increase the accuracy of the models.

12.5 Limitations and future improvements

In this study, the dataset used for training the CNN architectures is a small dataset that consists of only 349 images for the COVID-19 class and 397 images for the non-COVID-19 class. The dataset was then split into 3 parts for training, validation, and testing purposes. This caused the dataset used for training to become smaller. Generally, it is common that too little training data results in a poor approximation of deep learning algorithms due to the model complexity. There will be 2 conditions either overfitting or underfitting of training data. Also, too little testing data will cause a high variance estimation on the model's performance. This is demonstrated in this study, where the losses and accuracy graphs for validation showed the large amplitude oscillations compared to the training losses and accuracy. The validation data did not provide sufficient information for validating the models. The testing dataset used was also small for both classes with only 33 and 34 images, respectively. Though image augmentation techniques had been implemented to increase the dataset for both training and validation, a larger unseen dataset is still needed to ensure the trained deep learning models are more robust and generalize better.

Furthermore, in this study, the GradCAM visualization was only done using ResNet152 and ResNeXt models. The results demonstrated that the region of interest for each model was different, and that the abnormality localized by the models was inappropriate. This might be due to the insufficient training data. The models might need a larger dataset to learn more about the features, and thus more confident in classifying the images. Abnormality localization on different models should also be done to get more insights into the areas to which the models pay attention.

Few improvements can be done in the future to obtain more robust and reliable results in this study. Since the CNN architectures are deep and subject to model complexity, a large dataset is required, rather than an augmented dataset, allowing the networks to learn better with different unseen features, reducing the risk of overfitting. Besides, studies showed that extensive data augmentation techniques on a small dataset will affect the model's ability to generalize, as there will be bias towards the model's performance [5]. To overcome these issues, the larger dataset with higher diversity of images can be used in the future to increase the confidence and accuracy of the models. A comparison between trained models using a small dataset and a large dataset can also be analyzed.

In this study, only one transfer learning approach was used in training the dataset. Apart from finetuning the convolutional networks, fixing the convolutional networks as the feature extractors can also be applied to compare the model performance. A total of 10 pretrained models had been initialized for classification training. Different models can be explored and different hyperparameters tunings can be done in the future to improve the accuracy. Moreover, DarkNet, an open-source neural network framework can be used to train the dataset with CNNs, such as DarkNet-19 and DarkNet-53. This is because it is very fast and highly accurate especially for custom-trained model, as it is written in C and CUDA.

12.6 Conclusion

The ongoing pandemic of COVID-19 has greatly challenged the health care services over the world due to its highly transmittable nature. As of this time, there is no cure for this virus; vaccines may only reduce the severity of this disease, and the only way to reduce the rate of spreads is by interrupting the human-to-human transmission. As of now, the most efficient way is by isolating suspicious individuals from healthy ones to stop the transmission chains. To accomplish this, early detection of COVID-19 is needed in the epidemic conditions, where the spread is uncontrollable to ensure early prevention, isolation, and treatment.

RT-PCR tests are the key diagnosis method in detecting COVID-19. However, the tests are subjected to certain limitations. Hence diagnostic modalities in terms of imaging, such as CT, can be used in detecting the COVID-19, especially in the area where diagnosis needs to be done in celerity and monitor the progression of the disease during the treatment process. Comprehensive analysis of the patient's imaging manifestations and clinical manifestations are both necessary, as CT is easy to operate and provides fine-grained details on the region of infections in the lungs.

This study presented an automated method to classify the COVID-19 CT images from the non-COVID-19 images using different CNN through three stages procedures. A comprehensive analysis and benchmark of different transfer learning models' performance had also been done. In first stage, the dataset was split into three parts. The training and validation sets were then applied with data augmentation techniques to increase the dataset, while testing set remained with no augmentation. In stage 2, the binary classification of augmented dataset was implemented on 10 different pretrained models.

The results demonstrated that ResNet152, DenseNet201, GoogleNet, and ResNeXt had achieved the highest accuracy of 98.51%; VGG16 Net and SqueezeNet had an accuracy of 97.01%; ResNet50, ResNet101, VGG19 Net had 95.52% accuracy, and AlexNet's accuracy was 92.54%. The SqueezeNet had the least training parameters, and the training time per epoch was the shortest, with only 15.85 seconds per epoch. Although it had the smallest trainable parameters, it could outperform the other networks, such as AlexNet, which had 50 times more parameters, and ResNet50, ResNet101, and VGG19 Net, which had a lot more training parameters compared to it. Thus it had a low computation cost compared to other networks with the same level of accuracy.

The confusion matrix defines how well the classification models generalize on the testing data. The performance metrics, such as sensitivity, specificity, PPV, NPV, accuracy, and F1-score were computed to quantify the overall and individual class performance. All the classification models demonstrated higher NPV percentages than PPV percentages, except SqueezeNet and ResNeXt. This means that the models performed better in classifying the non-COVID-19 images than the COVID-19 images.

In stage 3, the trained models were then used for abnormality localization. To visualize the trained models, the localization approach, GradCAM was applied to understand why the neurons decided for the final classification results. It revealed the areas to which the models had paid attention.

The high-intensity regions, which were blue and red in color, showed the region of interest to the models. This increased the transparency of the models was useful in tuning the networks for further improvements.

Acknowledgments

We would like to thank Elsevier for giving us the opportunity to publish our book chapter and contribute to the content of book titled Digital Image Enhancement and Reconstruction. We appreciate the efforts of the editorial project manager for this book, Ms. Ivy Dawn Torre for managing our manuscripts.

This work was supported by the 2020 APT EBC-C (extra-budgetary contributions from China) Project on Promoting the Use of ICT for Achievement of Sustainable Development Goals and Universiti Malaya under IF015-2021. We appreciate this research opportunity given by Faculty of Engineering, Universiti Malaya.

References

[1] E.C. Abebe, T.A. Dejenie, M.Y. Shiferaw, T. Malik, The newly emerged COVID-19 disease: a systemic review, Virology Journal 17 (1) (2020) 96, https://doi.org/10.1186/s12985-020-01363-5.

[2] H. Chen, L. Ai, H. Lu, H. Li, Clinical and imaging features of COVID-19, Radiology of Infectious Diseases 7 (2) (2020) 43–50, https://doi.org/10.1016/j.jrid.2020.04.003.

[3] R. Ferrari, M. De Angelis, COVID-19 testing, European Heart Journal 41 (26) (2020) 2427–2428, https://doi.org/10.1093/eurheartj/ehaa483.

[4] N. Gupta, A. Rawal, S. Shiwani, Accuracy, sensitivity and specificity measurement of various classification techniques on healthcare data, IOSR Journal of Computer Engineering 11 (2013) 70–73.

[5] S.H. Kassania, P.H. Kassanib, M.J. Wesolowskic, K.A. Schneidera, R. Detersa, Automatic detection of coronavirus disease (COVID-19) in X-ray and CT images: A machine learning based approach, Biocybernetics and Biomedical Engineering 41 (3) (2021) 867–879, https://doi.org/10.1016/j.bbe.2021.05.013.

[6] Z.-Z. Jiang, C. He, D.-Q. Wang, H.-L. Shen, J.-L. Sun, W.-N. Gan, et al., The role of imaging techniques in management of COVID-19 in China: from diagnosis to monitoring and follow-up, Medical Science Monitor: International Medical Journal of Experimental and Clinical Research 26 (2020) e924582, https://doi.org/10.12659/MSM.924582.

[7] Y.-H. Jin, L. Cai, Z.-S. Cheng, H. Cheng, T. Deng, Y.-P. Fan, et al., A rapid advice guideline for the diagnosis and treatment of 2019 novel coronavirus (2019-nCoV) infected pneumonia (standard version), Military Medical Research 7 (1) (2020) 4, https://doi.org/10.1186/s40779-020-0233-6.

[8] D. Justus, J. Brennan, S. Bonner, A.S. McGough, Predicting the computational cost of deep learning models, in: 2018 IEEE International Conference on Big Data (Big Data), IEEE, December 2018, pp. 3873–3882.

[9] D. Müller, I.S. Rey, F. Kramer, Automated chest CT image segmentation of COVID-19 lung infection based on 3D U-Net, arXiv preprint, arXiv:2007.04774, 2020.

[10] I. Namatevs, Deep convolutional neural networks: structure, feature extraction and training, Information Technology and Management Science 20 (2017), https://doi.org/10.1515/itms-2017-0007.

[11] S. Vineth Ligi, S.S. Kundu, R. Kumar, R. Narayanamoorthi, K.W. Lai, S. Dhanalak-shmi, Radiological analysis of COVID-19 using computational intelligence: A broad gauge study, Journal of Healthcare Engineering 2022 (2022) 5998042, 25 pages.

[12] W.H. Organization, WHO Coronavirus (COVID-19) Dashboard, Retrieved from https://covid19.who.int/, 2021.

[13] H. Panwar, P.K. Gupta, M.K. Siddiqui, R. Morales-Menendez, P. Bhardwaj, V. Singh, A deep learning and grad–CAM based color visualization approach for fast detection of COVID-19 cases using chest X-ray and CT-Scan images, Chaos, Solitons and Fractals 140 (2020) 110190, https://doi.org/10.1016/j.chaos.2020.110190.

[14] R. Rs, A. Das, R. Vedantam, M. Cogswell, D. Parikh, D. Batra, Grad-CAM: Why did you say that? Visual explanations from deep networks via gradient-based localization, 2016.

[15] S. Ruder, An overview of gradient descent optimization algorithms, ArXiv, arXiv: 1609.04747 [abs], 2016.

[16] R.R. Selvaraju, M. Cogswell, A. Das, R. Vedantam, D. Parikh, D. Batra, Grad-CAM: Visual explanations from deep networks via gradient-based localization, in: 2017 IEEE International Conference on Computer Vision (ICCV), 22–29 Oct. 2017.

[17] P. Silva, E. Luz, G. Silva, G. Moreira, R. Silva, D. Lucio, D. Menotti, COVID-19 detection in CT images with deep learning: A voting-based scheme and cross-datasets analysis, Informatics in Medicine Unlocked 20 (2020) 100427, https://doi.org/10.1016/j.imu.2020.100427.

[18] M. Vihinen, How to evaluate performance of prediction methods? Measures and their interpretation in variation effect analysis, BMC Genomics 13 (4) (2012) S2, https://doi.org/10.1186/1471-2164-13-S4-S2.

CHAPTER 13

Brain tumor image segmentation using K-means and fuzzy C-means clustering

Munish Bhardwaj[a], Nafis Uddin Khan[a], Vikas Baghel[a],
Santosh Kumar Vishwakarma[b], and Abul Bashar[c]

[a]Jaypee University of Information Technology, Solan, India
[b]Manipal University, Jaipur, India
[c]Prince Mohammad Bin Fahd University, Al Khobar, Saudi Arabia

Contents

13.1 Introduction

The brain is an extremely important unit of the body, whose functioning influences the entire anatomical structure of the human being. If the human brain stops functioning for a while, then certainly the chances of death rise [1]. Therefore if there is any problem in the brain, then it must be accurately identified well in time. The tumor in brain is an extremely perilous disease, which is an unusual increase of tissues or mass in the brain [1]. It can also be defined as the uncurbed development of the cells, because of the failure of naturalistic cell development model [2]. The factors that cause the tumor in brain are mainly due to genetics or the excessive use of cell phones, power lines, and the effects of ionizing radiations. As per the data [3], older females and also those who have been affected by cancer previously are more susceptible to this disease. Such abnormal growth of tissues affects the proper functioning of the brain and can be the life-threatening [43]. The brain tumor, as per the biological definition is classified into two main

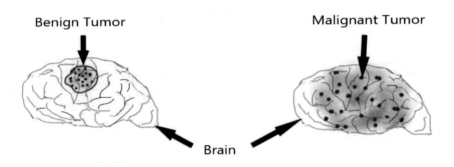

Figure 13.1 Malignant tumors and benign tumors.

types, which are scientifically known as *benign tumors* and *malignant tumors* [1,3,6,50]. The tumors that are noncancerous or do not contain cancer cells are termed as benign tumors. Such tumors can be easily removed and have a rare chance to grow again. These types of tumor cells do not transmit to the other parts of the body nor infect the surrounding tissues. The benign tumors are less harmful, slow-growing, and very rarely life-threatening. On the other hand, the malignant tumors are more harmful, rapid-developing, and quite serious, as they can become life threatening. Malignant tumors can grow very fast, and they attack on nearby healthy brain tissues. The two types of tumors discussed above are shown in Fig. 13.1.

Generally, the disease of brain tumor affects the human body in two stages, i.e., primary stage and secondary stage. The tumor can be eliminated in the primary stage. However, in the secondary stage, even after the elimination of the tumor, it continues to dilate and becomes a serious problem.

In 2016 a survey in the United States showed that approximately a total 23,800 adults, in which 13,450 were men and 10,350 women, were identified with tumors in the brain [4]. The analysis of the appearance of brain tumor or cancer is problematic because of the complex shape of brain and obscured tumor location and size [45–47]. But nowadays, the visual representation of the inner part of the brain is processed with the help of medical imaging techniques for medical research and analysis, which make it easier to identify the affected areas in the brain [10,11,31].

The main objective of the image processing in medical field is to find the meaningful and accurate details of the internal structure of the human body parts through images with utmost clarity. In brain tumor diagnosis, the imaging plays a central role in identifying the exact location and size of the tumor [4]. The various types of image processing methods are X-rays, ultrasound, computed tomography (CT) scan and magnetic resonance imaging (MRI). As compared to all other imaging techniques, MRI provides better visual quality and high-resolution images. MRI uses magnetic field and radio frequency for sensing human brain image without ionized radiations, and therefore MRI is exhaustive and efficient approach for tumor identification and detection of harmful cells [42]. In spite of better quality provided by MRI, still a lot of difficulties are faced by medical experts to detect the defects, because of the poor contrast of MRI images and complex structure of the brain. So, to exactly identify the brain tumor, proper image sensing and reconstruction algorithms are needed to get an enhanced image quality for better perception analysis. In this chapter, a comprehensive survey has been performed on brain tumor identification using image segmentation techniques.

The following contributions have been made in this chapter:

1. A comparative analysis has been done on two very popular methods, namely, K-means clustering (KMC) [14,9] and fuzzy C-means clustering (FCMC) [12] used for brain tumor image segmentation.
2. The fundamental steps involved in brain tumor extraction using image segmentation have been discussed.
3. Various quality assessment parameters and methods have been explored for the evaluation of brain tumor segmentation.
4. The possible future scopes and research issues in this field have also been discussed in detail.

The rest of the chapter is organized as follows: Section 13.2 describes the fundamentals of the brain tumor image segmentation. Comprehensive surveys on the traditional and advanced KMC methods and FCMC methods used for brain tumor image segmentation are presented in Section 13.3 and 13.4, respectively. Various image quality assessment parameters used for validation of these methods are detailed in Section 13.5. Discussions and observations for future research exploration are given in Section 13.6, and, finally, the chapter is concluded in Section 13.7.

13.2 Brain tumor extraction using image segmentation

The extraction of tumor affected area in the brain is based on image segmentation technique, which is the mechanism of partitioning the entire image into various segments, sections, or categories based on the particular application [1]. The region of tumor affected area in the brain (as shown in Fig. 13.1) is to be extracted out by proper selection of the pixels located at around that area. This requires the detection of edge pixels, which discriminate the tumor affected region with the rest of the image [4].

The process of detecting brain tumors through MRI images using image segmentation technique consists of mainly three steps shown in Fig. 13.2. The three functional steps are explained below.

13.2.1 Preprocessing

It is always desirable to perform preprocessing of the image before any specific task. The preprocessing of the image consists of eliminating the features from the image that are not important or which degrade the quality of the image. After the elimination of such undesirable artifacts from image, it may be processed efficiently and effectively. The usual exercise for preprocessing is to switch over to the grayscale image. When the image is converted to grayscale, the use of different filtering methods removes excess unwanted pixels from the image, which represent noise in image [4]. The MRI images are more sensitive to the speckle noise due to defects in image sensing devices. Therefore the image quality must be sufficiently enhanced by minimizing noise when it is used for brain tumor detection. The recovery of true and meaningful edges in MRI image is also very important along with removal of undesirable noisy pixels. For this purpose, median filter-based methods [59,56] are mostly used which help to reduce the noise along with proper edge preservation. It is a nonlinear filtering technique, where the image pixels are replaced by the median value of their corresponding neighbor pixel values. This is generally achieved in preprocessing of the image by using various gradient-based edge detection operators, such as Sobel, Prewitt, and Robert operators [59,56]. More promising and fruitful edge detection is obtained by Canny edge detection operator [59,56], which detects the edge pixels closer to the true edges and maintains proper edge localization.

The image after noise reduction along with edge and detail preservation is then used for brain surface extraction [32–34]. This includes removing background, skull, scalp, eyes, and all other structures that are not important for the analysis of brain tumor information. There are various brain surface extraction algorithms available in the literature, where the filters are utilized for removing irregularities, surface cleaning and masking, detecting edges, and performing morphological operations, such as erosion and dilation to isolate the brain region from the entire MRI image [34–37].

13.2.2 Brain tumor segmentation

After preprocessing and surface extraction, the images are fed to the segmentation process. The segmentation of image is extremely critical and difficult process as it needs to extract the feature of interest from a raw image. The extraction of pixels having common characteristics, edge detection, and boundary selection are challenging issues when segmenting the image. There are various techniques available in the literature for image segmentation, including region growing method [18,22,4] and edge-based segmentation [37,56], where the regions with identical pixels are extracted. For the given images, the seed selection is performed manually, and the neighbors of the seeds should be gathered along the field only if they are tantamount to the seed. This execution is made to continuously repeat till all the seeds cannot be assembled to the region, which makes this process quite lengthy and increases the execution time. The best way to extract out certain similar pixels from a raw image, which denotes a particular feature of interest in an image, is termed as *clustering* [6–9]. As far as the brain tumor extraction process is concerned, clustering techniques are most widely used techniques which are considered as unsupervised machine learning methods for image classification. The clustering based-brain tumor extraction from MRI image through an unsupervised classification of image pixels can be achieved efficiently through K-means clustering (KMC) method [9] and fuzzy C-means clustering (FCMC) method [12], which are discussed in Section 13.3 and Section 13.4 of this chapter, respectively.

13.2.3 Tumor contouring

The most challenging issue involved in brain tumor extraction from MRI images is poor contrast, which might get introduced in the image during image acquisition process. The images with poor contrast have their histogram concentrated over lower side of gray scale, which makes it very difficult to analyze the tumor affected area. Tumor contouring is also considered as a postprocessing operation in brain tumor segmentation as it provides the specific region of tumor in the image for proper medical analysis. Tumor contouring after image segmentation is the process to darken or highlight the tumor area and discriminate it from the background. It is an intensity-based thresholding or image binarization, where the extracted feature is usually displayed as light intensity, whereas the background is kept dark [36–38]. The restored image obtained after contouring has the advantages of smaller memory requirements, reduced execution time, and

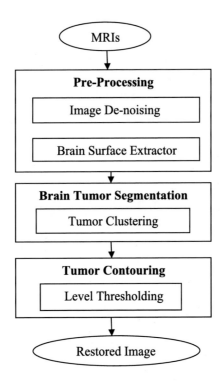

Figure 13.2 Functional block diagram of brain tumor extraction using image segmentation.

flexibility in manipulation as compared to gray-level image, which usually contains a large number of gray levels [28]. The complete functional block diagram of brain tumor extraction using image segmentation explained above is shown in Fig. 13.2.

In the next two sections of the chapter, a detailed review on clustering techniques used for tumor segmentation from brain MRI images are presented.

13.3 Review on K-means clustering

Clustering is an unsupervised learning process, which is applied to unlabeled data [6,7]. A cluster is defined as the collection of objects and data. In the cluster, the objects of similar characteristics are collected, but if the objects are of dissimilar characteristics, then they belong to other clusters. The general description of the clustering process is to organize objects in a group based on the likelihood properties. In K-means clustering (KMC), the image is arranged into K_u numbers of groups [4], where K_u is a positive integer. Basically, the function of this clustering technique in brain tumor segmentation is to extract the pixels of MRI image. These pixels are segmented in a group or a cluster by computing the Euclidean distance between the cluster centroid and pixel points to extract the tumor affected area. The following steps are used in the conventional KMC-based segmentation algorithm [7]:

a. Choose the initial number of cluster value, i.e., K_u where K_u is a positive integer. In KMC, the K_u cluster centers can be randomly selected initially. However, if K_u is large, the probability of error would be less; however, it may increase the risk of overfitting.

b. Center or mean of the cluster is calculated; it is termed as centroid.

c. Euclidean distance function (EDF) is used to compute the distance of each pixel from the centroid. If the distance is adjoining to the centroid, then it will relocate to that cluster. Otherwise, it will relocate to another cluster.

d. The rescheduling or reestimating of the position of centroid after each iteration.

e. The above process (b to d) is repeated several times until the position of centroid gets fixed, and all the pixels are gathered into a particular cluster.

The objective function M for KMC can be calculated by the following equations [9]:

$$M = \sum_{a=1}^{K_u} \sum_{b=1}^{L} \| O_b - C_a \|^2, \tag{13.1}$$

where L is number of events, O_b is case b or observed value, C_a is centroid for cluster, and $\| O_b - C_a \|^2$ is Euclidean distance function. To apply the KMC technique, initially we select the number of clusters and the values of centroid for each cluster randomly, i.e., $(C_a = C_1, C_2, \ldots, C_{K_u})$. For example, suppose we have the list of passengers of different age group of one-dimensional space. The observed values O_b are 14, 15, 17, 19, 21, 22, 23 with number of events L as 7, and number of clusters K_u is 2. In first step, take the initial random centroid for clusters: $C_1 = 14$ and $C_2 = 15$. D_1 is the distance between observed value and first centroid: $|O_b - C_1|$, and D_2 is distance between observed value and second centroid: $|O_b - C_2|$. On solving the Eq. (13.1), with the use of above data, the result is calculated with respect to smallest distance, and then it would be decided that

Table 13.1 The results decide the position of observed values in various clusters.

S. No.	Observed Value (O_b)	Initial Random Centroid (C_1)	Initial Random Centroid (C_2)	Distance (D_1)	Distance (D_2)	Observed value lies in Cluster
1	14	14	15	0	1	1
2	15	14	15	1	0	2
3	17	14	15	3	2	2
4	19	14	15	5	4	2
5	21	14	15	7	6	2
6	22	14	15	8	7	2
7	23	14	15	9	8	2

the data lie under which of the two clusters. The clustering result is shown in Table 13.1.

During the next iteration, the mean of the above observed values for cluster 1 (i.e., 14) and also for cluster 2 (i.e., 15, 17, 19, 21, 22, 23) are taken. The result of mean computation will provide the new centroids, such as for cluster 1 (C_1) is 14 and cluster 2 (C_2) is 19.5. The above process is repeated with new centroids ($C_1 = 14$ and $C_2 = 19.5$) and achieve new Euclidean distances D_1 and D_2. The result of these calculated values or object function will decide that the observed data, i.e., 14, 15 occurred in cluster 1 and the remaining present in cluster 2. In this way, the process is repeated again and again for a finite number of iterations till all the data points would gather into a particular cluster without further alterations. The above process of updating the centroids and corresponding clusters in this example is depicted in Table 13.2.

As per the result, the observed values (i.e., 14, 15, 17) lie under cluster 1 and remaining other go under cluster 2. Also, the centroid of clusters provides the same values for fourth and fifth iteration (i.e., $C_1 = 15.33333$ and $C_2 = 21.25$). So, the KMC technique is intended to partition number of events into K_u clusters. In brain tumor segmentation, the KMC technique has been used widely with lot of improvements, but still there are many critical aspects that need to be explored. KMC algorithms came into existence in 1967 by MacQueen [5], and since then they have been used for image segmentation purposes [8,14]. The more enhanced and self-adaptive KMC methods [9,10,14,16] were later developed for better efficiency. The major problem that the KMC approach suffered, when dealing with big datasets, is the criteria of randomly selecting the number of clusters, i.e.,

Table 13.2 The results decide the position of observed values in various clusters.

S. No.	Observed Value (O_b)	Initial Random Centroid (C_1)	Initial Random Centroid (C_2)	Distance (D_1)	Distance (D_2)	Observed value lies in Cluster
1	14	15.33333	21.25	1.33333	7.25	1
2	15	15.33333	21.25	0.33333	6.25	1
3	17	15.33333	21.25	1.666667	4.25	1
4	19	15.33333	21.25	3.666667	2.25	2
5	21	15.33333	21.25	5.666667	0.25	2
6	22	15.33333	21.25	6.666667	0.75	2
7	23	15.33333	21.25	7.666667	1.75	2

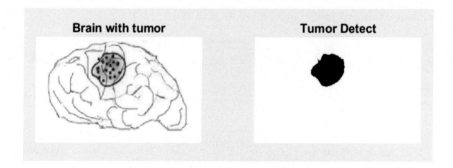

Figure 13.3 Brain tumor MRI image (left); result of KMC (right).

the K_u and the effect of noise. The image segmentation performance of KMC technique [18] has been far better and effective in terms of visual analysis. This can be easily observed in Fig. 13.3, where the tumor area in the image is quite easy to visualize through KMC.

The success of KMC method in brain tumor segmentation is mainly dependent on the selection of initial clusters and the positioning of centroid at the correct position. Keeping these issues in mind along with the issues of computational complexity, a lot of advancement have been made in KMC. The KMC has efficient computation time, but the starting cluster focal position is not very much effective in the conventional method. So, this method was further extended and used in 2-D space to develop the improved KMC algorithm [9,11]. The new formulation of mean vector for the new clusters is as shown in Eq. (13.2):

$$l_i = \sum_{x \in s(t)} \|y - S_o(t+1)\|^2,$$ (13.2)

where $o = 1, 2, 3 \ldots K_u$ and S_o is focal point, $\|y - S_o(t+1)\|$ is the distance measurement. This improved KMC is efficient as compare to conventional KMC in terms of stability and cluster precision. An automatic generation of K_u clusters [49] was developed in the standard approach, but the necessity of the memory space increases with large data points [49]. The method was further extended, which provided better computational time and also worked well for multidimensional vectors [27]. This approach has been utilized in MRI images as it is efficient for tumor detection in complicated MRI images. It minimizes the undesirable distortions by reducing the cost function, as shown in Eq. (13.3), (13.4), and (13.5) [27]:

$$W = \sum_{x=1}^{N} \sum_{p=1}^{K} T_{xp} \|X_n - Q_p\|^2,$$ (13.3)

$$Q_p = \frac{1}{G_p} \sum_{y \in Q_p} y,$$ (13.4)

$$T_{xp} = \begin{cases} 1 & \text{if } K = \arg\min_a \|X_n - Q_p\|^2, \\ 0 & \text{otherwise,} \end{cases}$$ (13.5)

where y and Q_p in Eq. (13.4) and (13.5) are data points and clusters, respectively. T_{xp} is the distance computation of data points with the cluster centers. However, the problem of artifacts appears in the output image, which degrades the quality. The brain tumor segmentation using KMC in most of the literature is evaluated in CIELAB color space or L*a*b color space [21,25,60], which is a three-axes coordinate system expressing the color relationship model among the four colors: red, green, blue, and yellow. The L*a*b color space consists of L*, which denotes lightness or luminance, where as a* and b* indicate chromaticity layers representing the fall of color in red-green axis and yellow-blue axis, respectively [21,60]. The L*a*b color model is the standard system used to quantify the color differences in an image. The color difference is the distance between the two color points and can be calculated as [21,60]:

$$\Delta D^* = \sqrt{(\Delta L^*)^2 + (\Delta a^*)^2 + (\Delta b^*)^2},$$ (13.6)

$$\Delta D^* = \sqrt{(L_1^* - L_2^*)^2 + (a_1^* - a_2^*)^2 + (b_1^* - b^*)^2},$$ (13.7)

where two colors denoted by '1' and '2' have coordinates $(L_1^* a_1^* b_1^*)$ and $(L_2^* a_2^* b_2^*)$ respectively [26]. The L*a*b* model is capable of expressing the colors perceived by human eyes. This model is also efficient for high color transition as compared to RGB model [26], and is quite helpful for retrieving the features of brain tumor segmentation and benefits the clustering process. The problem of detection of brain tumor position [18] in MRI images, along with removal of defective pixels, has been called intemplate-based KMC [27,29]. The identification of potential tumors on computer tomography images for the early-stage oral cavity cancer detection [28,29] was developed, but it requires suitable filtering in the preprocessing step. KMC has also been used in the detection and removal of undesirable speckles in tumor affected area [32,31], because the appearance of speckles on restored image reduces the perceived quality of visualization. Histogram threshold and watershed segmentation algorithms are used in conjunction with KMC for manual brain tumor segmentation [22,38,39], which helps to restore the image features. Semiautomatic and fully automatic segmentation algorithm were also developed, which are mostly based on deep learning methods [37,38,43,44,46–48,56]. In all these applications, there is a widespread use of KMC, which helps in defecting removal along with detail preservation. The efficiency of KMC is also affected due to large number of iterations used for updating the centroid position adjustment. This problem of KMC can be resolved by using the soft membership-based clustering algorithm, as proposed by Arora et al. [12], and it is called fuzzy C-means clustering (FCMC) algorithm, which is explained in the next section. The important key features of KMC methods explained above for brain tumor segmentation are shown in Table 13.3.

13.4 Review on fuzzy C-means clustering

The fuzzy C-means clustering (FCMC) algorithm is an unsupervised clustering algorithm, where the clustering operation takes place in an iterative manner, such as KMC [10,13]. However, FCMC is extremely better than KMC in the sense of computing the likelihood of data points. Unlike KMC where each data point belongs to one cluster, in FCMC, each data point would have membership degree belonging to all the clusters. In FCMC algorithm, the final cluster values depend on the choice of the preparatory membership value and preparatory cluster center [10,11]. So, the membership values are distributed in the normalized fashion. The FCMC algorithms may take less iterations to achieve the genuine cluster if an ap-

Table 13.3 Summary of features of KMC algorithms for brain tumor segmentation

Sr. No.	Method	Advantages	Disadvantages
1	NIC [19] DIV [24]	• The K-means clustering algorithms work efficiently on large datasets. • It offers low computational cost.	• In KMC the units of Ku should be known at prior. • To choose k_u values manually is a tough job.
2	DIV [24]	• It is a less complex method.	• The problem is with handling of categorical attributes.
3	NIC [19] DIV [24] MAD [42]	• KMC is an easy approach. • It restrains one image pixel in a single group.	• Its scalability decreases with the increase in dimensions. • Also, its result varies in the presence of outlier.
4	NIT [36]	• KMC implementation is simple. • KMC is faster than hierarchical clustering for larger number of variables. • For every iteration the clusters may change till the end result is achieved.	• The assumption of k_u is complicated. • The end output may get affected by the order of data.
5	UNN [52] KUL [55]	• The working of the KMC is good with numeric values because of the use of EDF. • In every cluster minimum, at least one item is present.	• If the data set is with noise, then KMC is not good enough. • This algorithm may have chance to enter into infinite rounds.

propriate set of preparatory membership value is chosen. But the main issue is to choose the appropriate set of preparatory membership values erratically. However, FCMC algorithm suffers from the computation time overhead and sensitivity to noise [10]. The FCMC algorithm has been efficiently used in many image applications, such as image segmentation, pattern recognition, and data mining [11,12,46,58]. The basic functioning procedure of the conventional FCMC algorithm is as follows:

a. Let us assume the finite dataset to be R (i.e., $R = r_1, r_2, \ldots, r_n$), whereas the number of clusters to be C (i.e., $C = C_1, C_2, \ldots, C_c$) [15]. The values of clusters are obtained from the user. Let V (i.e., $J = J_1, J_2, \ldots, J_c$) be the cluster centers based on the cluster C.

b. Randomly initialize the membership matrix w_{ik} of size $C * n$. The w_{ik} is the ith membership value of dataset R in the Kth cluster [15]. Then, randomly initialize the membership matrix using following equation:

$$\sum_{k=1}^{c} w_{ik} = 1, \qquad (13.8)$$

where the variables $(i, k) = 1, 2, 3 \ldots n$ are rows and columns, respectively. The n indicates the numbers of patterns in R. The sum in the membership degrees is equal to one for any given data points [11,22].

c. Calculate the cluster centroid using following equation:

$$J_K = \frac{\sum_i^n w_{ik}^q * r_i}{\sum_{i=1}^n w_{ik}^q}, \qquad (13.9)$$

where $k = 1, 2, 3, \ldots, C$, and $q > 1$ is a fuzzification parameter [12]. The Pal and Bezdek [57,58] suggested that q should lie in between 1.5 and 2.5. However, in most of the literature, the value of $q = 2$ has been taken without any special requirement [39].

d. Numerate the Euclidean distance $(dist.)_{ik}$ among dataset and cluster centroid using Eq. (13.10):

$$(dist.)_{ik} = \| r_i - J_k \|, \qquad (13.10)$$

where the r_i is the ith object and J_k is the kth cluster centroid.

e. Update the fuzzy membership and the new membership value would be calculated as [16,20]:

$$w_{ik} = \frac{\left[\frac{1}{(dist.)_{ik}} \right]^{\frac{1}{q-1}}}{\sum_{a=1}^{c} \left[\frac{1}{(dist.)_{ia}} \right]^{\frac{1}{q-1}}}, \qquad (13.11)$$

where $i = 1, 2, 3 \ldots n$; $k = 1, 2, \ldots, C$, and distance measurement $(dist.)_{ia}$ is same as used in Eq. (13.10). In first iteration for update the membership value, select the $k = 1$, and the i alters from 1 to n. In second iteration, the value of $k = 2$, and the i again alters from 1 to n.

f. Return to step b and continue the process till we get the same centroids. The cluster centers will be updated itinerantly with the membership values for datapoints [17]. Finally, each object will be grouped into a cluster following the highest level of membership [15].

Many efficient methods have been developed based on FCMC for brain tumor segmentation. The TKFCMC algorithm [29] can achieve results more efficiently than the conventional FCMC in terms of sensitivity, specificity, and accuracy. The equation of TKFCMC algorithm for segmentation is given below [29]:

$$f = \sum_{k=k+1}^{Q} \sum_{l=l+1}^{S} A(t_i, y_i) X \sum_{k=1}^{i} \sum_{l=1}^{O} P_{kl} \|t_i - O_l\|^2 X \sum_{l=1}^{J} \sum_{k=1}^{O} (g_{kl})^m d^2(t_l, a_k),$$

$$(13.12)$$

where P_{kl} is a binary image matrix, Q and S are the row and column of P_{kl}, i is number of data points, and $A(t_i, y_i)$ is the coarse image. The standard FCMC can be further extended by the SFCM algorithm [11], which increases the speed and minimize the overall calculations of the convention FCMC method. This algorithm is capable in identifying the efficient sets of beginning cluster centers [11]. The method [45] also performs good with respect to conventional FCMC method, but not sufficient for noisy environment. The FCMC and related methods for brain tumor detection are also measured with RGB and L*a*b color space [21,25,61,60] for perceptional analysis. A hybrid framework of KMC and FCMC was presented in [33], where hundreds of MRI images are executed, which shows satisfactory edge localization in tumor segmented areas. In [34], the performance comparison has been performed among various segmentation algorithms, where FCMC-based segmentation provides the best performance in terms of accuracy and selectivity as compared with the other three methods. The FCMC algorithm has also been compared with KMC, which shows that the accuracy and computation time is higher for FCMC than KMC, but MSE is less for FCMC than KMC algorithms [35]. The results show that the FCMC needs more computational time than KMC [36]. So, with the use of small number of clusters the FCMC algorithms can separate different tissue type, but in KMC, tissue types can be separated out with the use of large number of clusters. Also, the malignant tumor detects more accurately with FCMC algorithm as compared with KMC algorithm. The FCMC accurately predicts the tumor cells as compared to KMC in terms of accuracy and sensitivity, with less computational time [32]. To control the noise and reduced distortions, an improved FCMC algorithm is mentioned in the literature [53] for MRI images. It ameliorates the equality metering of the pixel severity and cluster center through vicinity allurement. The object function is given as [53]:

$$T = \sum_{e=1}^{c}\sum_{l=1}^{t} \mu_{el}^{i} d(f_l, a_e), \qquad (13.13)$$

where c is number of cluster centroids, t is the number of datapoints, f_l is the lth pixel, a_e is the centroid of eth cluster, μ_{el} is fuzzy membership. The description of region extraction and edge detection located at the tumor affected area are elaborated with the use of Otsu thresholding methods in FCMC [37]. All the above methods have accuracy more than 87.32% for finding out the tumor area, but the Otsu thresholding-based FCMC algorithm get the merit of fast execution time to compute the results.

A comparative summary and analysis of key FCMC methods as applied to brain tumor segmentation is provided in Table 13.4.

13.5 Performance analysis and assessment

To evaluate the performance of KMC and FCMC in brain tumor extraction, various image quality assessment (IQA) parameters [48,49,44] are available in the literature. The IQA parameters used for assessing and validating the performance of KMC and FCMC in brain tumor extraction are presented in this section.

MacQueen [5] uses *Pratt's figure of merit* (*FOM*) to calculate edge preservation in denoised images. FOM range is between 0 and 1, where 1 represents the best edge detection. FOM score decreases with an increase in the noise level.

$$FOM = \frac{1}{\max\{\hat{n},n\}} \sum_{i=1}^{\hat{N}} \frac{1}{1 + d_i^2 \gamma}, \qquad (13.14)$$

where $\hat{n}$ and n are detected and reference pixel, d_i is Euclidean distance between $\hat{i}^{th}$ edge pixel and its nearest neighbor, and $\gamma = 0.9$. Wang et al. [40] presented *mean structural similarity index measurement* (*MSSIM*) by combining luminance similarity, contrast similarity, and structure similarity between

Table 13.4 Summary of features of FCMC algorithms for brain tumor segmentation.

Sr. No.	Method	Advantages	Disadvantages
1	LAK [18]	• FCMC is reliable and robust diagnosis system.	• It offers high computational complexity
2	LAK [18] MAD [42] SYU [46]	• FCMC effectively handles uncertainty in segmentation. • Also, in FCMC each pixel may belongs to 2 or more clusters.	• For roughness measure, it is difficult to establish the upper and lower nearest value.
3	ANK [20]	• FCMC works good with noise image and intensity inhomogeneity.	• Its efficiency is slower.
4	NIT [36] SUG [54]	• No need of supervision. • FCMC is always converging. • Unsupervised	• It is very much sensitive towards the local minima and initial guess. • It needs more computational time.

reference image x and the distorted image y, as shown in Eq. (13.15):

$$MSSIM = [I_u(x, y)^\alpha . C_o(x, y)^\beta . S_t(x, y)^\gamma], \quad (13.15)$$

where I_u, C_o, and S_t are luminance, contrast, and structure measurement with α, β, and γ as constants [41]. Wang and Bovik [41] presented a simple and very popular *mean square error (MSE)* and *peak signal-to-noise ratio (PSNR)* error sensitivity metric [23], which can be calculated using Eq. (13.16) and (13.17) respectively:

$$MSE = \frac{1}{MN} \sum_{i=1,j=1}^{i=M,j=N} (f_o - f_d)^2, \quad (13.16)$$

$$PSNR = 20\log_{10}\left(\frac{Max_f}{\sqrt{MSE}}\right), \quad (13.17)$$

where f_o and f_d are original and denoised image, respectively. Max_f is the maximum possible pixel intensity (peak signal quality) of f_o. The segmented

MRI images are mostly validated in terms of sensitivity S_e, specificity S_p, and accuracy A_c for brain tumor detection [27]. The mathematical expressions of S_e, S_p, and A_c are given below [27,28]:

$$S_e = \frac{X}{X+Z} \times 100\%, \tag{13.18}$$

$$S_p = \frac{Y}{Y+Z} \times 100\%, \tag{13.19}$$

$$A_c = \frac{X+Y}{X+Y+Z+W} \times 100\%, \tag{13.20}$$

where X, Y, Z, and W are true positive, true negative, false negative, and false positive counts of the pixels taken in a cluster. The entropy-based evaluation is also quite popular in image segmentation assessment [5]. The execution time and computational cost are few meaningful performance measurements used for the evaluation of these methods.

The performance parameters discussed above are tabulated to compare the performance of the two clustering techniques demonstrated in Table 13.5.

The above observation reveals that the FCMC method can be considered preferable for better brain tumor segmentation as compared to the KMC algorithm. FCMC clustering is preferred for overlapped datasets, where it gives comparatively better results. The performance of the two methods indicated that at lesser number of clusters, both of the methods do not perform well, but as the number of cluster increases, both KMC and FCMC provide better and stable results. However, it does not signify that the greater number of the cluster guarantee better performance. The changes and updation in the position of the centroids in the cluster, needs an adaptive thresholding function for better image segmentation.

13.6 Observations and discussions

The goal of this study is to review existing KMC and FCMC algorithms and to address several challenging problems in MRI image segmentation for detection of tumor. KMC & FCMC algorithm-based brain tumor image segmentation is a growing field of research since it is a key factor for successful image enhancement [30,34], denoising, segmentation, classification, and recognition. A lot of work in this area has been done in past to improve the quality of restored images. However, there are still some new directions of research in this field for achieving better image segmentation

Table 13.5 Performance analysis of KMC and FCMC methods.

Sr. No.	Ref. No.	Parameters	KMC	FCMC	Remarks/Comments
1.	[21]	Execution time (sec.)	1.875	55.922	KMC has less execution time
	[25]	Execution time (sec.)	6.75	17.340	
2.	[27]	Sensitivity in percentage (S_e)	80	96	FCMC provide better sensitivity, accuracy, and specificity
		Accuracy in percentage (A_c)	83.3	86.6	
		Specificity in percentage (S_p)	93.12	93.3	
3.	[28]	PSNR	15.6479	14.1293	FCMC provides better PSNR
		Computational time	1.1232	5.4912	KMC has good computational time
		Accuracy in percentage (A_c)	12.8662	34.0088	FCMC has efficient segmentation accuracy
		PSNR (Ant Colony Optimization (ACO))	25.2458	24.5599	With the use of ACO, FCMC still provides better PSNR.
		Computational time	83.6945	83.3450	With the use of ACO, the CT is increased for both.
4.	[23]	PSNR	24.99	32.9	KMC is better
		MSE	13.65	0.07	FCMC is better
		Entropy	2.27	4.05	KMC is better
		Execution Time	13	129	KMC is better
		NCC	0.97	0.99	FCMC is better
		SSIM	0.93	0.97	FCMC is better

and region localization. Some properties of clustering techniques are not yet fully explored, and thus have sufficient scope to develop more effective brain tumor extraction with sufficient accuracy and scalability along with less computational time.

The important research issues in KMC are the selection of the number of initial clusters, position of centroid, and the computation of distance of all the datapoints from the cluster centroids. In most of the related literature [8,48,49,51–56,62–65] at the initial stage, the number of clusters and the position of corresponding centroids are chosen randomly. At the subsequent stages, number of clusters and the position of corresponding centroids are updated based on the increased number of iterations. However, in the case of low-contrast MRI images with edge abundant areas, this conventional scheme of clustering failed to protect maximum edges. In addition to this, the computation of distance between datapoints and centroid, which is mostly based on Euclidean distance, needs exploration for more robust tumor detection. Therefore, in this regard, a proper image content analysis is required for formulating the edge threshold function and the Euclidean distance function in clustering methods.

The parameter adjustments in many of the image segmentation methods [9,10,13–15,21,22,34,36,38] required lot of experimentations, and it also increases the computational costs. This reveals the need for the user to concern about the parameter settings for all the images in the entire experiment. However, it will be a good idea to explore the possibility of developing some optimization technique to optimize these parameters, which would also help in reducing the overall computational complexity. Another important issue where the computational complexity plays an important role is researching the better adaptive mechanism for neighborhood pixel operation in preprocessing of MRI images, which can perhaps provide efficient enhancement and denoising with reduced time and space requirements.

There are many emerging approximation and optimization tools available in the literature, where most of them are based on soft computing techniques, such as fuzzy logic and artificial neural network (ANN), Singular value decomposition (SVD), principal component analysis (PCA), swarm optimization (SA), and genetic algorithm (GA). These all are very useful in various fields of mathematical science and engineering, where parameter settings are required. However, there are very few techniques available in the literature [35,36,55,49], where these soft computing tools have been utilized in modifying the clustering technique. This motivates exploring the properties of the soft computing-based techniques to develop more approximated and optimized KMC and FCMC approaches, specifically for MRI image applications.

13.7 Conclusions

A comprehensive survey on brain tumor segmentation from MRI images by K-means and fuzzy C-means clustering methods is presented in this chapter. The basic background of K-means and fuzzy C-means clustering and their application in brain tumor image segmentation is discussed. The advancements of K-means and fuzzy C-means clustering in brain tumor extraction from MRI images have been explained. The possible future scopes and research issues in this field have been discussed in detail.

Clustering techniques are indeed the best option for MRI images in brain tumor segmentation. However, a strong and exhaustive exploration for defining clustering centroids and distance function for computing the likelihood of the pixels is required for edge abundant images. The main task is to ameliorate the quality of an image in a short time, without altering the original nature of MRI image. Moreover, a lot of improvement is needed for better accuracy and less computational time. The quality of restored segmented brain MRI images for medical applications can be improved by examining the image feature analysis to formulate the properties of clustering techniques. Furthermore, more advanced image quality metrics can be explored, depending upon the type and availability of image under processing.

References

[1] Mustofa AliSahid Almahfud, Robert Setyawan, Christy Atika Sari, De Rosal Ignatius Moses Setiadi, Eko Hari Rachmawanto, An effective MRI brain image segmentation using joint clustering (K-Means and Fuzzy C-Means), in: IEEE International Seminar on Research of Information Technology and Intelligent Systems (ISRITI), November 21–22, 2018, pp. 11–16.
[2] Priya Patil, Seema Pawar, Sunayna Patil, Arjun Nichal, A review paper on brain tumor segmentation and detection, International Journal of Innovative Research in Electrical, Electronics, Instrumentation and Control Engineering 5 (1) (2017) 12–15.
[3] https://www.thebraintumourcharity.org/brain-tumour-diagnosis-treatment/how-brain-tumours-are-diagnosed/brain-tumour-biology/what-causes-brain-tumours/.
[4] P.T. Gamage, Identification of Brain Tumor using Image Processing Techniques, Independent Study, Faculty of Information Technology, University of Moratuwa, 2017.
[5] J.B. MacQueen, Some methods for classification and analysis of multivariate observations, in: Berkeley Symposium on Mathematical Statistics and Probability, 1967, pp. 281–297.

[6] Nitesh Kumar Singh, Geeta Singh, Automatic detection of brain tumor using K-means clustering, International Journal for Research in Applied Science & Engineering Technology 5 (X1) (November 2017) 114–121.

[7] Rituja Mandhare, Jaya Nawale, Prabhanjan Kulkarni, Affan Ansari, Smita Kakade, Brain tumor segmentation using K-means clustering and fuzzy C-means algorithms and its area calculation and disease prediction using naive-Bayes algorithm, International Journal of Innovative Research in Science, Engineering and Technology 7 (6) (2018) 6518–6526.

[8] Vidya Dhanve, Meeta Kumar, Detection of brain tumor using k-means segmentation based on object labeling algorithm, in: IEEE International Conference on Power, Control, Signals and Instrumentation Engineering, 2017, pp. 944–951.

[9] Youguo Li, Haiyan Wu, A clustering method based on K-means algorithm, in: International Conference on Solid State Devices and Materials Science, in: Elsevier Procedia, vol. 25, 2012, pp. 1104–1109.

[10] Nor Ashidi Mat Isa, Samy A. Salamah, Umi Kalthum Ngah, Adaptive fuzzy moving K-means clustering algorithm for image segmentation, IEEE Transactions on Consumer Electronics 55 (4) (2009) 2145–2153.

[11] Ming-Chuan Hung, Don-Lin Yang, An efficient fuzzy C-means clustering algorithm, in: Proceedings of IEEE International Conference on Data Mining, San Jose, CA, 2001, pp. 225–232.

[12] Jyoti Arora, Kiran Khatter, Meena Tushir, Fuzzy C-means clustering strategies: a review of distance measures, Advances in Intelligent Systems and Computing 731 (2019) 153–162.

[13] Sandhya Prabhakar H, Sandeep Kumar, A survey on fuzzy C-means clustering techniques, International Journal of Engineering Development and Research 5 (4) (2017) 1151–1155.

[14] Fasahat Ullah Siddiqui, Nor Ashidi Mat Isa, Enhanced moving K-means (EMKM) algorithm for image segmentation, IEEE Transactions on Consumer Electronics 57 (2) (2011) 833–841.

[15] Min Ren, Peiyu Liu, Zhihao Wang, Jing Yi, A self-adaptive fuzzy c-means algorithm for determining the optimal number of clusters, Computational Intelligence and Neuroscience 3 (2016) 1–12, Hindawi Publishing Corporation.

[16] D. Maruthi Kumar, D. Satyanarayana, M.N. Giri Prasad, MRI brain tumor detection using optimal possibilistic fuzzy C-means clustering algorithm and adaptive k-nearest neighbor classifier, Journal of Ambient Intelligence and Humanized Computing 12 (4) (2020) 1–14.

[17] Soumi Ghosh, Sanjay Kumar Dubey, Comparative analysis of K-means and fuzzy C-means algorithms, International Journal of Advanced Computer Science and Applications 4 (4) (2013) 35–39.

[18] M. Angulakshmi, G.G. Lakshmi Priya, Automated brain tumour segmentation techniques – A review, Imaging Systems and Technology 27 (2017) 66–77, Wiley Periodicals.

[19] Nicer Navid K.R., K.C. James, A review of different segmentation techniques used in brain tumor detection, International Journal of Scientific & Engineering Research 7 (2) (February 2016) 106–113.

[20] Ankita Singh, Prerna Mahajan, Comparison of K-means and fuzzy C-means algorithms, International Journal of Engineering Research & Technology 2 (5) (2013) 1296–1303.

[21] K.M. Nimeesha, Rajaram M. Gowda, Brain tumour segmentation using K-means and fuzzy C-means clustering algorithm, International Journal of Computer Science & Information Technology Research Excellence 3 (2) (2013) 60–64.

[22] Heena Hooda, Om Prakash Verma, Tripti Singhal, Brain tumor segmentation: A performance analysis using K-means, fuzzy C-means and region growing algorithm, in:

Proceedings of IEEE International Conference on Advanced Communication Control and Computing Technologies, 2014, pp. 1621–1626.

[23] K. Rajesh Babu, Anishka Singal, Kandukuri Sahiti, Ch.V.S. Sai Jawahar, Syed Shameem, Performance analysis of brain tumor detection using optimization based FCM technique on MRI images, International Journal of Scientific & Technology Research 8 (11) (2019) 1717–1723.

[24] Divya Tomar, Sonali Agarwal, A survey on data mining approaches for healthcare, International Journal of Bio-Science and Bio-Technology 5 (5) (2013) 241–266.

[25] J. Vijay, J. Subhashini, An efficient brain tumor detection methodology using K-means clustering algorithm, in: Proceedings of IEEE International Conference on Communication and Signal Processing, 2013, pp. 653–657.

[26] Xin Zheng, Qinyi Lei, Run Yao, Yifei Gong, Qian Yin, Image segmentation based on adaptive K-means algorithm, EURASIP Journal on Image and Video Processing 68 (2018) 2–10.

[27] Rasel Ahmmed, Md. Foisal Hossain, Tumor detection in brain MRI image using template based K-means and fuzzy C-means clustering algorithm, in: IEEE International Conference on Computer Communication and Informatics, 2016, pp. 1–6.

[28] Sayali D. Gahukar, S.S. Salankar, Segmentation of MRI brain image using fuzzy C means for brain tumor diagnosis, Journal of Engineering Research and Applications 4 (4) (April 2014) 107–111.

[29] Md Shahariar Alam, Md Mahbubur Rahman, Mohammad Amazad Hossain, Md Khairul Islam, Kazi Mowdud Ahmed, Khandaker Takdir Ahmed, Bikash Chandra Singh, Md Sipon Miah, Automatic human brain tumor detection in MRI image using template-based K means and improved fuzzy C means clustering algorithm, Big Data and Cognitive Computing 3 (2) (2019) 27, pp. 1–18.

[30] S. Shanmuga Priyal, A. Valarmathi, Efficient fuzzy c-means based multilevel image segmentation for brain tumor detection in MR images, Design Automation for Embedded Systems 22 (14) (2018) 1–13.

[31] Sandeep Panda, Sanat Sahu, Pradeep Jena, Subhagata Chattopadhyay, Comparing fuzzy-C means and K-means clustering techniques: A comprehensive study, Advances in Computer Science, Engineering and Applications 166 (2012) 451–460.

[32] Eman Abdel-Maksoud, Mohammed Elmogy, Rashid Al-Awadi, Brain tumor segmentation based on a hybrid clustering technique, Egyptian Informatics Journal 16 (2015) 71–81.

[33] Karuna Yepuganti, Saritha Saladi, C.V. Narasimhulu, Segmentation of tumor using PCA based modified fuzzy C means algorithms on MR brain images, International Journal of Imaging Systems and Technology 30 (4) (2020) 1–9, Wiley.

[34] C. Latha, K. Perumal, Improved probability based fuzzy C-means and active contour using brain tumor images, in: IEEE International Conference on Power, Control, Signals and Instrumentation Engineering, 2017, pp. 880–887.

[35] K.S. Thara, K. Jasmine, Brain tumour detection in MRI images using PNN and GRNN, in: IEEE International Conference on Wireless Communications, Signal Processing and Networking (WiSPNET), Chennai, India, March 2016, pp. 1504–1510.

[36] Nitu Kumari, Sanjay Saxena, Review of brain tumor segmentation and classification, in: Proceeding of IEEE International Conference on Current Trends Toward Converging Technologies, 2018, pp. 1–6.

[37] Arashdeep Kaur, An automatic brain tumor extraction system using different segmentation methods, in: IEEE International Conference on Computational Intelligence & Communication Technology, 2016, pp. 187–191.

[38] Juntao Wang, Xiaolong Su, An improved K-Means clustering algorithm, in: IEEE International Conference on Communication Software and Networks, 2011, pp. 44–46.

[39] Leonardo Rundo, Lucian Beer, Stephan Ursprung, Paula Martin-Gonzalez, Florian Markowetz, James D. Brenton, Mireia Crispin-Ortuzar, Evis Sala, Ramona Woitek, Tissue-specific and interpretable sub-segmentation of whole tumour burden on CT images by unsupervised fuzzy clustering, Computers in Biology and Medicine 5 (April 2020) 1–13.

[40] Z. Wang, A.C. Bovik, A universal image quality index, IEEE Signal Processing Letters XX (2002) 1–4.

[41] Zhou Wang, Alan C. Bovik, Hamid R. Sheikh, Eero P. Simoncelli, Image quality assessment: from error visibility to structural similarity, IEEE Transactions on Image Processing 13 (4) (2004) 1–14.

[42] Madallah Alruwaili, Muhammad Hameed Siddiqi, Muhammad Arshad Javed, A robust clustering algorithm using spatial fuzzy C-means for brain MR images, Egyptian Informatics Journal 21 (1) (March 2020) 51–66, Elsevier.

[43] C. Jaspin Jeba Sheela, G. Suganthi, Automatic brain tumor segmentation from MRI using greedy snake model and fuzzy C-means optimization, Journal of King Saud University: Computer and Information Sciences (2019) 1–10.

[44] S.P. Lloyd, Least squares quantization in PCM, Technical Report RR-5497, Bell Lab, September 1957.

[45] V. Asanambigai, J. Sasikala, Adaptive chemical reaction based spatial fuzzy clustering for level set segmentation of medical images, Ain Shams Engineering Journal 9 (4) (2018) 1251–1262.

[46] Syu Jyun Penga, Cheng-Chia Lee, Hsiu-Mei Wud, Chung-Jung Lind, Cheng-Ying Shiau, Wan-You Guod, David Hung-Chi Pan, Kang-Du Liu, Wen-Yuh Chung, Huai-Che Yang, Fully automated tissue segmentation of the prescription isodose region delineated through the Gamma knife plan for cerebral arteriovenous malformation (AVM) using fuzzy C-means (FCM) clustering, Neuro Image: Clinical 21 (2018) 1–8.

[47] Heba Mohsen, El-Sayed A. El-Dahshan, El-Sayed M. El-Horbaty, Abdel-Badeeh M. Salem, Classification using deep learning neural networks for brain tumors, Future Computing and Informatics Journal 3 (2018) 68–71.

[48] Md Khairul Islam, Md Shahin Ali, Md Sipon Miah, Md Mahbubur Rahman, Md Shahariar Alam, Mohammad Amzad Hossain, Brain tumor detection in MR image using super pixels, principal component analysis and template-based K-means clustering algorithm, Machine Learning with Applications 5 (2021) 1–8, Elsevier.

[49] Sudhir Singh, Nasib Singh Gill, Analysis and study of K-means clustering algorithm, International Journal of Engineering Research & Technology 2 (7) (July 2013) 2546–2551.

[50] Mohiuddin Ahmed, Raihan Seraj, Syed Mohammed Shamsul Islam, The k-means algorithm: A comprehensive survey and performance evaluation, Electronics 9 (8) (2020) 1–12.

[51] Abhishek kumar K, Sadhana, Survey on K-Means clustering algorithms, International Journal of Modern Trends in Engineering and Research 04 (4) (2017) 218–221.

[52] Unnati R. Raval, Chaita Jani, Implementing & improvisation of K-means clustering algorithm, International Journal of Computer Science and Mobile Computing 5 (5) (2016) 191–203.

[53] Yogita K. Dubey, Milind M. Mushrif, FCM clustering algorithms for segmentation of brain MR images, Advances in Fuzzy Systems 2016 (2016) 1–14, Hindawi Publishing Corporation.

[54] R. Suganya, R. Shanthi, Fuzzy C-means algorithm – A review, International Journal of Scientific and Research Publications 2 (11) (November 2012) 1–3.

[55] Kuljit Kaur, A review paper on clustering in data mining, An International Journal of Engineering Sciences 3 (2014) 144–151.

[56] R.C. Gonzalez, R.E. Woods, Digital Image Processing, third edition, Prentice Hall, 2008.

[57] Xiangzhi Bai, Yuxuan Zhang, Haonam Liu, Zhiguo Chen, Similarity measure based possibilistic FCM with label information for Brain MRI segmentation, IEEE Transactions on Cybernetics 49 (7) (2019) 2618–2630.

[58] N.R. Pal, J.C. Bazdek, On cluster validity for the fuzzy c-means model, IEEE Transactions on Fuzzy Systems 3 (3) (1995) 370–379.

[59] A. Stella, B. Trivedi, Implementation of order statistic filters on digital image and OCT image: A comparative study, International Journal of Modern Engineering Research 2 (5) (2012) 3143–3145.

[60] A. Chitade, S.K. Katiyar, Color based image segmentation using K-means clustering, International Journal of Engineering Science & Technology 2 (10) (2010) 5319–5325.

[61] Sadia Basar, Mushtaq Ali, G.O. Ruiz, M. Zareei, Abdul Waheed, Awais Adnan, Unsupervised color image segmentation: A case of RGB histogram based K-means clustering initialization, PLoS ONE (October 2020) 1–21.

[62] C. Han, L. Rundo, R. Araki, Y. Nagano, Y. Furukawa, G. Mauri, H. Nakayama, H. Hayashi, Combining noise-to-image and image-to-image GANs: brain MR image augmentation for tumor detection, IEEE Access 7 (2019) 156966–156977.

[63] Q. Ye, Q. Zhang, Y. Tian, T. Zhou, H. Ge, J. Wu, N. Lu, X. Bai, T. Liang, J. Li, Method of tumor pathological micronecrosis quantification via deep learning from label fuzzy proportions, IEEE Journal of Biomedical and Health Informatics 25 (9) (Sept. 2021) 3288–3299.

[64] P.A. Govyadinov, T. Womack, J.L. Eriksen, G. Chen, D. Mayerich, Robust tracing and visualization of heterogeneous microvascular networks, IEEE Transactions on Visualization and Computer Graphics 25 (4) (1 April 2019) 1760–1773.

[65] T. Imtiaz, S. Rifat, S.A. Fattah, K.A. Wahid, Automated brain tumor segmentation based on multi-planar super pixel level features extracted from 3D MR images, IEEE Access 8 (2020) 25335–25349.

CHAPTER 14

Multimodality medical image fusion in shearlet domain

Manoj Diwakar[a], Prabhishek Singh[b], and Pardeep Kumar[c]

[a]Department of CSE, Graphic Era Deemed to be University Dehradun, Uttarakhand, India
[b]Amity School of Engineering and Technology, Amity University Uttar Pradesh, Noida, India
[c]CSE and IT Jaypee University of Information Technology, Solan, India

14.1 Introduction

In the present innovation scenario, image processing has a vast range to generate the best image and available features. Best quality image is crucial to gain good visual information [1]. Moreover, the fundamental image processing strategy using sampling and quantization are helpful to convert analog images into digital images. Digital images consist of information and data in two-dimensional (2D) signals in wave signs [2,3]. Additionally, the dividing into two types of images in the image processing may be analog image and digital image. The digital images are more demanding as compared to the analog signal. The digital image is in the matrix form that shows some values, and the analog image is a signal. The importance of zero and one image will be black & white, i.e., depending upon the zero and one; the present two variances from that the images are also known as binary images. Moreover, gray images are similar [4,5], ranging from 0 to 255 particular value ranges. The range from 0 to 255×3 patterns for the color image is in RGB (red, green, and blue). Medical images and remote sensing are suitable images examples. A wide variety of medical images is used to distinguish applications, such as CT, PET, and MRI images. The pixel is considered the crucial part of any the images, and it is the bit picture element with some coordinates values and intensity color values. It is essential for using the few processing operations block-wise. The pixel to pixel-wise on the particular image is the primary operation through which we can sort out the overlapping of some pixels [6–8].

According to extracting better image quality and some vital information from image processing operation, the output may be an image and signal dispensation or characteristics associated with it [9,10]. The two-dimensional (2D) images may be determined as the set for $f(x, y)$, where x

Digital Image Enhancement and Reconstruction
https://doi.org/10.1016/B978-0-32-398370-9.00021-4
317

and y are spatial coordinates and the amplitude of image signal at any pair of coordinates. The digital signal processing operations are performed on the digital images. The several operations performed are enhancement of the image, restoration of the image, compression of the image, segmentation of the image. This operation completes and focuses upon the image enhancement to enhance the quality of the image in the image processing. The following is the procedure of the image enhancement: 1. Image input, 2. Pre-processing of the image, 3. Spatial and transform domain technique, 4. Image output.

Image fusion is the method of merging the complementary information about the two or more images into a single output image. Image fusion is widely used in several applications related to remote sensing, medical imaging, military, and astronomy [11–14]. Image fusion is the technique for combining images to enhance the content information in the images. Image fusion methods are crucial for improving the performance in object recognition systems by combining images taken from different satellite images, airborne, and depending on the ground-based systems with the distinguished datasets [15–18]. Moreover, it is also essential in enhancement images. It shows better geometrical orientations and improves more features that are not visible in either of the images, removing the deformalities in the data and complementing the datasets for sound decision-making. It merges the critical information from two or more input images into a single output image that defines the visually better and maintains the crucial information from the given datasets of the input image [19,20]. The image fusion technique can be divided into frequency transform and spatial domain methods.

The frequency-domain techniques involve the various resolutions of the images. It disintegrates source images into multiscale coefficients. Therefore the several fusion approaches are used to get the fused image in spatial/transform domain. The significance of the frequency domain technique is that it reduces the effects of blocking in the images.

14.1.1 Frequency domain technique

The frequency-domain techniques that use the multiresolution methods are the pyramid transform and the wavelet transform. The distinguish approach for pyramids are Laplacian pyramid (LP), contrast pyramid (CP), and the gradient pyramid (GP), etc. [21]. The main problem in these techniques is lead to blocking effects in the outcome of the fusion [22–25]. The multiresolution fusion techniques in the wavelet depend on the methods used to deploy the distinct types of wavelet transforms in the fusion process.

14.1.2 Spatial domain techniques

In the spatial domain, methods are directly applied to the input images. A weighted average is one of the most accessible spatial domain techniques, which does not require any decomposition and transformation on the original input image. This technique is easy to implement for real-time processing. This domain increases the computation degree of focus in every pixel and block applying for the various focus measurements [26].

The significant contributions of this research work are the following:
- A unique approach, which includes bilateral filter processing and local energy-based fusion, is applied to acquire crisp and smooth features in low-frequency components.
- An SML algorithm (called sum modified Laplacian) combines the high-frequency coefficients to provide image fusion for high-frequency components.

The rest of the paper is as follows: Section 14.2 briefly explains different techniques of multimodality image fusion. Section 14.3 explains the proposed methodology. Section 14.4 shows the experimental result and discussion. Section 14.5 concludes the chapter.

14.2 Multimodality medical image fusion

Multimodality image fusion means the composition of the image taken from different medical sources and equipment acquired more detailed and reliable information about the image. In recent trends, the multimodality is the process adopted by the radiography synthesis in the medical diagnosis for the treatment and this methods cure, which is adopted for diagnosing or excluding the disease [27–30].

In the recent area of research, medical imaging that represents or imitates the object plays a crucial role in medical treatment. This leads to the quality of the image being of a big concern. Although, the complete structure of the spectrum in digital image processing is useful in medical diagnosis, for good treatment, radiologists have to combine organs or diseases. Moreover, because of designing constraints, instruments cannot give such information. For more superior image quality, distinguish conditions in image processing demand both high spatial and spectral information in a single image. In image processing, image fusion can deal with the quality of image issue gathered from all the distinguish images, and grouping of the image is called the fusion of the image of higher quality and better intensity. In the medical field, the significances of medical images are distinguished from other images. Image heterogeneity signifies body organs or living tissues present in the medical images [31]. The objects obtained with identical modality and size may vary from one patient to another. It is defined through standardized acquisition protocol, shape, internal structure, and sometimes various views of the identical patient with identical times. The objective of the multimodality medical image fusions process is to improve the quality of images by decreasing the error and redundancy to enhance [32]. Clinical detection in the medical image is used for the treatment and problem assessment.

Recently, image fusion methods are utilized in various applications and fields such as medical innovation, remote sensing fields, and military fields [33–36]. Achieving the crucial data in the image fusion is a more challenging and typical task, because the cost of instruments is high, and a vast amount of blur data is present. The main aspects of image fusion are to produce a fused image which have large information in compare to source images. The objective of image fusion is implemented in various applications in medical field. In medical field, Coronary Artery Disease (CAD) is a type of disease that will happen through a lack of blood supply to the heart, and image transparency is required. Hence to solve such problems, medical images such as CT image and MRI image can be fused to get more informative image for better treatment [37–39].

On the other hand, in the field of remote sensing particular portion of the earth should be visible from satellite channels. The missing information is saved with the help of multifocus image fusion. In remote sensing and military fields, many improvements and developments are made. Through the multiple sensors to improve the imaging systems, performance in each and every field is permitted. The data is easy to collect as a result of the higher number of sensors. When the data is merged, the merging of data is more suitable and useful, because the grouping can increase variability or apply complementary and essential information from several other resources. The computation of research work is without causing any damage to information or data, saving both money and time.

Multimodality medical image fusion is crucial for obtaining information from distinguished medical image modalities. For the best fusion outcome, the proposed methodology is introduced. The doctor is analyzes more details for the clinical diagnosis by images acquired through the combination of magnetic resonance imaging and computed tomography. In ten years, several fusion techniques vary according to vigor, complexity, and intelligence.

14.2.1 Principal component analysis

Despite the similarity with the intensity hue saturation transform, the principal component analysis technique can be used for the variable number of bands. The formation of low-resolution multispectral images can be obtained through the uncorrelation principal component analysis. The information about the panchromatic images gives more variance and information. Meanwhile, the inverse principal component analysis transform can get the high-resolution multispectral image.

14.2.2 Pyramid technique

In the human visual system, the image fusion using the selective pattern approach can be performed to get the more informative images in spatial/transform domain. To get the resultant image through the inverse transform pyramid, combine all images to form the composite image. The fused pyramid decomposition is applied at every level to obtain the fusion image.

14.2.3 Discrete wavelet transform (DWT)

The discrete wavelet transform depends on the coding of the subband. The less important information in the signal appears in very low amplitudes, and the more important aspects in the signal are conveyed in high amplitudes. The technique is simple. The discrete wavelet transform is divided into four subbands (LL, LH, HL, and HH). The original size of the image, the bands, becomes half of the size. The LH, HL, and HH subbands can be considered a detailed component of the image, whereas the LL subbands can be considered the approximation part. It is implemented and designed quickly, can reduce the computation time and resources required, and provides fast computation advantages of the discrete wavelet transform.

14.2.4 Artificial neural networks (ANN)

The nonlinear response function is used in the artificial neural network. The pulse-coupled neural network (PCNN) is used in the feedback network. The network is divided into three types: pulse generator, modulation field, and respective field. The input image of each pixel corresponds to every neuron. The external input to the pulse-coupled neural network (PCNN) is used to match the pixel's intensity. This technique is helpful in bridging minor intensity variations in the patterns of the input, independence of geometric variations, and hardness against noise. It gives real-time system performance, and the method is user-friendly; the pulse-coupled neural network has importance in biological and medical imaging.

14.3 Proposed methodology

This proposed methodology uses NSST transform, bilateral filter, and SML to perform multimodality medical image fusion. Algorithm 14.1 has shown the complete proposed methodology step by step.

14.4 Results and discussion

The experimental evaluation was done using the MATLAB® 2018a software. The resolution of all the images used for experimental results was 512 × 512. There are numerous multimodality effects seen in Figs. 14.1–14.4. For fair analysis, a comparative study is performed using similar and recent methods, and the methods for comparison are [13], [36], [15], [17], [25], [28], and [35].

In Figs. 14.1–14.4, the first two are the input medical images. From Fig. 14.1, it is apparent that the results of [13] and [17] are satisfactory; however, edges over the high-textured area are not up to the mark. Similarly, results of [36] and [15] also give satisfying results, but near high contrast, the strength of edges is not so strong. In [25], [28], and [35], the results are good. However, the proposed methodology results are excellent compared to existing methods.

Based on Fig. 14.2, it can be concluded that the outcomes of [13] and [17] are good; nevertheless, the edges over the high-textured area are not up to par. Similarly, [36] and [15] provide satisfactory results, although the strength of edges near high contrast is not as strong as it is at lower contrast. The findings in [25], [28], and [35] are satisfactory. The outcomes of the suggested approach, on the other hand, are outstanding when compared to existing methods.

Fig. 14.3 shows that the results of [13] and [17] are satisfactory; nevertheless, the margins over the high textured region are inadequate. Similarly, the findings of [36] and [15] are good, albeit the strength of edges near

---

Algorithm 14.1 A proposed multimodal scheme using NSST domain.

Input: Input images, i.e., CT and MRI images. The CT and MRI images are depicted as A and B in the proposed methodology.

Output: Fused image

Step 1: For $i = 1$ to 3, $i =$ decomposition level, do: apply NSST on A and B separately.

Step 2: Decomposition of A into two subbands, low-pass subbands (LP1, LP2, LP3) and high-pass subbands (HP1, HP2, HP3).

Step 3: The low-pass subbands (LP1, LP2, LP3) are processed using bilateral filter processing and local energy-based fusion.

$$LPSB^{filtered}(x) = \frac{1}{W_p} \sum_{a_i \in \Omega} I_0(a_i) f_r \left(\| I_0(a_i) - I_0(a) \| \right) g_s \left(\| a_i - a \| \right). \qquad (14.1)$$

Step 4: The high-pass subbands (HP1, HP2, HP3) are processed using sum modified Laplacian (SML), as given below:

$$SML(i,j) = \sum_{h=-N}^{N} \sum_{g=-N}^{N} \left[SL(i+h, j+g) \right]^2, \qquad (14.2)$$

$$SL(i,j) = \left| 2HP(i,j) - HP(i-1,i) - HP(i+1,j) \right| \\ + \left| 2HP(i,j) - HP(i,j-1) - HP(i,j+1) \right|.$$

The fusion approach for the high-frequency subbands is

$$HP_c^{g,h}(i,j) = \left\{ \begin{array}{ll} HP_A^{g,h}(i,j) & \text{if } SML_A^{g,h}(i,j) > SML_B^{g,h}(i,j) \\ HP_B^{g,h}(i,j) & \text{if } SML_A^{g,h}(i,j) \le SML_B^{g,h}(i,j) \end{array} \right\}, \qquad (14.3)$$

where $HP^{g,h}(i,j)$ represent coefficient at pixel (i,j) of the g-th scale and h-th direction subband.

Step 5: Apply inverse NSST to get the final fused image.

The proposed technique decomposes input images using the nonsubsampled shearlet transform (NSST) to extract low- and high-frequency components from the low- and high-frequency components of the images. A novel approach that includes bilateral filter processing and local energy-based fusion is used to acquire crisp and smooth features in low-frequency components. An SML algorithm (sum modified Laplacian) combines the high-frequency coefficients to provide image fusion for high-frequency components.

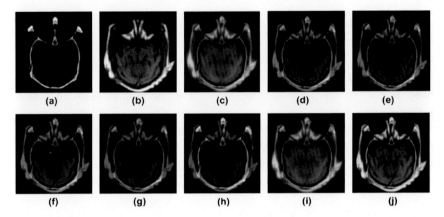

Figure 14.1 Result analysis: (a) and (b) are source medical images, (c) [13], (d) [36], (e) [15], (f) [17], (g) [25], (h) [28], (i) [35], and (j) proposed approach.

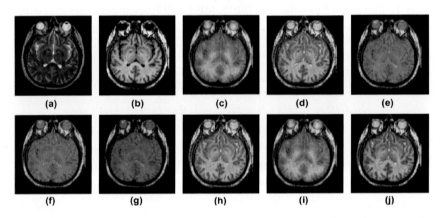

Figure 14.2 Result analysis: (a) and (b) are source medical images, (c) [13], (d) [36], (e) [15], (f) [17], (g) [25], (h) [28], (i) [35], and (j) proposed approach.

high contrast is not as strong as near low contrast. The findings in [25], [28], and [35] are acceptable. Compared to existing approaches, the proposed methodology results are exceptional.

However, the outcomes of [13] and [17] are excellent, as shown in Fig. 14.4. However, the margins over the high-textured region are insufficient, as shown in Fig. 14.4. As with [36], the findings of [15] are also encouraging, albeit the strength of edges near high contrast is not as robust as the strength of advantages near low contrast. Findings [25], [28], and [35] are acceptable in light of the circumstances.

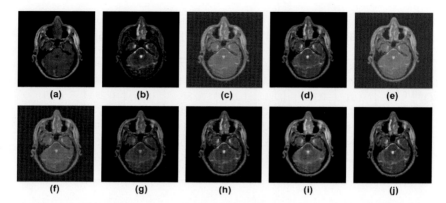

Figure 14.3 Result analysis: (a) and (b) are source medical images, (c) [13], (d) [36], (e) [15], (f) [17], (g) [25], (h) [28], (i) [35], and (j) proposed approach.

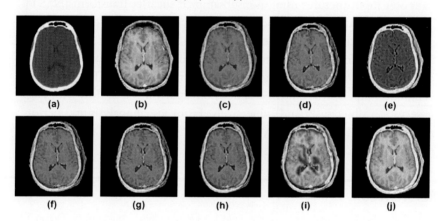

Figure 14.4 Result analysis: (a) and (b) are source medical images, (c) [13], (d) [36], (e) [15], (f) [17], (g) [25], (h) [28], (i) [35], and (j) proposed approach.

For result analysis, visual results alone are not adequate; consequently, the outcomes of the current techniques are checked and assessed using measures of their performance. The findings were evaluated using 70 pairs of medical images, and the average value is presented in Table 14.1. Based on Table 14.1, it can be concluded that the transform domain techniques produce superior results.

14.5 Conclusions

The integration of crucial imaging data has become vital for many medical applications. This paper proposes a novel multimodality medical picture

Table 14.1 Performance metrics result analysis (average outcome of 70 pairs).

Parameter	[13]	[36]	[15]	[17]	[25]	[28]	[35]	Proposed Method
M.I.	2.38	2.19	2.12	2.10	2.52	2.17	2.19	2.97
S.D.	62.45	61.21	63.13	66.11	62.3110	65.18	61.08	68.52
$Q^{AB/F}$	0.61	0.52	0.62	0.66	0.86	0.36	0.22	0.85
S.F.	22.67	24.73	25.40	22.84	25.88	25.45	25.74	26.21
Mean	53.39	52.26	52.12	52.12	52.28	53.51	53.88	54.71
Entropy	6.34	6.56	6.55	6.82	6.56	7.17	6.85	7.83
Time (in seconds)	6.34	6.56	6.12	6.45	6.34	6.57	6.66	7.03

fusion technique called the shearlet domain. The proposed method decomposes input pictures using nonsubsampled shearlet transform (NSST). Combining bilateral filter processing and local energy-based fusion with a novel approach provides sharp and smooth low-frequency components. This study examines the outcomes of testing and analysis of numerous medical modalities on the multimodal medical image dataset. The proposed technique outperforms cutting-edge fusion algorithms that deal with edge preservation objectively and subjectively. From visual analysis and performance metrics, it can be clearly concluded that the proposed methodology gives better outcomes than existing methods.

References

[1] Z. Xu, Medical image fusion using multi-level local extrema, Information Fusion 19 (2014) 38–48.

[2] P. Zhang, Y. Yuan, C. Fei, T. Pu, S. Wang, Infrared and visible image fusion using co-occurrence filter, Infrared Physics & Technology 93 (2018) 223–231.

[3] S. Li, H. Yin, L. Fang, Group-sparse representation with dictionary learning for medical image denoising and fusion, IEEE Transactions on Biomedical Engineering 59 (12) (2012) 3450–3459.

[4] G. Bhatnagar, Q.J. Wu, Z. Liu, Human visual system inspired multi-modal medical image fusion framework, Expert Systems with Applications 40 (5) (2013) 1708–1720.

[5] M. Yin, W. Liu, X. Zhao, Y. Yin, Y. Guo, A novel image fusion algorithm based on nonsubsampled shearlet transform, Optik 125 (10) (2014) 2274–2282.

[6] P. Ganasala, V. Kumar, Multi-modality medical image fusion based on new features in NSST domain, Biomedical Engineering Letters 4 (4) (2014) 414–424.

[7] W. Kong, J. Liu, Technique for image fusion based on nonsubsampled shearlet transform and improved pulse-coupled neural network, Optical Engineering 52 (1) (2013) 017001.

[8] P. Ganasala, V. Kumar, Feature-motivated simplified adaptive PCNN-based medical image fusion algorithm in NSST domain, Journal of Digital Imaging 29 (1) (2016) 73–85.

[9] R. Singh, R. Srivastava, O. Prakash, A. Khare, Multi-modal medical image fusion in dual tree complex wavelet transform domain using maximum and average fusion rules, Journal of Medical Imaging and Health Informatics 2 (2) (2012) 168–173.

[10] Q. Xiao-Bo, Y. Jing-Wen, X.I.A.O. Hong-Zhi, Z. Zi-Qian, Image fusion algorithm based on spatial frequency-motivated pulse coupled neural networks in nonsubsampled contourlet transform domain, Acta Automatica Sinica 34 (12) (2008) 1508–1514.

[11] J. Du, W. Li, K. Lu, B. Xiao, An overview of multi-modal medical image fusion, Neurocomputing 215 (2016) 3–20.

[12] T. Zhou, S. Ruan, S. Canu, A review: Deep learning for medical image segmentation using multi-modality fusion, Array 3 (2019) 100004.

[13] S.D. Ramlal, J. Sachdeva, C.K. Ahuja, N. Khandelwal, An improved multi-modal medical image fusion scheme based on hybrid combination of nonsubsampled contourlet transform and stationary wavelet transform, International Journal of Imaging Systems and Technology 29 (2) (2019) 146–160.

[14] S. Liu, M. Shi, Z. Zhu, J. Zhao, Image fusion based on complex-shearlet domain with guided filtering, Multidimensional Systems and Signal Processing 28 (1) (2017) 207–224.

[15] H. Ullah, B. Ullah, L. Wu, F.Y. Abdalla, G. Ren, Y. Zhao, Multi-modality medical images fusion based on local-features fuzzy sets and novel sum-modified-Laplacian in non-subsampled shearlet transform domain, Biomedical Signal Processing and Control 57 (2020).

[16] L. Wang, B. Li, L.F. Tian, Multi-modal medical image fusion using the inter-scale and intra-scale dependencies between image shift-invariant shearlet coefficients, Information Fusion 19 (2014) 20–28.

[17] X. Liu, W. Mei, H. Du, Multi-modality medical image fusion based on image decomposition framework and nonsubsampled shearlet transform, Biomedical Signal Processing and Control 40 (2018) 343–350.

[18] N. Mehta, S. Budhiraja, Multi-modal medical image fusion using guided filter in NSCT domain, Biomedical and Pharmacology Journal 11 (4) (2018) 1937–1946.

[19] S. Maqsood, U. Javed, Multi-modal medical image fusion based on two-scale image decomposition and sparse representation, Biomedical Signal Processing and Control 57 (2020).

[20] Q. Hu, S. Hu, F. Zhang, Multi-modality medical image fusion based on separable dictionary learning and Gabor filtering, Signal Processing. Image Communication 83 (2020) 115758.

[21] Z. Zhu, Y. Chai, H. Yin, Y. Li, Z. Liu, A novel dictionary learning approach for multi-modality medical image fusion, Neurocomputing 214 (2016) 471–482.

[22] Z. Zhu, H. Yin, Y. Chai, Y. Li, G. Qi, A novel multi-modality image fusion method based on image decomposition and sparse representation, Information Sciences 432 (2018) 516–529.

[23] Y. Cao, S. Li, J. Hu, Multi-focus image fusion by nonsubsampled shearlet transform, in: 2011 Sixth International Conference on Image and Graphics, IEEE, August 2011, pp. 17–21.

[24] G. Guorong, X. Luping, F. Dongzhu, Multi-focus image fusion based on nonsubsampled shearlet transform, IET Image Processing 7 (6) (2013) 633–639.

[25] Z. Fu, Y. Zhao, Y. Xu, L. Xu, J. Xu, Gradient structural similarity based gradient filtering for multi-modal image fusion, Information Fusion 53 (2020) 251–268.

[26] S. Goyal, V. Singh, A. Rani, N. Yadav, FPRSGF denoised non-subsampled shearlet transform-based image fusion using sparse representation, Signal, Image and Video Processing 14 (4) (2020) 719–726.

[27] J.R. Benjamin, T. Jayasree, An efficient MRI-PET medical image fusion using nonsubsampled shearlet transform, in: 2019 IEEE International Conference on Intelligent

Techniques in Control, Optimization and Signal Processing (INCOS), IEEE, April 2019, pp. 1–5.

[28] X. Luo, Z. Zhang, B. Zhang, X. Wu, Image fusion with contextual statistical similarity and nonsubsampled shearlet transform, IEEE Sensors Journal 17 (6) (2016) 1760–1771.

[29] C. Zhao, Y. Guo, Y. Wang, A fast fusion scheme for infrared and visible light images in NSCT domain, Infrared Physics & Technology 72 (2015) 266–275.

[30] A.U. Moonon, J. Hu, S. Li, Remote sensing image fusion method based on non-subsampled shearlet transform and sparse representation, Sensing and Imaging 16 (1) (2015) 23.

[31] G. Ghimpețeanu, T. Batard, M. Bertalmío, S. Levine, A decomposition framework for image denoising algorithms, IEEE Transactions on Image Processing 25 (1) (2015) 388–399.

[32] R. Hou, D. Zhou, R. Nie, D. Liu, X. Ruan, Brain CT and MRI medical image fusion using convolutional neural networks and a dual-channel spiking cortical model, Medical & Biological Engineering & Computing 57 (4) (2019) 887–900.

[33] C.S. Asha, S. Lal, V.P. Gurupur, P.P. Saxena, Multi-modal medical image fusion with adaptive weighted combination of NSST bands using chaotic grey wolf optimization, IEEE Access 7 (2019) 40782–40796.

[34] A. Tannaz, S. Mousa, D. Sabalan, P. Masoud, Fusion of multi-modal medical images using nonsubsampled shearlet transform and particle swarm optimization, Multidimensional Systems and Signal Processing 31 (1) (2020) 269–287.

[35] M. Yin, X. Liu, Y. Liu, X. Chen, Medical image fusion with parameter-adaptive pulse coupled neural network in nonsubsampled shearlet transform domain, IEEE Transactions on Instrumentation and Measurement 68 (1) (2018) 49–64.

[36] H. Ouerghi, O. Mourali, E. Zagrouba, Non-subsampled shearlet transform based MRI and PET brain image fusion using simplified pulse coupled neural network and weight local features in YIQ colour space, IET Image Processing 12 (10) (2018) 1873–1880.

[37] R. Dhaundiyal, A. Tripathi, K. Joshi, M. Diwakar, P. Singh, Clustering based multi-modality medical image fusion, Journal of Physics. Conference Series 1478 (1) (2020), IOP Publishing.

[38] P. Kumar, M. Diwakar, A novel approach for multimodality medical image fusion over secure environment, Transactions on Emerging Telecommunications Technologies 32 (2) (2021).

[39] M. Diwakar, P. Singh, A. Shankar, Multi-modal medical image fusion framework using co-occurrence filter and local extrema in NSST domain, Biomedical Signal Processing and Control 68 (2021).

CHAPTER 15

IIITM Faces: an Indian face image database

K.V. Arya[a] and Shyam Singh Rajput[b]

[a]ABV-Indian Institute of Information Technology and Management, Gwalior, India
[b]Department of Computer Science and Engineering, National Institute of Technology Patna, Patna, India

15.1 Introduction

In the field of multilabel classification, identifying every facial attribute from a single given image is a classical problem. Face-attribute detection is meant to specify these attributes. The attributes give necessary information about the midlevel representations of facial images that are analyzed between features of very low-pixel rates and labels of high identity. The attributes to be extracted from the face include much variety. These diverse attributes are the gender of the person, whether facial hair (beard or mustache) are present or not, the color of the hair on the head, and the density of the hair. The aim to have an intuitive and human interpretable face description model, and for serving this purpose, identification of these attributes with considerable reliability is very important. Today as the human-computer interaction (HCI) is increasing, the development of such a model plays a crucial role in designing HCI systems, which need to be aware of various features of the user to respond accordingly.

For this purpose, a dataset of Indian faces named IIITM Faces is being presented in this chapter. A total of 107 subjects, which include the student and the staff members at ABV-IIITM Gwalior have participated to make IIITM Face dataset possible. The images of the subjects are captured in all possible combinations of 6 emotions and 3 different orientations (see Fig. 15.2). In this dataset, there is a total of 1928 images which are captured with a high-resolution camera. As shown in Fig. 15.1, constant facial attributes of the subjects are also marked. All these images have been labeled to capture face-attributes, such as the presence of mustache or eyeglasses, presence and density of beard and hair, the gender of the subject along with what he/she is wearing. Table 15.1 provides a detailed description of the dataset across all the attributes.

Digital Image Enhancement and Reconstruction
https://doi.org/10.1016/B978-0-32-398370-9.00022-6

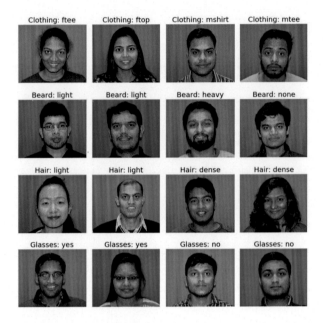

Figure 15.1 Diversity of attributes in IIITM Faces.

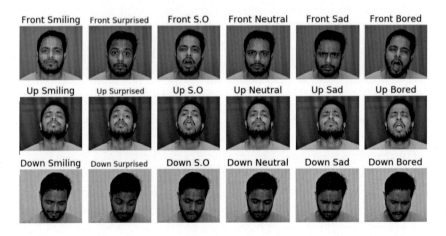

Figure 15.2 Variation in emotion and poses in the IIITM Faces.

The classification of these facial attributes has been achieved by using three classifiers, namely logistic regression (LR), support vector machine (SVM) [1], and ResNet [2]. The implementation details and hyperparameters used are outlined in Section 15.4.

The major contribution of the work can be summarized as follows: (i) We release the IIITM Face dataset, a face-attribute dataset, labeled extensively and with Indian faces. (ii) The dataset is rigorously benchmarked through main multi-attribute classification metrics. (iii) We compare the classification performance on the IIITM Face dataset.

15.2 Related work

In the early days of face attribute detection study, the sizes of the datasets were small (only about 500–1000 images with 20–120 participants) and had a comparatively lesser number of attributes for face identification task [3–5]. These were aptly suited for the computational power available at that time. As algorithms improved after receiving a boost from the enhancement in computation power, these algorithms grew data-hungry.

Given the large availability of data, bigger datasets have been constructed in recent years. The Labeled Faces in the Wild (LFW) dataset [6] is one of the first such datasets, which consists of 13,233 images of 5749 people by scraping from the Internet. Furthermore, CelebA [7] dataset made of 200K images of celebrity faces (each celebrity with 40 attribute annotations) is introduced, which dominates all other previous databases because of its larger size. Another dataset, VGGFace [8], one of the largest datasets available to the public, contains 2.6M images of 2622 subjects. The dataset was again released as VGGFace2 dataset [9]. The size of this dataset was further increased to contain 3.3M images of 9131 subjects. VGGFace2, along with UMDFaces [10] are among the very few large-scale datasets publicly accessible, which contain pose information corresponding to each face image instance. Another class of datasets focuses entirely on facial emotion detection.

However, there has been a relative paucity of data in the Indian case. To make the facial recognition systems more reliable, a very crucial element is to include racial diversity. For instance, the datasets VGGFace2 [9] and FairFace [11] have focused to include diversity in the dataset. They have increased the proportion of the ethnically diverse population and also more number of faces from different professional groups were added. The earliest dataset having the Indian faces is called the Indian Face dataset [12]. This contains 11 images of each of the 40 different people in poses and emotional attributes. Some other datasets are also available like the Indian Face Age database (IFAD) [13], which contains the information of the attributes of Indian celebrities. The drawback of the data is that it has a very limited

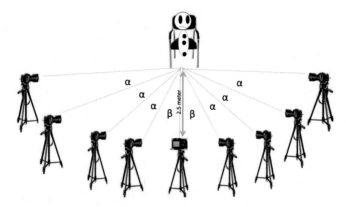

Figure 15.3 Illustration of the camera positions while capturing the images. The values of angle α and β are 20 degrees and 30 degrees, respectively, while the distance of the camera stand from the center point of the subject's chair is 2.5 meter.

number of subjects and images of low resolution. In the Indian Spontaneous expression [14] dataset, video frames of subjects are presented while they were watching the emotional video clippings. This gives rich information on the emotion transitions of the subjects. Another very large dataset available is for Indian personalities, called the Indian Movie Face database [15]. It contains 34,512 images of 100 Indian celebrities. The attribute labels consist of gender, pose, age, expression, and amount of occlusion. But all of these datasets on Indian faces are constrained in either image resolution, attribute diversity, or dataset size.

One of the major problems often examined on these datasets is the description of facial attributes [16–18]. This can be described as a multitask joint learning question or can be learned by using an ensemble of models for each attribute. The advantage of joint learning is that a relationship among the attributes can be established. This fact is essentially helpful as facial attributes having a high correlation. It can also be noted that when large facial variations are present, the separate models fail. This work explores both the ensemble of models approach and multitask joint learning approach on the proposed IIITM Face dataset.

15.3 Methodology

15.3.1 Camera setup

In a photographic studio, a Nikon HD digital camera is used to capture the face images of resolution 4096×2160 pixels. In this setup, the distance of the camera is approximately 2.5 meters from the center of the chair on which the subject is sitting. Moreover, to capture the images from different angles, the stand of the camera is moved manually by the cameramen with angle α and β, as shown in Fig. 15.3.

15.3.2 Overview of IIITM Face dataset

The IIITM Face Dataset comprises 1928 images of 107 subjects with a wide range of facial attributes including pose, emotion, gender, the hair on the face, glasses, hairstyle and density, and clothing style. The people who participated in the dataset are the students and staff members of the ABV–IIITM Institute. Each subject has at least 18 pictures in this dataset. As the facial features and clothes worn in the image are the same in all the images of one subject, the permutations of three poses and six emotion features cover all possible combinations of images. The Face dataset was taken in three different colored backgrounds. The green color background was used to capture the subject with the front pose, blue background with the up pose, and white background with the down pose. Six emotions have been recorded under each background color. The different colors in the background are used to make the dataset properly segmented.

The dataset is designed to serve as a benchmark for facial matching tasks across poses and emotions and also for facial attribute classification tasks. More specifically, it is designed keeping in mind the lack of high–resolution facial data from the Indian context. Most large scale datasets have either a very low number of subjects of Indian ethnicity or the images are scraped from the Internet, and thus are not in high resolution.

Table 15.1 gives the comparison of the introduced IIITM Face dataset with other Indian facial image datasets that are publicly available for experimentation.

Table 15.1 Comparison of the IIITM Faces with other existing Indian Face databases.

Dataset	# Subjects	# Images	Resolution	Emotion	Pose	Facial Attributes
IITK Face	40	440	640 × 480	Yes	Yes	No
IMFDB	100	34,512	Varying	Yes	Yes	Yes
IFAD	55	3296	128 × 128	Yes	Yes	No
ISED	50	428	1920 × 1080	Yes	No	No
IIITM Face	107	1928	2992 × 2000	Yes	Yes	Yes

Table 15.2 Attribute-wise illustration of the IIITM Faces.

Attributes			
Orientation	**Gender**	**Emotion**		**Beard**
Down: 642	Female: 360	Neutral: 322	Surprised: 322	Heavy: 288
Up: 642	Male: 1568	Sad: 321	S.O: 321	None: 792
Front: 644		Smiling: 321	Bored: 321	Light: 848
Mustache	**Glasses**	**Cloth**		**Hair**
Yes: 1135	Yes: 180	F. Tee: 36	M. Shirt: 775	Light: 180
No: 793	No: 1748	F. Top: 324	M. Tee: 793	Dense: 1748

15.3.3 Attribute descriptions

In IIITM Face dataset, each face image is labeled for the following eight attributes:

- Gender: female, male
- Pose: front, up, and down
- Emotion: neutral, sad, smiling, surprised, surprised with open mouth (S. O.), Bored
- Beard: heavy, light, none
- Mustache: yes, no
- Glasses: yes, no
- Hair: light, dense
- Cloth 1: male shirt (M. Shirt), female top (F. Top), Polo T–shirt (Polo), male T–shirt (M. Tee), none
- Cloth 2: sweater, jacket, hoodie, none

Beard, hair, and mustache are subjective of those eight attributes mentioned. The five human annotators have voted to assign labels and the majority vote across them is chosen as the final label. There is no ambiguity in labeling the emotion as the subjects were asked to show a particular emotion, and this was marked along with the image. The spectrum of emotions was selected to have as much variety as possible in terms of how different regions of the face are animated to represent all these emotions. (See Table 15.2.)

15.3.4 Problem formulation

The proposed IIITM Face dataset comprises of m samples of facial images, where each sample x_i ($i \in \{1, \ldots, m\}$) is an RGB image with dimensions $h \times w$.

Each sample has been labeled for k features (attributes), and a_j ($j \in \{1, \ldots, k\}$) denotes the exhaustive set of valid labels for feature j. The aim is to train a classifier

$$H : [0, 255]^{h \times w \times 3} \to \{\{0, 1\}^{|a_j|}, j \in \{1, \ldots, k\}\}. \qquad (15.1)$$

Now, the problem in hand can be dealt with a variety of approaches. This work accomplishes this task by treating it as a multilabel prediction problem requiring simultaneous identification of the present features. To achieve this, A is formulated as the union set of all feature label exhibited in any of the training sample across all features. This is defined as

$$A = \bigcup_{j=1}^{k} a_j. \qquad (15.2)$$

This work considers the training labels y_i as a binarized vector of length $|A|$. We therefore construct a label matrix $\mathbf{Y} \in \{0, 1\}^{m \times |A|}$, where each y_{ij} is 0 or 1, indicating the presence or absence of jth feature label in the ith training instance. Thus the multilabel classifier H becomes

$$H : [0, 255]^{h \times w \times 3} \to \{0, 1\}^{|A|}. \qquad (15.3)$$

This work explores an alternate approach to train k individual multiclass predictors for each feature. These predictors are then expected to output $H = \{h_1, \ldots, h_k\}$, where each $h_j(x_i)$ will give probability distribution over labels $l \in a_j$.

15.3.5 Evaluation metrics

Evaluation of multilabel classification performance is significantly different from single-label counterpart. The task is inherently more difficult as multiple labels can occur in any permutation in a given sample. This requires the use of specially crafted metrics that captures the complexity of this fundamentally difficult task. In this work, we use 9 such key metrics that have been introduced in previous works and focus on capturing the effectiveness of these classifiers from different perspectives. The following presents a detailed account of the metrics used:

The coverage loss, zero-one loss, and Hamming loss have been assessed in a group of works, such as [19–21], whereas AUC and F1 score in the multilabel systems can be grown to instance level (averaging on each instance), microlevel (averaging on prediction matrix), and macrolevel (averaging across each label) metrics. For a harmonious perspective on these metrics for multilabel classification and their significance, see [22].

15.4 Experimental setup

On our dataset we do the following experiments: Firstly, we train a logistic regression without dimensionality reduction (**LR-MT**), with PCA (**LR-PCA-MT**), with LDA (**LR-LDA-MT**), support vector machine without dimensionality reduction (**SVM-MT**), with PCA (**SVM-PCA-MT**), with LDA (**SVM-LDA-MT**), and deep neural network model (ResNet-50) without dimensionality (**RN-MT**). These models are trained by binarizing the attributes, and multilabel classification is performed as a multitask (MT) learning (as discussed in Section 15.3.4). Thereupon, the best-performing model is picked in multitask learning (ResNet in our case, refer to Table 15.3), and then 8 such models per single attribute are trained individually. An ensemble of these 8 models is created to get a classifier for all attributes, referred to as **RN-Ens**. In all experiments, all pictures of 85 subjects are kept in the train set and that of 22 subjects in the test set. We conduct 2 set of experiments on our new dataset. In the first experiment, we train 8 individual classifiers on each of the 8 labels present in our dataset. For this, we use a ResNet-50 architecture proposed in [2]. This sets a very strong baseline for our multilabel classification problem. In the second experiment, we deal with the multilabel classification task, as detailed in Section 15.3.4. For this, we employ 3 popular classification models: logistic regression, support vector machine and ResNet-50. The implementation details are described below.

15.4.1 Implementation details

In this work, three algorithms, namely a) logistic regression (LR), b) support vector machine (SVM), and c) deep neural network using ResNet-50 architecture are used for multilevel classification prediction. The predictors, employing LR and SVM as learning algorithms, are trained as One vs. Rest classifiers across the union set of all the labels. The input to these classifiers is all training samples of dimension $100 \times 100 \times 3$. Subsequently, they are flattened to a 2-dimension feature vector, which are then passed to the model. Since it results in a very high dimensional feature space (i.e., a vector of size 30,000), a dimensionality reduction techniques e.g., principal component analysis (PCA) and linear discriminant analysis (LDA) are

Table 15.3 Benchmarking performance of different techniques in the classification of face attribute on IIITM Faces.

Techniques				Multi-Attribute Detection				
Database				IIITM Face				Ensemble of Models IIITM Face
Metrics	LR-MT	LR-PCA-MT	LR-LDA-MT	SVM-MT	SVM-PCA-MT	SVM-LDA-MT	RN-MT	RN-Ens
Hamming Loss	0.216	.233	.233	0.246	.241	.241	0.119	0.147
Coverage Loss	23.5	29.0	29.0	24	29.0	29.0	13.87	14.71
Zero-one Loss	0.991	1	1	1	1	1	0.876	0.959
Instance F1	0.671	.587	.548	0.508	.461	.461	0.813	0.778
Micro F1	0.671	.586	.550	0.508	.461	.461	0.812	0.774
Macro F1	0.499	.367	.259	0.142	.116	.116	0.744	0.687
Instance AUC	0.753	.702	.682	0.661	.641	.641	0.887	0.863
Micro AUC	0.753	.702	.682	0.661	.641	.641	0.887	0.863
Macro AUC	0.636	.604	.536	0.5	0.5	0.5	0.839	0.811

utilized to reduce the dimensional vector to size of 100. The PCA and LDA are separately used for both SVM and LR predictors. For all these predictors, the L2 regularization is employed, and $C = 1$ while initializing the other hyper-parameters with default values [23].

For the ResNet-50 (hereafter referred to as **ResNet** only) based classifiers, we coherently follow the architecture described in [2] with some modifications to the hyperparameter values, as described below. The training samples are resized to possess the dimensions $224 \times 224 \times 3$ and the predictor is instantiated with learned weights on ImageNet [24], as suggested by Yosinski et al. [25]. This helps the classifier inherit a notion of real-world geometry and the corresponding geometrical constraints and relations, which are difficult to learn from a relatively small sized dataset. The predictor is fine-tuned using Adam optimizer [26], and the images are fed in batches of size 64. The learning rate find mechanism introduced in [27] is employed to configure the initial learning rate. The cyclical learning rate update mechanism is used for tweaking the learning rate for subsequent epochs. To prevent bias in pose detection based on the background color, the background color is removed from all the training samples.

For RN-MT, hinge loss is employed as the loss heuristic since multiple labels are predicted simultaneously can mathematically be represented as follows:

$$L_i = \sum_{j \neq y_i} \max(0, s_j - s_{y_i} + \Delta), \tag{15.4}$$

where s_j is the score representative of a correct prediction, s_{y_i} is the score representative of an incorrect prediction, and Δ is a margin/bias term.

In the case of RN-Ens, loss is calculated on per sample basis, L_i corresponding to the number of classes C in each label as given in Eq. (15.5):

$$L_i = \begin{cases} -(y \log(p) + (1-y)\log(1-p)) & \text{if } C = 2, \\ -\sum_{c=1}^{C} y_{o,c} \log(p_{o,c}) & C > 2, \end{cases} \tag{15.5}$$

where y (or $y_{o,c}$) is a binary indicator (0 or 1) of the correct classification of class label c in the given sample o.

15.5 Results

In this section, various key observations are presented based on the results shown in above tables. Initially, according to our experiments, ResNet is much better than LR, LR-PCA, LR-LDA, SVM, SVM-PCA, and SVM-LDA on the basis of multi-attribute classification on image datasets. It is also seen that RN-MT is much superior to RN-Ens during various evaluations. Therefore this ability makes RN-MT able to make correlations among various attributes (multi-attribute). In the case of RN-Ens, zero-one loss is slightly high and that strengthens our claim. As we know, absolute correctness of all attributes is measured by zero-one loss, hence it gives the clear picture that our single model is able to capture correlations accurately.

15.5.1 Application areas

Following are the major research fields where the IIITM Face dataset can be employed for experimental purposes:

- Face recognition [28–34]
- Face super-resolution [35–40]
- Biometric
- Surveillance [41–43]

15.6 Conclusions

In this work, a new dataset of Indian faces in the context of Indian faces is released for the research community to explore in the future. This dataset is enriched with high-resolution images, so it can be used to model low-resolution images on high-resolution datasets and to compare the performance of different models. Moreover, it can be used in emotion recognition to evaluate state-of-the-art techniques in the context of Indian faces.

Acknowledgments

We are grateful for Department of Science and Technology, New Delhi, India to support part of this work under the Technology System Development Program project: DST/TSG/NTS/2013/19-G. We are also thankful to the undergraduate and Ph.D. students of IIITM Gwalior and the library staff for posing for the camera to help us collect the dataset.

References

[1] M.A. Hearst, Support vector machines, IEEE Intelligent Systems 13 (4) (1998) 18–28.

[2] K. He, X. Zhang, S. Ren, J. Sun, Deep residual learning for image recognition, in: 2016 IEEE Conference on Computer Vision and Pattern Recognition (CVPR), 2016, pp. 770–778.

[3] A.S. Georghiades, P.N. Belhumeur, D.J. Kriegman, From few to many: Illumination cone models for face recognition under variable lighting and pose, IEEE Transactions on Pattern Analysis and Machine Intelligence 6 (2001) 643–660.

[4] H. Wechsler, J.P. Phillips, V. Bruce, F.F. Soulié, T.S. Huang, Face Recognition: From Theory to Applications, vol. 163, Springer Science & Business Media, 2012.

[5] O. Jesorsky, K.J. Kirchberg, R.W. Frischholz, Robust face detection using the Hausdorff distance, in: International Conference on Audio- and Video-Based Biometric Person Authentication, Springer, 2001, pp. 90–95.

[6] G.B. Huang, M. Mattar, T. Berg, E. Learned-Miller, Labeled faces in the wild: A database for studying face recognition in unconstrained environments, in: Workshop on Faces in 'Real-Life' Images: Detection, Alignment, and Recognition, 2008.

[7] Z. Liu, P. Luo, X. Wang, X. Tang, Deep learning face attributes in the wild, in: IEEE Conference on Computer Vision and Pattern Recognition (CVPR), 2013.

[8] O.M. Parkhi, A. Vedaldi, A. Zisserman, Deep face recognition, in: BMVC, vol. 1, 2015, p. 6.

[9] Q. Cao, L. Shen, W. Xie, O.M. Parkhi, A. Zisserman, VGGFace2: A dataset for recognising faces across pose and age, in: 2018 13th IEEE International Conference on Automatic Face & Gesture Recognition (FG 2018), IEEE, 2018, pp. 67–74.

[10] A. Bansal, A. Nanduri, C.D. Castillo, R. Ranjan, R. Chellappa, UMDFaces: An annotated face dataset for training deep networks, in: 2017 IEEE International Joint Conference on Biometrics (IJCB), IEEE, 2017, pp. 464–473.

[11] K. Kärkkäinen, J. Joo, FairFace: Face attribute dataset for balanced race, gender, and age, arXiv:1908.04913 [abs].

[12] V. Jain, A. Mukherjee, The Indian face database, http://vis-www.cs.umass.edu/vidit/IndianFaceDatabase/index.html.

[13] R. Sharma, M.S. Patterh, Indian Face Age Database: A database for face recognition with age variation, International Journal of Computer Applications 126 (2015) 21–27.

[14] S. Happy, P. Patnaik, A. Routray, R. Guha, The Indian spontaneous expression database for emotion recognition, IEEE Transactions on Affective Computing 8 (1) (2015) 131–142.

[15] S. Setty, M. Husain, P. Beham, J. Gudavalli, M. Kandasamy, R. Vaddi, V. Hemadri, J.C. Karure, R. Raju, B. Rajan, V. Kumar, C.V. Jawahar, Indian Movie Face Database: A benchmark for face recognition under wide variations, in: National Conference on Computer Vision, Pattern Recognition, Image Processing and Graphics (NCVPRIPG), 2013.

[16] Z. Liu, P. Luo, X. Wang, X. Tang, Deep learning face attributes in the wild, in: Proceedings of the IEEE International Conference on Computer Vision, 2015, pp. 3730–3738.

[17] F. Taherkhani, N.M. Nasrabadi, J. Dawson, A deep face identification network enhanced by facial attributes prediction, in: Proceedings of the IEEE Conference on Computer Vision and Pattern Recognition Workshops, 2018, pp. 553–560.

[18] Y. Sun, J. Yu, Deep facial attribute detection in the wild: From general to specific, in: BMVC, 2018, p. 283.

[19] R. Schapire, Y. Singer, A boosting-based system for text categorization, Machine Learning 392 (3) (1999) 135–168.

[20] S.-J. Huang, Y. Yu, Z.-H. Zhou, Multi-label hypothesis reuse, in: Proceedings of the 18th ACM SIGKDD International Conference on Knowledge Discovery and Data Mining, ACM, 2012, pp. 525–533.

[21] M.-L. Zhang, L. Wu, LIFT: Multi-label learning with label-specific features, IEEE Transactions on Pattern Analysis and Machine Intelligence 37 (1) (2014) 107–120.

[22] X.-Z. Wu, Z.-H. Zhou, A unified view of multi-label performance measures, in: Proceedings of the 34th International Conference on Machine Learning – Volume 70, JMLR.org, 2017, pp. 3780–3788.

[23] F. Pedregosa, G. Varoquaux, A. Gramfort, V. Michel, B. Thirion, O. Grisel, M. Blondel, P. Prettenhofer, R. Weiss, V. Dubourg, J. Vanderplas, A. Passos, D. Cournapeau, M. Brucher, M. Perrot, E. Duchesnay, Scikit-learn: Machine learning in Python, Journal of Machine Learning Research 12 (2011) 2825–2830.

[24] J. Deng, W. Dong, R. Socher, L.-J. Li, K. Li, L. Fei-Fei, ImageNet: A large-scale hierarchical image database, in: 2009 IEEE Conference on Computer Vision and Pattern Recognition, IEEE, 2009, pp. 248–255.

[25] J. Yosinski, J. Clune, Y. Bengio, H. Lipson, How transferable are features in deep neural networks?, Advances in Neural Information Processing Systems (2014) 3320–3328.

[26] D.P. Kingma, J. Ba, Adam: A method for stochastic optimization, arXiv preprint, arXiv:1412.6980.

[27] L.N. Smith, No more pesky learning rate guessing games, arXiv:1506.01186.

[28] K.V. Arya, S.S. Rajput, Recognition of facial images via self-organizing landmark location with approximate graph matching, in: A. Dhawan, V.S. Tripathi, K.V. Arya, K. Naik (Eds.), Recent Trends in Electronics and Communication, Springer Singapore, Singapore, 2022, pp. 1043–1055.

[29] S.S. Rajput, K.V. Arya, CNN classifier based low-resolution face recognition algorithm, in: 2020 International Conference on Emerging Frontiers in Electrical and Electronic Technologies (ICEFEET), 2020, pp. 1–4, https://doi.org/10.1109/ICEFEET49149.2020.9187001.

[30] K.V. Arya, S.S. Rajput, S. Upadhyay, Noise-robust low-resolution face recognition using sift features, in: N.K. Verma, A.K. Ghosh (Eds.), Computational Intelligence: Theories, Applications and Future Directions – Volume II, Springer Singapore, Singapore, 2019, pp. 645–655.

[31] Y.K. Mydam, S. Singh Rajput, P. Chanak, Low rank representation based discriminative multi manifold analysis for low-resolution face recognition, in: 2018 Conference on Information and Communication Technology (CICT), 2018, pp. 1–5, https://doi.org/10.1109/INFOCOMTECH.2018.8722393.

[32] K.V. Arya, A. Rajawat, M.K. Pandey, S.S. Rajput, Very low resolution face recognition using fused visual and texture features, in: 2017 Conference on Information and Communication Technology (CICT), 2017, pp. 1–5, https://doi.org/10.1109/INFOCOMTECH.2017.8340642.

[33] A. Rajawat, M.K. Pandey, S.S. Rajput, Low resolution face recognition techniques: A survey, in: 2017 3rd International Conference on Computational Intelligence Communication Technology (CICT), 2017, pp. 1–4, https://doi.org/10.1109/CIACT.2017.7977381.

[34] S.S. Rajput, K.V. Arya, P. Sharma, Face recognition in low-resolution space, in: The Biometric Computing: Recognition and Registration, CRC Press, 2019, pp. 263–279.

[35] S.S. Rajput, K.V. Arya, A robust face super-resolution algorithm and its application in low-resolution face recognition system, Multimedia Tools and Applications 79 (33) (2020) 23909–23934, https://doi.org/10.1007/s11042-020-09072-5.

[36] S.S. Rajput, K.V. Arya, A robust facial image super-resolution model via mirror-patch based neighbor representation, Multimedia Tools and Applications 78 (2019) 25407–25426, https://doi.org/10.1007/s11042-019-07791-y.

[37] S.S. Rajput, K.V. Arya, V.K. Bohat, Face image super-resolution using differential evolutionary algorithm, in: N.K. Verma, A.K. Ghosh (Eds.), Computational Intelligence: Theories, Applications and Future Directions – Volume II, Springer Singapore, Singapore, 2019, pp. 635–644.

[38] S.S. Rajput, K.V. Arya, Noise robust face hallucination via outlier regularized least square and neighbor representation, IEEE Transactions on Biometrics, Behavior, and Identity Science 1 (4) (2019) 252–263.

[39] S.S. Rajput, V.K. Bohat, K.V. Arya, Grey wolf optimization algorithm for facial image super-resolution, Applied Intelligence 49 (2019) 1324–1338, https://doi.org/10.1007/s10489-018-1340-x, 2019.

[40] S.S. Rajput, Mixed Gaussian-Impulse noise robust face hallucination via noise suppressed low-and-high resolution space-based neighbor representation, Multimedia Tools and Applications 81 (2022) 15997–16019, https://doi.org/10.1007/s11042-022-12154-1.

[41] S.S. Rajput, K.V. Arya, V. Singh, V.K. Bohat, Face hallucination techniques: A survey, in: 2018 Conference on Information and Communication Technology (CICT), 2018, pp. 1–6.

[42] S.S. Rajput, K. Arya, V. Singh, Robust face super-resolution via iterative sparsity and locality-constrained representation, Information Sciences 463–464 (2018) 227–244.

[43] S.S. Rajput, A. Singh, K. Arya, J. Jiang, Noise robust face hallucination algorithm using local content prior based error shrunk nearest neighbors representation, Signal Processing 147 (2018) 233–246.

Index

Printed in the United States
by Baker & Taylor Publisher Services